Globalization, Labor Markets and Inequality in India

India started on a program of reforms, both in its external and internal aspects, sometime in the mid-eighties and going on into the nineties. While the increased exposure to world markets ('globalization') and relaxation of domestic controls has undoubtedly given a spurt to the GDP growth rate, its impact on poverty, inequality and employment have been controversial.

This book examines in detail these aspects of post-reform India and discerns the changes and trends which these new developments have created. Providing an original analysis of unit-level data available from the quinquennial National Sample Surveys, the Annual Surveys of Industries and other basic data sources, the authors analyze and compare the results with other pieces of work in the literature. As well as describing the overall situation for India, the book highlights regional differences, and looks at the major industrial sectors such as agriculture, manufacturing and tertiary/services. The important topic of labor market institutions – both for the formal or organized and the unorganized sectors – is considered and the possible adverse effect on employment growth of the regulatory labor framework is examined carefully. Since any reform of this framework must go hand in hand with better state intervention in the informal sector to have any chance of acceptance politically, some of the major initiatives in this area are critically explored.

The book is based on the results of a collaborative research project carried out at the Institute for Human Development (IHD), New Delhi, which is an autonomous institution specializing in labor markets, employment and human development issues. The Munk Centre for International Studies (MCIS) of the University of Toronto provided administrative support for the project funded by the International Development Research Centre (IDRC), Ottowa.

Overall, this book will be of great interest to development economists, labor economists and specialists in South Asian Studies.

Dipak Mazumdar is Senior Research Associate, Munk Centre for International Sudies at the University of Toronto, Canada and Visiting Professor, Institute for Human Development, New Delhi. He is the author of numerous publications on development economics. His co-authored book, with Ata Mazaheri, *The African Manufacturing Firm* was also published by Routledge, in 2003. **Sandip Sarkar** is currently working as a Fellow with the Institute for Human Development (IHD), New Delhi, India. His main areas of research interest are industry, poverty, labor and employment on which he has experience of over two decades. His recent major research project was on the impact of globalization on the labor market in India which is sponsored by the International Development Research Centre (IDRC), Canada. He has been extensively involved in several large research projects funded by reputed national and international agencies.

Routledge studies in the growth economies of Asia

1 **The Changing Capital Markets of East Asia**
Edited by Ky Cao

2 **Financial Reform in China**
Edited by On Kit Tam

3 **Women and Industrialization in Asia**
Edited by Susan Horton

4 **Japan's Trade Policy**
Action or reaction?
Yumiko Mikanagi

5 **The Japanese Election System**
Three analaytical perspectives
Junichiro Wada

6 **The Economics of the Latecomers**
Catching-up, technology transfer and institutions in Germany, Japan and South Korea
Jang-Sup Shin

7 **Industrialization in Malaysia**
Import substitution and infant industry performance
Rokiah Alavi

8 **Economic Development in Twentieth Century East Asia**
The international context
Edited by Aiko Ikeo

9 **The Politics of Economic Development in Indonesia**
Contending perspectives
Edited by Ian Chalmers and Vedi R. Hadiz

10 **Studies in the Economic History of the Pacific Rim**
Edited by Sally M. Miller, A.J.H. Latham and Dennis O. Flynn

11 **Workers and the State in New Order Indonesia**
Vedi R. Hadiz

12 **The Japanese Foreign Exchange Market**
Beate Reszat

13 **Exchange Rate Policies in Emerging Asian Countries**
Edited by Stefan Collignon, Jean Pisani-Ferry and Yung Chul Park

14 **Chinese Firms and Technology in the Reform Era**
Yizheng Shi

15 **Japanese Views on Economic Development**
Diverse paths to the market
Kenichi Ohno and Izumi Ohno

16 **Technological Capabilities and Export Success in Asia**
Edited by Dieter Ernst, Tom Ganiatsos and Lynn Mytelka

17 **Trade and Investment in China**
The European experience
Edited by Roger Strange, Jim Slater and Limin Wang

18 **Technology and Innovation in Japan**
Policy and management for the 21st century
Edited by Martin Hemmert and Christian Oberländer

19 **Trade Policy Issues in Asian Development**
Prema-chandra Athukorala

20 **Economic Integration in the Asia Pacific Region**
Ippei Yamazawa

21 **Japan's War Economy**
Edited by Erich Pauer

22 **Industrial Technology Development in Malaysia**
Industry and firm studies
Edited by Jomo K.S., Greg Felker and Rajah Rasiah

23 **Technology, Competitiveness and the State**
Malaysia's industrial technology policies
Edited by Jomo K.S. and Greg Felker

24 **Corporatism and Korean Capitalism**
Edited by Dennis L. McNamara

25 **Japanese Science**
Samuel Coleman

26 **Capital and Labour in Japan**
The functions of two factor markets
Toshiaki Tachibanaki and Atsuhiro Taki

27 **Asia Pacific Dynamism 1550–2000**
Edited by A.J.H. Latham and Heita Kawakatsu

28 **The Political Economy of Development and Environment in Korea**
Jae-Yong Chung and Richard J Kirkby

29 **Japanese Economics and Economists since 1945**
Edited by Aiko Ikeo

30 **China's Entry into the World Trade Organisation**
Edited by Peter Drysdale and Ligang Song

31 Hong Kong as an International Financial Centre
Emergence and development 1945–1965
Catherine R. Schenk

32 Impediments to Trade in Services
Measurement and policy implication
Edited by Christoper Findlay and Tony Warren

33 The Japanese Industrial Economy
Late development and cultural causation
Ian Inkster

34 China and the Long March to Global Trade
The accession of China to the World Trade Organization
Edited by Alan S. Alexandroff, Sylvia Ostry and Rafael Gomez

35 Capitalist Development and Economism in East Asia
The rise of Hong Kong, Singapore, Taiwan, and South Korea
Kui-Wai Li

36 Women and Work in Globalizing Asia
Edited by Dong-Sook S. Gills and Nicola Piper

37 Financial Markets and Policies in East Asia
Gordon de Brouwer

38 Developmentalism and Dependency in Southeast Asia
The case of the automotive industry
Jason P. Abbott

39 Law and Labour Market Regulation in East Asia
Edited by Sean Cooney, Tim Lindsey, Richard Mitchell and Ying Zhu

40 The Economy of the Philippines
Elites, inequalities and economic restructuring
Peter Krinks

41 China's Third Economic Transformation
The rise of the private economy
Edited by Ross Garnaut and Ligang Song

42 The Vietnamese Economy
Awakening the dormant dragon
Edited by Binh Tran-Nam and Chi Do Pham

43 Restructuring Korea Inc.
Jang-Sup Shin and Ha-Joon Chang

44 Development and Structural Change in the Asia-Pacific
Globalising miracles or end of a model?
Edited by Martin Andersson and Christer Gunnarsson

45 **State Collaboration and Development Strategies in China**
The case of the China-Singapore Suzhou Industrial Park (1992–2002)
Alexius Pereira

46 **Capital and Knowledge in Asia**
Changing power relations
Edited by Heidi Dahles and Otto van den Muijzenberg

47 **Southeast Asian Paper Tigers?**
From miracle to debacle and beyond
Edited by Jomo K.S.

48 **Manufacturing Competitiveness in Asia**
How internationally competitive national firms and industries developed in East Asia
Edited by Jomo K.S.

49 **The Korean Economy at the Crossroads**
Edited by MoonJoong Tcha and Chung-Sok Suh

50 **Ethnic Business**
Chinese capitalism in Southeast Asia
Edited by Jomo K.S. and Brian C. Folk

51 **Exchange Rate Regimes in East Asia**
Edited by Gordon de Brouwer and Masahiro Kawai

52 **Financial Governance in East Asia**
Policy dialogue, surveillance and cooperation
Edited by Gordon de Brouwer and Yunjong Wang

53 **Designing Financial Systems in East Asia and Japan**
Edited by Joseph P.H. Fan, Masaharu Hanazaki and Juro Teranishi

54 **State Competence and Economic Growth in Japan**
Yoshiro Miwa

55 **Understanding Japanese Saving**
Does population aging matter?
Robert Dekle

56 **The Rise and Fall of the East Asian Growth System, 1951–2000**
International competitiveness and rapid economic growth
Xiaoming Huang

57 **Service Industries and Asia-Pacific Cities**
New development trajectories
Edited by P.W. Daniels, K.C. Ho and T.A. Hutton

58 **Unemployment in Asia**
Edited by John Benson and Ying Zhu

59 **Risk Management and Innovation in Japan, Britain and the USA**
Edited by Ruth Taplin

60 **Japan's Development Aid to China**
The long-running foreign policy of engagement
Tsukasa Takamine

61 **Chinese Capitalism and the Modernist Vision**
Satyananda J. Gabriel

62 **Japanese Telecommunications**
Edited by Ruth Taplin and Masako Wakui

63 **East Asia, Globalization and the New Economy**
F. Gerard Adams

64 **China as a World Factory**
Edited by Kevin Honglin Zhang

65 **China's State Owned Enterprise Reforms**
An industrial and CEO approach
Juan Antonio Fernandez and Leila Fernandez-Stembridge

66 **China and India**
A tale of two economies
Dilip K. Das

67 **Innovation and Business Partnering in Japan, Europe and the United States**
Edited by Ruth Taplin

68 **Asian Informal Workers**
Global risks local protection
Santosh Mehrotra and Mario Biggeri

69 **The Rise of the Corporate Economy in Southeast Asia**
Rajeswary Ampalavanar Brown

70 **The Singapore Economy**
An econometric perspective
Tilak Abeyshinge and Keen Meng Choy

71 **A Basket Currency for Asia**
Edited by Takatoshi Ito

72 **Private Enterprises and China's Economic Development**
Edited by Shuanglin Lin and Xiaodong Zhu

73 **The Korean Developmental State**
From dirigisme to neo-liberalism
Iain Pirie

74 **Accelerating Japan's Economic Growth**
Resolving Japan's growth controversy
Edited by F. Gerard Adams, Lawrence R. Klein, Yuzo Kumasaka and Akihiko Shinozaki

75 **China's Emergent Political Economy**
Capitalism in the dragon's lair
Edited by Christopher A. McNally

76 **The Political Economy of the SARS Epidemic**
The impact on human resources in East Asia
Grace O.M. Lee and Malcolm Warner

77 **India's Emerging Financial Market**
A flow of funds model
Tomoe Moore

78 **Outsourcing and Human Resource Management**
An international survey
Edited by Ruth Taplin

79 **Globalization, Labor Markets and Inequality in India**
Dipak Mazumdar and Sandip Sarkar

Globalization, Labor Markets and Inequality in India

Dipak Mazumdar and Sandip Sarkar

Routledge
Taylor & Francis Group
LONDON AND NEW YORK

International Development Research Centre
Ottawa • Cairo • Dakar • Montevideo • Nairobi • New Delhi • Singapore

First published 2008
by Routledge
2 Park Square, Milton Park, Abingdon, Oxon OX14 4RN

Simultaneously published in the USA and Canada
by Routledge
270 Madison Ave, New York, NY 10016

Routledge is an imprint of the Taylor & Francis Group, an informa business

Published in association with the International Development Research Centre
PO Box 8500, Ottawa, ON K1G 3H9, Canada
www.idrc.ca
ISBN: 978-1-55250-373-7 (ebk)

Typeset in Times by Wearset Ltd, Boldon, Tyne and Wear
Printed and bound in Great Britain by TJ International, Padstow, Cornwall

British Library Cataloguing in Publication Data
A catalogue record for this book is available from the British Library

Library of Congress Cataloging in Publication Data
A catalog record for this book has been requested

ISBN10: 0-415-43611-7 (hbk)
ISBN13: 978-0-415-43611-3 (hbk)

Contents

Figures

Tables

Maps

1 Introduction

An overview of globalization, reforms and macro-economic developments in India

The process of economic reform and globalization in India

India embarked on a policy of liberalization and globalization in the latter part of the last century. There has been some discussion in the literature as to when India took steps to move away from the regime of comprehensive state control of the economy and dismantle the restrictive structure. A distinction has been made in this connection between 'reforms' and 'globalization'. Strictly speaking the former is supposed to emphasize the process of easing control of the domestic economy, while the latter refers to the attempts at liberalization on the external account. It is useful to keep the two sets of policy distinct, and will be referred to below.

In practice the former entails the latter. As Nayar (2006a, p. 10) observes:

> Economic liberalization within a country creates pressures to integrate the national economy with the world economy ... Say, for example, a country commences economic reform and removes restrictions on production by the private sector to accelerate growth. Eventually the state would have to allow imports of capital goods and intermediate goods to increase production – and that means integration into the world economy. And if it allows imports of these goods, then it must also promote exports in order to pay for them – further integration into the world economy.

In fact the process is more extensive than suggested in the above quotation. External liberalization also involved removing a good deal of restrictions on the import of *consumer* goods, not just capital and intermediate goods to aid production. The motivation for this was to promote competition in the domestic economy, and bring the efficiency levels in the Indian economy nearer the levels of the world economy.

It is clear that reforms of the domestic economy started earlier in India. Rodrick and Subramanain (2004) date the beginning of this process to the return of Indira Gandhi to power at the beginning of the 1980s. They ascribe the new direction to an 'attitudinal' shift in the perception of the leaders after the Congress Party had been 'chastened' by its electoral defeat in the earlier election of the late seventies. They also find a 'structural break' in several key indicators including GDP growth in this period. When the party was returned to power in January 1980 it became more inclined to support growth with the help of a more dynamic private sector. Nayar (2006b) maintains that the reform process started earlier in 1975–1976 during the regime of Indira Gandhi herself. The leadership was jolted partly by the turmoil created by the excesses of the 'dirigist' policy followed in the years 1969–1973 (including large-scale nationalization of banking and industry), and partly by external shocks (including war, droughts and oil price inflation). Besides adopting deflationary policy to stabilize the economy, the Gandhi administration undertook deregulation and export-promotion measures on top of the earlier devaluation (Joshi and Little 2000, p. 56).

While the period of 'creeping liberalization' might have been a prolonged one, it was not till the economic crisis of 1991 that there was an open endorsement of 'paradigm shift' embracing a policy of integration with the world economy and recognition of the need to follow the path of the South-East Asian growth strategy. It involved a sharp devaluation of the rupee; removal of quantitative restrictions on imports; reduction of import tariffs; and a unification of the exchange rate as the rupee was made convertible for current-account transactions. On the domestic front of the reform process the system of industrial licensing was removed and the list of items reserved for the small-scale producers was shortened considerably. The program also saw fiscal reforms though the maintenance of important subsidies, particularly on the agricultural front, continued to plague the budget (Ahluwalia 2002; Joshi and Little 2000).

The removal of quantitative restrictions on imports (QRs), an important feature of the controlled economy, came gradually in the decade of the nineties. QRs on intermediate and capital goods were removed in 1991, but they remained significant on a range of consumer goods. Over the next ten years, a series of international negotiations, starting with the 'Uruguay Rounds' of the WTO, saw a gradual whittling down of these barriers. Tariffs do, however,

Table 1.1 Custom duty rates in India and other developing countries, various years

	All goods	*Agriculture*	*Manufacturing*
India 2001/2002 (CD only)	32.3	41.7	30.8
India 2002/2003 (CD only)	29.0	40.6	27.4
India 2002/2003 (CD + SAD: est.)	35.0	47.1	33.3
India 2003/2004 (CD + SAD: est.)	32.7	46.8	30.7
Brazil 2000	14.1	12.9	14.3
China 2000	16.3	16.5	16.2
Korea 2000	12.7	47.9	6.6
105 developing countries (1996–2000)	13.4	17.4	12.7

Source: World Bank (2003). 'India: Sustaining Reforms, Reducing Poverty', *Development Policy Review*, 14 July, Washington, D.C.

Notes
Unweighted average rates, CD = custom duty, SAD = special additional duty, est. = estimated.

remain as a deterrent to imports on a variety of goods. Table 1.1 is taken from a World Bank Report (Dahlman and Utz 2005) give the extent of the tariff barrier relative to some comparators in the early years of the century.

India's tariff rates remain high by the standards of other developing countries (Table 1.1). But a fair amount of integration with the world economy has been achieved. The following paragraphs briefly discuss the extent of the integration both in terms of the current and capital account of the balance of payments.

External trade

India's merchandise exports had a steep decline during the autarkic regime going down from 2.17 percent of world exports in 1949 to 0.44 in 1980. It hovered around 0.50 percent throughout the decade, and started going up only after 1991. Liberalization of trade has certainly had the impact of starting an upward trend and the share had reached a high of 0.8 in 2004. The share still remains quite low relative to comparator countries in Asia. China increased its share from under 2 percent in 1990 to close to 6 percent in 2003. Even a much smaller country like Korea had a share of 2.8 percent at this date (Table 1.2).

Manufactured exports have been a substantial part of the Indian export growth – reaching 74 percent in 2004 (government of India, Economic Survey – 2005–2006). India seems to have performed relatively better in service exports. The gap between India and comparator countries in service exports, particularly vis-à-vis China, is not as large. India's progress in exports in computer and communications services has been much more than China's – which has done better in travel and related services (Figure 1.1).

Table 1.2 Export growth and share in world exports of selected countries

	Percentage growth rate			*Share in world exports*			*Value (US $ billion)*
	1995–2001	*2003*	*2004*	*2001*	*2003*	*2004*	*2004*
China	12.4	34.5	35.4	4.3	5.9	6.6	593.0
Hongkong	3.6	11.9	15.6	3.1	3.0	2.9	259.0
Malaysia	6.6	6.5	26.5	1.4	1.3	1.4	125.7
Indonesia	5.7	5.1	11.2	0.9	0.9	0.8	71.3
Singapore	4.1	15.2	24.5	2.0	1.9	2.0	179.6
Thailand	5.9	17.1	20.0	1.1	1.1	1.1	96.0
India	8.5	15.8	25.7	0.7	0.8	0.8	71.8
Korea	7.4	19.3	30.9	2.5	2.6	2.8	254.0
Developing countries	7.9	18.4	27.1	36.8	38.8	40.7	3,685.1
World	5.5	15.9	21.2	100.0	100.0	100.0	9,049.8

Source: IFS statistics, IMF.

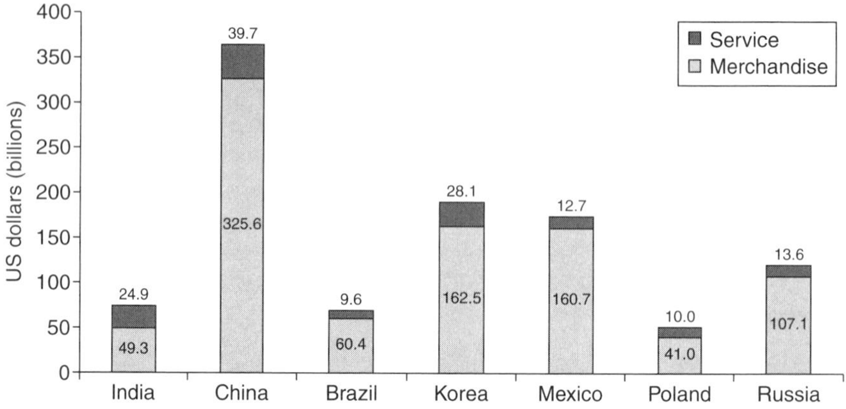

Figure 1.1 Merchandise and service exports, India and comparators, 2002 (source: World Bank staff analysis using World Bank internal database).

Import volume has generally kept slightly ahead of export volume (Table 1.3). India has been helped in its current account by the terms of trade tilting in its favor in a majority of the years (though in very recent years there is a threat of significant deterioration of the TOT). But in any event the balance of payments position has been helped, increasingly so in recent years, by substantial inflow of foreign funds. This is due to another aspect of India's globalization – the substantial emigration of its nationals and the inflow of remittance from the overseas residents of Indian origin.

Foreign-capital inflow other than remittance has in fact not been significant. In fact India has been a significant laggard in attracting foreign direct investment. Even though the actual value of FDI in India has increased several times from its level before liberalization, it is quite small compared with global trends.

Table 1.3 Performance of the foreign-trade sector (annual percentage change)

Year	*Export growth*			*Import growth*			*Terms of trade*	
	Value (in US dollar)	*Volume*	*Unit value*	*Value (in US dollar)*	*Volume*	*Unit value*	*Net*	*Income*
1999–2000	7.7	10.6	8.4	8.3	12.4	7.2	1.5	11.7
1990–1995	8.1	10.9	12.6	4.6	12.9	7.6	5.0	16.5
1995–2000	7.3	10.2	4.3	12.0	11.9	6.9	–2.0	7.0
2000–2001	21.0	23.9	3.3	1.7	–1.0	8.2	–4.5	18.3
2001–2002	–1.6	3.7	–1.0	1.7	5.0	1.1	–2.1	1.5
2002–2003	20.3	21.7	0.3	19.4	9.5	10.7	–9.4	10.3
2003–2004	21.1	6.0	8.5	27.3	20.9	–0.1	8.6	15.1
2004–2005	26.2	13.2	8.9	39.7	8.8	25.7	–13.0	–2.0

Source: The Directorate General of Commercial Intelligence and Statistics, India.

At its height in recent years it has perhaps been no more than 1 percent of GDP – compare to 4.7 percent in China in 2001 and 4.4 percent in Brazil. In value terms India received $4.26 billion in FDI in 2003, compared with $53.5 billion for China (Dahlman and Utz 2005, pp. 30–31). Dahlman, however, reports that according to the *Foreign Direct Investment Confidence Index* (by A.T. Kearney) India's attractiveness to foreign investors is rapidly rising – although it has been well below China's for sometime.

It is clear from this capsule account that globalization in the sense of integration with the world economy has been significant both on the trade and the capital account. It is equally clear that it has been accompanied by a spurt in the growth rate of GDP. Further, the efficiency of the economy has increased in the aggregate. The slow growth of India's constant price investment ratio (increasing from around 22 percent in the 1970s and the 1980s to no more than 24 percent at the end of the 1990s), while GDP growth was accelerating suggests that the marginal capital–output ratio must have been rising significantly. According to one author this ratio was a meager 0.12 in India's worst decade 1965–1974, but it had doubled to 0.246 in the decade of 1991–2000 (Berry 2006, p. 3).

In spite of this positive effect of globalization, doubts are widespread about the success of the economy in achieving greater equity and acceptable levels of poverty reduction. In the next section we shall review, equally briefly, the major thrust of the literature speculating on the possible links between growth and equity. While this review of the theoretical literature is not to provide exact guidelines to our empirical investigation to follow, some of the ideas explored might help to illuminate or emphasize specific results in the chapters to follow.

Labor markets, poverty and inequality in the growth process

The theoretical discussion on the changes in the incidence of poverty and inequality in the growth process of agrarian economies from low levels of income has been a major topic in development economics. The impact of growth is delineated through the labor market, and any predictions about the impact on poverty and inequality must be based on some implicit or explicit view of the structure of labor markets and their functioning.

Homogeneous labor

The classical view on economic development and its impact on inequality is found in the Lewis model and its elaboration in the early work of Kuznets and of Ranis-Fei. All these models consider the growth process to be driven by a shift of labor from the 'traditional to the developing sector', (variously identified as 'rural and urban', 'subsistence and capitalist'; 'agricultural and industrial'). Ranis and Fei in their work on Taiwan formalized the three different elements in this story which together determine the dynamics of inequality over time. First, there is the 'reallocation effect' of labor moving out of agriculture to the secondary and tertiary sectors. This shift will tend to increase inequality if the distribution is less equal in the latter. Second, we have the 'functional distribution effect' in the 'commercialized' sector (the income accruing to the agricultural sector is best treated as mixed income comprising returns to both labor and capital in family farms). An increase in the share of wages will typically increase equality. Before the 'turning point' in the labor market in the Lewis sense, the unlimited supply of labor at constant wages should induce technological change in labor-using direction and should prevent any increase in technology in a capital-deepening way that shifts the functional distribution towards capital. But after the 'commercialization point' in the labor-surplus economy the trend in the functional distribution of income depends on the nature of technical progress. Thus we have the third element in the dynamics: the 'innovation-intensity effect' that might be sufficiently biased against labor to decrease the share of labor over time and tend to increase inequality. The course of inequality through time depends on the relative strength of all these three effects. In fact the 'innovation-intensity effect' depressing the share of wages in the commercialized sector might not be delayed till after the 'turning point' as suggested by Ranis and Fei, but might already be working in a labor-saving way if entrepreneurs in the commercialized sector choose to adopt imported capital-using technology for a variety of reasons.

The Kuznets hypothesis of the U-shaped pattern of inequality dynamics follows from a theory embodying the above three elements. In the early adages of development the reallocation effect is strong and the share of labor also might, fall inducing a rising inequality. The trend is reversed when the reallocation effect weakens and the rise in wages overwhelms any effect coming from continuing bias towards capital-using technological progress.

Since the reallocation effect shifts labor from the low-income sector, the prediction is that in the early stages of the Kuznets process poverty should decline but inequality has an upward trend. We draw particular attention to this prediction because this is the trend we see in a number of developing countries in recent development history – including China and India.

Labor with different skill-levels

The basic model: skilled and unskilled labor

The economic literature in the last decade has paid a great deal of attention to the reason for rising wage inequality in a number of developed countries (including the USA). A feature of the increase in inequality has been the sharp rise of wages of 'skilled' workers relative to the 'unskilled'. The reversal of the trend towards narrowing wage differentials, which had been going on for much of the twentieth century, coincided with the increase in the share of manufactured exports going from the developing countries to USA and Japan in particular. It was natural for a number of US economists to jump to the conclusion that the critical role in this phenomenon was being played by the increase in imports of labor-intensive goods. A well-know theorem within the framework of the

Heckscher–Ohlin model states that when trade is opened up, since each country tends to export the commodity using the more abundant factor, the relative price of the more abundant factor in each country will tend to increase. In developed countries, which shift to more skill-intensive products, the relative price of skilled labor would increase. The corollary of this proposition is that in developing countries the opposite will happen – the wages of unskilled labor would increase relative to those of the skilled, and wage inequality could be expected to fall.

The last corollary is less persuasive than would appear at first sight. The assumption of a homogeneous labor market, which transmits the impulses originating in the tradable manufacturing sector throughout the economy-wide labor market, even if partially acceptable in a developed economy, is wide of the mark in developing countries. The manufactured exports from developing countries originate in the formal sector. The extent to which this sub-sector is linked to the informal manufacturing sector varies from country to country, and in any case it is a small part of the labor market properly considered, which is dominated by the self-employed. We will come back to this point later on. But for the moment let us confine ourselves to some additions to the model as it is applied to the wage-labor market.

Extensions of the model: technological progress

THE DEVELOPED-COUNTRY SCENARIO

The static Heckscher–Ohlin theory is formulated in static terms with trade impacting the economy with an unchanged production function. But the recent decades have seen not only a great deal of technological progress, but of such progress being biased towards skilled labor.

Apart from considerations based on general observations, economists have noted that all explanations of rising wage inequality in the 'North' 'leave unexplained the rising skill intensity in non-traded goods as traded goods sector. In spite of having to pay more for skilled workers, employers in almost all sectors (traded as well as non-traded goods) chose to hire more skilled workers' (Gottschalk and Smeeding 1997, p. 649). 'Only technological change is consistent with rising skill intensity in the face of rising skill prices' (ibid., p. 650).

Daron Acemoglu (2002) has recently surveyed the vast literature on the technical progress and rising wage inequality in the North. The broad facts are clear. While the past 60 years have seen a vast increase in the supply of more educated and skilled workers, the returns to education in the U.S. among other countries fell during the seventies, but have begun a steep rise during the 1980s. This stylized fact is consistent with either a slowing down of the rate of increase of the supply of more skilled workers with a constant pace of technological progress, or alternatively with an accelerated pace of skill-intensive technical progress since the 1980s. It might indeed be a combination of supply and demand side factors.

Acemoglu hypothesizes that technical change is to a very large extent induced by factor market conditions. In the nineteenth century when the North had a plentiful supply of unskilled labor, technical change (e.g., during the industrial revolution) was directed to saving the use of skilled labor. With the rapid growth of education, the supply of skilled labor took a jump in its rate of growth, and the inducement for technical progress shifted towards saving the use of unskilled labor. The skill premium could be held in check as long as the pace of technical progress did not exceed that of the growth of skilled labor. But it is to be expected that with the vast growth of educated labor, its rate of growth in the North had to slow down. In fact, it is possible that the large expansion of international trade might have been a factor in increasing the pace of skill-biased technical progress. As the basic trade model noted, expansion of exports of skill-intensive products from the North tend to increase the relative price of such goods, leading to a search for technology biased towards increasing the productivity in such industries.

THE DEVELOPING-COUNTRY SCENARIO

What have these developments in the North got to do with wage-inequality trends in the South – the developing countries? The availability of a large pool of unskilled labor could be expected to promote technological progress that will economize on the use of skilled labor, as in the nineteenth century North. But there are several important factors which might suggest why this has not happened as a widespread phenomenon.

First, and foremost, it is clear from recent economic history that R&D expenditure is heavily concentrated in the North, and it seems to have the highest payoff in the advanced economies. Thus a more plausible scenario is that, rather than each country and region developing its own technology, new technology is developed in the leading economies of the North and spreads across countries.

Second, we need to emphasize that the techniques of production are not determined only by the relative supplies of different types of labor, but also by the quality of product which the market accepts. It has been noted in the literature that techniques which make use of less capital and less skilled labor often produce a final product which has attributes catering to the demand of low income consumers (Little *et al.* 1987, chapter 13). When a developing country enters export markets in a big way, the final consumer is located in the affluent North, and the technique of production has to be geared to producing items with superior attributes in the quality spectrum. Often these superior quality ranges would need more mechanized techniques with more skill-intensive labor. The point is reinforced by the need to achieve timeliness and homogeneous quality in the batches exported.

Third, it is useful to think in terms of different stages of production for the market. The stage of physical production might indeed be allocated to dispersed units using techniques which make use of labor of the type that is in plentiful supply (of low or traditional skills), but these have to be integrated with organizational, financial and marketing units to be able to supply the export market effectively. The garment industry, which has played such an important role in the export expansion from the South in recent decades, is a case in point. The tertiary activities needed in this export activity often use labor of high or non-traditional skills, which might be in short supply.

Fourth, the last point brings into focus an important part of the story of export expansion from the South. This is the role of outsourcing. Feenstra and Hanson (1999) among others have emphasized that the change in the degree of inequality or the relative wage of unskilled to skilled labor should be analyzed in terms of a foreign outsourcing model, which emphasizes trade in intermediate products, and not exclusively in terms of trade in final products which the H–O model stresses. The production of a final manufactured good can be broken down into several stages which can be arranged in ascending order of the skill intensity of the activity. Outsourcing from the developed country means that the some of the lower ranges of skill intensity in this chain are shifted out to developing countries. But these activities which are shifted, although they are of relatively low skill intensity in the North, are relatively in the higher rung of skill intensity in the South. The net effect of the outsourcing is then to *reduce* the relative demand for less skilled workers in the North, but to *increase* the demand for more skilled workers in the South. Thus while we can expect the skill premium in the North to increase, wage inequality in the South would also tend to increase, contrary to the predictions of the simple H–O model. This kind of outsourcing effect will, of course, be particularly important when the increase in manufactured exports from the South is being driven by direct investment by Northern businesses.

Extensions of the model: several grades of skill

Another dose of realism could be added to the basic H–O model by extending the model to accommodate more than just two types of labor – skilled and unskilled, with the former being complementary to capital in twentieth century technology. Adrian Wood (1994) makes a distinction between at least three types of labor: labor without any modern industrial skill – 'raw labor' which is found in agriculture or low services, but not adapted to work in modern factories or businesses; labor with some basic skills for factory work; and labor with higher skills to perform more complicated tasks in the modern sector. Wood believes education is the basis of this classification – he calls the first category *NO-ED*, the second *BAS-ED* (those with at least primary or low-secondary education) and *SKILD* (with higher levels of education) the third category of labor. But the distinction need not be defined by levels by schooling alone. It is known that a significant wage gap exists in favor of labor of low skill in the 'modern' sector even in the face of plentiful supply of labor in the traditional sector (see the section below on 'segmented labor markets'). Wage inequality within the large-scale industrial sector might be squeezed but the over-all wage inequality increases because of the wage of BAS-ED labor increasing relative to that of NO-ED labor.

Even this limited prediction might be thwarted, if technological progress is skill-biased as discussed above, or alternatively, if we introduce factors of production other than labor and capital. Another strand in Wood's set of hypotheses is that factors of production in addition to labor and capital are critical in the comparative advantage of an economy – most notably land and the availability of natural resources. Countries with relatively large endowments of natural resources will tend to export more land-intensive products, while those with a shortage of such resources will tilt towards more manufactured activities. But the land-intensive primary products lead into processing industries which use less skilled labor than other industrial products. Thus expansion of industrial exports in land-abundant countries *ceteris paribus* would tend to dampen wage inequality, and to increase it in resource-poor economies. This is, of course, only the demand side of the story. The final outcome depends on the relative supply of educated or skilled labor over time – which is to large extent the result of autonomous state policies.

Extensions of the model: shifting boundary of the non-traded sector

In the original discussions of the H–O model there was an implicit assumption that the boundary between the traded and non-traded sectors coincided with that between the manufacturing and the tertiary sector. (For some theorists the implicit assumption was extended further to the distinction coinciding with that between the formal (modern) and informal (traditional) sectors.) Recent developments in the world economy have made this distinction quite unrealistic. For one thing, the services sector has emerged as a major exporter. Second, some products of the non-traded service sector are in close relationship to the traded sector.

Liberalization of the external sector, including devaluation which might accompany it, increases the relative price of traded goods and pushes more resources into the traded sector. But two other effects need to be considered. The first is that some non-traded goods might be complementary to the export sector. Such for instance might be infrastructure, including transport and some supporting services. An increase in the developing countries' exports, even if they are more low-skill intensive than the exports from developed countries, induces complementary expansion of infrastructure which is more skill intensive. Thus the net impact on the demand for labor of different skill levels is uncertain. Second, we should allow for substitution on the consumption side. Consider a developing country with abundant supply of unskilled labor, in which low skill services are close substitutes for the more skill-intensive traded goods (e.g., washing machines). Liberalization reduces the relative price of the latter, leading to a lower demand for low-grade services, and hence a lower demand for low-skill labor, which might offset the increase in demand for such labor induced by the expansion of labor-intensive exports.

The upshot of this discussion is that when the basic trade model is extended by successive doses of realism no definitive prediction about the movements of relative prices of skill, and hence the direction of change in the degree of wage inequality, is possible. This is not to say that empirical analysis would not yield patterns which are uniform over sets of countries or regions. Some work which has been done already has contained the intriguing suggestion that greater openness has decreased wage inequality in East Asian experience in the seventies in the expected way of the simple model, but that in several Latin American countries the opposite has been the case in the eighties. Commenting on this possible generalization, Wood (1997, p. 47) offers a hypothesis apparently based on a suggestion by Jeffrey Sachs:

> It might be the case that all manufactures were import substitutes in Latin America, but only skill-intensive manufactures were import substitutes in East Asia. In that case, non-traded sectors (of a given skill intensity) might be more skill-intensive than import-competing sectors in Latin America and less skill-intensive than import competing sectors in East Asia. Hence, if greater openness (through substitution in consumption) caused non non-traded as well as export sectors to expand (and import-competing sectors to contract), the net effect might be to increase the relative demand for skilled labor in Latin America, but to decrease it in East Asia.

Education policies and the supply of skilled labor

While the evolution of the demand for skilled labor is important, countries differ enormously in the way the formal educational system develops over time. Even if skill formation is heavily influenced by on-the-job training, basic formal education is a critical variable. The impact of education on wage inequality has two different effects. The growth of educated population has a 'compositional effect' which yields an inverted U-shaped pattern à La Kuznets. Until a certain proportion of the population belongs to the more educated (and higher wage) groups, an increase in the proportion of the latter will increase inequality, but after the critical point is passed inequality falls as a larger proportion already belongs to the high wage group. The rising inequality in the earlier part of this process will be moderated if the rate of return to education does not increase, and a fall in the returns of sufficient magnitude will in fact reduce inequality. The latter possibility in fact turns on the supply of educated labor running ahead of the inversing demand as the modern sector develops. It has been noted in the literature that the decrease in wage inequality in Korea and Taiwan during their process of export-led industrialization could be traced in large measures to the prior investment in secondary education (see, for example, Gindling and Sun on Taiwan, and Fields and Yoo on Korea). The experience in these East Asian economies contrasts strongly with the development in Thailand, where post-primary education was neglected till the nineties. Thus over the period 1976–1988, Thailand had a strong upward trend in the inequality index as the export-led boom of the latter eighties put strong pressure in the market for skilled labor (World Bank 1996).

Segmented labor markets

The discussion so far has concentrated on the wage-labor market, and for the most part on labor markets differentiated by levels of measurable skills (e.g., education). But in developing countries much of the labor force is self-employed. Even within the wage-labor market discussions in the mainstream literature are generally concentrated on the formal part of the market – which typically excludes the small and micro sectors, if only because the informal sector is poorly served by regular statistical surveys on wages. If labor markets were reasonably homogeneous, trends in the formal wage-labor market would indicate trends in other parts of the labor market as well. But typically labor markets in such economies are segmented. Labor with the same measurable human capital earns significantly different incomes in different segments of the market. The trends in earnings might also diverge as between the different segments of the market.[1]

A schematic picture of the labor market in a developing country looks like Table 1.4 (A and B refer to the formal and the informal sectors respectively). There are large gaps in the levels of earnings between the segments of the labor market shown in the table. These gaps persist even after we have controlled for measurable human capital differences between the workers found in the different

Table 1.4 A schematic picture of the labor market in developing countries

Urban	*Rural*
UA. The formal sector: 1 Public-sector employees 2 Employees in private large enterprises	*RA. The formal sector:* 1 Public-sector employees 2 Regular (round-the-year) workers in larger farms, plantations or non-agricultural enterprises
UB. The informal sector: 1 Wage labor in small firms 2 Self-employed workers (outside the professions) 3 Casual wage workers	*RB. The small-scale farm sector:* 1 Wage workers, daily and round-the-year 2 Self-employed: owners and tenants 3 Part-time workers in non-farm sector
	RC. Non-agriculture: 1 Self-employed 2 Casual wage employees

Notes

i The urban informal sector is generally demarcated by somewhat arbitrary, but not unreasonable statistical criteria. For example UB1 is defined as enterprises employing less than five workers or those not covered by the official Industrial Census of the large-scale sector. UB2 excludes those with more than middle secondary education.

ii In the rural labor market there is widespread prevalence of multiple occupations. Thus the distinction between RB3 and RC (1 and 2) has to be fixed arbitrarily in statistical sense. Usually workers in the farm sector receive some of their income from the farm activities, and some from the non-agricultural sector. If the proportion of the latter exceeds 50 percent they are placed in the non-agricultural sector.

sectors. The extent of the earnings differences would of course vary from country to country, and one of the tasks of country studies would be to quantify the more important of the wage gaps.

The impact of liberalization or other aspects of globalization on the over-all distribution of income would depend on:

a the distribution of labor between the different segments and the way it changes in response to the developments in the external sector;
b the direction and extent of the changes in the inter-sectoral wage gaps (differences in mean earnings) over time; and
c the change in the distribution of earnings within each sector.

First, the observed levels of employment and earnings in each segment of the stylized classification given above are the product of the intersection of demand and supply curves of labor in that segment. Thus one should be aware that factors affecting the derived demand for labor, as well as the supply conditions of labor, would be instrumental in affecting the outcomes in the segment.

Second, it should be apparent that the movements of these variables over time would be influenced, not only by the way markets for labor of different skills behave over time, but also by the working of the markets of co-operant factors, particularly land and capital. Thus the earnings of the self-employed will be more equally distributed if they are able to accumulate capital more easily over time. A more restrictive capital market would on the other hand both depress their mean earnings relative to those in the formal sector, and also perhaps lead to a more unequal distribution in this sector. For those in the farming sector, the distribution of land and of the basic inputs like fertilizer and water are of crucial significance.

Accounting for the earnings difference between the formal and the informal sectors

The formal–informal sector divide in the labor market cuts through the entire range of non-agricultural industries – both in the tertiary and secondary sectors, and in some economies even in agriculture where there is a large concentration of large Farms or plantations. In view of the importance of this phenomenon it might be useful to review the various hypotheses accounting for the gap in the levels of earnings between the two. In general these hypotheses are not mutually exclusive. They might co-exist in different degrees in any particular economy.

The institutional hypothesis

An important strand in the literature has asserted that labor in the formal sector is 'protected' in the sense that its wage level cannot be undercut by competition from outside labor. This type of 'protection' might be supported by institutions like labor laws or trade unions working independently or working hand-in-hand with the state's labor-regulatory framework. In this case, in so far as wage levels are significantly above alternative earnings outside, entry into the sector is rationed. There is an elastic supply of job seekers but only a fraction can be admitted.

The wage–efficiency hypothesis

The literature has recognized for sometime that the wage–efficiency relationship sets a floor to the wage rate in the formal sector. The most straightforward version is the nutritional one. Efficiency increases with the level of wages because better-fed workers are able to work harder. Thus no employer with a stable body of workers will offer a wage below a level at which efficiency decreases proportionately more than wages. Such a floor to wages is undermined in the informal sector because of a number of factors which include: (i) casual labor without attachment to specific employers; and (ii) self-employment working from households in which earnings of different working members are pooled together. Further, if we do not interpret the wage–efficiency relationship strictly in nutritional terms it will vary with the type of work, quality of machinery used and of goods produced, and the organization of labor. In fact it may become a hazy notion depending very much on the perception of employers. Large formal-sector employers, wary of possible labor unrest or adverse laws protecting job security, might opt for a labor system in which a small elite body of workers produces at a high rate of efficiency in exchange for stable employment at high wages. In any event a significant difference in wage per man is established between the formal and the informal sector although the difference in wage cost per efficiency unit of labor might not be that large. The extent of the differential clearly depends on the quality of labor supplied in the market as well as the institutional setting of the formal labor market.

How does this set of factors affecting the wage differential with respect to the informal sector relate to the discussion above about the skill/education related differentials? The mechanism discussed here in fact establishes a higher wage in the formal sector for all levels of education/skill. This does not, however, mean that formal-sector employers would not use education as a screening or signaling device for the selection of their workforce. If this happens we might find that the educational distribution of the workforce in the formal sector is much more skewed to the higher groups than in the informal. In addition to the wage–efficiency mechanism it would be a supplementary influence enhancing the premium enjoyed by skilled workers in the formal sector.

Constraints in the supply of co-operant factors in the informal sector

As indicated the self-employed constitute a major component of the workforce in the informal sector. Their earnings are in the nature of mixed income, consisting of returns to labor as well as to the co-operant factors used, principally capital (perhaps more of working than fixed capital). It is well known that credit constraints are more severe for the players in the informal sector. Thus the earnings profile in this sector would be critically influenced by the supply function of capital in this sector. It would affect not only the level but the shape of the earnings distribution in the informal sector. The differential with respect to formal-sector earnings is likely to be different for different parts of the distribution – and would also vary from country to country depending on the severity of the credit constraint in this sector.

Regional differences in earnings and employment

In recent work on post-reform developments spatial differences have come to the forefront of discussions. In fact the basic problem of uneven economic growth spatially is in some sense the heart of the subject of development economics. Post-reform developments in the rapidly growing economies like China have drawn renewed attention to the problem. Globalization is heavily directed in the first place to limited areas where producer links to external markets can be most advantageously established and entrepreneurs can exploit important external economies of scale. In fact the concern about unequal development exists equally in a relatively closed economy where major innovations might favor some regions more than others in a cumulative way – as might have happened in the spread of the green revolution in Indian agriculture.

It would be wrong to assume that processes of economic growth necessarily worsen inter-regional inequality. Even if the growth process is concentrated in some regions or enclaves to begin with, rising costs and links to other internal markets can and do produce incentives for producers to diversify to other areas. The net outcome in the dynamic process depends on the relative strength of these centrifugal forces and the process of cumulative causation favoring increased localization.

Plan of the work

The brief review of some of the more important theoretical ideas in the last section provides a background to the empirical investigation of the impact of the reform process and globalization on labor markets, poverty and inequality in India. The major data sources of the data utilized are the 'Thick' rounds of the National Sample Survey (NSS) which are conducted every five years. The latest round available for analysis is the 55th round for 1999–2000. At the time of the completion of this work the subsequent 'thick' round for 2004–2005 is not available for analysis with the unit-level records. But we are able to indicate some broad trends form the published reports issued by the NSS on a limited set of tabulations. This is done in the Epilogue. For the most part the bulk of the work relates to the period ending at the close of the last century.

The book is in four parts. Part I discusses the broad trends for the economy as a whole. Part II focuses on differences between major states and 'broad regions' of the country. Part III carries the analysis to the major sectors – agriculture, manufacturing and the tertiary industries. Part IV discusses issues in labor institutions – both in the formal and the informal sectors.

The analysis for All-India begins with the changes in the incidence of poverty – contrasting in particular the trends in the pre-reform years between the two thick rounds of the NSS before the 55th, and the post-reform period between 1993/1994 and 1999–2000. We discuss, within the framework of a decomposition model, the relative importance of rural–urban shift of labor, growth of the two sectors of the economy and changes in inequality within each. The varying experiences of the urban areas of different population-size groups as well as of the major states in the process are also discussed.

Chapter 3 presents the basic trends in employment and earnings over the period covered, contrasting the post-reform years with the previous periods. It goes on to document the emerging trends in inequality, both for wage earners and all wage- and non-wage-earning households together. We also document the increase in 'rural–urban dualism' in the post-reform years, which had already been suggested by the poverty analysis of Chapter 2.

Part II turns to the analysis of regional differences. This topic is of vital interest in a large country like India. We can do this regional analysis in two ways. First, we can look at differences between major states. This is important because states are political units with a good deal of autonomy in the implementation of economic policies. They are, however, not homogeneous areas in terms of agro-ecological areas. The latter are of great importance in Indian conditions as they have significant impact on productivity and incomes in the large agricultural sector in particular. From this point of view, working with NSS regions which are more homogeneous in character would seem to be more pertinent. We pursue the analysis at both levels. Chapter 5 is a contribution to the analysis of inter-state differences in labor-market outcomes. In the following chapter we work with NSS regions and look at differences in rural poverty in particular. Since the number of NSS regions is large, an attempt is to group them into seven 'broad regions' defined in terms of agro-economic conditions and geographical contiguity. This attempt at the analysis of rural poverty in terms of grouped NSS regions is, we believe, the first such attempt at regional analysis, and will undoubtedly be improved upon by other researchers.

Part III of the book shifts attention to individual industrial sectors of the economy. The problem of labor absorption at reasonable levels of earnings in agriculture is discussed in Chapter 7. Two important questions related to the performance of the agricultural sector are also addressed. The first is the relationship of agricultural productivity to off-farm activities; and the second is the trends in household welfare of different classes of farmers, especially in the post-reform period. The unit-level data available from the NSS are analyzed to throw light on these major issues. The last three chapters in Part III are on the performance in the non-agriculture sector. Chapter 8 is a detailed analysis of the low elasticity of employment with respect to output in the formal manufacturing sector. The fact that the (relatively) high productivity formal sector has been able to create only a low rate of employment growth, in spite of the fairly high rate of output growth, has meant that labor going into the manufacturing sector has been largely absorbed in the low-productivity informal sector. Chapter 9 in fact shows that the developments in Indian manufacturing have been somewhat more complicated than that. Apart from the labor absorption in the truly informal sector – consisting of household enterprises employing none or only a few hired workers, employment has been disproportionately concentrated at the small end of the formal sector, in units employing 6–9 workers (the so-called DME sector). The bi-modal distribution of employment in Indian manufacturing (with concentration at the smallest and the highest size-groups) has given rise to the problem of dualism in Indian manufacturing. This issue is discussed in detail in Chapter 9 – where we analyze the adverse impact of the phenomenon of the 'missing middle' on healthy manufacturing growth, and also the causes leading to its origin and persistence. Chapter 10 takes on the tertiary sector which has been the major source of labor absorption from agriculture.

In the last part of the book – Part IV – labor-market institutions are studied. A critical evaluation of labor laws affecting the formal sector is followed by a review of on-going initiatives to tackle the difficult question of state intervention to improve the conditions of the large numbers of workers eking out a living in India's informal sector.

Part I

Trends in poverty, inequality, employment and earnings

2 Poverty, growth and inequality in the pre- and post-reform periods and the patterns of urbanization in India

An analysis for all-India and the major states

This chapter[1] attempts to assess the impact of the economic reforms (including liberalization) on the incidence of poverty in India. It does so by comparing the changes over the period 1993–1994 to 1999–2000 with the course of poverty decline in the previous quinquennial 1987–1988 to 1993–1994. These are the two periods covered by the six yearly ('thick') rounds of the National Sample Survey (NSS) household expenditure surveys.

A number of researchers have already worked on these particular data sets. Major contributions have been published by Sundaram and Tendulkar (2000, 2001 and 2003) and by Deaton and Dreze (2002). Our work builds on and extends these important pieces of research.

In the first section of the chapter we outline the methodology of decomposition changes in the incidence of poverty used elsewhere by Mazumdar and Son (2002). It seeks to quantify the components of the change between any two periods between those due to growth in mean income (or expenditure), those due to distribution of income, and those due to a shift of population between sectors of the labor market (e.g., the rural and the urban sectors). The first section also undertakes a reassessment of the data on measured poverty for the NSS rounds in question. As is well known from the work referred to above, there are two important issues in the empirical use of the NSS data. First, we have the problem of the correct assessment of the poverty line for different sectors, dates and regions of India. Second, we have the problem of comparability of the measured household expenditure per capita over time due to some changes in the recall period in the successive NSS surveys. In the first section we extend the Deaton and Dreze method of assessing the poverty lines, and the Sundaram–Tendulkar approach to deriving consistent estimates of the average per capita expenditure (APCE) of households at different dates. New estimates of the incidence of poverty are presented.

The second section discusses the main results for all-India. An important extension to previous work is the explicit distinction made in the analysis between metro and non-metro towns.

The third section contains a detailed analysis of the state-level data, and some progress is made in the unraveling of critical inter-state differences in the changes in the incidence of poverty over the periods studied.

The final section presents the major conclusions of the work.

The decomposition of poverty

The conventional method of understanding the dynamism of changes in poverty is done through various inequality measures including that of Lorenz curve and various Entropy measures. The decomposition exercise undertaken here does not require us to specify an inequality measure. It uses an idea of shift in that part of the Lorenz curve, which affects the poor.

A brief exposition of decomposition methodology

To get better understanding about dynamics of changes in poverty, the change in the incidence of poverty can be broken down into three elements: (i) any shift in population between the different segments with different degrees of poverty; (ii) the growth in income in each of the segments; and (iii) the change in the distribution of income, particularly at the lower end where the poor households are located. The methodology of such decomposition is set out in Appendix 1. To summarize the result, the percentage change in poverty for the whole economy can be expressed as:

$$\frac{\Delta P}{P} = \sum_i \frac{\bar{f}_i \bar{P}_i}{P} \frac{(\Delta P_i)_m}{P_i} + \sum_i \frac{\bar{f}_i \bar{P}_i}{P} \frac{(\Delta P_i)_I}{P_i} + \sum_i \frac{\bar{P}_i \bar{f}_i}{P} \left(\frac{\Delta f_i}{f_i} \right)$$
$$= \textit{Growth Effect} + \textit{Inequality Effect} + \textit{Population Shift} \qquad (1)$$

where f_i and P_i are the population share and poverty index of the ith group respectively;

$$\bar{f}_i = \frac{f_{i1} + f_{i2}}{2} \text{ and } \bar{P}_i = \frac{P_{i1} + P_{i2}}{2};$$

the subscript m denotes the change in poverty due to mean income growth and the subscript I gives the measure of poverty change due to change in inequality.

The first term in equation (1) measures the effect of growth within each group on overall change in the poverty incidence, when the distribution within each group remains the same over time. This first term can be further decomposed into two terms:

$$\sum_i \frac{\bar{f}_i \bar{P}_i}{P} \frac{(\Delta P_i)_m}{P_i} = \sum_i \frac{\bar{f}_i \bar{P}_i}{P} \frac{(\Delta P_i)_g}{P_i} + \sum_i \frac{\bar{f}_i \bar{P}_i}{P} \frac{(\Delta P_i)_{bg}}{P_i} \qquad (2)$$

The first term on the right-hand side of above equation measures the effect of growth on percentage change in poverty under the counter-factual that all groups enjoyed the same uniform growth rates and the second term in the right-hand side measures the effect of differential growth rates within groups.

So substituting (2) into (1), we get a decomposition that expresses the percentage change in the poverty incidence as the sum of four components:

(1) overall growth effect when inequality in the distribution does not change; (2) effect of differential growth rates in different groups; (3) effect of change in inequality within different groups; and (4) effect of changes in population shares between groups. This is an exact decomposition and, therefore, there will not be any residual term.

The database

The database used in this analysis is the 'consumption expenditure survey' of various quinquennial rounds of National Sample Survey Organisation (NSSO).[2] The purpose of this study is a comparison of the incidence in poverty between the pre- and post-liberalization periods in India. We have done our analysis on the basis of the three quinquennial rounds, i.e., 43rd (1987–1988), 50th (1993–1994) and 55th (1999–2000). We intend to capture the impact of liberalization by comparing the change in poverty for the first period (1987–1988 to 1993–1994) with that in the second period (1993–1994 to 1999–2000). The decomposition exercise for the Head Count Ratio (HCR), the poverty gap ratio (PGR) and the squared poverty gap ratio has been carried out for 16 major states and for all India (16 states combined).

Adjustment made in the database

We have used average monthly per capita consumption expenditure (APCE) as the proxy for per capital income. However, certain adjustments were made to APCE for the year 1993–1994. Expenditures of all consumer items of 1987–1988 and 1993–1994 are based on a 30-day recall period, known as uniform recall period (URP). For 1999–2000, all but five items are based on the 30-day recall period. The expenditures on the five remaining items are based on 365-day recall periods. These items are clothing, footwear, education, institutional medical expenses and consumer durables. So for 1999–2000, the reference period is known as the mixed reference period (MRP). In the year 1993–1994, for these five consumer items, expenditure data were collected for both 30-day and 365-day reference period. To make 1993–1994 data comparable with 1999–2000 data we replaced 30-day expenditures of these five items with 365-day expenditure.[3] In this fashion, we could change 1993–1994 URP (uniform reference period) expenditures into MRP (mixed reference period) expenditure. A comparison of APCE on these five items by the 30-day and the 365-day reference periods for the year 1993–1994 showed that in both rural and urban areas the change of the reference period from 30-day to 365-day made substantial difference largely in clothing.

We could not convert 1987–1988 consumer expenditure data into MRP in a similar fashion because the expenditure data on the above-mentioned five items were not collected for both the 30-day and the 365-day reference periods. Hence the decomposition analysis for changes in poverty for the period 1987–1988 to 1993–1994 (pre-liberalization period) will be based on URP and for the period

1993–1994 to 1999–2000 will be based on MRP. We will surely lose continuity of poverty estimates in this fashion but avoiding this important issue would otherwise lead to an upward bias in the reduction of poverty in the post-liberalization period relative to the pre-liberalization one.

It might be objected that flow expenditure on low-frequency articles like durables might be reported differently by poor people than by rich consumers for the two alternative recall periods. In fact experiments performed in the 'thin' samples of the 51st to the 54th rounds showed that on the 365-recall period, lower-income households reported higher annual rates compared to the 30 day recall method, but richer households had exactly the opposite bias. At the same time there is an expectation that there has been a large increase on durables affecting all classes. A comparison of the change in APCE based on the 30-day recall as for the first period might not be strictly comparable to the change in the second period based on the 365-day recall. One might be missing less at the mean in the first change than in the second change.[4] An examination of the detailed data on consumption by items and income groups, however, showed that the major difference for poorer groups in the reported expenditure by the two recall periods was in clothing, not in all durables. In the lowest eight income groups, ranging up to the 35–40 fractile, in the 1993–1994 (50th round) survey, the highest difference was Rs.2.5 for durables compared with Rs.17.25 for clothing (the full data are given in Mazumdar and Sarkar 2004). Thus the income-related bias in reported flow of expenditure on durables might not quantitatively of great importance in the two periods of comparison with different recall periods.

Choice of poverty line

In choosing the poverty line we deliberately did not choose the official poverty line as given by the Planning Commission of India. Historically, the rural–urban price differential as incorporated in the official poverty lines at all-India level was around 15 percent level. But the 1993 Expert Group Report recommended separate rates for each state (based on studies of interstate price differentials) and did not explicitly consider the urban to rural differentials. As a result, in 1999–2000, the urban to rural differential implicit in the official lines was around 39 percent and it is astonishingly large for some states (Deaton 2003). The effect of the adoption of the Expert Group lines was to raise measured poverty in urban relative to rural areas. The poverty-line figures, by state and sector, are calculated by using the Tornqvist price index presented by Deaton (2003).[5]

Following Deaton's procedure, the starting point for calculation of poverty indexes is the official rural all-India poverty line for the 43rd round, 1987–1988. The figure is Rs.115.7 per capita per month. First, rural poverty lines for states are obtained by multiplying this base poverty line by *rural price indexes for each state relative to all India*. Urban poverty lines, for each state as well as for all-India, are calculated from the rural poverty lines by scaling up by the respective *urban relative to rural price indexes*.

Similarly, for the 50th round (1993–1994), the all-India rural poverty line of 115.7 of the 43rd round is scaled up by the index for all-India rural for the 50th round relative to the 43rd round. The figure thus calculated is 196.5. Rural poverty lines for states are obtained by multiplying this base poverty line by rural price indexes for each state relative to all-India. Urban poverty lines, for each state as well as all-India, are calculated from rural poverty lines by scaling up by the respective *urban relative to rural price indexes* (see Mazumdar and Sarkar 2004 for the table of poverty lines by states and rural–urban location).

Results for all-India

We first discuss the pattern of poverty decline in the two periods for the whole of India – based on the new figures for the 16 states considered. The results for the decomposition analysis are presented in Table 2.1.

According to our estimates the head-count ratio (HCR) was reduced at a perceptibly higher rate in the more recent period – the decline was about 20 percent higher. This apparent acceleration is, however, largely due to the smaller base of the HCR at the beginning of the second period. The absolute decline in HCR was 6.3 percentage points in 1987–1993 and 5.3 in the 1993–2000 periods. Thus our figures support the conclusion of Deaton and Dreze that 'poverty decline has been fairly evenly spread between the two sub-periods (before and after 1993–1994) in contrast with the pattern of acceleration in the second sub-period associated with the official estimates' (p. 3734).

Growth of mean consumption accelerated in the second period, and played a larger role in the poverty reduction in this period. It can be seen that the inequality effect overall (i.e., taking the rural and urban areas together) continued to play a contributory role to poverty reduction, but the share of this factor in the reduction was much reduced.

Important changes, however, emerged in the relative importance of the rural and the urban areas in the process of poverty reduction. The share of the urban areas in the overall poverty decline increased in the later period (from 12 percent

Table 2.1 Decomposition of poverty change of HCR in rural and urban areas of India

	Uniform growth	*Differential growth*	*Mean growth*	*Inequality*	*Population shift*	*Total*
India (1987–1988 to 1993–1994)						
Rural	−10.67	0.85	−9.82	−3.54	−2.21	−15.57
Urban	−2.39	−0.45	−2.84	−0.41	1.27	−1.83
Total	−13.06	0.40	−12.66	−3.95	−0.94	−17.40
India (1993–1994 to 1999–2000)						
Rural	−18.83	6.62	−12.21	−4.69	−0.37	−17.27
Urban	−4.35	−2.15	−6.50	1.66	0.19	−4.65
Total	−23.18	4.47	−18.71	−3.03	−0.18	−21.92

Source: Unit-level data of consumption schedules of 43rd, 50th and 55th rounds of NSS.

of the total *percentage* decline to 21 percent). This bigger role of the urban sector in poverty decline was, however, *not* due to accelerated population shift to the urban sector. In fact, the 'population shift' effect, while playing a minor role in both periods, actually decreased significantly in the 1993–2000 period.

The crucial element was the higher growth rate in the urban sector. Both the sectors increased the rate of mean growth, but it can be seen from the third column of Table 2.1 that the differential effect of growth rates reduced the incidence of poverty significantly in the urban areas, but increased it in the rural areas. If the latter had grown at the same rate as the rest of the economy, poverty reduction in the 1993–2000 periods would have been 30 percent higher.

The impact of the differential growth rate was balanced to some extent by the impact of changes in inequality in the two sectors. While inequality (in the relevant range of the Lorenz curve) decreased in the rural sector, it deteriorated somewhat in the urban sector, thus canceling out some of the poverty-reduction effect of the differential growth in the sector. But the inequality effects were not as strong as the differential growth effect. This explains the larger role of the urban areas in poverty reduction in this period.

Elasticity of poverty decline and the poverty gap ratio

We have seen that both the growth rate of mean consumption and the rate of decline in the headcount ratio of poverty accelerated in the second period of our study. The elasticity of the change in HCR with respect to the growth in consumption is of interest. Table 2.2 shows the numbers for the two periods. The values of the elasticity in the rural and urban areas are very close together. In both sectors there has been a significant fall in the elasticity in the post-reform period. The results of the decomposition analysis given in Table 2.1 suggest that the reasons for this decline are different in the two sectors. In the rural economy the inequality effect increased its *negative* value, suggesting that *ceteris paribus* the effect on HCR of growth would be strengthened. But there was a significant fall in the shift of the labor force out of this sector, which weakened the impact on poverty. By contrast the urban areas – where the change in HCR benefited from the fall in the intake of labor – suffered from an adverse distributional effect.

The HCR of course only measures the number of people below the poverty line, and does not take account of the economic distance of the poor from the poverty line. This is addressed in the group of measures called the 'poverty gap ratio' (PGR) and its variants. Table 2.3 shows the values of the elasticity of

Table 2.2 Elasticity of head-count ratio with respect to mean consumption growth

Period	*Rural*	*Urban*
1987–1988 to 1993–1994	–3.41	–3.49
1993–1994 to 1999–2000	–2.52	–2.58

Table 2.3 Elasticity of poverty-gap ratio with respect to mean consumption growth

Period	*Rural*	*Urban*
1987–1988 to 1993–1994	–5.33	–4.14
1993–1994 to 1999–2000	–3.21	–3.47

PGR with respect to mean consumption growth in the two periods. It is seen that the elasticity of the PGR with respect to growth is much higher than that of the HCR in both periods and both sectors. This partly reflects the fact that the absolute value of the initial PGR is much lower than that of the HCR. But it also draws attention to the substantive point that the growth process has affected people further below the poverty line strongly – not just those slightly below the threshold.

A second interesting point to note is that as with the HCR the elasticity of PGR fell in the second period in both sectors. However, the decline in elasticity in case of PGR seems to have been much stronger in the rural areas suggesting that the poorest of poor were worse hit.

Table 2.4 gives the results for the decomposition analysis for the poverty gap measure. The different components of the poverty reduction appear to behave in much the same way for this measure as for the HCR. As already pointed out the percentage decrease in PGR is larger than in the HCR, but qualitatively the role of all three components of poverty decline is the same in the two cases. In the post-reform period the role of population shift is much reduced. The urban areas gain in the strength of the growth effect, but inequality increases, offsetting the effect of growth to some extent. The relative slowdown in growth in the rural sector is partly countered by a favorable inequality effect.

There are differences in the relative magnitudes of the various effects. One interesting difference is that in the recent period the inequality effect on the PGR seems to be stronger than on the HCR in the rural areas, but the other way round

Table 2.4 Decomposition of change in poverty-gap ratio in rural and urban areas

	Uniform growth	*Differential growth*	*Mean growth*	*Inequality*	*Population shift*	*Total*
India (1987–1988 to 1993–1994)						
Rural	−14.05	1.37	−12.68	−7.67	−2.14	−22.49
Urban	−2.72	−0.53	−3.23	−0.23	1.15	−2.32
Total	−16.77	0.84	−15.91	−7.90	−0.99	−24.81
India (1993–1994 to 1999–2000)						
Rural	−23.23	8.26	−14.98	−7.83	−0.35	−23.17
Urban	−4.74	−2.48	−7.23	1.15	0.19	−5.90
Total	−27.97	5.78	−22.21	−6.68	−0.16	−29.07

Source: Unit-level data of consumption schedules of 43rd, 50th and 55th rounds of NSS.

in the urban sector. In the rural sector the inequality effect is 38 percent of the growth effect in the HCR decomposition, but 52 percent in the PGR analysis. The offsetting effect of increased inequality is, however, weaker for the PGR in the urban areas (15 percent of the growth effect as against 25 percent for the HCR decomposition).

We are inclined to agree with the Deaton–Dreze conclusion that very little additional insight is to be gained from the detailed analysis of the poverty- gap ratio or its further refinements over and above what we learn from the simple analysis of the HCR (Table 2.5). In view of this we will make no further reference to the measures other than HCR in the subsequent discussions.

Metro and other urban areas

An interesting question pertains to the relative importance of metropolitan (population > one million) and other urban areas in poverty reduction.

The decomposition of HCR was done for metro and other areas separately. Out of the 16 major states considered for the decomposition analysis, only seven states had a metro city in the year 1987–1988, ten states in the year 1993–1994 and 11 states in the year 1999–2000. So to maintain uniformity, we analyzed seven states separately that had a metro city throughout our period of analysis. However, separate analysis was undertaken for the three states that had a metro area only since 1993–1994.

The incidence of poverty is as expected higher in the non-metro areas. We studied changes in the incidence of poverty over the two sub-periods between 1987–1988 and 1993–1994, and 1993–1994 and 1999–2000 and these have been worked out on the basis of both the URP and the MRP criteria (Mazumdar and Sarkar 2004, Table II.3).

For the seven states the decline in poverty incidence in absolute terms does not differ much between metro and non-metro areas in the 1987–1993 period. This implies that in proportionate terms the decline is much more in the metro areas. But the trend seems to have been reversed in the later sub-period.

Table 2.5 Decomposition of change in squared poverty-gap ratio in rural and urban areas

	Uniform growth	*Differential growth*	*Mean growth*	*Inequality*	*Population shift*	*Total*
India (1987–1988 to 1993–1994)						
Rural	−15.83	1.59	−14.24	−10.94	−2.09	−27.27
Urban	−2.83	−0.57	−3.40	−0.05	1.09	−2.36
Total	−18.66	1.02	−17.64	−10.99	−1.00	−29.63
India (1993–1994 to 1999–2000)						
Rural	−25.33	9.06	−16.28	−11.10	−0.35	−27.73
Urban	−4.99	−2.55	−7.54	0.47	0.17	−6.90
Total	−30.32	6.51	−23.82	−10.63	−0.18	−34.63

Source: Unit-level data of consumption schedules of 43rd, 50th and 55th rounds of NSS.

The absolute decline is much smaller in the metros as the HCR seemed to be nearing the floor level, though the difference in percentage terms is not all that much.

Our decomposition analysis was applied to the data for the metro and the non-metro areas in the same way that we had done for the rural and the urban areas as a whole. The results are set out in Table 2.6.

It is seen that a major change in the more recent period was registered by the non-metro urban sector. Differential growth rate favored poverty reduction in a more pronounced way in the non-metros. The non-metro sector also suffered relatively much more from an increase in inequality which seemed to have affected the urban areas as a whole. Combined with a more positive contribution from population shift to poverty reduction, almost the entire decrease in urban HCR in the 1993–2000 period was accounted for by the non-metro sector.

The urban sector by size classes of towns

For some purposes it might be better to classify the urban sector by more size classes than just two. We distinguished three sub-groups: towns with a population of less than 50,000 (small); those larger than this but with less than ten lakhs or one million (medium and large); and those more than one million (metro).

For the country as whole, there is a remarkable difference between the two periods. For the 1987–1993 period the rate of growth of APCE was directly related to the size of towns, the largest towns having the highest growth rate. Accordingly the rate of decline in HCR was also varied directly with the size groups – and in fact this positive relationship was much stronger. *In the post-*

Table 2.6 Decomposition of poverty change of HCR in metro and non-metro areas

	Uniform growth	*Differential growth*	*Mean growth*	*Inequality*	*Population shift*	*Total*
India (1987–1988 to 1993–1994) for 7 states						
Metro	−3.60	−0.60	−4.20	−0.40	0.48	−4.18
Non-metro	−16.44	1.54	−14.85	−1.72	−1.05	−17.62
Total	−20.04	0.94	−19.05	−2.12	−0.57	−21.80
India (1993–1994 to 1999–2000) for 7 states						
Metro	−5.73	0.53	−5.20	1.65	3.23	−0.32
Non-metro	−29.89	−7.46	−37.35	8.35	−7.14	−36.14
Total	−35.62	−6.93	−42.55	10.00	−3.91	−36.46
India (1993–1994 to 1999–2000) for 3 additional states						
Metro	−3.00	−1.60	−4.57	4.36	−0.15	−0.36
Non-metro	−28.60	−9.50	−38.02	3.03	0.29	−34.70
Total	−31.60	−11.10	−42.59	7.39	0.14	−35.06

Source: Unit-level data of consumption schedules of 43rd, 50th and 55th rounds of NSS.

reform years 1993–2000 the relationship has been reversed remarkably. The reversal again is much more prominently revealed in the variations in the rates of decline of the HCR. The small towns had a rate of decline 50 percent higher than the largest group.

This interesting result poses the question: what aspect of the post-reform growth process has been responsible for this reversal of the fortunes of the small towns relative to the larger ones? It is possible to hypothesize that the result might be the consequence of either a strong 'trickle down' effect powered by a decentralization of non-agricultural activities in the urban sector. Alternatively the smaller towns might have enjoyed a stronger growth rate (and poverty reduction) in the post-reform years because of the impact of the growth and commercialization of the agricultural economy. It is probable that both influences have been present in the process observed.

It should be noted that some of the individual states show trends different from the one just mentioned for all-India. There are, in particular, five states in which the rate of growth of APCE and HCR are *directly* related to the size class of towns – the opposite of the result for India as a whole. These are: Gujarat; Karnataka; Maharashtra; Rajasthan; and Tamil Nadu. As it happens, these are the states which have been the largest recipients of Foreign Direct Investments. Since it is well known that FDI goes almost exclusively to metro cities, the hypothesis suggested strongly is that FDI has given an uplift to the growth rate of metro areas in those states where it has played a significant role – and that this impact has raised the growth rate of mean consumption sufficiently induce a higher rate of poverty decline than would be expected by looking at the average for all-India.

The relevant data on FDI per capita in metros by states are plotted along with the rate of growth of APCE in the individual states for the 1993–2000 period in the scatter diagram of Figure 2.1. The relationship is found to be a very strong one.

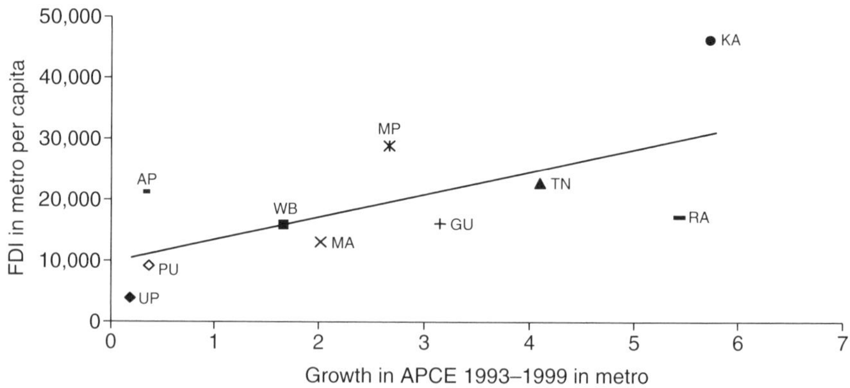

Figure 2.1 Relationship between FDI and growth rates of APCE in metro areas.

Note
See full names of different states like WB, MP, AS, etc. in first column of Table 2.8.

This result suggests that there are two different aspects to the impact of the post-reform developments including globalization on growth and poverty decline in the urban metro sector. On the one hand, there has been a distinct trend towards decentralization of economic activities to smaller towns and cities. This has led to the inverse relationship between growth and the size of towns observed in many states and in India as a whole. There are, however, a group of states in which the role of FDI is strong, and the impact is seen in a high growth rate in metro areas, so that a *direct* relationship between growth (and poverty reduction) and town size is observed. The only exception to this two-way classification of states is Rajasthan. The inflow of FDI per capita in metros in this state is low, yet it shares the characteristics of the high FDI states in having a relatively high growth rate in the larger towns (see Figure 2.1). It is, however, well known that even if the inflow of FDI is small Rajasthan has participated in the globalization process strongly through the promotion of international tourism in particular.

The implication of the argument of the last paragraph is that the 'trickle down' effect on smaller towns has been more important in the states with a lower level of international connection. The reform process has encouraged decentralization in these states. But what about the impulse to growth in small towns coming from the rural sector? Figure 2.2 plots the growth rate of APCE in small towns (with population of less than 50,000) against the growth of APCE in rural areas of individual states. There is indeed a positive relationship, but it is a relatively weak one.

Trends in the rural–urban dualism

An important issue in the development literature is the rural–urban gap in levels of income (and consumption) and in the incidence of poverty. Post-reform developments and globalization are sometimes viewed with concern as acting towards increasing the degree of this dualism.

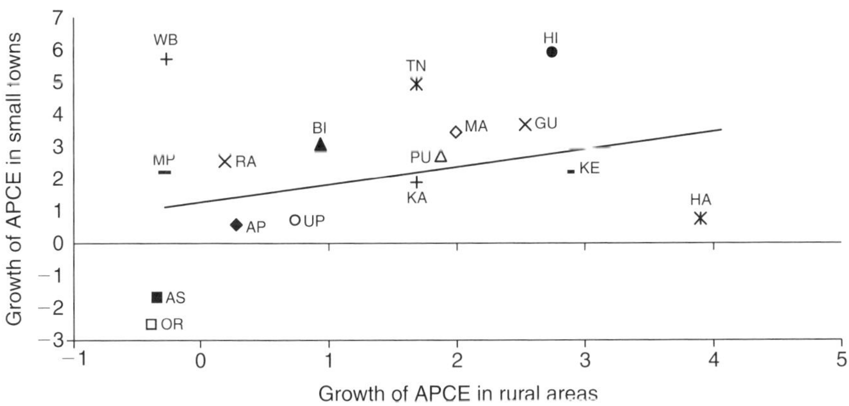

Figure 2.2 Relationship between growths of APCE in small towns and rural areas.

Note
See full names of different states like WB, MP, AS, etc. in first column of Table 2.8.

We tried to throw some light on the variations in the gap between the incidences of poverty between rural and the urban areas across states. The variable to be explained is the ratio of the HCR in rural areas to that in the urban areas. Since the rural economy is large in all Indian states, a higher level of development in a state would generally imply a higher rural APCE. Also, with economic growth urbanization increases. A little reflection shows that the net impact of both these variables on the relative rural–urban gap depends on whether or not 'trickle down' is confined to the sector in question, or extends to the other sector. Take the expected sign of APCE (rural) first. If the impact is largely confined to the rural sector, then the relative gap would be reduced (the sign would be negative), but in so far as it reduces the level of the urban poor through higher demand for urban goods and services, the sign of the variable would be positive. The final outcome depends on the relative strength of the two forces. Similarly a higher rate of urbanization would mean a larger relative gap if urbanization has only a limited effect on rural incomes at the lower end of the scale, but would go the other way if the urban to rural linkage is strong. Second, as far as urban poverty is concerned, the size distribution of cities also matters since the incidence of poverty is inversely related to city size. We can use the summary measure of the share of metro population in the urban sector as a variable to capture this effect. The prediction about the sign of this variable, as with the other variables, depends on the relative strength of the linkage with the economies of sectors outside the metros. Generally, the incidence of poverty is lower in metro cities, so a greater preponderance of metro population would imply a *higher* relative gap in poverty incidence between the rural and the urban sector. But if 'trickle down' in states with a larger metro population is weak, the higher development of metro towns would have a limited effect on poverty incidence in non-metro urban areas, thus pushing up the HCR in the urban sector as a whole, i.e., the rural–urban ratio in HCR could be *lower*. The regression model with these variables is fitted to inter-state variations in the rural–urban HCR ratio for different dates of the NSS rounds, and the results are reported in Table 2.7.

The results show that in the pre-reform years, between 1987–1988 and 1993–1994, the impact of the rate of urbanization is significantly *negative*: 'trickle down' extends to the rural economy. But the sign of the variable measuring the share of the metro in urban population is significantly *positive*: the growth of metro towns apparently reduces HCR in the urban sector as a whole, not so much in the rural areas. The sign of APCE (rural) is positive but not very significant.

In the post-reform years both the urbanization and metro share variables lose their significance, and the APCE is even less significant. Evidently factors other than those connected with the rural–urban 'trickle down' process discussed above now explained inter-state variations in the poverty gap. We have already seen that in the post-reform years urban growth was more important in reducing poverty across a wide range of states. This process reduced the inter-state variations in the relative poverty-gap even as it reduced the overall value of this gap.

Table 2.7 Regression of relative rural–urban poverty across major 16 states in different years

Sl.	*Year*	*Independent variable*	*Regression results*				
I	1987–1988	Relative gap in poverty	=216.79+ (1.04)	1.87 $APCE_{ru}$ (1.54)	−19.50 UR (−2.94)***	+8.87 SHMET (2.02)*	;R^2= 0.435
II	1993–1994 URP	Relative gap in poverty	=314.86+ (2.67)**	0.53 $APCE_{ru}$ (0.71)	−11.82 UR (2.65)**	+5.18 SHMET (1.76)*	;R^2= 0.411
II	1993–1994 MRP	Relative gap in poverty	=341.43+ (1.46)	1.20 $APCE_{ru}$ (1.44)	−26.68 UR (−2.81)**	+11.36 SHMET (1.84)***	;R^2= 0.424
IV	1999–2000	Relative gap in poverty	=384.78– (3.80)***	0.30 $APCE_{ru}$ (–0.90)	−4.62 UR (–0.99)	+3.38 SHMET (1.30)	;R^2= 0.311
V	1999–2000	Relative gap in poverty	=378.88– (4.16)***	0.47 $APCE_{ru}$ (–1.82)*	−1.98 UR (–0.72)	+0.01 FDI_{urpc} (2.20)**	;R^2= 0.439

Notes

1 Relative gap in poverty is defined as the ratio of rural to urban HCR; $APCE_{ru}$ is level of APCE in rural areas; UR is the urbanization rate from respective NSS rounds; SHMET is share of metropolitan population in urban population and FDI_{urpc} is cumulative FDI approved (1991–98) urban per capita.

2 ***, ** and * denoted significance at 0.01, 0.05 and 0.1 level and figures in parentheses () are t-values corresponding to estimated coefficients.

We have also seen that within urban areas there was a distinction between the states which received a relatively large flow of FDI and those who did not. In the FDI states, it will be recalled, the pattern of poverty decline in urban areas by size of towns was different. It was inversely related to the size group of towns and was lowest in the largest cities. The relationship between HCR and town size was just the reverse in 'non-FDI' states. We tried to see if this difference was in any way related to the pattern of inter-state variability of the rural–urban poverty gap. The last equation of Table 2.7 shows that it is indeed so. FDI (urban) per capita is the only significant variable in the estimated equation and is *positive*, implying that those states which have a large FDI inflow have a significantly *lower* incidence of urban poverty relative to the rural sector. In other words, the effect of metro towns in increasing the relative poverty gap – which was true of the entire range of states in the pre-1993–1994 years – is now significant only in the FDI states. It draws attention to the point that FDI is an important player in the poverty scene in spite of the total inflow being much smaller in India than in other countries like China. FDI inflow reduces poverty significantly in the largest cities, but its 'trickle down' effect is limited outside the metro areas.

Differences by states

It is well known that Indian states differ substantially in the incidence of poverty. Also the distribution of population among the different states is uneven. The trend in the all-India measure of poverty, such as the HCR, will then be affected by the way the pattern of the difference in poverty reduction between more and less populous states. It has been hypothesized that growth rates and hence the rate of poverty reduction have not been generally stronger in the states with a larger share of the poor. The following paragraphs explore this hypothesis in more detail for the two periods we are considering.

Table 2.8 gives the shares of the individual states in the total count of those below the poverty line for the three dates (corresponding to the 38th, 50th and the 55th rounds of the NSS).

Seven states – Andhra Pradesh, Bihar, Madhya Pradesh, Maharashtra, Orissa, Uttar Pradesh and West Bengal – accounted for over 70 percent of the total poor in the rural areas in 1999–2000. Just three states – Bihar, Madhya Pradesh and Uttar Pradesh – accounted for over 40 percent of the rural poor. It is interesting to note that the same states to a large extent account for the bulk of the urban poor as well. The only difference between the two sets is Orissa which accounts for only 2.6 percent of the urban poor, reflecting the relative underdevelopment of the state. Looking back to 1987–1988 it is seen that there is not much difference in the spatial distribution of the poor – the same states account for the bulk of the rural and the urban poor. Perhaps the concentration of the poor in these states was a little higher in the earlier period.

It is interesting to see which states fell behind the all-India average in APCE growth rate in the most recent post-reform period. Because of its weight we look especially at the rural areas. The lagging states are: Assam, Andhra Pradesh,

Table 2.8 Distribution of persons below poverty line across states (percentage of total)

State	*1987–1988*		*1993–1994 (URP)*		*1993–1994 (MRP)*		*1999–2000*	
	Rural	*Urban*	*Rural*	*Urban*	*Rural*	*Urban*	*Rural*	*Urban*
Andhra Pradesh (AP)	**6.9**	**8.1**	6.8	7.7	6.9	8.3	**7.7**	**7.1**
Assam (AS)	N.A.	N.A.	3.4	0.8	3.2	0.8	4.6	1.3
Bihar (BI)	**16.4**	**8.6**	17.9	7.6	18.5	7.5	**17.9**	**9.5**
Gujarat (GU)	4.3	4.6	4.2	5.3	4.2	4.8	3.1	2.7
Haryana (HA)	0.7	0.9	1.0	1.1	0.9	1.0	0.3	1.0
Himachal Pradesh (HP)	0.3	0.0	0.4	0.0	0.3	0.0	0.2	0.1
Karnataka (KA)	5.2	7.2	5.6	7.4	5.3	7.3	4.5	5.5
Kerala (KE)	2.1	2.7	2.0	2.5	1.8	2.9	1.4	2.6
Madhya Pradesh (MP)	**8.9**	6.2	9.0	7.1	8.8	6.6	**11.4**	**7.8**
Maharashtra (MA)	**8.7**	**12.7**	9.9	14.1	10.4	14.6	**8.1**	**15.6**
Orissa (OR)	5.6	1.7	5.7	1.6	6.1	1.8	**7.9**	**2.6**
Punjab (PU)	0.4	0.8	0.4	1.2	0.4	1.1	0.3	0.9
Rajasthan (RA)	4.8	3.9	3.8	4.6	3.5	4.1	2.7	2.9
Tamil Nadu (TN)	**7.4**	**10.2**	6.4	10.2	6.8	10.4	6.1	8.7
Uttar Pradesh (UP)	**15.8**	**15.8**	15.6	15.1	15.1	15.1	**13.3**	**17.8**
West Bengal (WB)	**7.2**	**8.3**	5.9	7.1	5.9	7.1	**7.7**	5.5
India	100.0	100.0	100.0	100.0	100.0	100.0	100.0	100.0
Share of 16 states in all-India	94.6	91.8	98.0	93.4	97.9	93.5	97.1	91.4
Number of poor All-India (in Lakh)	2,335	462	2,181	431	1,787	342	1,582	270

Source: Unit-level data of consumption schedules of 43rd, 50th and 55th rounds of NSS.

Note
URP is uniform reference period and MRP is mixed reference period.

Bihar, Madhya Pradesh, Orissa, Rajasthan, Uttar Pradesh and West Bengal (for details see Mazumdar and Sarkar 2004, pp. 24–25). These states coincide with the set accounting for the bulk of the rural poor. The only state with large HCR missing in the set is Maharashtra – which is fairly close to the growth rate rural all-India. We conclude that the spatial pattern of growth rates in the 1993–2000 period was *not* favorable to the cause of poverty decline in the rural sector.

Poverty decline in the two periods

Further light can be shed on the experience of inter-state differences in poverty decline in the post-reform period by looking directly at the changes in the HCR. In Figures 2.5 through 2.8 we present the scatter diagrams of the state-level changes in the HCR over the two time periods between the NSS surveys – 1987–1988 to 1993–1994 and 1993–1994 to 1999–2000. We plot the change in the HCR on the y-axis against the level of HCR in the initial year of the respective period on the x-axis. The graphs are drawn separately for the rural and the urban areas.[6]

We would expect that the decline in HCR would be higher in the states where the absolute value of the HCR is higher. The percentage decline in HCR is given by the ratio of the two magnitudes. Convergence between states in the incidence of poverty will occur only if the percentage decline *increases* with the initial value of the HCR – i.e., the relationship between the two magnitudes in the scatter diagram is non-linear. The graphs (Figures 2.3 to 2.6), however, show that there is at best a linear relationship between the decline in HCR and its initial value. There is no evidence of inter-state differences in poverty incidence to converge over time in either sector.

Second, it is seen that while the slope of the line relating the initial HCR to its absolute change is more or less the same in the urban areas, it has definitely become flatter in the rural areas in the post-reform years. For the rural sector as a whole we can no longer say that the percentage decline in poverty is directly related to the absolute value of HCR in the rural areas of the state in the 1993–1994 to 1999–2000 period. The reason for this is that several of the states suffered from a deceleration of poverty decline in their rural sector in the post-reform areas. There is naturally an overlap between the states lying significantly below the regression line of Figure 2.6 and those identified earlier in this section as being laggards in rural APCE growth. They include Andhra Pradesh, Assam, Madhya Pradesh and West Bengal.

Table 2.9 showing the classification of states into four groups and

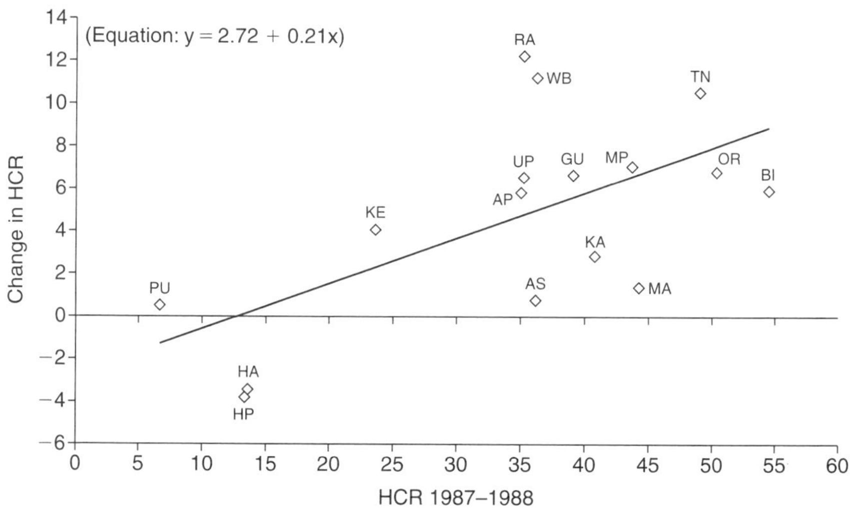

Figure 2.3 Poverty (HCR) and declines in HCR from 1987–1988 to 1993–1994 (rural) across states.

Note
See full names of different states like WB, MP, AS, etc. in first column of Table 2.8.

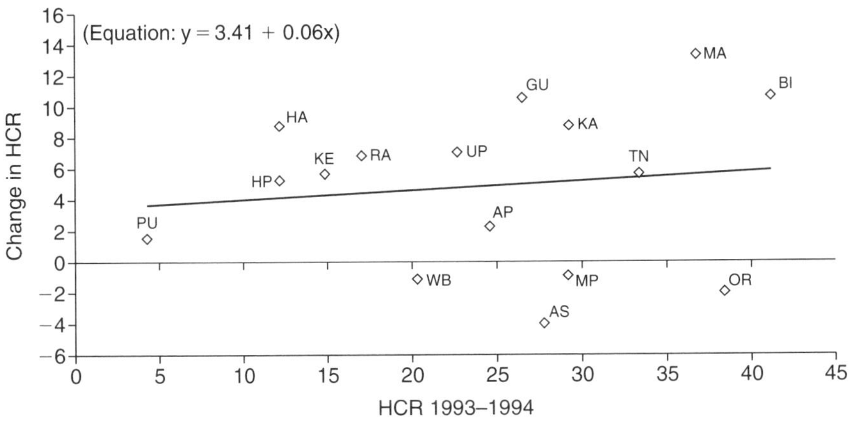

Figure 2.4 Poverty (HCR) and declines in HCR from 1993–1994 to 1999–2000 (rural) across states.

Note
See full names of different states like WB, MP, AS, etc. in first column of Table 2.8.

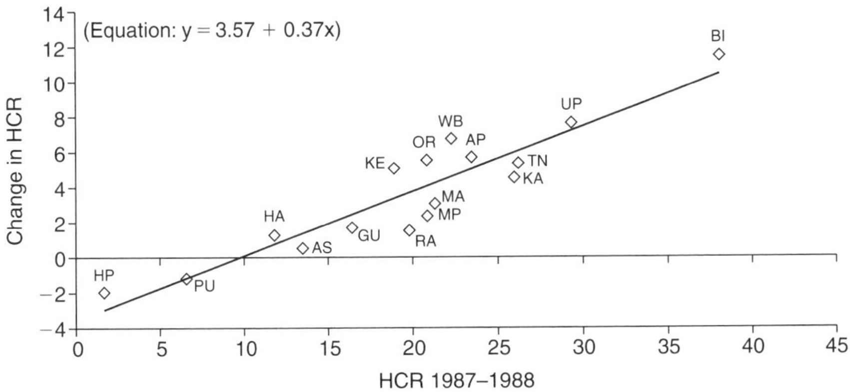

Figure 2.5 Poverty (HCR) and declines in HCR from 1987–1988 to 1993–1994 (urban) across states.

Note
See full names of different states like WB, MP, AS, etc. in first column of Table 2.8.

their changes over the two periods might help to throw some further light on state-level changes in *rural* poverty decline. The groupings are from I to IV in descending order of poverty decline. Table 2.9 confirms that the flattening of the regression line in Figure 2.4 is largely due to four states slipping from Category I (high HCR decline) and category II (middling decline) in the pre-reform period to category IV in the post-reform one. This adverse effect is balanced to some extent by Maharashtra moving from IV to I, and Karnataka from IV to II.

Further details on the change in the HCR between the two periods for individual states is provided in Table 2.10 which reproduces the results of the

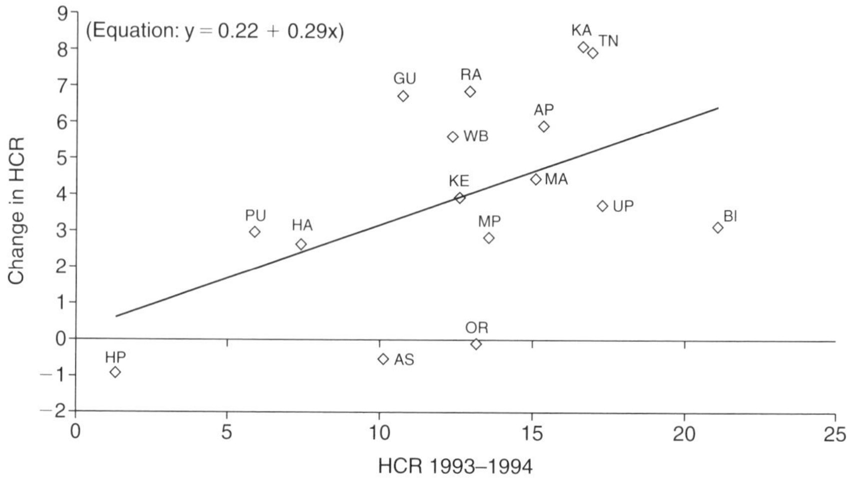

Figure 2.6 Poverty (HCR) and declines in HCR from 1993–1994 to 1999–2000 (urban) across states.

Note
See full names of different states like WB, MP, AS, etc. in first column of Table 2.8.

Table 2.9 Patterns in decline of rural poverty among four groups of states over two periods

1987–1993 /1993–1999	*I*	*II*	*III*	*IV*
I	BI	TN		MP OR
II		GU RA UP		AP WB
III			PU KE	
IV	MA	KA	HA	AS

decomposition analysis applied to the data for each state. The total *percentage* change in poverty for the state as a whole (rural and urban combined) is given in column 10, while the components of this statistic are found in the six columns preceding it. The column of %D gives the component due to differential growth, while %I is that due to change in inequality. The differences between HCR change and the sum of %D and %I in each sector are the sum of two elements: (i) 'Uniform growth' – the hypothetical growth if the APCE in each sector had grown at the same rate as in the state as a whole; (ii) the effect of the rural–urban shift (the latter has been small in most states). The last two columns of Table 2.10 give the *percentage* change in HCR in each of the two sectors – rural and urban separately.

Table 2.10 Decomposition of percentage change in head-count ratio (HCR)

Group	*Year*	*State*	*Rural HCR change*	*Of which*		*Urban HCR change*	*Of which*		*Total HCR change*	*% change in HCR*	
				%D	*%I*		*%D*	*%I*		*Rural*	*Urban*
1	1993–1999	Bihar	–25.0	0.0	–9.5	–0.5	0.4	0.1	–25.5	–25.9	–14.9
1	1987–1993	Bihar	–9.4	3.6	–8.2	–3.0	–	0.1	–12.4	–10.9	–30.0
1	1993–1999	Gujarat	–32.8	2.5	2.3	–10.3	–	–0.4	–43.2	–39.7	–62.8
1	1987–1993	Gujarat	–19.6	7.5	1.2	0.8	–	6.8	–18.8	–17.0	–10.3
1	1993–1999	Maharashtra	–30.2	3.1	–5.9	–5.3	–	2.0	–35.4	–36.2	–29.5
1	1987–1993	Maharashtra	–7.5	5.3	–2.4	–0.6	–	0.2	–8.1	–3.1	–14.4
1	1993–1999	Karnataka	–23.8	10.9	0.0	–9.3	–	2.5	–33.0	–29.8	–48.8
1	1987–1993	Karnataka	–5.2	3.0	–1.9	–3.8	–	0.2	–9.0	–7.0	–17.5
1	1993–1999	Haryana	–59.9	–0.4	–7.5	–5.5	2.1	7.1	–65.4	–71.9	–35.5
1	1987–1993	Haryana	14.4	3.4	19.9	1.7	–	4.0	16.2	25.3	–10.8
1	1993–1999	Punjab	–24.9	7.4	10.0	–16.5	–	7.3	–41.4	–36.5	–50.4
1	1987–1993	Punjab	–7.2	3.5	–26.0	6.8	–	3.2	–0.3	–7.7	18.2
2	1993–1999	Tamil Nadu	–12.9	18.4	6.4	–10.3	–	6.8	–23.2	–17.0	–46.9
2	1987–1993	Tamil Nadu	–16.3	–4.5	–0.8	–4.8	2.0	–1.6	–21.1	–21.5	–20.4
2	1993–1999	Rajasthan	–32.0	12.6	–30.6	–10.1	–	–1.1	–42.1	–40.0	–53.1
2	1987–1993	Rajasthan	–32.0	–6.0	–9.0	0.4	2.2	–0.8	–31.6	–34.7	–7.8
2	1993–1999	Uttar Pradesh	–26.9	2.9	–14.0	–2.8	–	0.7	–29.7	–31.1	–21.6
2	1987–1993	Uttar Pradesh	–16.7	0.0	1.7	–3.3	–	–0.9	–20.0	–18.6	–26.0
2	1993–1999	Kerala	–31.1	–2.1	13.9	–5.6	0.2	6.7	–36.7	–38.2	–31.1
2	1987–1993	Kerala	–21.6	0.0	4.3	1.1	–	–1.3	–20.5	–17.2	–26.7
3	1993–1999	Andhra Pradesh	–10.4	12.5	–1.3	–5.7	–	1.6	–16.1	–9.1	–38.5
3	1987–1993	Andhra Pradesh	–17.8	–1.3	–7.2	–1.5	0.7	–3.7	–19.3	–16.6	–24.3
3	1993–1999	Madhya Pradesh	4.2	10.9	–2.4	–3.1	–	2.5	1.1	3.2	–20.8
3	1987–1993	Madhya Pradesh	–18.3	–1.8	–2.8	0.8	1.2	–0.7	–17.6	–16.2	–11.3

continued

Table 2.10 continued

Group	*Year*	*State*	*Rural HCR change*	*Of which*		*Urban HCR change*	*Of which*		*Total HCR change*	*% change in HCR*	
				%D	*%I*		*%D*	*%I*		*Rural*	*Urban*
3	1993–1999	Orissa	0.7	–3.0	–0.6	1.4	0.2	–0.8	2.1	5.1	0.8
3	1987–1993	Orissa	–13.9	1.5	–7.5	–1.0	–	–0.2	–14.9	–13.5	–26.6
3	1993–1999	West Bengal	6.6	18.6	–2.0	–7.8	–	–0.7	–1.1	5.3	–45.4
3	1987–1993	West Bengal	–25.0	0.0	–0.5	–5.5	–	0.9	–30.5	–30.9	–30.3
3	1993–1999	Assam	13.8	7.5	6.3	0.2	–	1.5	14.0	14.4	5.3
3	1987–1993	Assam	–4.2	1.9	–23.7	0.7	–	0.1	–3.5	–2.1	–3.9
	1993–1999	India	–17.3	6.6	–4.7	–4.7	–	1.7	–21.9	–19.8	–32.9
	1987–1993	India	–15.6	0.9	–3.5	–2.0	–	–0.4	–17.5	–15.8	–21.6

Note
D and I denote the differential growth effect and inequality effects.

We can use the table to classify the states into three groups in terms of the *percentage change in HCR* over the two periods we are considering (taking the rural and the urban sectors together):

1 states which accelerated the decline in HCR in the post-reform period markedly (more than doubled the percentage decline): Bihar, Gujarat, Maharashtra, Karanataka, Haryana, and Punjab;
2 states which had a less spectacular, but still substantial, decline in HCR relative to the earlier period: Tamil Nadu, Rajasthan, Uttar Pradesh and Kerala;
3 states which suffered retardation in HCR decline (or actually registered an increase in HCR) Andhra Pradesh, Madhya Pradesh, Orissa, West Bengal and Assam.

It is to be noted that the list in group 3 is identical to the group already mentioned earlier as the laggards in *rural* poverty decline. It shows the quantitative importance of the rural sector in the overall trend in poverty reduction.

While the growth of the rural sector is naturally the dominant influence on the overall decline in HCR (the share of the rural sector in the incidence of poverty being so much more), it is important to note that the urban sector became a much more important player in several states. We have already seen in section II that this is true for all-India in the post-reform years. But some individual states stand out. The urban sector of Gujarat, Karnataka and Punjab among the group 1 states, and Tamil Nadu and Rajasthan among the group 2 states contributed to the total HCR decline of to an extent of a third or more of the contribution of the rural sector. In all these states the differential rate of growth was higher in the urban sector, contributing to the HCR decline (%D in the urban sector was negative).

Of the states in which HCR declined Bihar and Uttar Pradesh are the only ones in which the rural sector increased its contribution to the decline. Rural growth also contributed strongly to HCR decline in Kerala, but it was offset to some extent by a substantial increase in inequality in the sector, so that the contribution of the urban sector increased in the 1993–1999 period. In the case of Bihar (and to some extent Uttar Pradesh, in so far its Eastern districts are really an extension of the economy of Bihar) the strong rural growth in APCE causing poverty decline is less due to the growth rate of its domestic rural economy, as it is to the remittance sent back home by migrant labor participating in the rural economy of the North-Western states and in urban areas scattered all over India.

We have already underlined in the third section the point about the increased inequality in the urban sector in the post-reform period for India as a whole. Its relative impact in retarding poverty decline is significant, but quantitatively not substantial. The state-level data reveal that the inequality effect has been more important in some states. Running down the column (9)–%I for the urban sector – it is seen that this has been so in Tamil Nadu, Gujarat, Haryana, Kerala and Punjab. It should not, however, be concluded that inequality increased only in the urban economy of some states. There was substantial inequality increase retarding poverty decline in the rural sector of a few states as well. These include Tamil Nadu, Kerala, Punjab, and to some extent Gujarat. It is interesting to note that these states are also the ones which experienced the adverse inequality effect in the urban sector as well.

It is important to comment on the experience of the *group 3* states. Andhra Pradesh suffered from a slight retardation in the rate of decline in HCR, but the incidence of poverty actually increased in the other states in this group. It is seen that all these states suffered from adverse movements in the HCR in the *rural* sector. The figures of column (5) reveal that the crucial problem was the differentially lower growth in the rural economy which contributed to an increase in HCR. In the case of three of three states – Andhra Pradesh, Madhya Pradesh and West Bengal – the poverty incidence would have been worse but for the stronger performance of the urban sector. Assam stands out in registering an increase in inequality both in the rural and the urban sectors. An increase in urban inequality also contributed to HCR decline in Madhya Pradesh, but its relative importance was much less than that of the slow-down in rural growth.

Conclusions

In this chapter we have contrasted the change in poverty incidence in the 1987–1993 period with that in the 1993–1999 years. The second period could be seen as one in which the impact of the reforms tied to liberalization of the economy could be expected to have had some impact. We have based this comparison from several angles on the 'consumption expenditure survey' data generated by the NSS for three quinquennial rounds: the 43rd (1987–1988), the 50th (1993–1994) and the 55th (1999–2000). We have addressed the methodological problems involved in the surveys, and produced a new set of consistent data on mean consumption of the survey households, and the incidence of poverty. The differences between our estimates and those of other researchers have been spelled out in the first section and the Appendices.

We have a used a decomposition analysis of the percentage change in poverty over the two successive periods. This method used elsewhere by Mazumdar and Son (2002) enables us to quantify the relative contribution of three elements to the overall change in poverty incidence: mean growth of consumption, population shift between defined sectors and the change in inequality. The analysis is applied to the economy as a whole and to its rural and urban sectors. It is done for all-India and for the individual states.

The more important conclusions are the following:

1 At the all-India level the absolute change in the HCR was about the same in the post-reform period as in the previous one, but the rate of change was higher because the initial base was smaller. However, the growth rate of

APCE increased rather more so that the elasticity of poverty change with respect to income fell. This is true even more for the poverty gap measure.

2 The share of the urban sector in poverty reduction increased in the second period. This was not due to a larger shift of population to urban areas – in fact the rate of this shift decreased. The major reason for the change was the higher differential growth rate of the urban sector. It was offset, but only partially, by an increase in urban inequality. However, the relative impact of rising urban inequality in retarding poverty decline in the late nineties was quantitatively not substantial.

3 Turning to poverty decline by size of towns there are two different aspects to the impact of the post-reform developments including globalization. On the one hand, there has been a distinct trend towards decentralization of economic activities to smaller towns and cities. This has led to the inverse relationship between growth and the size of towns observed in many states and in India as a whole. There are, however, a group of states in which the role of FDI is strong, and the impact is seen in a high growth rate in metro areas, so that a *direct* relationship between growth (and poverty reduction) and town size is observed, as was the case generally in the urban sector as whole in the previous period.

4 State-level analysis showed that the states could be divided into three groups when we compare the change in HCR in the post-reform years with the period preceding it:

group 1 are those which accelerated the decline in HCR in the post-reform period markedly (more than doubled the percentage decline): Bihar, Gujarat, Maharashtra, Karanataka, Haryana, Himachal Pradesh and Punjab;

group 2 states had a less spectacular, but still substantial, decline in HCR relative to the earlier period: Tamil Nadu, Rajasthan, Uttar Pradesh and Kerala;

group 3 states suffered retardation in HCR decline (or actually registered an increase in HCR): Andhra Pradesh, Madhya Pradesh, Orissa, West Bengal and Assam.

It is seen that the unhappy performance of the group 3 states is largely due to retardation in the rate of growth of the *rural* economy of these states. The growth of the urban sector, however, played a significant role in the poverty decline of group 1 and group 2. We have already seen that at the all-India level, urban growth in the post-reform years was higher than rural growth. Although the urban economy is still a small part of the economy, its contribution to poverty reduction started being important in several states. The urban sector of Gujarat, Karnataka and Punjab among the group 1 states, and Tamil Nadu and Rajasthan among the group 2 states contributed to the total HCR decline to as much as a third or more of the contribution of the rural economy.

5 Increased inequality seems to have been associated with the higher growth rate in the urban sector in the post-reform period for India as a whole. Its relative impact in retarding poverty decline is significant, but quantitatively not substantial. The state-level data reveal that the inequality effect has been more important in some states. They include Tamil Nadu, Gujarat, Haryana, Kerala and Punjab. It should not, however, be concluded that inequality increased only in the urban economy of some states. There was substantial inequality increase retarding poverty decline in the rural sector of a few states as well. Theses include Tamil Nadu, Kerala, Punjab, and to some extent Gujarat. It is interesting to note that these states are also the ones which experienced the adverse inequality effect in the urban sector as well.

Appendix 1

Poverty-decomposition methodology

Let us divide the total population into k mutually exclusive socioeconomic and demographic groups. For decomposable poverty measures, then, we can write the total poverty as the weighted average of poverty within each group.

$$P = \sum_i f_i P_i$$

where f_i and P_i are the population share and poverty index of the ith group, respectively. Further, define the change in poverty between two periods as

$$\Delta P = P_2 - P_1 \tag{1}$$

where $P_1 = \sum_i f_{1i} P_{1i}$ and $P_2 = \sum_i f_{2i} P_{2i}$., P_{1i} and P_{2i} being the poverty incidence in the group in years 1 and 2, respectively, and f_{1i} and f_{2i} are the population shares of the ith group in years 1 and 2, respectively.

Equation (1) can be written as

$$\Delta P = \frac{1}{2}\left[\sum_i f_{1i}(P_{2i} - P_{1i}) + \sum_i f_{2i}(P_{2i} - P_{1i})\right]$$

$$+\frac{1}{2}\left[\sum_i P_{1i}(f_{2i} - f_{1i}) + \sum_i P_{2i}(f_{2i} - f_{1i})\right]$$

which shows that the change in total poverty can be written as the sum of two components. The first component measures the effect on total change in poverty due to changes in within-group poverty and the second component estimates the change in total poverty due to possible shifts in population between groups.

The percentage change in total poverty, thus, can be written as follows:

$$\frac{\Delta P}{P} = \sum_i \frac{\bar{f}_i P_i}{P}\left(\frac{\Delta P_i}{P_i}\right) + \sum_i \frac{\bar{P}_i f_i}{P}\left(\frac{\Delta f_i}{f_i}\right) \tag{2}$$

where $\bar{f}_i = \dfrac{f_{1i} + f_{2i}}{2}$ and $\bar{P}_i = \dfrac{P_{1i} + P_{2i}}{2}$.

Note that the first term in Equation (2) estimates the percentage change in total poverty explained by changes in poverty within groups. The second term estimates the percentage change in total poverty due to a shift in population between groups. The shift in population is deemed pro-poor if the second term is negative because it leads to a reduction in poverty. This situation is likely to occur if migration occurs from rural to urban areas. If migration takes place from urban to rural areas, on the other hand, the second component is likely to make a positive contribution to poverty. In this case, the population shift is not pro-poor.

Kakwani (2000) has proposed a decomposition, which explains the percentage change in poverty as a sum of two components: one is the growth effect, measuring the change in poverty when mean income changes but inequality remains fixed and the other component is the inequality effect, which measures changes in poverty when inequality changes but the mean income remains constant. This methodology can now be applied within each group.

A general poverty measure is characterized as

$$P = P(z, \mu, L(p))$$

where z is the poverty line, μ is the mean income of society, and $L(p)$ is the Lorenz curve. The Lorenz curve measures the effect of inequality on poverty. Following from Kakwani (2000), the percentage change in poverty can be written as

$$\Delta P = (\Delta P)_m + (\Delta P)_I = \textit{Mean effect} + \textit{Inequality effect} \tag{3}$$

where $(\Delta P)_m$ is the change in poverty if mean income changes from μ_1 in period 1 to μ_2 in period 2 but the Lorenz curve remains fixed. Thus, $(\Delta P)_m$ can be written as

$$(\Delta P)_m = \frac{1}{2}\big[P(z, \mu_2, L_1(p)) - P(z, \mu_1, L_1(p)) + P(z, \mu_2, L_2(p)) - P(z, \mu_1, L_2(p))\big]$$

where $L_1(p)$ and $L_2(p)$ are the Lorenz curves in periods 1 and 2, respectively. Note that in deriving the mean effect, we can either fix the Lorenz curve for the initial period or for the terminal period. Because we do not know a priori which period of the Lorenz curve we should fix, we have taken the average of the two periods.[7]

Similarly, the inequality component can be derived as

$$(\Delta P)_I = \frac{1}{2}\big[P(z,\mu_1,L_2(p)) - P(z,\mu_1,L_1(p)) + P(z,\mu_2,L_2(p)) - P(z,\mu_2,L_1(p))\big]$$

which estimates the change in poverty if inequality measured by the Lorenz curve changes from $L_1(p)$ in the initial period to $L_2(p)$ in the terminal period but mean income is fixed between the two period. The sum of the mean and inequality effects gives rise to the total changes in poverty.

We apply the decomposition in (3) within each group, which results in

$$\frac{\Delta P_i}{P_i} = \frac{(\Delta P_i)_m}{P_i} + \frac{(\Delta P_i)_I}{P_i} \quad \text{for } i = 1, 2, 3, \ldots\ldots\ldots, k. \tag{4}$$

where

$$(\Delta P_i)_m = \frac{1}{2}\big[P(z,\mu_{2i},L_{1i}(p)) - P(z,\mu_{1i},L_{1i}(p)) + P(z,\mu_{2i},L_{2i}(p)) - P(z,\mu_{1o},L_{2i}(p))\big]$$

and

$$(\Delta P_i)_I = \frac{1}{2}\big[P(z,\mu_{1i},L_{2i}(p)) - P(z,\mu_{1i},L_{1i}(p)) + P(z,\mu_{2i},L_{2i}(p)) - P(z,\mu_{2i},L_{1i}(p))\big]$$

i^{th} group in year t (t = 1,2).

From (2) and (4), the percentage change in total poverty can be expressed as

$$\frac{\Delta P}{P} = \sum_i \frac{\bar{f}_i P_i}{P}\frac{(\Delta P_i)_m}{P_i} + \sum_i \frac{\bar{f}_i P_i}{P}\frac{(\Delta P_i)_I}{P_i} + \sum_i \frac{\bar{P}_i f_i}{P}\left(\frac{\Delta f_i}{f_i}\right)$$

= *Within Group Growth Effect* + *Within Group Inequality Effect* + *Population Shift* (5)

The first term in equation (5) measures the effect of growth within each group on overall change in the poverty incidence, when the distribution within each group remains the same over time. This first term can be further decomposed into two terms:

$$\sum_i \frac{\bar{f}_i P_i}{P} \frac{(\Delta P_i)_m}{P_i} = \sum_i \frac{\bar{f}_i P_i}{P} \frac{(\Delta P_i)_g}{P_i} + \sum_i \frac{\bar{f}_i P_i}{P} \frac{(\Delta P_i)_{bg}}{P_i} \tag{6}$$

where

$$(\Delta P)_g = \frac{1}{2}\Big[P(z, \mu^*_{2i}, L_{1i}(p)) - P(z, \mu_{1i}, L_1(p))$$

$$+ P(z, \mu^*_{2i}, L_{2i}(p)) - P(z, \mu_{i1}, L_{2i}(p))\Big]$$

$$(\Delta P)_{bg} = \frac{1}{2}\Big[P(z, \mu_{2i}, L_{1i}(p)) - P(z, \mu^*_{2i}, L_1(p))$$

$$+ P(z, \mu_{2i}, L_{2i}(p)) - P(z, \mu^*_{2i}, L_{2i}(p))\Big]$$

and $\mu_{2i} = \mu_{1i}(1 + g)$ where g being the average growth rate of the whole population is the mean income of the ith group in year 2 if the income of the ith group were growing at the same rate as the average growth rate of the whole population.

The first term in the right-hand side of (6) measures the effect of growth on percentage change in poverty under the counter-factual that all groups enjoyed the same uniform growth rates and the second term in the right-hand side measures the effect of differential growth rates within groups. Thus, substituting (6) into (5), we arrive at our poverty decomposition that expresses the percentage change in the poverty incidence as the sum of four components: (1) overall growth effect when inequality in the distribution docs not change, (2) effect of differential growth rates in different groups; (3) effect of change in inequality within different groups; and (4) effect of changes in population shares between groups. This is an exact decomposition and, therefore, there will not be any residual term. This decomposition does not require us to specify an inequality measure. It uses the idea of shift in that part of the Lorenz curve, which affects the poor.

The first component will always be negative if there is a positive growth in the economy. The second component can be either negative or positive. If it is positive (negative), the disparity in growth rates of different groups has contributed to an increase (decrease) in total poverty. The third component can again be either positive or negative. If it is positive (negative), it indicates that a change in inequality within group has contributed to an increase (decrease) in the total poverty incidence. Finally, the fourth component measures the effect of migration of population between groups on the total poverty incidence.

Appendix 2

This appendix compares our calculation of HCR based on the adjustments made to the NSS figures on Average Per Capita expenditure (APCE) with others in the literature. We campared the APCE by fractile erxpenditure groups in rural and urban areas for the year 1993–1994 as given by Sundaram and Tendulkar 2003a (S&T) and our own calculation. It was observed that some differences exist only in highest fractile (95–100) but not for other lower fractiles. The effect on estimation on Level of HCR would be minimal.

In this regard, it is interesting to note that Sen and Himanshu (2004), following the S&T procedure, found all-India HCR for all areas to be 35.9 percent using URP and 30.6 percent using MRP for the year 1993–1994. S&T in their revised estimates found the corresponding figures to be 37.35 percent (URP) and 32.15 percent (MRP). This is probably because S&T use a somewhat different poverty line than the official poverty line. Sen and Himanshu (2004) further corrected the 55th round estimates of food and intoxicants for possible 'contamination' from the 7-day questionnaire. They used information from early NSS rounds to arrive at some estimates. At the lower bound, the extent of such contamination was found to be small but even then the authors calculated that the 55th round all-India poverty incidence using MRP was 27.8 percent as against the official figure of 26.1 percent. Thus they found the measured decline between 1993–1994 (MRP) and 1999–2000 (MRP revised) to be at most 2.8 percent implying an *increase* in the absolute number of the poor by five million. Their results are quite opposite to the official calculation of poverty decline (in HCR) by 9.8 percent implying a *fall* in the number of poor by 60 million and to the S&T revised estimates showing a fall of 4.83 percent denoting reduction in number of poor by 13 million in the period.

3 Trends in employment and earnings 1983–2000

In Chapter 2 the focus was on households. We looked at trends in household welfare – and the changes in the incidence of poverty at the household level in particular. But household welfare is the result of the working of factor markets, and for households near the poverty line, trends in labor markets are of paramount importance. In this chapter our attention shifts to individuals. We begin to address the question: are the observed developments in the labor market consistent with and illuminate the results obtained in the previous chapter on household-level poverty trends?

Trends in aggregate employment

The Task Force on Employment Opportunities appointed by the Planning Commission reported a sharp decline in the labor-force growth rates between the 1980s (1983 to 1993–1994) and the 1990s (1993–1994 to 1999–2000). Its estimates from the NSS showed that the growth rate fell from 2.05 percent per annum to 1.03 (GOI July 2001). Taken in conjunction with the increase in measured rates of open unemployment, this slow-down has been widely interpreted to have been the result of 'discouragement' of potential workers from entering the labor force. There are, however, two basic problems with this estimate: (i) is the question of using the correct age-structure of the population; and (ii) the question of appropriate employment category on which the estimates are based.

On (i) it has been maintained that the survey-based age-structure, on which the weighted employment rates of the NSS are based is less reliable than the age-structure reported by the nearest Census of population figures; and on (ii) the Planning Commission estimates of employment growth are based on the UPSS figures of the NSS, and does not distinguish adequately the supply side aspects of the labor force from the effects originating from changes in the demand for labor. Research on both these questions has been extensive, and we shall begin by summarizing the major conclusions from this research.

The age-structure issue

Sundaram and Tendulkar (2006) have looked carefully at the NSS-based age distribution and compared it with the data reported by the Censuses of 1981, 1991 and 2001. They reported that

> using the survey-based age-distribution results in a sharp slow-down in the growth of prime-age (15–59) population in the nineties … . [But] in the context of the observed slow-down of population growth reflecting the decline in fertility – from 2.09 percent per annum (pcpa) to 1.97 pcpa – over the same period, equally problematic is the acceleration in the growth of population in the 0–9 age group – from 1.17 to 1.33 pcpa – between the two periods that shows up with the use of the survey-based age distribution.

It is generally accepted by researchers that, while surveys like the NSS are more reliable at getting at participation or employment rates for different age–sex groups, the age-structure of the population itself is better measured by the Population Censuses. Sundaram and Tendulkar thus use the age–sex-sector specific worker-population rates produced by the NSS and re-weight them by the appropriate demographic structure obtained from the Population Censuses. This adjustment has the effect of substantially moderating the slow-down in the growth rate of the labor force: from about 2.06 percent in the 1980s to 1.58 percent in the 1990s.[1]

The problem of measuring the labor force

The NSS distinguishes those who participate in the labor market on the basis of several criteria. A major difference is the estimate on the basis of Usual Principal Status (UPS – the activity in which the individual spent most of his time in the reference period of the last 365 days) and of the Secondary Status (SS – the activity defined in terms of some part of time spent in the reference year). Usual Principal and Secondary Status (UPSS) workers are then the principal workers as well as part-timers of various kinds. Clearly the number of SS workers could vary with changes in conditions affecting the supply of secondary workers as well as the demand for them. There is no way of judging from the numbers per se if any change observed is due to predominantly supply or predominantly demand conditions. This is particularly true of secondary women workers who form a substantial but varying part of the UPSS labor force reported by the NSS (Rustagi 2005). This important issue will be analyzed in detail in the next chapter.

Trends in employment by industry

Economic Development, in the history of both today's developed economies, and in the recent growth of developing economies, has been associated with a relative increase of employment away from the agricultural sector. This process is associated with an increase in labor productivity because the relative productivity is generally lowest in agriculture. Our first task, then, is to see how far India has been following this traditional pattern of transformation in recent decades.

Multiple occupations

We need to clarify at the outset the issue of multiple occupations in the Indian economy. How do we trace the changing structure of employment by industry or occupation when a significant number of households have members who pursue more than one occupation? There are in fact two distinct aspects of this issue. First, households would contain more than one earner of 'usual principal status' (UPS at the individual level). Second, a 'principal status' earner might have more than one activity. The first possibility creates a difference between the occupational or industrial classification of *households* (in terms of the activity of the 'main earner', defined as the main contributor to the household pot), and the occupations or industrial classification of *individuals*. The second point creates a distinction between the occupational classification of *individuals* based on the UPS and the UPSS status. The issue of occupational distribution by households is of importance when we are considering household income levels in different occupations. Since income (or expenditure) is available for the household as a whole we would need to define the occupation of the household by the activity of the main earner. We have done this in our work on the tertiary sector (Chapter 10). It is seen that the difference in changes in occupational classification over time by the household and the individual definitions is marginal. Here in this chapter we discuss the changes in the distribution for individuals only by the two alternatives of UPS and UPSS.

Trends in the industrial structure of individuals

It is apparent from the data in Table 3.1 that agriculture has indeed been shedding labor and it would appear that the process seems to have accelerated in the post-reform years of the 1990s. It is equally clear that the absorption of labor in manufacturing has been quite slow – even though it might have increased a bit in the nineties – and much of the increase in the labor force has been accounted for by the various types of tertiary activities, as well as construction.

We can infer from the discussion above that the decline in the share of the labor force in agriculture might have been exaggerated with the UPSS definitions because of the inclusion of secondary workers in the count. This category of workers might be disproportionately represented in agriculture which has a larger component of the self-employed. In so far as this reduction is partly due to supply-side changes affecting secondary workers or indeed due to fluctuations in the pace of technology spread in agriculture (see Chapter 7), the basic shift away from agriculture in the nineties might be overestimated. We therefore looked at the industrial distribution for labor defined on the UPS criterion. This might provide an estimate of the lower limit of the shift from agriculture.

Table 3.1 Industrial distribution of UPSS workers (percentage of total)

Industry code and description	*1983*	*1993–1994*	*1999–2000*	*Average annual increments*	
				1983–1993/1994	*1993/1994–1999–2000*
0 Agriculture	68.5	64.0	60.4	44.8	5.6
1 Mining and quarrying	0.6	0.7	0.6	1.3	–1.9
2–3 Manufacturing	10.7	10.6	11.0	10.4	16.4
4 Electricity, gas, etc.	0.3	0.4	0.3	0.7	–0.6
5 Construction	2.3	3.3	4.4	7.4	21.8
6 Trade, hotels, etc.	6.3	7.6	10.2	13.0	49.8
7 Transport, etc.	2.5	2.8	3.7	4.3	16.2
8 Financial services, etc.	0.7	1.0	1.2	2.2	4.4
9 Personal, business and community services	8.2	9.6	8.3	15.9	–11.6
Tertiary (6 to 9)	17.6	21.0	23.4	35.4	58.8
Total	100.0	100.0	100.0	100.0	100.0

Source: Calculated from unit-level data of employment and unemployment schedule of NSS rounds of 38th, 50th and 55th rounds.

A comparison of the two sets reveals that the UPSS definition does show a substantially larger decline in the incremental share of labor absorbed by agriculture. The UPS definition gives the decline in the incremental share in agriculture from 42.07 in the first period to 27.55 in the second. But even confining ourselves to principal workers, as the UPS definition does, the data confirm that there was a significant decline in labor absorption by agriculture in the nineties compared to the eighties. The gain of the tertiary sector in the incremental share under the alternative UPS definition was from 37.49 to 45.41.

Unemployment

What can we say about the level and trends in the rates of open unemployment in the Indian economy? The NSS data can be used to calculate unemployment rates based on either the CDS or UPS status of the labor force. The CDS estimates measure the rates of *person-days* which are being spent as 'not working but available for work', measured in half-day units over the reference week (see Appendix 2). These rates differ from the unemployment rates based on the UPS counts describing the 'usual status' of workers. (Note that subsidiary workers are by definition employed, still there can be estimate of UPSS rates of unemployment different from the UPS rates.) We can say that the CDS rates capture *open underemployment* during the week – as distinct from *disguised unemployment* on family farms or businesses (when some members of the household workforce are 'unproductively' employed but not declaring themselves available for work). The unemployment rate provided by the UPS measure will be necessarily less than the CDS rate since it measures the proportion of the labor force which is 'usually' unemployed during the major part of the year.

The rates of CDS unemployment in 1999–2000 was 7.2 percent in the rural areas and 7.7 percent in the urban. The UPS unemployment rates were, however, only 1.43 and 4.65 respectively (Government of India (2001), Tables 2.7 and 2.10(a)). It is apparent that underemployment, rather than round-the-week open unemployment is the real issue in rural areas. The difference, although significant, is less striking in the urban economy in the post-reform years between 1993 and 1999. It increased substantially in the rural sector – from 5.6 to 7.2. (The increase in the urban sector was hardly apparent – of the order of 0.3 percent.) A part of the increase could be attributed to the increased 'casualisation' of the labor force – the rise in the proportion of casual labor relative to the self-employed. It cannot be maintained that this is necessarily the result of deteriorating labor-market conditions. It might be partly the result of increased commercialization, as marginal farmers shifted more to wage labor. The income levels of the latter are often higher.

In any event the evidence suggests that even CDS unemployment is very much a problem of the youth, perhaps a result of waiting and job searching in the labor market. The unemployment rates for both sectors and for all rounds fall off sharply for age groups 30 and above. The increase of the unemployment rate between the 50th and the 55th rounds, after a fall between the 38th and the 50th in most age groups, perhaps does indicate a slight deterioration of labor-market conditions, but the phenomenon is one of lesser importance than other issues discussed in the book.

Trends in labor productivity by industry

The data given in the last section shows some movement outside agriculture – even though it has not been as fast as in many other Asian countries during the process of their economic transformation.

Another special feature of the changing employment structure in India has been the overwhelming importance of the tertiary sector in the absorption of labor outside agriculture. This at once raises the question: is the transformation of the employment structure – slow as it is – has really been of the type that has increased earnings of labor. A detailed examination of this point is attempted in the later part of this chapter and also in the chapters on individual major sectors in Part III. Here it is sufficient to note the relative mean productivity per worker in the major sectors and their changes over time – based on the figures given in the National Account estimates.

It is clear from the mean value of labor productivity that they are between 2.5 and 3.5 times higher in the manufacturing and tertiary sectors relative to those in agriculture – even if we take the more moderate estimates based on the UPS estimates (i.e., excluding the secondary workers who are relatively more abundant in agriculture), and even if we are looking at the less productive sub-sectors within tertiary activities (Table 3.2). Further, the productivity differential with respect to agriculture seems to have increased over time. This first cut at the data does strongly suggest that the movement of labor away from

Table 3.2 Labor productivity by broad sectors 1983–2000 (Based on UPS estimates of employment)

Industry code and description	*Labor productivity (UPS)*				*Labor-productivity index (UPS)*			
	55th	*50th*	*43rd*	*38th*	*55th*	*50th*	*43rd*	*38th*
0 Agriculture	13,349	11,752	10,116	10,223	100	100	100	100
1 Mining and quarrying	129,579	73,754	64,802	62,920	971	628	641	615
2–3 Manufacturing	46,999	34,444	27,547	24,801	352	293	272	243
4 Electricity, gas, etc.	239,870	139,433	111,410	93,247	1,797	1,186	1,101	912
5 Construction	34,406	34,492	25,551	37,543	258	294	253	367
6 Trade, hotels, etc.	42,838	36,593	32,298	31,866	321	311	319	312
7 Transport, etc.	60,537	48,310	42,871	38,468	453	411	424	376
8 Financial services, etc.	303,895	259,820	184,626	171,029	2,276	2,211	1,825	1,673
9 Personal, business and community services	47,729	27,137	26,387	22,588	358	231	261	221
Tertiary (6 to 9)	61,216	44,144	37,985	33,950	459	376	375	332

Source: National accounts (various years) and NSS (own calculations from unit-level data).

agriculture – at a slow pace as it has been – has in fact in the direction of enhancing earnings of worker. We will see later in this chapter if this tentative conclusion is borne out by more direct evidence on wages and earnings levels.

Is India out of line with the experience of other Asian economies?

The exceptional nature of the absorption of labor moving out of agriculture in the tertiary rather than the secondary sector is seen to have been a feature of Indian development in recent decades. At the same time we have found that aggregate figures show that the relative income per worker in the tertiary sector is relatively high. Can we learn something from international experience if the Indian pattern of change is out of line with the observed pattern of development and, if so, in what way?

Papola (2005) discussed in detail the theory in the literature about sectoral shift of GDP and employment. Classical economists like Fisher and Clark explain the shift from industry to services by the changing demand patterns predicted by Engel's law. Fisher argued that services are 'luxuries' with more than a unitary elasticity of demand and so at a higher level of income increasing share of expenditure is absorbed by them and thus leads to high share of services in output and labor force. He assumed that the increase in the share of services in final demand proportionately lead to increase in the share of employment. However, Clark attributes the increase in the share of service employment

Table 3.3 International comparison of GDP and employment share

Country	*GDP share (in %)*						*Share in employment (in %)*					
	Agriculture		*Industry*		*Services*		*Agriculture*		*Industry*		*Services*	
	1960	*2002*	*1960*	*2002*	*1960*	*2002*	*1960*	*2002*	*1960*	*2002*	*1960*	*2002*
China*	30	15	49	51	21	34	69	47	18	21	13	31
Indonesia	50	18	25	45	25	38	75	44	8	17	17	39
Thailand	40	9	19	43	41	48	84	46	4	21	12	33
Malaysia	39	9	18	47	43	44	40	19	12	32	48	50
India	55	24	16	25	29	51	74	60	11	18	15	22

Source: Papola (2005). The original source is the *World Development Report* (various years).

Note
* The figure for China in the first year is for 1980.

additionally to low relative productivity in services relative to manufacturing. Later economists like Bamoul and Fucho ascribed the rise in the share of service employment primarily to productivity differentials between industry and services resulting from technological, scale and geographical concentration of production in services. Further, increase in the share of service employment is also explained by the increased tendency of industry to outsource intermediate inputs used by industry to the service sector.

Popola refers to the experience of some Asian economies for comparison with India. The data for the shares of both employment and GDP and their change over the second half of the last century are given in Table 3.3.

It can be seen from the table that the share of workforce in industry increased along with is share of GDP in all countries including India, but it produced a much larger share of GDP in all other Asian developing countries other than India. It shows that the relative sectoral productivity of labor in India has been strikingly low by international comparison. By 2002 the tertiary sector in India contributed more than half the GDP in India but its contribution to employment was only 22 percent. It shows that service-sector growth has been productivity led but not employment led, contradicting views of some economists that employment grow in services because of low productivity vis-à-vis industry.[2]

The picture presented in Figure 3.1 of relative productivity in services vis-à-vis industry in the comparator Asian countries brings out the striking point that it is only in India – among all the countries represented – that the relative productivity in services has *increased* over the 40-year period. A second important point to note is that – with the exception of Thailand in 1960 when it had hardly any industry at all – the productivity in services exceeds that in industry only in India in both years, and that by a substantial percentage.

It shows that service-sector growth in India has been productivity led and not employment led, contradicting views of some economists that employment grew

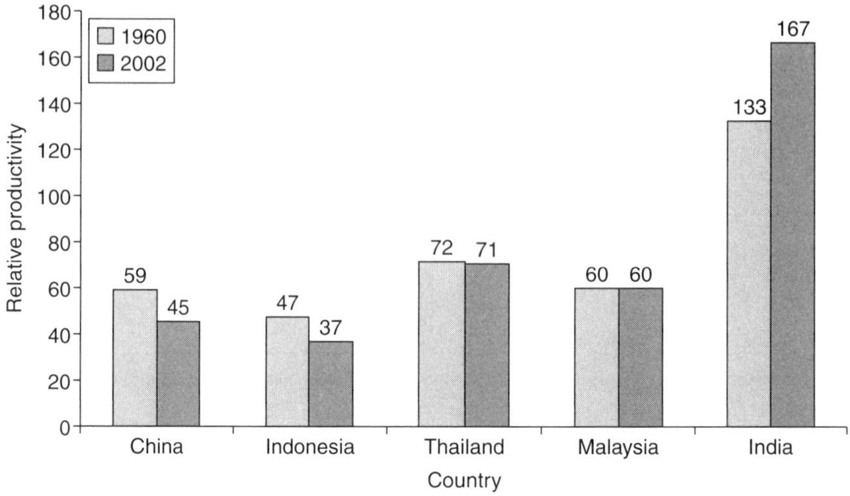

Figure 3.1 Relative productivity in services and industry, various Asian countries 1960–2000.

in services because this sector has been a repository of low income labor 'pushed out' of agriculture. The heart of the employment problem in India would thus seem to be *not* an excess absorption of labor in the tertiary sector, but the relatively low productivity of the manufacturing sector, and its persistence over time. It is this low performance of manufacturing which has prevented it from being the dynamic sector playing a central role in productivity growth as well as the reallocation of labor as in other countries in the history of successful economic development.

How much of this productivity differential in favor of the tertiary sector is due to the recent developments of the information technology sector? The answer would appear to be not very much. For one thing the productivity differential in favor of the tertiary sector was substantial even in 1960 when the IT sector was non-existent. Second, in terms of the numbers employed the tertiary sub-sector dealing with IT is quite small even in recent years. Table 3.4 gives an estimate of employment in this sector based on enterprise surveys, and Table 3.5 provides the estimate from the household surveys of the NSS. The Manufacturing sub-sector includes hardware, central processing units (CPUs), communications equipment, electronic components and industrial control and supervision equipment manufacturing (not including medical equipment). The tertiary segment includes telecommunications services, computer and related services (IT and software), research and development services and also start-up companies.

The estimates show that the total employment in the IT tertiary sector is of the order of 400,000 to 600,000 (Tables 3.4 and 3.5). Considering that the total employment in the tertiary sector (in the UPS count of the NSS) was around

Table 3.4 Employment in the IT sector on the basis of enterprise survey

Sector	*Organized*	*Unorganized*	*All*
Manufacturing	241,199	60,502	301,701
Trade	4,143		4,143
Telecommunication	227,822	35,542	263,364
IT and enabled services	36,071	115,799	151,870
ICT sector	509,235	211,843	721,078

Source: Sarkar and Mehta (2006). Original source is Annual Survey of Industries (ASI) and Employment Review of DGE&T.

Note
Manufacturing refers to the year 2000–2001, organized-service sector refer to the March 1998 and unorganized-service sector refer to the year 2001–2002.

Table 3.5 Employment in the IT sector on the basis of household survey (1999–2000)

Sector	*Rural*	*Urban*	*Total*	*% share of rural*
Manufacturing	54,766	416,305	471,071	11.63
Trade	1,151	34,644	35,795	3.22
Telecommunication	118,390	199,135	317,525	37.29
IT and ITES	13,688	249,393	263,081	5.20
Total	187,995	899,477	1,087,472	17.29

Source: Sarkar and Mehta (2006). Original source is National Sample Survey, Unit-level data, 55th round (1999–2000).

Note
Employment includes that of Usual Principal Status (UPS) workers only.

150 million, the percentage of tertiary employment in the IT sector was at best 0.4 per cent.

It is necessary to turn our attention to the denominator of the ratio and consider the possible reasons for the low labor productivity of the manufacturing vis-à-vis the tertiary sector in India.

Table 3.6 draws attention to the 'dualism' that exists in Indian manufacturing. The household enterprises (not employing any hired labor) contribute more than half of manufacturing employment whereas establishments with 500 and above employees contribute more than two-fifths of gross value added but employ less than one-tenth of employment. Consequently there is a tremendous difference in relative labor productivity between these two size groups and it is this which leads to very low level of labor productivity in the manufacturing sector. Such a situation does not exist in other developing countries in Asia, as will become clear from the evidence presented in Chapter 9. Unless there is substantial growth of small (10–100 employees) and medium (100–500 employees) that are relatively labor-intensive and have substantially higher labor productivity than household enterprises leading to substantial increase in the share of manufacturing in GDP with some increase in employment share in the Indian economy, we

Table 3.6 Share of household enterprises (OAME) and of establishments with 500 plus workers in manufacturing employment and GVA

Variable and size	*1984–1985*	*1989–1990*	*1994–1995*	*2000–2001*
Employment				
Household enterprises	62	57	54	56
500 and above	8	7	8	7
Value-added				
OAME	17	13	9	10
500 and above	40	41	43	42
Relative labor productivity, OAME = 1				
500 and above	17	24	33	33

Source: Calculated from respective years ASI and NSS unorganized manufacturing data.

are unlikely to follow the sectoral pattern of growth as other countries experienced in the development process.

Further discussion of this important issue will be found in Chapters 8 and 9 in Part III of this work.

Employment in the organized sector

It might be useful at this point to put the size of the *formal or organized* sub-sector in manufacturing in the context of total employment in the formal sector. In Chapter 10 we will examine the formal–informal distinction within the tertiary sector in detail. But for the present purposes the official estimates of different types of employment within the formal sector put out by the Ministry of Finance of GOI will suffice. These are given in Table 3.7. The stagnation of manufacturing in the formal sector is apparent from this table, as is the relatively small share of manufacturing in total formal sector employment. The total including all sectors is itself very small in 2001 – only about 7 percent of all employment. The public sector still dominates the scene in formal employment in spite of India having embarked on a process of encouragement of the private sector since the early 1980s.

Table 3.7 Employment in the organized sector (millions)

	1981	*1991*	*2001*	*2003*
Private-sector total	7.4	7.7	8.7	8.4
of which manufacturing	4.5	4.5	5.0	4.7
Public-sector total	15.5	19.1	19.1	18.6
of which manufacturing	1.5	1.9	1.4	1.3
Private and public sectors	22.9	26.8	27.8	27.0
of which manufacturing	6.0	6.4	6.4	6.0

Source: Employment Review of DGE&T.

Patterns of urbanization and the quality of employment

A feature of economic growth has been the increasing absorption of labor in the urban sector. The rate of urbanization has been slow in India – consistent with the slow transformation of the employment structure. There has been some concern in the literature if the reallocation of labor to higher-quality jobs in non-agriculture has been disproportionately achieved only in the urban economy. We can also refer at this point to the finding in Chapter 5 that there have been important changes in recent decades in the size structure of towns, with a redistribution of population to smaller towns. How does in the change in the industrial structure of employment differ between small and large towns – as well as between rural and urban areas? To throw light on this question we present in Table 3.8 the way the *incremental flow* of labor in each of the three broad sectors was distributed between the rural, and the three classes of towns. The data are presented separately for the 1980s (1983 to 1993/1994) and the nineties (1993/1994 to 1999/2000), but the classification by size of town is not available for the earlier period. Of particular interest is the relative importance of the flows of new employment in the secondary and the tertiary sectors. The importance of the secondary sector even in the most recent period is higher in the urban areas as whole, and in large towns. In 1990–2000 the share of manufacturing was 27 percent in large towns compared to 19 percent in small towns and only 7 percent in the rural areas. But it is apparent from the figures on *incremental* flows in Table 3.8 that a redistribution of employment in the secondary sector has been taking place in the recent period in favor of small towns, and also the shares of the rural and the urban sectors in the new employment has been almost the same. The importance of the small towns in the tertiary sector has, however, been increasing faster. The small towns have clearly witnessed a substantial swing away from employment in the primary sector. The redistribution of employment to small towns, which has been noticed, has been driven by non-agriculture.

Expansion of education and the quality of employment

The expansion of employment outside agriculture – and the concomitant upgrading of jobs – is closely related to the expansion of education. It has been maintained that the lopsided development of education outside the rural sector has in fact hindered the diversion of employment in the rural economy (Chadha and Sahu 2002).

Table 3.9 in particular brings out the point that it is at the education level 'graduate and above' that the urban economy plays an overwhelming role in attracting the educated. But it is also of great importance to note that the major proportionate shifts in the *additional* flows of educated labor are to be observed in the smaller towns in the post-reform period. These towns have been able to attract a large proportion of educated labor – with secondary as well as college qualification – in major way in the 1993–1999 period. This is another interesting

Table 3.8 Distribution of the increment of worker by size of community: broad sectors (percentages)

Industry	*Period I (1983/1984–1993/1994)*					*Period II (1993/1994–1999/2000)*				
	Rural	*Urban*	*Small towns <50,000 thousand*	*Medium towns 50,000–1,000,000*	*Large towns >1,000,000*	*Rural*	*Urban*	*Small towns <50,000*	*Medium towns 50,000–1,000,000*	*Large towns >1,000,000*
Primary	62.0	7.0				46.1	–12.5	–56.5	–2.1	–0.5
Secondary	14.6	27.8				29.0	31.6	39.0	31.1	29.2
Tertiary	23.4	65.2				24.9	80.9	117.5	71.0	71.3
Total	100.0	100.0				100.0	100.0	100.0	100.0	100.0

Source: Calculated from unit-level data of employment and unemployment schedule of NSS rounds of 38th, 50th and 55th rounds.

Note

The data for filling in the flows by size of towns do not exist for the first period.

Table 3.9 Distribution of average annual increment of labor force by educational level and community size (%)

Level of Education	*Period I (1983/1984–1993/1994)*					*Period II (1993/1994–1999/2000)*				
	Rural	*Urban*	*Small towns <50,000*	*Medium towns 50,000–1,000,000*	*Metro >1,000,000*	*Rural*	*Urban*	*Small towns <50,000*	*Medium towns 50,000–1,000,000*	*Metro >1,000,000*
Not literate	13.0	10.7				–14.4	0.4	–243.7	–3.2	9.4
Literate and up to primary	29.9	13.9				15.3	–0.5	–272.2	–4.9	13.0
Middle	24.4	15.6				46.6	27.9	173.5	19.3	26.0
Secondary	26.6	34.0				28.7	24.4	163.9	28.3	17.4
Higher Secondary						12.8	13.5	102.0	15.9	8.9
Graduate	6.4	26.0				10.1	33.9	173.0	44.0	25.2
Not specified	–0.2	–0.1				1.0	0.4	3.5	0.6	0.2
Total	100.0	100.0				100.0	100.0	100.0	100.0	100.0

Source: Calculated from unit-level data of employment and unemployment schedule of NSS rounds of 38th, 50th and 55th rounds.

Note

The data for filling in the flows by size of towns do not exist for the first period.

part of the increasing role played by the smaller towns in recent years – which had already been noticed in Chapter 2.

India has made rapid progress in upgrading the quality of its labor force. The number of workers with less than five years of education has come down steeply from 80 percent in 1983 to 65.5 in 1999–2000. But even then it is significantly behind most of the rapidly developing countries in Asia. The average years of schooling for the population aged 25 and over in China around 2000 were 5.7, and in East Asia 6.5 compared with 3.6 in India. The proportions with no schooling were 20.9, 22.8 and 44.5 respectively. Equally damaging is the low proportion of those with secondary schooling – known to be a critical group in the development of manufacturing and other modern-sector activities. In India it is only 17 percent at this date, much lower than India's income level would predict. It is only half that of China, and the proportion is worse for females (World Bank 2007, Table 1.3). It will be suggested in Chapter 9 that its relative neglect of primary and post-primary education in earlier years might have been a major cause of the persistence of 'dualism' and the slow growth of the dynamic manufacturing sector in India.

Trends in wages and wage inequality

Wages of casual and regular workers

The wage sector in India is substantial – even in the rural areas. Regular workers (those with a more permanent contract for varying periods of time) are more important in the urban areas, and casual wage workers (those hired on day-to-day contract as work is available) are in a majority in the rural economy.

Regular workers have several days of work during the week – the NSS data show that the average is between 5.6 and 5.9. Casual workers get work for fewer days of the week – generally less than four. Part of the difference in the earnings per worker between the two categories, therefore, reflects the difference in the number of days of work secured in the week of enumeration. For casual workers the seasonal element is likely to be of great importance. When making comparison between the two groups – which could be used to reflect an aspect of the formal–informal dichotomy in the labor market – it is important to be clear as to the objective if the comparison: are we interested in the levels of income of the two classes or in the returns to a unit of work?

Average wages (earnings) per day

The NSS collected data on the earnings of the workers for the preceding week (seven days) of the survey, and it also recorded in the same field the number of person-days thc worker was actually at work. These data give us the earnings per day for both casual and regular workers. The casual–regular wage difference varies by rural–urban location, by gender and also by occupation (i.e., manual or non-manual). In the rural areas there were about ten million casual workers according to the 55th round of the NSS (Census adjusted 15–59 age group) and only two million regular. The corresponding figures for the urban sector were 1.4 and 2.5 million. Females were a third of the total in the rural casual labor market, but in all other segments, in the regular category and in urban areas, the representation of females is much smaller – of the order of 15–20 per cent. It is to be noted that not all regular workers were classified as non-manual. In fact both in the rural and the urban sectors almost half of the regular were manual workers. On the other hand, only 10–15 per cent of the casual workers were non-manual.

We examined the data from the NSS showing the difference in mean wages per day for different categories of workers in the 15–59 age group for the 55th round 1999–2000. For casual workers the manual wage rates are close to the non-manual, for both sexes, in both the rural and the urban areas. On the other hand, the difference between the two categories of workers for the *regular* wage earners is huge (between twice and three times as high). It shows the importance of human capital attainments in the determination of regular wages.

It is important to note, however, that even for manual workers alone, regulars earn nearly double the amount of casuals – except for females in rural areas, where the differential is more like 50 per cent higher. Since regular workers get a significantly larger number of days of work in the week (also get paid for the whole week), the difference in earnings would be even higher. While a part of this difference – even for manual workers – might reflect measured human capital attributes, a good deal of the differential really pertains to the formal-informal sector dichotomy in the labor market. This differential is partly due to institutional factors (employment in large establishments, or in the public sector) and partly due to the operation of the wage-efficiency relationship for 'established' workers with low turnover.

Distribution of wages

The data on wages from the NSS have been analyzed by Puja Vasudeva-Dutta (2004). Vasudeva noted that the dispersion in wages among casual workers is much smaller than among regular wages. This is confirmed by the graphs in Figure 3.2, which also suggests that the dispersion seems to have increased over time for regular wage workers, but not for the casual. A major reason for the difference is, of course, is that regular wage workers have a much greater variance in human capital attributes, particularly education. There is a big difference between manual and non-manual wage difference for regular workers, but not for the casual, reflecting the dispersion by skill and education for the former category.

Growth rate of wage rates

The figures 3.3a and 3.3b give a picture of the growth rates of real wage rates for different categories of labor namely rural male (RM), rural female (RF), urban male (UM) and urban female (UF).

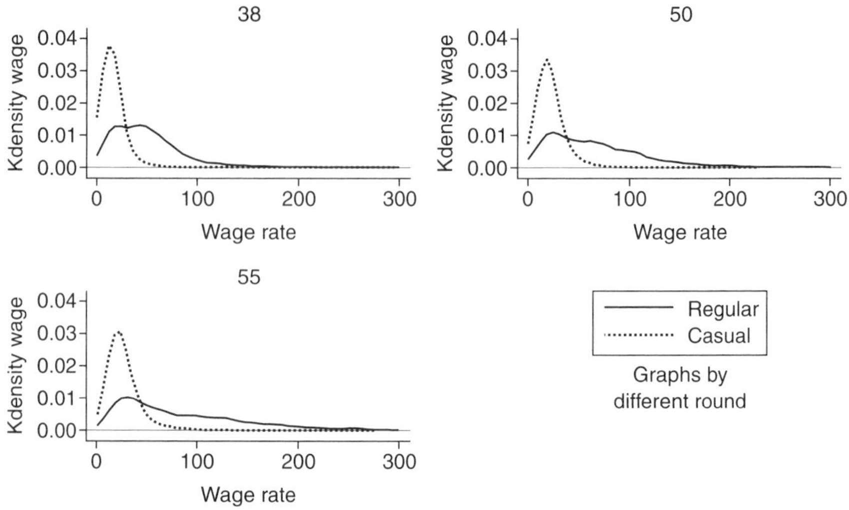

Figure 3.2 KDF distribution for regular and casual workers for different NSS rounds.

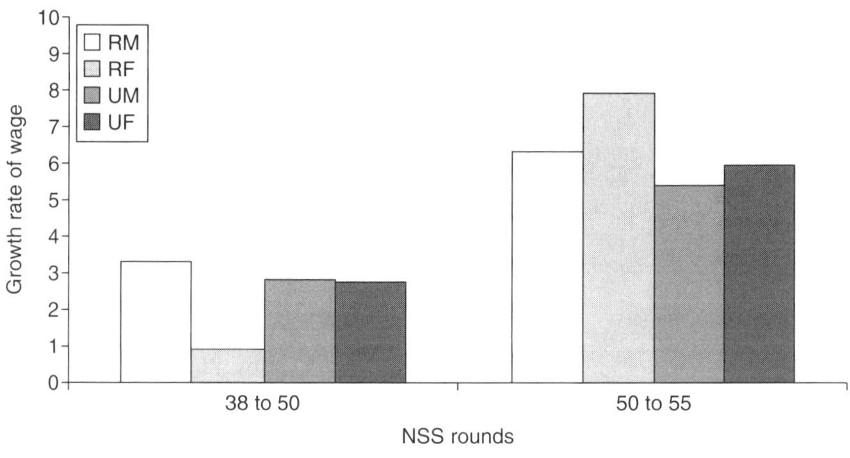

Figure 3.3a Growth rate of wage of regular non-manual wage earners.

The wages of regular non-manual workers in the second period increased at around twice the rate of the pre-liberalization era, but there was little change in the growth rates of casual manual workers. This is an aspect of the increase in inequality in the labor market in the nineties.

Trends in wage inequality

It can be inferred from Figure 3.2 that there is strong suggestion from the KDF` graphs that wage inequality is higher for regular workers and has increased over

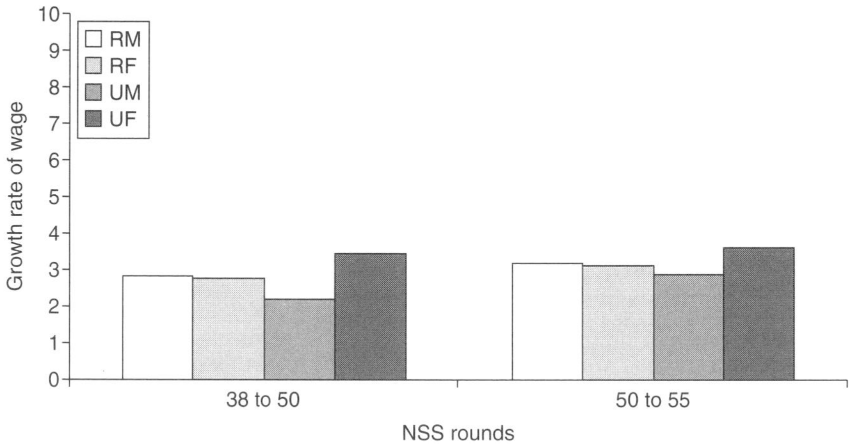

Figure 3.3b Growth rate of wage of casual manual wage earners.

time. Vasudeva's summary measures for wage inequality indicated that, for regular workers, GE(0) went up from 0.286 to 0.337 between 1983 and 1999, and GE(2) increased from 0.381 in 1983 to 0.430 in 1999. The level of inequality was much less for casual workers and it also declined over time. The values of GE(0) were 0.143 in 1983 and 0.117 in 1999.

It is interesting to note that while inequality among regular workers increased significantly between 1993 and 1999 – and more so at the upper end as evident from the larger increase in the GE(2) measure – the 'between group inequality' for educational groups did not change by all that much. Much the more important part of the inequality increase was accounted for by the 'within group' component. This is in line with the evidence from other countries which have experienced increase in wage inequality in the globalization era. While returns to formal education do increase, it is the differential valuation of the individual worker's non-formal attributes which seem to be more important in the increase in inequality.

Vasudeva has used the regression-based methodology of Fields to study the 'factor inequality shares' of different explanatory variables in the earnings functions estimated separately for the regular and the casual workers (Field 2000). The 'factor inequality share' gives a quantitative estimate of the total inequality in the dependant variable (in this case 'wage earnings') explained by the different explanatory variables in the earnings function.

A semi-logarithmic Mincerian (standard or augmented) wage determining function can be written as:

$$\ln(w_i) = \sum_{j=1}^{J+1} a_j' Z_{ij} = \mathbf{a'Z} \qquad (1)$$

where $\mathbf{a} = [\beta_1.....\beta_j, 1]$ and $\mathbf{Z} = [Z_1.....Z_j, \varepsilon]$ are vectors of coefficients and explanatory variables respectively. An inequality index I can be defined on the vector of wages (**w**). Applying Shorrocks' theorem the relative factor inequality weights (i.e., the percentage of inequality that is accounted for by the *j*th factor) can be calculated as follows:

$$s_j[\ln(w)] = \frac{\text{cov}[a_j Z_j, \ln(w)]}{\sigma^2 \ln(w)} = \frac{a_j \times \sigma(Z_j) \times cor[Z_j, \ln(w)]}{\sigma \ln(w)} \tag{2}$$

where *cov[.]* denotes the covariance, *cor(.)* the correlation coefficient and $\sigma(.)$ the standard deviation.

The major results from Vasudeva's exercise can be summarized as follows:

1 As far as regular workers are concerned just over half of the variance in the log of wages are explained by the earnings function. The same variables explain much less – a third – of the variance for casual workers.
2 In terms of the explained part of the variance, human capital variables were most important for regular workers. Age accounted for about a quarter and education a third of the explained variance in 1999. The other important factor in line was industry affiliation – contributing another quarter.
3 By contrast, human-capital factors were of much less importance for casual workers – only age, and not education having any positive contribution, but at a much lower level of around 7 percent. The single most important explanatory variable was geographical difference – the state of residence contributing no less than 62 percent for casuals as against only 3.5 percent for regulars.
4 Although for regular workers the wage gap between those with graduate and primary-school qualifications increased between 1983 and 1999 (see 'Rural–urban differences' section below), the share of education in the explanation of the variance declined from 23 to 17 percent. The importance of age increased as did that of industry affiliation. Further, Vasudeva confirms that the increase in the 'contribution of selection coupled with the fall in that of education suggest a rising importance of unobservable for regular workers, possibly linked to the process of trade liberalization'.

Inequality in household welfare

Although substantial wage employment in India is still only a part of total employment, and a good deal of households are outside the wage-sector – mostly self-employed. We would want to know if the experience of non-wage households mirrors that of the wage earners. This section therefore looks at the trends of welfare of *all* households irrespective of the type of employment. We choose as our measure the average (mean) per capita expenditure (APCE) of the households as recorded by the NSS of successive rounds. Figure 3.4 portrays the movement of the KDF distribution of APCE over time, separately for the rural and the urban areas.

It is apparent that while the modes of the distribution have shifted outward in both sectors, but more so in the urban sector, there has been a more pronounced

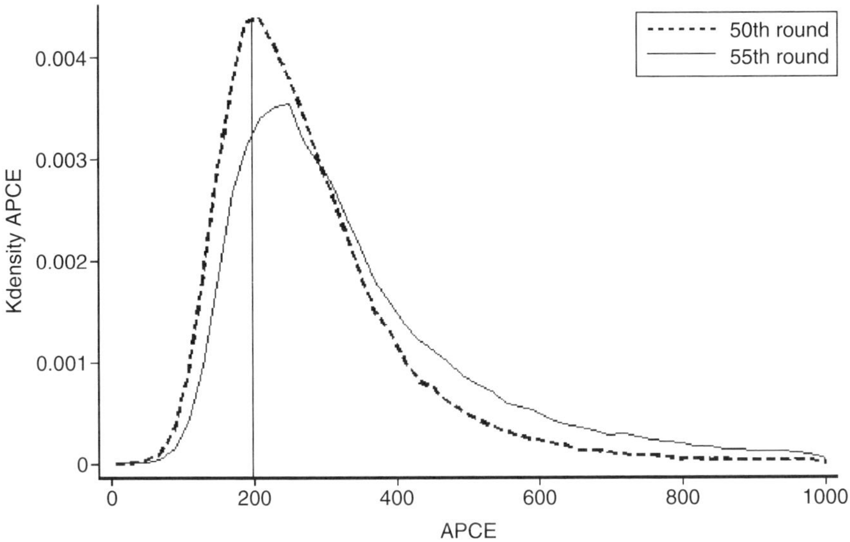

Figure 3.4a KDF distribution of APCE, Rural (poverty line: Rs.196.50, at 1993–1994 = 100).

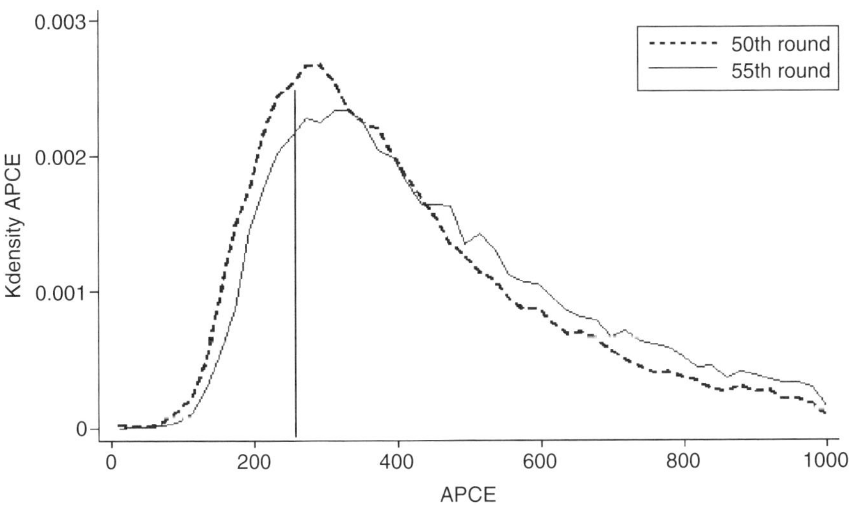

Figure 3.4b KDF distribution of APCE, Urban (poverty line: 227.20, at 1993–1994 = 100).

'flattening' of the distribution in the urban sector signifying an increased degree of inequality.

Table 3.10 gives the measures for overall inequality. Note the large values for GE(2) which is more sensitive to high incomes. While this measure has decreased substantially in the rural areas it has increased in the urban.

Table 3.10 Inequality measures for APCE, 50th and 55th rounds of NSS

	Rural		*Urban*	
	1993	*1999*	*1993*	*1999*
GE(0)	0.111	0.113	0.165	0.191
GE(1)	0.132	0.129	0.184	0.222
GE(2)	0.329	0.207	0.305	0.442

Source: Unit level data from consumption schedule of 38th, 50th and 55th rounds of NSS.

Rural–urban differences

The discussion in the last section has suggested that inequality has increased more strongly in the urban economy, at least in the post-reform era. Thus the disparity in household welfare between the two sectors has increased, we now look a bit more intensively at the rural–urban difference. Has the disparity increased more for some groups rather than others? Can we isolate more concretely the factors responsible for it?

Figure 3.5 brings out clearly the point that the *relative d*ifference in household welfare has increased for higher expenditure groups. We can compute the 'Blinder–Oaxaca' decomposition of mean outcome differential between the rural and the urban sectors, The difference between two groups can be decomposed into three parts: i) due to differences in endowment (E); ii) due to differences in coefficients including the intercept (C); and iii) due to interaction between

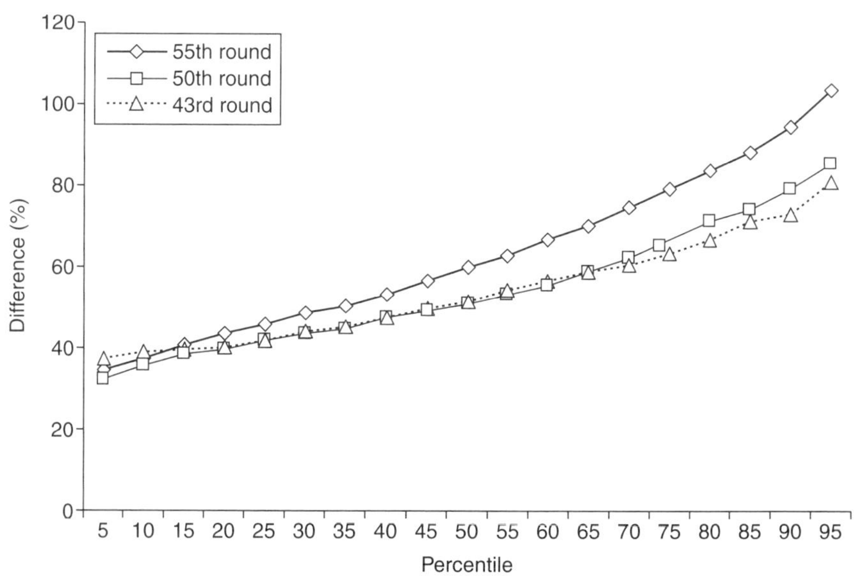

Figure 3.5 Urban–rural difference in APCE by percentile.

Table 3.11 Summary of Oaxaca decomposition results for APCE (as %)

	55th	*50th*	*43rd*
Amount attributable:	30.2	14.5	7.4
due to endowments (E)	21.1	22.7	21.1
due to coefficients (C)	9.1	−8.2	−13.7
Shift coefficient (U)	17.7	28.1	31.7
Raw differential (R) {E+C+U}	47.9	42.6	39.1
Adjusted differential (D) {C+U}	26.8	19.9	18.0
Endowments as % total (E/R)	44.1	53.3	53.9
Discrimination as % total (D/R)	55.9	46.7	46.1

Notes

U = unexplained portion of differential (difference between model constants).

D = portion due to discrimination (C+U).

+ sign indicates advantage to high group.

– sign indicates advantage to low group.

coefficient and endowment (CE). Depending on the model that is assumed to be 'true' model (absence of discrimination), the three-fold decomposition can be used to determine the explained (Q) and unexplained (U). By using the low group (rural APCE) as the no-discrimination base we calculated Q = E and U = C + CE.

Table 3.11 summarize the results for the 'Oaxaca decomposition' for APCE between the rural and urban areas. The calculations show that there has been a substantial increase in the 'discrimination' factor for urban households in the post-reform years between the 50th and 55th rounds. The increase in the rural–urban disparity is due not to the better endowments of the urban workers but to the higher returns to the human-capital factors secured by them in the urban economy.

Returns to education

The results discussed above suggest that educational developments have been a major player in the increase in inequality and in the growing rural–urban disparity. The increments to income from successive levels of education could be approximated by the difference in co-efficient to the education dummies in a fitted earnings functions for regular wage earners. These are reported in Table 3.12 and graphed in Figures 3.6a and 3.6b separately for the rural and the urban areas.

The difference between rural and urban economies is brought out dramatically in Figures 3.6a and 3.6b. The lift to the returns to education in the post-reform years occurs at different levels of education in the two areas. In the rural economy the sharp increase occurs at the level of secondary education, while in the urban sector the lift is observed at the college graduate level. The curves for the successive rounds, however, intersect at lower education levels in both sectors, showing that at levels less than middle, the returns to education are in fact depressed for the later years. They are nearly at the same level for middle-school leavers in the rural sector, and for secondary-school leavers in the urban. All this is consistent with

Table 3.12 Private returns to different levels of education (in %) of regular wage workers

	Rural			*Urban*		
Educational level	38th	50th	55th	38th	50th	55th
Literate	5.6	19.9	−8.8	5.5	13.3	4.3
Primary	24.2	14.3	12.4	7.6	0.4	2.9
Middle	17.4	13.2	16.0	14.1	16.3	14.4
Secondary	33.1	35.4	44.8	35.0	33.9	34.7
Graduate	25.7	29.4	27.5	34.5	38.7	43.7

Notes
1 The figures are the difference in coefficients of the successive dummies of education levels used in the estimation of the earnings function. The base is 'Illiterate'. Other variables included in the regression were age, age square, regional dummies, sex dummies.
2 Manual workers are excluded.

expectations about what might happen with the increase in the supply of educated labor. Demand outstrips supply in the post-reform period in the rural areas for secondary-school leavers, and for college graduates in the urban.

Analysis of the returns to education by age-groups revealed an interesting finding about the urban labor market. For the 20–29 group the marginal returns to secondary education actually fell in the 50th and the 55th rounds while those for college graduates showed a sharp upward movement. By contrast for the older 30–39 group there was a milder increase for both the secondary and college graduates in both the 50th and the 55th rounds. It is clear that the demand for the more educated has been soaring in recent years and has affected the new entrants to the urban labor market more strongly.

The literature has drawn attention to the increased demand for more educated labor in the era of globalization in a number of countries and has stressed the importance of skill-intensive technical change in manufacturing in particular,

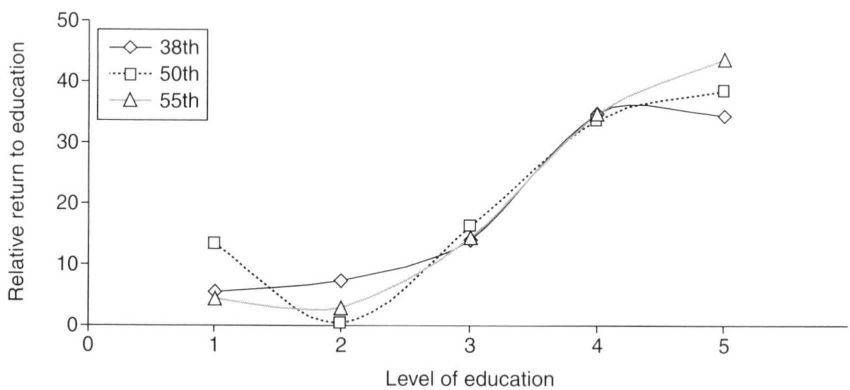

Figure 3.6a Private return to different levels of education (urban).

Note
1, 2, 3, 4 and 5 denote the levels of education namely literate, primary, middle, secondary and graduate respectively.

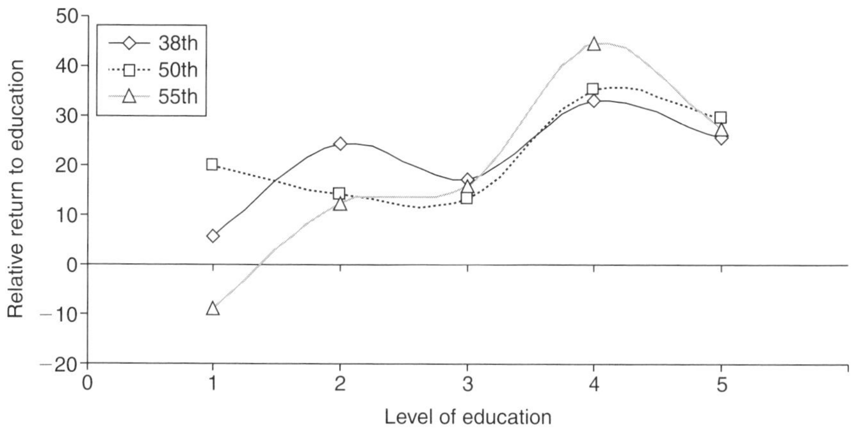

Figure 3.6b Private return to different levels of education (rural).

Note
1, 2, 3, 4 and 5 denote the levels of education namely literate, primary, middle, secondary and graduate respectively.

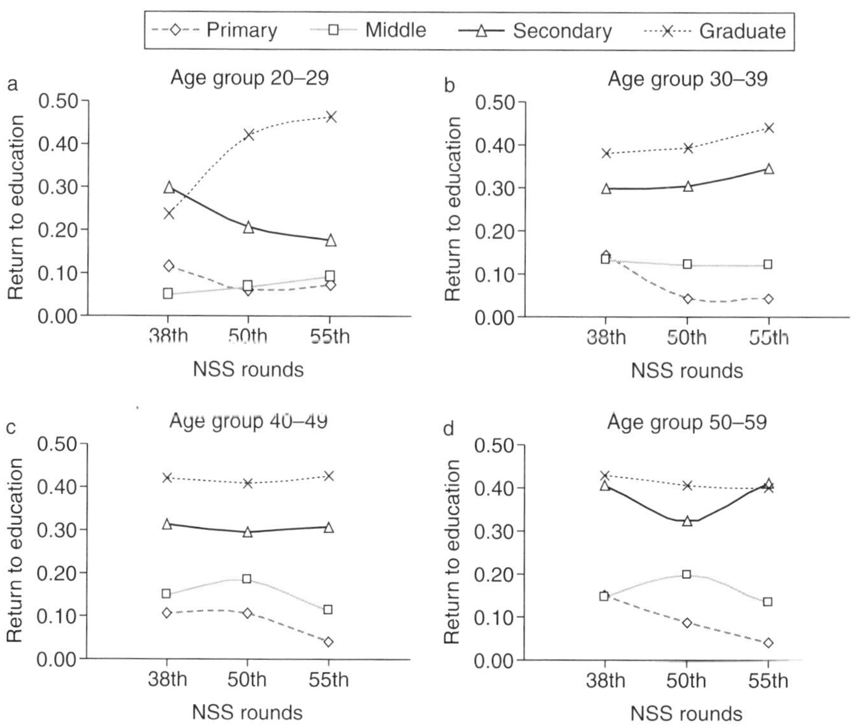

Figure 3.7 Returns to education in urban areas by age-groups.

Table 3.13 Distribution of incremental work force by educational level and broad industry group in urban areas, UPSS (15–59)

Level of Education	*1983–1993*			*1993–1999*		
	Primary	*Secondary*	*Tertiary*	*Primary*	*Secondary*	*Tertiary*
Not literate	17.7	11.6	9.1	56.6	7.9	5.6
Literate and up to primary	31.1	10.2	13.3	41.9	4.3	4.0
Middle	14.2	18.5	14.6	3.6	30.9	23.3
Secondary	24.5	38.9	32.9	−1.7	34.1	33.8
Graduate and above	12.7	20.7	30.2	−0.6	22.3	33.1
Not specified	0.0	0.1	−0.2	0.2	0.5	0.3
Total	100.0	100.0	100.0	100.0	100.0	100.0

Note
During 1993–1994 and 1999–2000 there is a decline in absolute number of UPSS workers in primary sector, so negative figures mean positive increase.

and/or the importance of more skill-intensive manufactured goods in international trade (see Chapter 1 above). But we have seen that the employment expansion in post-reform India has been concentrated not so much in skill-intensive manufacturing as in the tertiary sector. It is therefore useful to ask the question: is the expansion of demand for educated labor which we witness particularly in the market for college graduates in the urban areas originating mostly in the tertiary sector? Table 3.13 gives the distribution of the *addition* to the UPS workforce by industry for different levels of educational attainments.

It is apparent that the market for college graduates in particular has expanded relatively more in the tertiary sector. A somewhat unexpected finding is that this trend had been going on since the eighties. Equally revealing is the finding that labor with less than middle level of schooling is now almost entirely absorbed in the primary sector. The difference between NO_ED and BASE_ED education stressed in the Introduction to the book would seem to be drawn at the boundary of primary education in the Indian labor market in the late nineties. Entry into the non-primary sector would now seem to require post-primary education.

We will discuss in Chapter 10 in particular that the bias in Indian policies towards tertiary education has encouraged the growth of skill-intensive industries. It is seen from the evidence presented here that the demand for labor with college education seems to be outrunning the supply with this pattern of development – even with the historical bias in education policies. It is very likely that the return to college education has continued to increase in the years since 1999–2000.

Appendix

Employment estimates based on current daily status (CDS)

Current daily status of all individuals above the age of five is coded in the NSS for each half-day over the seven days preceding the survey. The activity of each half-day could be classified as (i) employed (ii) unemployed or (iii) out of labor force. Even if an individual is not classified as unemployed under the usual status in the week, some half-days of unemployment are possible if they are available for work for those units of time. Thus apart from the 'usual' unemployed the unemployment days would be contributed by casual workers; the self-employed who are working generally; and even by those 'usually' outside the labor force. The CDS unemployment rate is calculated by adding up these person-days of unemployment as a proportion of all days of employment plus unemployment.

There has been a school of thought in the Planning Commission and other GOI circles which has favored the use of CDS for the estimates of employment. This generally produces estimates which are much lower for 1999–2000 than those calculated on the UPS or UPSS basis. Thus the growth rate of employment shows a significantly higher rate of decline than the other estimates. For example, Srinivavsan (2005, Table 4) gives the growth rate of employment in the 1987–1999 period (between the 43rd and 55th rounds) *in the rural areas* at −4.59 percent on the CDS basis against −1.48 percent on the UPSS basis. But Srinivasan comments:

> The total number of *person-days* of employment is not the same as the total number of employed *persons*. The reason is that a given total number of *person-days* of employment could be distributed among the same number of persons in many ways so as to lead to different numbers of *persons* employed. For example, consider a four person economy in which all four participate in the work force and together they were employed for ten person-days in the week. This yields a person-day rate of employment of 10 out of 28 or 36%. If the ten person-days are distributed in a way that one person is employed for seven days, another for three days and the remaining two are unemployed, then person-rate of employment is two out of four or 50%. On the other hand, if it is distributed in a way that three persons work for three days each and one person works for just a day, the person rate of employment is four out of four or 100%, given the priority given to the status of employment!

We know that the NSS estimates of the numbers of persons in different demographic groups are underestimated, so we have to get the population figures from the Census counts. It is inappropriate to apply the employment rates based on *person-days* to the count of *persons* obtained from the Census of Population to arrive at the total number of employed persons.

4 Accounting for the decline in labor supply in the 1990s

It has already been mentioned in the last chapter that the Task Force of the Planning Commission on Employment Opportunities (July 2001) had in its Report (popularly known as the 'Ahluwalia Report') focused attention on the sharp decline in employment growth. The Committee rightly pointed out that while a part of the slowdown in employment growth was due to an increase in the rate of unemployment, much the more important part of the decline has to be ascribed to a slow down in the growth of the labor force. This is largely because of a fall in the participation rates (PRs) as measured by the NSS.

The Committee did not take a firm position on the reasons for the fall in participation rates, but the arguments presented included non-economic factors. e.g., the expected shift in the activity status of the younger age group towards education; increase in the share of the population aged 60 and over; a reversal or 'correction' of the increase in PRs of certain age groups recorded in the 1993–1994 NSS (p. 45). At the same time its assertion that the decline in the PRs in the prime age group is 'within the margin of sampling errors', while partly applicable to males, is, as we shall see, certainly not true for females.

A follow-up Report by a 'Special Group' of the Planning Commission (May 2002) firmly put its emphasis on a slowdown in the growth of demand for labor as the culprit on the observed trends in labor force and employment growth. Noting that the fall in employment growth was accompanied by a higher rate of GDP growth, the Committee concluded: 'It means that the capacity for job creation per unit of output went down about three times compared with that in the 1980s and the early 90s' (ibid., p. 336). It suggested that the nature of economic growth had become more capital-intensive, both due to structural changes, and the 'rightsizing' of labor use.

In this chapter we shall go into some detail into the reasons for the fall in participation rates which is the main cause of the observed decline in employment rate. Our major purpose would be to see if we can confirm in any conclusive way if this is the result more of demand-side developments (as implied by the 'Special Group' *Report*).

The theoretical perspective

The measured labor force at any point of time (and the volume of employment) is determined by the equation of the demand and supply functions of labor. If the observed magnitude changes over time it might be because of the shift of the demand or the supply functions or by a combination of the shifts in both. Thus if the labor force or employment growth falls over time we cannot conclude that it is because of a fall in the demand for labor. It might easily be caused more by a fall in the supply of labor. We cannot measure the contribution of supply and demand factors to the observed slowdown without a fully specified and estimated model. While this might be difficult to achieve we can at least infer the relative importance of the two sets of factors *qualitatively* by looking at trends in wage levels over the time periods covered. This can be illustrated by Figure 4.1.

The Figure 4.1 shows the supply-and-demand framework for wage determination in a dynamic setting. The x-axis measures participation rate while the y-axis measures the wage per worker. The participation rate in effect measures the *flow of labor per unit of time* out of the potential stock. The demand function is then downward sloping: the lower the wage level the more is the flow of labor sought by employers from the existing stock. The upward sloping supply function is propelled by the 'substitution effect' of changes in wage levels. A higher wage will see a higher rate of allocation of time to the labor market at the expense of other activities, like leisure, household work or education.

As we have seen the post-reform period in India saw a significant fall in the rate of growth of employment compared to the previous decade. It will be shown in the next section that this decline was the counterpart of a decline in the participation rate In the competitive labor-market framework presented in Figure 4.1, this must imply that, if this decline has been caused by a shift in the demand function with a relatively unchanged supply function, the wage per worker must fall in the second period (situation 2 in Figure 4.1). We have already seen in the

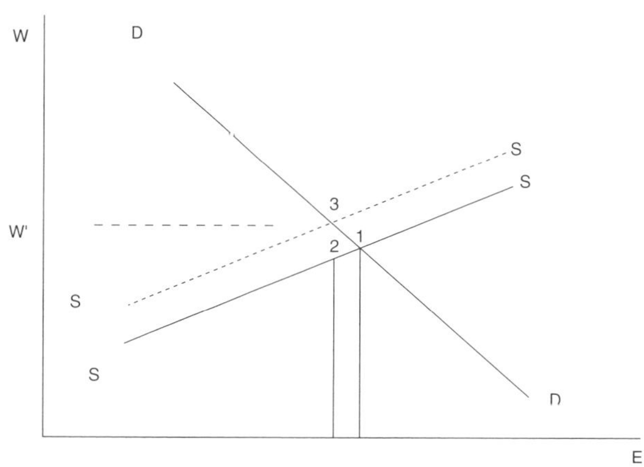

Figure 4.1 Wage-determination framework.

last chapter that this has not been the case. The real wage has increased in the post-reform period. This outcome is only possible if the supply function has shifted upward. Such a shift is possible if the 'income effect' of higher welfare levels causes household members to supply less labor to the market for a given wage growth. An increasing growth rate of wages could indeed both cause and sustain such an increase in household income levels.

In the empirical work presented below we shall be investigating the possibility of such an income effect for different demographic groups and sectors.

It is of course possible that the wage determination in the Indian economy cannot be interpreted within the competitive labor-market framework in the post-reform years. The higher rate of wages might have been the result of institutional factors. In this case the rate of employment growth (and consequently participation) could fall in response to the higher wage growth, and the gap between the growth of labor supply and of labor demand would have opened up leading to a higher rate of unemployment (situation 3 in the Figure 4.1). In fact the second Report of the Planning Commission hinted at this possibility without actually analyzing it in detail. There are two objections to this alternative hypothesis. The rate of unemployment did increase in the post-reform years, but we shall see in the discussion below that the magnitude of this increase was not really large enough to account for the large fall in the growth rate of employment. Second, and more crucially, it is hard to believe that institutional determination of the higher growth rate of wages would be at all realistic in an economy in which the bulk of employment is in the 'unorganized' sector.

There is a third possibility which is suggested by the 'segmented labor market' model. Segmentation implies that labor markets in the different segments are subject to different sets of supply-and-demand factors. In this case falling demand in one segment causing reduced participation might coexist with increased demand in other segments putting an upward pressure on wages. If, then, the observed data refer to participation in the first segment and wages in the second, we might indeed have the apparently inconsistent picture referred to above with slackening demand coexisting with rising wages in the aggregate. Segmentation might be caused by many factors and depending on the focus of our analysis could refer to gender, formal-informal, caste and many others. In the context of the current issue the factor we should emphasize is the distinction between primary and secondary earners. In the methodology of the NSS the former is called Usual Principal Status (UPS) and the latter Subsidiary Status (SS). This distinction is important in the context of the issue being discussed, because as we shall see a substantial part of the fluctuation in participation has taken place in the market for SS workers, while the wage or earnings data which are reported are for the markets of UPS workers.

The SS labor market is dominated by females, the majority in self-employed status, who are generally part of agricultural households and divide their time between household activity and work on the family farm as required. The amount of time spent on the latter is not measured by the NSS which only records the number such workers during the period of the survey. During an upsurge in economic activity, as might have happened during the introduction of new technology in paddy in the early eighties, the increase in demand for labor might be partly met by an increase in workers of secondary status working for varying lengths of time. Over a period of time as the labor market settles down to the new level of activity if the technical change is of a lasting kind, a new deployment of labor would normally be worked out by farmers in which some of the secondary workers used would be replaced by UPS workers on more permanent basis. Since the time spent by the latter on economic work is normally much larger than that by secondary workers, the numbers recorded as employed by the total (including both UPS and USS workers) might actually fall although the number of UPS workers might have increased. Thus the total employment figure might give a misleading idea of the change in demand in the labor market. We have to look specifically to the numbers in UPS status to see how the employment change in relate the recorded change in wage levels.

We will follow this line of analysis in the empirical work reported below.

It might be objected that in the discussion above we might have overemphasized the importance of wage workers in the Indian labor markets. In so far there is a large presence of self-employed workers, an analysis focused on wage trends might be misleading.

How important is wage labor in the Indian labor market?

The share of wage workers in UPS (principal) employment is more than half – slightly less in rural areas. Some part of wage labor is, however, supplied by secondary workers. It is important to get an idea about what proportion of the UPSS employed (principal and subsidiary together) actually participate in the labor market as wage labor either as a first or a second job. This total gives us the proportion of the employed who actually respond to wage signals in the labor market directly. Looking at the (larger) UPSS labor force as a whole, it was seen that the proportion of wage workers goes up (relative to the UPS count) by 3.5 percent in rural areas but it marginally declines in the urban areas. Evidently in rural areas more of the total enter the labor market as wage workers in subsidiary employment. In the urban areas relatively more workers in secondary status are to be found in the non-wage employment segment.

Decline in labor-force growth and distribution of fall in LFPR among different demographic groups

The fall in the rate of growth of employment in the post-reform period can be shown to be basically due to the fall in the participation rate. It has already been pointed out in the last chapter that the rate of unemployment in the Indian labor market is low, either with or without the secondary workers. Even if the rates of unemployment might have gone up in the post-reform era a bit its overall impact on the employment growth is small.

Our discussion in this section, therefore, concentrates on the changes in the participation rates, and the possible reasons for these changes.

Table 4.1 Growth of UPSS labor force (annual compound in percentages)

Rounds	*Rural*		*Urban*		*Rural*	*Urban*	*Male*	*Female*	*Total*
	Male	*Female*	*Male*	*Female*					
38th–50th (1983 to 1993–1994)	1.62	1.06	2.70	3.19	1.42	2.80	1.89	1.35	1.71
50th–55th (1993–1994 to 1999–2000)	1.15	0.41	2.63	1.35	0.89	2.37	1.55	0.55	1.23
50–55th derived	1.81	1.93	3.06	3.69	1.85	3.19	2.14	2.20	2.16

Source: Calculated from unit-level data of employment and unemployment schedule of 38th, 50th and 55th rounds.

Note
Derived figures are hypothetical labor force if there was no change of LFPR of 12 age groups (five-year interval) during 50th to 55th rounds.

We first set out the change in the rates of growth of the total (UPSS) labor force between the different NSS rounds.

Table 4.1 suggests that there was substantial decline in the labor-force growth from the 1980s (38th to 50th round or 1983 to 1993–1994) to the 1990s (50th to 55th round or 1993–1994 to 1999–2000) from 1.71 percent to 1.23 percent. The decline in the labor force could be due to decline in the working-age population or due to the decline in the labor-force participation rate (LFPR). Keeping the LFPR of 1999–2000 the same as 1993–1994 we find that hypothetical labor-force growth would have been much higher at 2.16 percent – much higher that even in the 1980s. It clearly shows that it is the decline in the LFPR that is mainly responsible for slower growth of employment in the 1990s.

We examined separate graphs for the age-specific LFPRs for all the three rounds for rural male, rural female, urban male and urban female.

The overall impression from the four profiles of age-specific PRs is that the most important change in the post-reform period is the decline in female participation, particularly in the rural economy. As far as males are concerned, the profiles for both the rural and the urban areas showed marginal declines in LFPR in age groups 5–19 years and 59+ age groups in 1990s. The decline in male LFPR in 5–19 years was substantial in the 1980s but slowed down in the 1990s – in both rural and urban areas. By contrast, the female LFPR showed a decline in all age groups between 1993–1994 and 1999–2000. In the previous period between 1983 and 1993–1994 the decline in both rural and urban areas were sharper in 5–19 age groups, but there was no substantial changes in the older age groups. The distinctive change in the latest period is the marked decline in female LFPR in the working age group as well.

As a substantial proportion of females participate in the labor market in a subsidiary capacity (i.e., enter the labor market only for a part of the year) it is worthwhile to look at female LFPR separately for UPS (Principal) and SS (Subsidiary) categories. This is portrayed in Figures 4.2a to 4.2d.

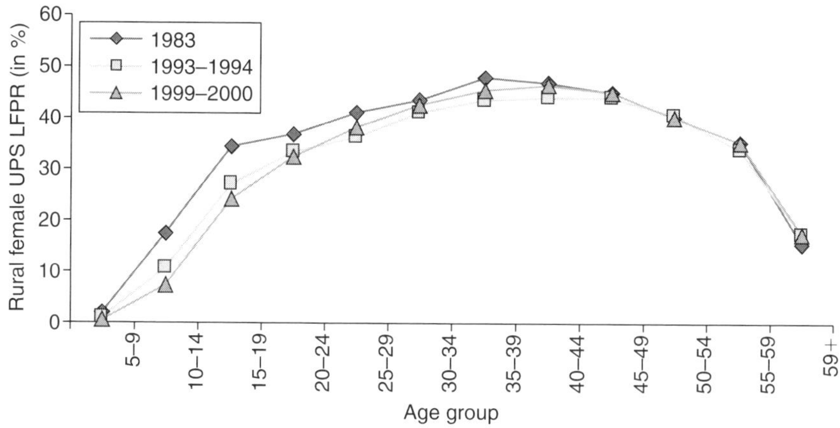

Figure 4.2a Rural female UPS labor-force participation rate.

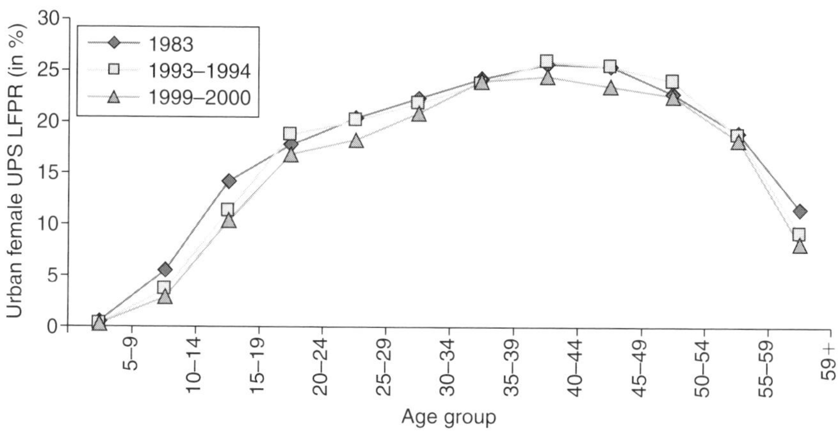

Figure 4.2b Urban female UPS labor-force participation rate.

As in the case of males, the UPS female LFPR in all areas showed marginal decline only in the 5–19 age group in the 1990s most of the decline having taken place in the earlier decade. In the urban areas a marginal decline was observed in other age groups as well. But the real dramatic changes seem to have taken place in the category of subsidiary female labor. The LFPR graphs in both rural and urban areas showed shift inwards in the 1990s – signifying a decline in LFPR in all age groups. This contrasts strongly with the movement in the previous period in the 1980s, the adult age groups of 25–49 years showing a substantial increase in LFPR in both rural and urban areas. The patterns and the nature of shift of the LFPR graphs suggest that there was an upsurge in female subsidiary labor demand in the period between 38th and 50th rounds and females belonging to

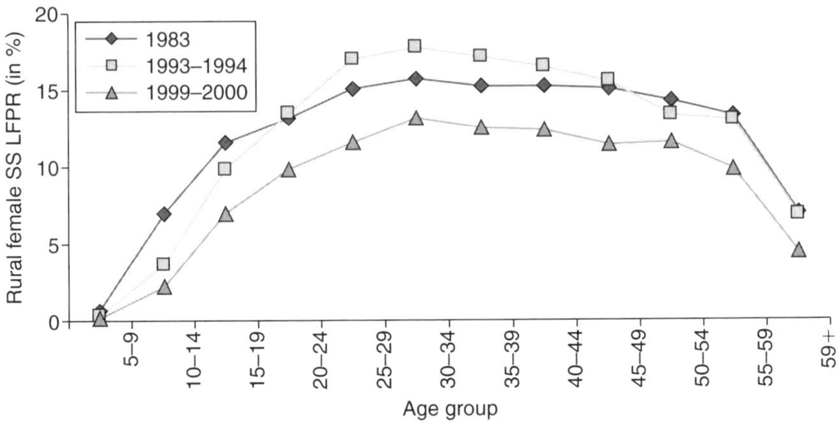

Figure 4.2c Rural female subsidiary labor-force participation rate.

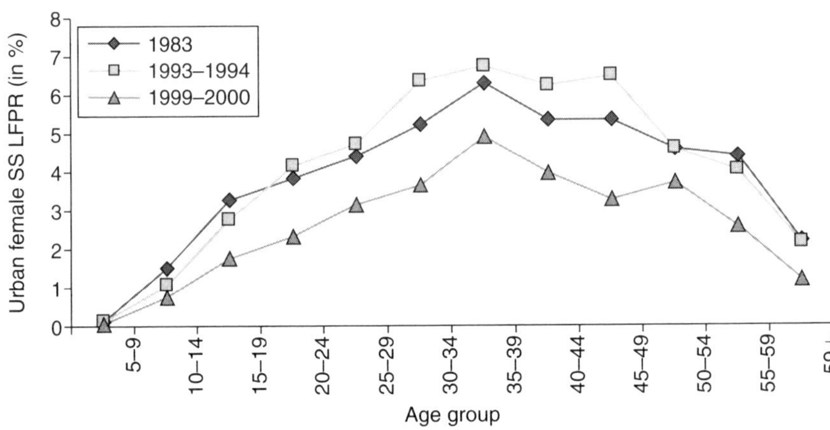

Figure 4.2d Urban female subsidiary labor-force participation rate.

the age group 25–49 were in the best position to respond to it. However, between the 50th and the 55th rounds there seems to have been a substantial decline in the demand for subsidiary workers and it is reflected in the inward movement of the entire LFPR curve for female subsidiaries (It is to be remembered that for the subsidiary labor force there is no unemployment, all are employed.) This is an important point – which is valid both for the rural and the urban sectors, but quantitatively more so for the rural.

Accounting for the decline in the labor force in the nineties

Three significant points emerged from the discussion in the last section: First, the decline in the 5–19 age group of the primary labor force (UPS); Second, a

Table 4.2 Actual and derived labor force

Sl. no	*Labor force*	*Derived (D)*	*Actual (A)*	*(D–A)*	*Ratio of (D–A) to UPSS (in %)*
1	UPSS 55th	425,060,597	402,446,304	22,614,292	100
2	SS 55th female	25,908,883	36,622,565	10,713,682	47.38
3	UPS 5–19	44,194,706	50,877,018	6,682,312	29.55
4	UPS 59+	29,481,191	31,892,790	2,411,599	10.66
2 + 3 + 4	Total	99,584,781	119,392,373	19,807,593	87.59

Source: Calculated from unit-level data of employment and unemployment schedule of 38th, 50th and 55th rounds.

Note
Derived figures are hypothetical labor supply when there is no change of age groupwise LFPR from 50th to 55th rounds. See Appendix 2 for detailed procedure.

marginal decline in the 59+ UPS labor; last, a substantial decline in female subsidiary labor supply.

The question is what is the relative contribution of each of these segments to the total decline in labor supply in the 1990s? Table 4.2 throws light on this question. It presents the actual (A) and hypothetical (D) labor force, the latter on the assumption of no change in age-group specific LFPRs between the 50th and 55th rounds.[1]

The results show that decline in LFPR actually contributed to a fall of 23 million in the labor force. The last column shows that female subsidiary labor force (of all ages) contributed 47 percent of the total decline. The 5–19 UPS LFPR contributed 30 percent and aged LFPR (59+) contributed another 10 percent. These three factors combined accounted for as much as 88 percent of the total hypothetical labor force decline in the 1990s. Clearly the first component – the withdrawal of subsidiary females from the labor force – leads the list in terms of the diagnosis of the observed fall in employment growth. But before coming to this topic, we discuss briefly the fall in LFPR in the 5–19 and 59+ age groups.

5–19 UPS labor-force participation rate

The distribution of all persons in this age group in different principal activities is given in Table 4.3.

One can clearly see that the increase in proportion of students is the main factor responsible for decline in the work participation rate in both the rural and the urban sectors. There is a difference between the two periods: between 1983 and 1993–1994 and the subsequent period of the 1990s. The earlier period experienced substantial jump in the category of students but the shift was relatively more from the category of 'nowhere children' (doing nothing). In the latter period, it was largely a shift from UPS worker and domestic work. However, the withdrawal from work in absolute term was higher in the 1980s compared with the 1990s. We conclude that it is either demand for education and/or better educational facilities

Table 4.3 Distribution of UPS persons in the age group 5–19 (UPS)

Year	*Sector*	*Principal status*				
		UPS workers	*Students*	*Domestic work*	*Doing nothing*	*Others**
1983	Rural	19.5	38.9	13.5	26.9	1.3
1993–1994	Rural	15.6	55.1	10.2	18.3	0.9
1999–2000	Rural	12.7	60.4	8.4	17.6	0.9
1983	Urban	10.6	62.5	10.8	13.9	2.3
1993–1994	Urban	9.1	73.8	7.3	8.3	1.5
1999–2000	Urban	8.0	74.8	6.6	9.1	1.5

Source: Calculated from unit-level data of employment and unemployment schedule of 38th, 50th and 55th rounds.

Note
* Others include unemployed.

that seem to be the prime reason for decline in labor-force participation in this age group. However, increase in the students' participation rate in this age group seems to be tapering off in the urban areas in the 1990s (Table 4.3).

We examined the relationship of the participation of this demographic group to the levels of the expenditure per capita of the households to which they belonged. The tabulation was done separately for the rural and the urban households. Participation was found to be negatively related to household expenditure levels in both sectors, but the negative relationship was stronger in the urban areas. The slope of the negative relationship clearly decreased over time, but was still strong in the 1999–2000 survey, particularly in the urban sector.

Aged 59+ labor-force participation rate (LFPR)

The post-liberalization years saw a reversal in participation trends in the rural sector for both males and females, *but not in the urban areas.* Participation rates fell in contrast to the positive trend in the previous decade. In the urban sector the relatively slow decline in participation already noticed in the previous decade continued at more or less the same pace. Overall the share of the post-retirement workers in the total withdrawal from the labor force in the 1993–2000 years is small.

In the 59+ age group it is generally argued that income effect predominates when withdrawal from labor force is observed over time. Only in the case of urban females do we see a consistent decline in LFPR over the three rounds and also for the top three quintiles. The trends are much more mixed for the other categories, though for both rural and urban males the decline in participation in the 1990s seems to have been strongest in the top two quintiles.

It should be emphasized that this result, although suggestive, cannot be conclusive about the income effect on the participation of seniors. This is because the earnings of the seniors staying on in market activity itself affect the expenditure level of their household.

Female subsidiary labor force

Change in the demand for subsidiary labor

As argued earlier, there was a sudden upsurge of female subsidiary labor demand in the 1980s followed by a contraction of labor demand in the 1990s. This fluctuation requires further probe. Tables 4.4a to 4.4b present the distribution of subsidiary female employment by major industries and occupations.

As we can see subsidiary female employment is concentrated in a few agricultural and allied activities, i.e., growing of cereals and animal husbandry. They contributed 80 percent of female subsidiary employment in rural areas and even a sizeable part of such employment in the urban labor market.

We, therefore, looked specifically at the growing of cereals sector in rural areas since it constituted the largest chunk of female subsidiary labor supply. This sector contributed 4.9 million out of six million of additional subsidiary female employment between the 38th and 50th rounds. At the same time it contributed

Table 4.4a Share of selected occupation in female subsidiary labor supply

Occupation	*Rural*			*Urban*		
	1983	*1993–1994*	*1999–2000*	*1983*	*1993–1994*	*1999–2000*
Cultivators	34.2	42.0	37.9	14.0	13.2	8.8
Livestock, poultry and dairy farmers	32.1	23.2	28.6	29.5	26.8	23.0
Agricultural labor	14.5	19.7	15.5	5.5	0.8	1.1
Total	80.8	84.9	82.0	49.0	40.8	32.9

Source: Calculated from unit-level data of employment and unemployment schedule of 38th, 50th and 55th rounds.

Table 4.4b Share of selected industries in female subsidiary labor supply

Industry	*Rural*			*Urban*		
	1983	*1993–1994*	*1999–2000*	*1983*	*1993–1994*	*1999–2000*
Growing of cereals	48.1	60.2	53.6	19.0	20.2	13.0
Cattle breeding and production of milk	33.2	21.5	27.0	23.7	15.7	14.2
Total	81.3	81.7	80.6	42.7	35.9	27.2

Source: Calculated from unit-level data of employment and unemployment schedule of 38th, 50th and 55th rounds.

5.8 million out of 6.3 million of decline in female subsidiary employment between the 50th and 55th rounds.

However, analysis across states for this sector show that four states Karnataka, Madhya Pradesh, Maharashtra and West Bengal[2] played the major role in absorption of female subsidiary labor in this sector in the 1980s and subsequent decline in the 1990s. These states include the districts which experienced a spread of the green revolution in the 1980s. Thus this piece of evidence gives credence to the argument that the spread of labor absorbing green revolution technologies in the 1980s bumped up the demand for labor in these areas, which in the short run could only be met by increasing use of female secondary labor. Subsequently in the 1990s as rising labor costs led to the introduction of labor replacing technologies, the additional demand for female labor subsided. This process might have been also helped by hurdles faced by oilseed development program in the 1990s in parts of this region.

It should be noted that most of this adjustment took place, not in the wage-labor market, but among the self-employed workers. It can be seen from Table 4.4a that agricultural wage labor accounted for a small portion of total female subsidiary employment in the rural areas, and even less so in the urban sector. Further examination of the NSS data by employment status showed that casual wage labor accounted for only 16.9 percent of all female subsidiary workers (in the age group 15 and above) in the rural areas in the 55th round – down from 21.7 percent in the 50th. The corresponding percentages in the urban sector were 12.1 and 20.6. Much the more substantial share of such employment in both sectors was accounted for by the 'self-employed' and the 'helpers' categories.

Evidence on the 'income effect'

If there is a significant income effect affecting participation then we would expect the opportunity cost of leisure to increase at all household welfare (or income) levels – but it would presumably increase more at higher levels of welfare. Consider a supply function of labor-relating participation rate (of, say, prime-age females) to the household welfare level. At any point of time, for a given distribution of household incomes, we would expect this curve to turn down quite sharply as the effect of higher household welfare begins to overshadow the substitution effect. When at a later date average income of all household increases, the supply curve relating participation of this group to the household welfare level is pushed downwards. Thus there is less participation at all welfare levels – but the point at which there is a significant fall in the slope of the curve comes earlier in the lower part of the household welfare distribution. We have seen that a very important portion of the change in participation in the post-liberalization period is accounted for by the fall in the number of females of subsidiary status. We can try to see which household welfare groups have typically contributed to the withdrawal of labor in the female subsidiary status. The index for household welfare used is the mean per capita expenditure level. We use the groupings as provided by the NSS reports.

Table 4.5 Distribution of subsidiary employment across APCE groups for ages 5+

Consum. expen. class (in percentile)	APCE groups	50th round						55th round					
		Rural			Urban			Rural			Urban		
		Male	Female	Total	Male	Female	Total	Male	Female	Total	Male	Female	Total
0–5	1	2.2	3.2	3.1	5.6	7.1	6.9	4.5	5.6	5.5	2.4	2.6	2.6
5–10	2	2.2	3.6	3.4	2.3	6.3	5.8	2.3	4.9	4.7	1.3	2.0	1.9
10–20	3	6.0	7.8	7.6	8.9	**12.5**	**11.9**	6.8	8.7	8.5	2.1	4.2	3.8
20–30	4	8.0	9.9	9.7	6.2	9.8	9.3	8.2	9.7	9.6	2.8	7.1	6.4
30–40	5	6.9	8.5	8.3	**11.3**	**13.1**	**12.9**	9.3	**10.2**	**10.1**	6.1	5.6	5.7
40–50	6	**10.4**	9.7	9.8	**10.4**	**10.5**	**10.5**	9.2	8.7	8.8	2.6	**10.4**	9.2
50–60	7	**10.5**	**10.7**	**10.7**	**14.4**	9.5	**10.2**	**11.6**	**10.9**	**10.9**	6.5	**10.8**	**10.1**
60–70	8	**10.3**	**10.1**	**10.1**	**11.7**	**11.1**	**11.2**	9.1	**10.1**	10.0	**10.9**	8.4	8.8
70–80	9	**13.1**	**11.6**	**11.8**	8.8	7.8	8.0	**11.4**	**11.3**	**11.3**	8.0	**10.5**	**10.1**
80–90	10	**13.0**	**11.4**	**11.6**	**11.9**	7.4	8.0	**12.1**	**10.4**	**10.6**	**16.9**	**17.4**	**17.4**
90–95	11	6.6	6.1	6.2	3.6	2.8	2.9	6.5	4.8	5.0	**10.4**	9.1	9.3
95–100	12	**10.0**	6.8	7.2	4.7	1.6	2.1	8.9	4.8	5.1	**29.9**	**12.0**	**14.7**
Not mentioned	13	0.7	0.6	0.6	0.2	0.5	0.5						
Total		100.0	100.0	100.0	100.0	100.0	100.0	100.0	100.0	100.0	100.0	100.0	100.0
0–20 (P1)		10.4	14.7	14.2	16.9	25.9	24.6	13.7	19.1	18.6	5.8	8.8	8.3
80–100 (P2)		29.7	24.3	24.9	20.2	11.8	13.0	27.4	20.0	20.7	57.3	38.5	41.4
P2/P1		2.9	1.7	1.8	1.2	0.5	0.5	2.0	1.0	1.1	10.0	4.4	5.0

Source: Unit-level data of 50th and 55th rounds of employment and unemployment schedule.

It is seen that in the rural sector the female subsidiary workers in the 55th round area coming much more from a lower expenditure group than those in the 50th round. Notice in particular that the P2/P1 ratio, as defined in Table 4.5, has fallen from a value of 1.66 to 1.04 in the post-liberalization years. The value of this ratio for rural males has also fallen, but not by as much.[3] The evidence strongly suggests that the withdrawal of subsidiary workers – which was identified as a dominant feature of the change in the rural labor markets over this period – came increasingly from higher household expenditure groups. Interestingly enough, the trend in the urban sector is the exact reverse. The P2/P1 ratio increased substantially both for males and females, suggesting that the withdrawal observed for subsidiary workers in the urban labor markets came increasingly from *lower* expenditure groups. We conclude that the 'income effect' seems to have been a factor in the fall in participation of subsidiary workers, particularly females, in the rural areas, but that other factors (e.g., education or social connection) might have been more important in the falling participation rate in the urban economy.

Principal-status labor-force participation

Let us now see how the supply of labor in the UPS category behaves in contrast to the supply in the UPSS status discussed in the last section. The change in the growth rates of UPS labor by gender and sector are shown in Table 4.6.

Unlike in the case of the UPSS labor force no decline in the growth rate is observed in the 1990s compared with the 1980s. However, there is an important gender difference. The male labor-force growth fell in in the 1990s, whereas female labor-force growth increased by 50 percent. The last row in Table 4.6 shows the hypothetical growth rate which would have occurred if the PRs had remained at the same levels as in the 50th round. The significant point to note is that in the rural labor market although the actual growth rate for female principal workers between the 50th and the 55th rounds was below the 'derived' growth rate for this group, it had nevertheless increased compared with the previous period between the 38th and the 50th rounds. Further scrutiny about changes in age-specific participation rates for principal females shows that this increase is really due to an *increase* in PRs for the prime age groups 25–59 (see Figure 4.2a).

Table 4.6 Growth of UPS labor force (annual compound in percentage)

Rounds	*Rural*		*Urban*		*Rural*	*Urban*	*Male*	*Female*	*Total*
	Male	*Female*	*Male*	*Female*					
38th–50th	1.67	0.80	2.76	3.01	1.42	2.80	1.95	1.13	1.73
50th–55th	1.29	1.77	2.67	2.49	1.42	2.64	1.66	1.89	1.72
50th–55th derived	1.79	1.92	3.05	3.70	1.83	3.17	2.13	2.22	2.16

Source: Calculated from unit-level data of employment and unemployment schedule of 38th, 50th and 55th rounds.

We did a D–A analysis for rural females in the 55th round by broad age groups, showing the difference between the derived figure of the labor force (on the assumption of PRs being unchanged from the 50th round) and the actual labor force reported. A negative figure indicates that the PR for the relevant age group has increased. It was seen that the D–A statistic for the 25–59 age group was *minus* two million compared to the positive 0.5 million for the total rural female workers of UPS status. Thus while for the rural principal females as a whole there was a net marginal decline in PRs, the PRs for the prime age groups had increased to a significant degree, relative to the trends in all other age–sex groups in the rural labor market for UPS workers.

Considering that there had been a substantial fall in the PRs for the rural females in secondary status in this period (see Figure 4.4a), we conclude that there was some shift of employment from subsidiary to principal status during this period. It is quite consistent with rationalization of the labor force where principal workers are preferred compared with the subsidiary labor force when growth is sustained over a period of time.

It is clear, therefore, that the observed decline in the labor force – and the attendant fall in employment – has not affected the principal labor market. On the contrary the evidence suggests a tightening of labor conditions in this market. Since the reported wage rates refer to this labor market, we would expect this tightening to be reflected in an increase in real wages. This is indeed what we see across the board for different classes of principal workers.

Evidence on wage trends

We have already seen in Chapter 3 that the growth rate of the manual casual wage per day shows a slight acceleration in the *rural* sector as a whole, for both males and females. More detailed statistics are given in Table 4.7 for the manual

Table 4.7 Growth rates of manual and non-manual wage per day (casual workers)

	38th to 50th			*50th to 55th*		
	Male	*Female*	*Total*	*Male*	*Female*	*Total*
Rural wage						
Manual	2.85	2.77	2.91	3.18	3.11	3.14
Non-manual	2.70	2.53	2.54	3.09	3.83	3.25
Total	2.84	2.76	2.90	3.17	3.15	3.16
Urban wage						
Manual	2.23	3.43	2.51	2.91	3.61	3.51
Non-manual	2.04	0.60	1.78	4.18	3.38	4.09
Total	2.22	3.32	2.45	3.01	3.72	3.59

Source: Calculated from unit-level data of employment and unemployment schedule of 38th, 50th and 55th rounds.

as well as the non-manual parts of the casual labor market. The wage rate accelerated substantially in the second period for both sexes in non-agriculture in rural areas and in the urban areas.

While all groups seem to have experienced an upward trend, the acceleration in the second period was stronger for non-manual workers and in the urban areas. The evidence suggests that the increase in demand for labor in the non-manual labor market supplemented the relative increase in demand for female principal workers, which seems to have been caused by the rationalization of labor deployment in the manual agricultural labor market.

Conclusion on withdrawal of labor

The observed fall in the supply of labor in the 55th round due to decrease in PRs has three major components: the 5–19 age group in UPS status (30 percent of the total decrease); the older 59+ age group in UPS (11 percent); and the females of working age group in subsidiary status (47 percent). It is the last which has been the subject of extended discussion and alternative explanations. Our analysis based on a reading of the historical record suggests that the key to an understanding of this phenomenon is the upsurge in the demand for labor in the early eighties due to the second wave of the green revolution in paddy cultivation and also in oilseed cultivation. This increase in demand was met in the short run by a lift in the participation of SS females as shown in the data for the 38th and 50th rounds. As the economy adjusted to the new level of labor demand in agriculture labor deployment was gradually changed with more use of female labor of a more regular kind. Thus we get a shift from SS females to UPS females between the 50th and the 55th rounds. Since the supply of effort by UPS workers is at a substantially higher level than for the SS workers, this led an overall decrease in female *number* of workers over all. While this restructuring of the female labor demand is the basic cause of the observed fall in PRs of SS females, we can also discern an element of the income effect leading to a withdrawal of female secondary workers from higher income groups. As explained the wage rates in agriculture are determined in the market for the more regular (UPS) workers. It seems that the increase in demand for such workers continued to keep ahead of the increase in supply due to natural growth of the working-age population, so that the rate of increase in wages increased in the nineties.

Appendix 1 concept of different types of labor force

Usual Principal and Subsidiary Status (UPSS) include persons in the labor force by both major and minor time criteria. In other words, it includes both principal and subsidiary status categories of persons in the labor force.

UPS labor force refers to the persons those who are included in the labor force by major time criterion.

> 5.0.15 ***Usual activity status:*** The usual activity status relates to the activity status of a person during the reference period of 365 days preceding the date of survey. The activity status on which a person spent relatively longer time (major time criterion) during the 365 days preceding the date of survey is considered the *principal usual activity status* of the person. To decide the principal usual activity of a person, he/she is first categorized as belonging to the labor force or not, during the reference period **on the basis of major time criterion** .... For the persons belonging to the labor force, the broad activity status of either 'working' or 'not working but seeking and/or available for work' is then ascertained again on the basis of the relatively longer time spent in the labor force during the 365 days preceding the date of survey.
>
> (Instruction manual, 55th round, schedule 10, section 5.0.15.)

In this study, the Subsidiary Status (SS) labor force is defined as persons who are pursuing non-economic activities (out of labor force) by major time criterion (UPS) but belong to the labor force by minor time criterion. It excludes persons who are included in labor force by UPS to avoid double counting. Since unemployment status is determined by major time criterion, those belonging to labor force only on the basis of subsidiary status by default are all workers.

> 5.0.16 ***Subsidiary economic activity status:*** A person whose principal usual status is determined on the basis of the major time criterion may have pursued some economic activity **for a relatively shorter time** (minor time) during the reference period of 365 days preceding the date of survey .... It may be noted that engagement in work in subsidiary capacity may arise out of the two following situations:
>
> i a person may be engaged for a relatively longer period during the last 365 days in economic/non-economic activity and for a relatively shorter period in another economic activity and
> ii a person may be pursuing one economic activity/non-economic activity almost through-out the year in the principal usual activity status and also simultaneously pursuing another economic activity for a relatively shorter period in a subsidiary capacity.
>
> (Instruction manual, 55th round, schedule 10, section 5.0.16.)

In our concept of subsidiary status labor force we have only included the persons who are engaged in non-economic activity for a 'relatively longer period during the last 365 days' but engaged in economic activity for a 'relatively shorter period' or 'pursued non-economic activity almost throughout the year in principal usual activity status' but pursued another economic activity for 'relatively shorter period in a subsidiary capacity'. In this fashion we managed to get UPSS labor force = UPS labor force + SS labor force which is additive.

Table 4A.1 NSS rounds and their mid-year dates

NSS Rounds	*Period*	*Mid-year*
38th	1983	1 July 1983
50th	July 1993–June 1994	1 January 1994
55th	July 1999–June 2000	1 January 2000

Appendix 2: estimating the absolute number of the labor force

NSS rounds are sample surveys. They do calculate India's population but these are generally underestimated and the level of underestimation is going up over the year. We can get corrected population estimates for these three mid-year dates by interpolating population figures from three decadal population census of India – 1981, 1991 and 2001.

NSS differs from decadal census in terms of age-group distribution population. To adjust for the 38th, 50th and 55th rounds of NSS we have used the five-year age-group distribution of the 1981 Census, 1991 Census and National Health and Family Welfare Survey-II (NFHS) 1998 respectively. The 13 age groups that we have considered are 0–5, 5–10, 10–15, 15–20, 20–25, 25–30, 30–35, 35–40, 40–45, 45–50,50–55, 55–60 and 60 and above. NSS also differs from decadal census in terms of rate of urbanization rate and sex ratio. To get around this problem we used the Census-adjusted NSS mid-year population and age-group distribution separately for rural male (RM), rural female (RF), urban male (UM) and urban female (UF). Thus, we calculated population for these four sections of population for 13 age groups separately.

Labor-force participation rate (LFPR) for each of these four sections of population for all three rounds have been generated for all 12 age groups (for 0–5 age group LFPR is not calculated) from unit-level data. By multiplying LFPR for each of them with the respective population cohort gives us the labor force for each of this population cohort. By adding up the labor force of all age groups and dividing it by its respective population we could derive the LFPR at more aggregate levels. Our calculated LFPR at aggregate level marginally differs from published LFPR figures of NSS.

A similar procedure has been adopted for calculating the number of workers in Chapter 3 and elsewhere.

Part II

Regional dimensions

5 Some implications of regional differences in labor-market outcomes in India

Ahmad Ahasan and Carmen Pages[1]

Introduction

This chapter attempts to examine and understand the determinants of key labor-market indicators by looking at the experience across Indian states and regions by analyzing the NSS thick round data from 1983–2000.[2] It does so in two parts. First, it shows how states and regions display considerable variation in labor-market outcomes: some states and regions have been able to provide significantly more employment opportunities, and thus show higher employment and participation rates.[3] Others states, not all in the same group, have lower unemployment rates.

Wage rates also vary significantly across regions leading to large differences in earnings. This leads to the second part of the chapter, which attempts to understand these patterns by trying to answer three key questions, two from the demand and the other from the supply side of labor markets. First, what are the factors that have enabled some states to create more jobs, and specifically what role did differences in economic activity and economic growth play in creating these jobs? Second, a related issue is, the role of differences in economic activity in affecting the quality of jobs as measured by earnings of workers. On the supply side the key issue that we address is the determinants of the variation in participation rates and especially in female participation rates across states and regions.

It may be useful to highlight the four main findings of this chapter. First, regional level differences in employment indicators are significant across regions and display a geographical clustering: 34 out of 78 NSS regions have statistically significantly different – better or worse – employment and unemployment outcomes than all India averages. Further, not only are these differences significant, but they have persisted over time. A related finding is that employment outcomes are clustered within certain states and regions: regions in the North Eastern states, Bihar and parts of UP, Jammu and Kashmir and Arunachal Pradesh, the coastal belts of Orissa and states such as Goa and Pondicherry have significantly worse employment outcomes. On the other hand Western and Southern States show better employment outcomes (see the third section below).

Second, wage and earning trends across regions present a complex picture with two countervailing aspects. On the one hand, significant differences in wages across regions are being balanced to some extent by evidence of convergence in wages across regions and between rural and urban areas. This finding is consistent with observations that not only are migration rates in India surprisingly low, but they have shown little signs of increasing in the 1990s. Further urbanization rates have also been much lower than predicted (Mohan and Dasgupta, 2004) and lower than in many other comparable countries. If wage rates are converging across regions and between rural and urban areas, then, other things remaining the same, the incentives to migrate to other states and to urban areas will decrease. On the other hand, dualism in wages between the formal, salaried sector and the informal, casual sector persists in that there remains a substantial premium for salaried workers (around 16 percent of the labor force) over casual labor (about 36 percent of the labor force) even after controlling for human-capital characteristics across all regions.

Third, we take up the issue of job content of growth by relating employment and earnings to GSDP levels across states as well as to changes in GSDP across four rounds from 1983 to 2000. Although GSDP growth is significant in explaining the growth of employment it cannot, per se, explain much of the variation in employment growth.[4] However, we find that income differences across states and growth of income within states exert substantial positive effect on female employment levels while it also reduces unemployment rates for females in rural areas; but they are not significant in explaining employment-level differences for men. However, GSDP level changes across states do have a significant impact on raising rural earnings for males.

Fourth, regional variations in employment outcomes can be explained on the supply side, by differences in female employment and participation rates. Although female employment rates are uniformly lower than those of males, the variance in regional participation rates is also much higher for female workers. In addition, female participation rates have declined in the 1990s, a trend difficult to reconcile with the declining fertility and increasing education rates of female workers, factors that have contributed to rising female participation in other regions.[5] In this chapter, we test two competing hypotheses to explain differences across regions and time in female participation: The first is that changes in participation are driven by income effects – increasing spouse earnings are driving female workers out of the labor force (see Sundaram and Tendulkar 2005b). The second hypothesis is that women are withdrawing from the labor market due to lack of opportunities (substitution effect). We find that while both forces are at work, the lack of opportunities, as indicated by unemployment rates and low expected earnings, have a greater role in explaining this trend.

The rest of this chapter is organized in the following manner: the second section briefly discusses the methodology used here and how the Chapter advances the literature. The third section documents the remarkable variance in labor-market outcomes across Indian states and regions. The following section analyzes these differences focusing on the role played by GSDP in affecting employment and earnings and the differences in participation rates. The final section concludes.

Methodology and how this chapter advances the literature

The evident disparities in economic conditions, growth and human development across Indian states have attracted considerable attention over the last few years. A sizeable literature has developed attempting to explain differences in growth and poverty-reduction performance across states. However, the cross-state and, particularly, the regional dimensions of employment remain relatively unexplored.

The literature on cross-state growth has highlighted the importance of differences in the investment climate in explaining differences in total factor productivity across states (Dollar *et al.* 2004); other studies have emphasized the differences in infrastructure and regulations (Lall and Mengistae 2005), the decline and variations in plan expenditures, the greater use of private capital flows and the wide variations in credit utilization (Dev 2002); the degree of urbanization (Sach *et al.* 2002); differences in land reforms, access to credit, education and labor-market related regulatory policies (Besley and Burgess 2004) as factors that have led to divergences in growth across Indian states. While most papers have confined their analysis to the state level, an important paper by Palmer-Jones and Sen (2004) has extended the analysis to the regional level, highlighting agro-ecological factors, irrigation and the interaction between these factors to explain divergence in agricultural growth rates. Overall the literature appears to have converged on a consensus that there is growing divergence in economic performance across states.

As noted, the literature on labor-market differences across states is relatively less developed. Some of the papers have presented at some length the differences in employment and unemployment rates across regions and have emphasized the role of divergent labor-market outcomes being a driving factor behind regional inequality (Bhattacharya and Sakkhivel 2004). A paper by Kijima and Lanjwou (2004) has estimated differences in agricultural wages across different regions. Another by Besley and Burgess (2004) has analyzed the effects of labor regulations in explaining state-wise variations in manufacturing output and employment growth. Hasan *et al.* (2003) estimated the effect of trade on labor-demand elasticity in industry and showed it to be positive. Extending further, they have shown how regulatory policies in states affect these demand elasticity adversely. At a broader level, the literature on labor-market differences has stopped short at two important points. First, the literature has focused more on describing differences in employment indicators across states and less on analyzing these differences, with Besley and Burgess (2004) and Hasan *et al.* (2004) being important exceptions. Second, the discussion has stayed focused at the state level except for Palmer-Jones and Sen (2004).

This chapter contributes to the literature on regional labor-market analysis in India in four ways. First, we construct synthetic panel data set on labor-market indicators at the regional and state levels to identify the extent of state and regional differences in Indian labor-market outcomes. The panel-based research on employment in India has so far mainly focused on using the annual survey of industries or smaller sample based data such as the NCAER surveys (e.g., Foster and Rozenweig 2004). By definition such research has excluded more than 80 percent of the Indian labor force or has been based on small nationally unrepresentative surveys. In this chapter we use the nationally representative panel to present the regional differences in employment, wages and participation, and analyze their determinants.

Second, this chapter takes the analysis beyond the state level to the (NSS-sample-based) regional level. Hitherto, analysis of regional level has been confined to a few studies on poverty and agricultural wage rate estimates. This is important since significant differences in employment indicators lie at the regional level. An examination of the data of the 55th round, as many as ten out of 32 states display a higher within state variation (as measured by the coefficient of variation) than the variation across states. Similarly, eight regions show higher within state variation in rural casual wages than the all-India variation.

Third, this chapter extends the discussion to the smaller states of the North-east such as Arunachal Pradesh, Mizoram, Nagaland and Himachal Pradesh, where much of the variation in employment is found.

Fourth and last, this chapter uses a variety of panel data-estimation techniques using region-level data to examine the drivers of regional variations. These include estimating equations of varying degrees of complexity, fixed-effects models, and using instruments to account for endogeneity of employment, participation, wages and GSDP.

How different are labor-market conditions across states? Some stylized facts

Labor-market outcomes are significantly different across India in a number of respects. In what follows we focus on regional differences in employment, participation and earnings.

Stylized fact 1: striking regional clustering of employment

The first stylized fact is the clustering of low employment rates in the north-eastern states of Arunachal Pradesh, Assam, Nagaland, Tripura and Manipur. In addition, the lagging states of UP and Bihar have particularly lower employment rates (Figure 5.1). This trend is largely mirrored in the low participation rates as shown in Figure 5.2. In general one finds a high correlation between employment rates and participation rates (0.95). This correlation is stronger for females (at 0.99 percent) than for men (0.95 percent). The relationship between these variables can be in both directions. Participation can lead to employment. Most workers seeking work in a poor developing-country labor market such as India can find work even if it is in a low-productivity job or a self-employed job. That is supply of labor creates its own demand. On the other direction, low employment rates in a region can lead to a discouragement of workers and lower participation. We examine this issue at some length later in the section 'Understanding differences across states and regions', where we try to analyze some key regional differences and trends in labor-market outcomes.

Participation rates for males and females are shown for all states in Figure 5.2. The relatively lower participation and employment rates in states such as Delhi, Kerala and West Bengal are puzzling (employment rates are presented in Figure 5.1). Given their higher income levels, the low employment rates in these states need more explanation. On the other hand, and more predictably, the prosperous states of the South and West, Tamil Nadu, Karnataka, Gujarat and Andhra Pradesh show significantly higher employment and participation rates. An interesting exception is Rajasthan where employment and participation rates are high.

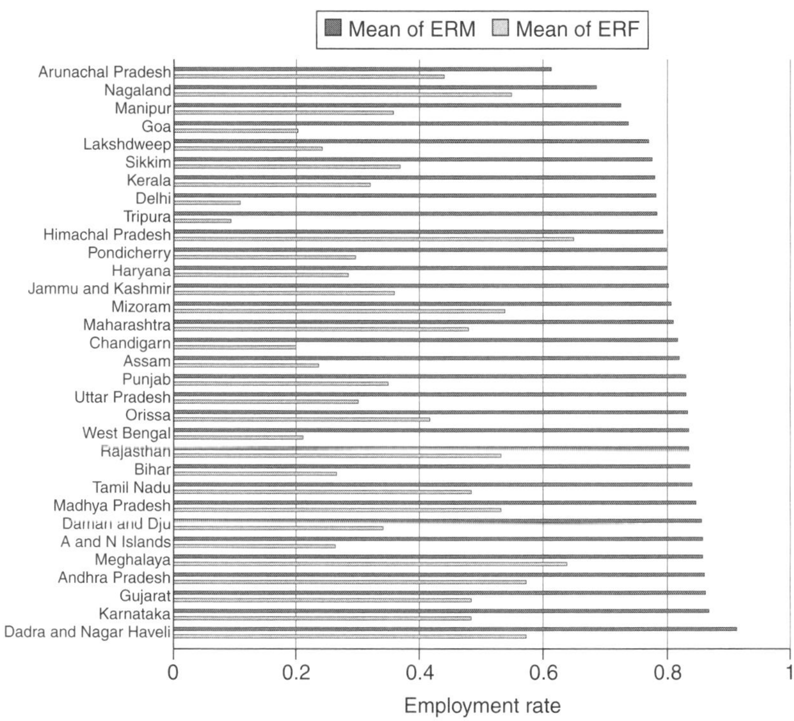

Figure 5.1 Employment rates for males and female, 55th round (source: Authors estimates. *Erm* and *Erf* refer to employment rate of males and females respectively (measured in 0 to 1 scale; i.e. 0.8 refers to 80 percent employment rate). Employment rates for males and female are defined as workers in 15–59 age group as a share of the population in their age group. Derived from NSS 55th Round data).

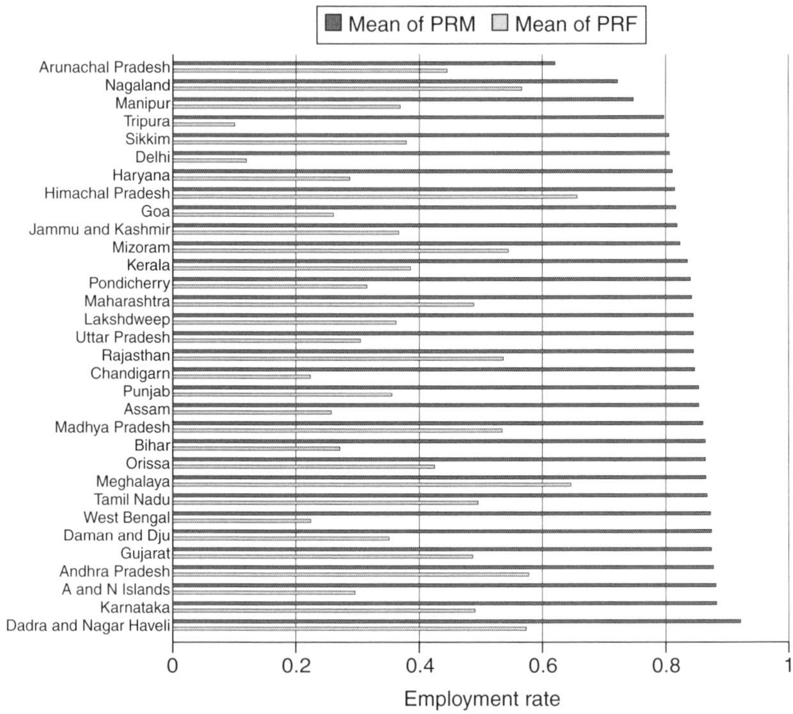

Figure 5.2 Participation rates for males and female, 55th round (source: Authors estimates). Participation rates for men (prm) and women (prf) are defined as workers and unemployed in 15–59 age group as a share of the population in their age group (units are scaled to 0 to 1). Derived from NSS 55th Round data.

This could be one factor explaining why poverty rates in Rajasthan are low despite its relatively lower level of income.

Stylized fact 2: cross-regional differences in employment rates are much larger for women than for men

The second interesting stylized fact emerging from state and regional analysis is that the variation in female employment rates is significantly higher than for men: the coefficient of variation of female employment and participation rates is nearly four times as large as for men. However, the regional patterns in these variations are not as clear as the ones for males. In addition to low employment and participation rates in the North-eastern regions (including Tripura), and the low rates in UP and Bihar, female employment rates are also very low in West Bengal, and perhaps not so surprisingly in prosperous Punjab. But once again female employment and participation rates are much higher in the prosperous Southern and Western states of Gujarat, Maharashtra, Karnataka, AP and Tamil Nadu. One implication of this grouping is that it will be difficult to attribute low participation rates in West Bengal to schooling rates, as these are also high in the Western and Southern regions.

Stylized fact 3: regional differences in employment rates have persisted

The third stylized fact is that the divergence in employment rates across regions is persistent. We use the threshold of one standard deviation from the Indian mean to classify regions as being significantly different from all-India averages. For most variables, the number of regions significantly different from the mean have either stayed the same or increased in the 55th round (1999–2000) compared with the 50th round (1993–1994). Particularly noteworthy is the increasing divergence in rural employment rates in the 55th round compared with the 50th round. This is also confirmed when we see that employment and participation rates are highly correlated across consecutive rounds: employment and participation rates in the 55th round are closely correlated to those in the 50th round and so on. That is employment and participation rates tend to show very high persistence across regions, in sharp contrast to the case for real wages, which show a small (and negative) correlation across rounds (Table 5.1).

Another and perhaps better way to look for convergence would be to run unconditional convergence regressions (as done in the section 'Understanding differences across states and regions').

Stylized fact 4: there are some signs of convergence in wages for casual workers

As Table 5.1 has hinted, in contrast to employment indicators, there are signs of convergence in wages across regions at a time when wage growth has taken place in most regions. First, wage inequality is falling across regions for all categories of casual wages (see Table 5.2). There is a drop in the coefficient of variation and Gini coefficients in all casual wage categories – rural and urban non-agricultural between 1993 and 2000. However, there was an increase in regional inequality in salaried wages, although it was low to begin with.

Second, convergence in wages is also suggested by econometric tests of convergence that show wages in all categories to have unconditional convergence

Table 5.1 Correlation of employment and participation rates by regions across rounds

Correlation between one round and previous round								
Employment rate		*Participation rate*		*Unemployment rate*		*Urban salaried*	*Urban casual*	*Rural casual*
Male	*Female*	*Male*	*Female*	*Male*	*Female*			
0.8266	0.8971	0.7955	0.8924	0.6485	0.5581	–.1143	–.0547	–.0819

Table 5.2 Trends in regional distribution of real wages

Rounds	*Mean*	*Median*	*CV*	*Gini*	*90/10*	*50/10*
Rural non-agriculture salaried						
1983	43.06	42.52	0.25	0.14	1.91	1.40
1987–1988	57.92	57.72	0.26	0.14	1.85	1.48
1993–1994	62.33	63.13	0.22	0.12	1.64	1.35
1999–2000	86.37	84.66	0.26	0.15	1.96	1.42
Rural non-agriculture casual						
1983	22.43	20.56	0.36	0.20	2.63	1.48
1987–1988	22.97	19.82	0.40	0.22	2.60	1.38
1993–1994	30.27	28.31	0.40	0.18	2.12	1.41
1999–2000	37.11	35.42	0.33	0.17	2.09	1.38
Urban non-agriculture salaried						
1983	51.22	51.64	0.15	0.08	1.47	1.23
1987–1988	60.84	60.83	0.16	0.09	1.46	1.23
1993–1994	74.49	74.83	0.13	0.08	1.39	1.19
1999–2000	100.67	99.19	0.19	0.11	1.61	1.28
Urban non-agriculture casual						
1983	25.84	24.46	0.29	0.16	2.13	1.40
1987–1988	29.26	27.48	0.28	0.16	2.08	1.38
1993–1994	32.11	30.70	0.28	0.15	2.03	1.41
1999–2000	38.55	39.01	0.25	0.14	1.90	1.49

Source: Wages have been derived from NSS data and deflated by CPIAL and CPIIW with 1993–1994 prices for rural and urban areas respectively.

across regions between 1983 and 2000 (see Table 5.3). Growth rates of real wages are robustly negatively related to initial real wages in all categories. Significantly, the convergence is least for wages in agricultural operations. Given that agricultural productivity will vary widely depending on agro-ecological conditions, a slower degree of convergence is not unexpected.

Third, there is evidence that dualism between rural and urban areas has either mildly declined or, at least, it has not increased. The ratio of real casual wages in urban and rural (non-agricultural sector) shows a decline in all states except Nagaland, Manipur and Orissa, all states in the Eastern and North-eastern part of India. Similarly there are declines in the ratio of salaried to casual wage differentials between 1993 and 2000 within each region in both rural and urban areas. Most states show these trends, excluding West Bengal, UP, Meghalaya, Nagaland, Orissa and Tripura, where the ratio of salaried to casual wages have increased in the 55th round compared with the 50th.

However, the raw differential between rural and urban wages can be misleading as one needs to take into account human-capital characteristics in analyzing wage differentials. Urban–rural premium for both casual and salaried workers fell in the 1990s and largely disappears once human-capital characteristics are taken into account. In terms of regions, the number with significantly higher premium (say more than 20 percent) has fallen from 28 to five regions in the

Table 5.3 Regional convergence: beta coefficients of real-wage growth regressed on initial real wages

Rounds	*Urban casual industry*	*Urban salaried industry*	*Rural casual industry*	*Rural casual agriculture and allied*	*Rural casual agricultural operations*	*Rural salaried industry*
38–50	–1.06	–0.64	–1.07	–1.21	–0.19	–0.68
50–55	–1.13	–1.24	–0.97	–0.95	–0.20	–0.92
38–55	–1.03	–1.03	–0.87	–0.99	–0.24	–0.97

Note
All coefficients are statistically significant.

case of casual workers, and from 12 to six in the case of salaried workers. However, as far as the more difficult issue of salaried to casual workers is concerned, marked dualism still remains. Even after accounting for education, age and gender, there is no evidence of a narrowing premium, which remain high at about 30 percent.

To summarize, there is a large heterogeneity in employment and in earnings both across and within states. The dispersion in employment outcomes is higher for women than for men. And while there are few signs of employment convergence across regions, regional divergences in wages, as well as in urban–rural wage gaps, are declining. This leads to the next important theme in Indian labor markets: low migration and urbanization rates.

Stylized fact 5: economic migration between regions and urbanization rates are very low

Given the significant differences in labor-market conditions across the different regions, India's unusually low economic migration rates present somewhat of a puzzle. Overall while about 1.8 percent of India's population migrated on average each year between 1997 and 2000, only about 0.3 percent points of this were due to economic factors. Also a similarly small share, 0.3 percent points, migrated outside of their districts or states. In comparison some 5.5 percent of the US population migrated across county or state lines in a similar period.[6]

A look at the pattern of migration from and to different regions in Map 5.1 confirms that migration rates are low across many regions. In three years from 1998 to 2000, most regions show less than 1 percent net in- or out-migration. Chandigarh, Goa, Daman and Diu, Haryana, Punjab, Delhi, Mumbai and the Kolkata areas show the maximum inflow, exceeding 1 percent of the labor force in the three years from 1998 to 2000. Overall though Maharashtra and Gujarat show in-migration to be around 0.5 percent and 0.2 percent respectively, Northern Tamil Nadu, AP and parts of MP, and, less expectedly, Mizoram and Nagaland, also show in-migration. The main out-migration regions are Bihar, western Rajasthan and J&K. Kerala, Karnataka and Southern Tamil Nadu are also regions from where out-migration takes place.

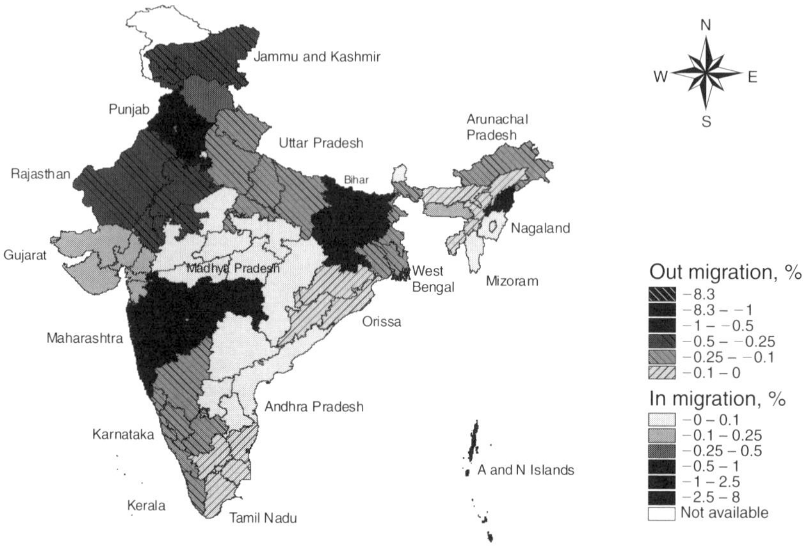

Map 5.1 Economic migration across states and regions, 1997–2000 (source: Estimated from NSS data, 55th Round).

The convergent trend of wages across regions and growing unemployment rates in the major urban areas can help to explain why migration rates have not picked up. While wage differences are high, they are converging and do not appear to significantly affect migration, though urban casual wages – the best proxy of spot-market wages – are positively related with in-migration. On the other hand, unemployment rates are significantly inversely related to net economic migration rates.

Another issue related to labor markets is India's low urbanization rates. Even in the larger metropolitan areas of Mumbai, Delhi, Kolkata and Chennai that attract the highest rates of migrants, the in-migration rates, about 1.5 percent of the population per annum, are low. Further, the share of economic migration to urban areas has been stagnant from 66 percent in the mid-1990s to 62 percent. Compared with Asian countries such as China, Indonesia, Vietnam, Pakistan and Bangladesh, India has the lowest rate of urban population growth. China provides a dramatic contrast: urban population grew by some 190 million over 1990 to 2003. In India the corresponding number was 80 million or less than half.

Urbanization slowed down in India in the 1980s and 1990s as casual wages in rural and urban areas converged. Demographic projections in 1981 estimated that India's urban population would be about 31 percent in 2001. In reality, it turned out to be 27 percent of the population, i.e., lower by about 40 million persons.[7] Part of the answer behind low urbanization rates would appear to lie in the converging trend in rural–urban wages. As the gap between rural and urban wages narrow and urban unemployment rates are growing, the expected earnings from migrating are falling. It follows that the incentives to migrate to the cities are declining accordingly.[8] An important implication could be that urban infrastructure and service development may not be proceeding fast enough to create jobs that are better paying than rural areas. This may have further implications: because economic growth shows up in the growth of cities and towns, this slow urbanization has the potential to slow down growth.

Not only has urbanization slowed down, there is also evidence that job and population growth has shifted away from the large metropolitan cities and rural areas to mid-size towns. Decomposing urban growth by size of cities (Table 5.4) we see that there is significant shift of jobs from the rural centre and large cities to secondary towns and to a lesser degree in peri-metro areas. The implication of these developments has to be interpreted carefully. The growth of the large cities (100,000 or more) is not fast enough to accommodate the movement of labor and population out of rural areas to secondary cities with population between 20,000 to 50,000 persons. Given that these town sizes are probably too small to take advantage of economies of scale, there is a particular need to develop peri-metro areas.

Understanding differences across states and regions

In this section, we attempt to answer three key questions regarding differences in labor market performance across regions. We first study how economic growth has affected job creation and address the question of whether growth has been jobless and driven mainly by productivity growth. For this we estimate the impact of GSDP growth and GSDP levels on employment and unemployment across regions and across four time periods corresponding to the last four thick rounds (1983, 1987, 1993–1994, 1999–2000). Second, we use the state and regional variation to estimate the effect of GSDP and economic activity on earnings. Third, we analyze the determinants of regional differences in female participation rates to understand the variation in participation rates and its declining trend.

Explaining differences in employment performance across regions

In the broadest terms the relationship between GSDP growth and employment growth while significant in urban areas but is not by itself able to explain much of the variation across regions. We used estimates of the correlation between changes in GSDP and changes in employment across regions for rural and urban areas and for the total population (Table 5.5).[9] To filter away changes in employment that can result from secular changes in schooling and marriage decisions by females, we take the labor force for persons age 25 and above. Finally, in some specifications we account for unobservable differences across states and rounds by including state and round fixed effects.

Our results presented in Table 5.5 indicate that growth of GSDP is significantly correlated to employment growth, but the effect is confined to urban areas. Overall 1 percent point increase in GSDP growth is associated with a 0.28 to 0.42 percentage point increase in employment growth rates. Two points are

Table 5.4 Growth of population and manufacturing jobs by size of town

District type	*Number*	*Population (1991, mill.)*	*% share of population*	*% share of manufacturing employment 1989*	*% share of manufacturing employment 1996*	*% share of urban population in 1991*	*% share of urban population in 2001*
Metropolitan centers (100,000 +)	7	40.4	5.1	15.7	13.5	65.2	61.7
Peri-metro (50,000 to less than 100,000)	7	21.7	2.7	3.9	8.3	10.9	12.3
Secondary cities (20,000 to less than 50,000)	32	100.2	12.6	10.4	21.1	13.2	15.0
Tertiary cities (10,000 to less than 20,000)	36	86.5	10.9	7.5	10.2	7.8	8.1
Towns and rural centers (less than 10,000)	306	549.2	68.8	62.4	46.9	2.9	2.9

Source: Staff estimates from Census and other sources.

Table 5.5 Growth of employment (UPSS) and GSDP across regions and time. Dependent variable: growth of employment

	OLS			*OLS with round effects*			*OLS with state effects*		
	1	*2*	*3*	*4*	*5*	*6*	*7*	*8*	*9*
	Rural	*Urban*	*All*	*Rural*	*Urban*	*All*	*Rural*	*Urban*	*All*
Growth of GSDP	0.076	0.638	0.28	0.092	0.499	0.292	–0.099	0.931	0.425
	(0.67)	(2.96)**	(2.22)*	(0.54)	(1.90)+	(2.02)*	(0.64)	(3.17)**	(2.76)**
Urban dummy			0.008			0.008			0.011
			(0.27)			(0.26)			(0.35)
Dummy for 1993–1994				0.028	0.23	0.13	0.079	0.129	0.102
				(0.5)	(3.61)**	(2.68)**	(1.57)	(1.99)+	(2.45)*
Dummy for 1999–2000				–0.16	–0.106	–0.132	–0.116	–0.209	–0.166
				(2.98)**	(1.61)	(3.11)**	(2.27)*	(3.17)**	(4.09)**
Constant	0.045	–0.149	–0.056	0.044	–0.149	–0.056	0.06	–0.248	–0.1
	(1.41)	(2.24)*	(1.58)	(1.58)	(2.32)*	(2.03)*	(1.07)	(3.64)**	(2.47)*
Observations	212	213	425	212	213	425	212	213	425
R^2	0	0.09	0.02	0.13	0.29	0.18	0.38	0.43	0.27
Adjusted R^2	0	0.03	0.02	0.12	0.28	0.17	0.27	0.33	0.21

Notes

Robust ‘t’ statistics in absolute values calculated using robust standard errors clustered at the state level reported in parentheses; + denotes significant at 10%; * significant at 5%; ** significant at 1%.

worth stressing. The employment effects of GSDP takes place mainly in urban areas. Second, however, growth, by itself, can explain very little in the variation in employment growth; only about 2 percent overall and about 9 percent in urban areas (columns 3 and 2 in Table 5.5). Our results indicate that employment growth fell significantly in the 1990s as the round dummies for 1999–2000 in columns 6, 8 and 9 have a negative and statistically significant sign.

Although these estimates suggest a strong correlation of employment with economic growth they can be misleading as these do not account for changes in wages or other factors. They do not account either for the endogeneity of economic growth and wages to changes in economic growth. We, therefore, make additional estimates of the relationship between output and employment by means of estimating labor-demand functions, for male and female workers, and for rural and urban areas.[10] These relate employment levels in different states to output, wages and other factors after trying to account for endogeneity – i.e., by attempting to account for possibility that wages and output can be related to each other in both directions or be related through the impact of a third factor, e.g., investment.[11]

Once again we find a strong relationship between output and employment across the difference regions and periods. In the Appendix, Table 5A.1 presents our estimates for males and females separately. We find that the elasticity of employment to output, i.e., the effect of a percentage increase in GSDP on *male* employment levels, across all states and periods and after accounting for wage changes, is estimated to be about 0.4 percent on average, 0.2 percent in rural areas and 0.8 percent in urban areas (columns 1–3 in Table 5A.1). Thus, across India, richer states employ more workers because GSDP is positively and statistically related to employment. As we saw previously in Table 5.5, employment effects are here also stronger in urban areas than in rural areas.

We then make the same estimates for males including state dummies (columns 4 to 6 in Table 5A.1). These variables absorb all the unobserved heterogeneity across states. This implies that the estimated relationship between output and employment would now main measure the effect of employment within states across and across time. Once we do this it turns out the relationship is much weaker. After including state dummies the elasticity of output-employment is positive and sizeable – though smaller than the one estimated without state dummies – but not statistically significant. These results imply that while there is a sizeable relationship between income and employment across regions, within states such relationship is less clear. Increases in state income are not necessarily related to an increase in employment in that state. While this may be evidence of jobless growth in recent periods, it may also reflect the low cyclical variation of male employment rates: i.e., most male workers have to find work of some kind.

Hence we next turn to see the effect of output change on females, who may have more flexibility. Making the same estimates for female employment (Table 5A.1, columns 7 through 12), we find that the elasticity of female employment with respect to GSDP levels is significant and higher (0.7 on average, 0.5 in rural areas and 0.8 in urban areas) than that for male employment. Thus, across states, there is an unambiguously higher impact of GSDP on female employment.

This suggest that female employment responds more significantly to changes in the levels of GSDP across states partly accounting for the variations in participation we see across the regions. The estimates also suggest that within regions, increases in output *are* associated with larger increases in female than in male employment *in the rural areas*. Instead, we don't find much of a relationship between time changes in employment and output within urban areas. As in the case of male workers, despite a sizeable and robust regional correlation between income and employment *across* regions, there is no evidence that *within* states increases in output lead to increasing employment for females in urban areas. This latter result may be the result of a weakening relationship between income and employment in urban areas. It could also be driven by the fact that an expanding output may increase household income and allow women to buy more leisure (and therefore not increasing their labor participation and employment rates). We examine this point in more detail below.

It is also worth noting that as for males, female employment is substantially lower in urban areas than in rural ones and that the difference between urban and rural employment rates is much larger for women. Our results also suggest that the decline in employment registered in the latest round (1999–2000), and also shown in Table 5.5 is mostly due to a decline in the employment rates of women in rural areas (columns 7 and 10 of Table 5A.1).

Finally, our results also provide some estimates for wage-elasticities – i.e., how sensitive is employment to wages. Our results (in columns (1)–(3) of Table 5A.1) suggest that states with higher urban wages for males tend to register a lower demand for male urban salaried employment. There is, however, no evidence of such negative relationship between the price of labor and employment across states for male casual rural workers or for women in general.

Explaining differences in earnings

We next assess the impact of economic activity on real weekly earnings of males. Earnings are defined as the product of actual employment in a week and wages received.[12] The results, presented in Table 5A.2, show an interesting contrast to the previous result on employment. There is little evidence, when we do not take into account state specific effects, that weekly earnings in rural or urban areas are higher in richer states (Table 5A.2 columns (1–4)). Once we control for overall state differences, we find that within states, earnings increase with output in rural but not in urban areas. This may reflect the much more significant presence of the formal and public sector (which provides for two-thirds of formal-sector jobs) in urban areas, which are less sensitive to cyclical changes in GSDP. It may also indicate that labor supply in rural areas is more elastic than in urban areas: an increase in economic activity in rural areas may require a higher increase in wages to pull people into the labor market. Combining these findings with those related to employment, we find that while an increase in economic activity increases employment and earnings for males in rural areas, not much change is registered in the urban areas.

We also find interesting results about the effects of caste and education on earnings. We find that regions with higher shares of scheduled tribe and caste people in population experience lower casual agriculture earnings and higher wages for salaried workers. Finally, we find the share of labor force with primary education to be positively correlated with higher earnings in rural areas, while the share of workers with post-primary education is positively correlated with earnings in urban areas.

Understanding regional variation and trends in participation rates

One key issue in determining employment outcomes is the variation in female participation rates across the different regions and time. As we have seen earlier in Figures 5.2 to 5.3, the main variation across regions takes place in female rates of participation. This is also evident in Map 5.2.

Map 5.2 shows that participation rates are particularly low in Bihar and UP, the Northern parts of Madhya Pradesh, parts of Punjab, and coastal Orissa and Goa. Interestingly, except for one region in Assam, participation rates are not particularly low in the North-east. On the other hand, parts of Tamil Nadu and Kerala show relatively lower participation rates. In general, as Table 5.7 shows, while participation rates for women are markedly lower than for men in both rural and urban areas in all regions, the variation in participation for females across regions is 15 to 20 times higher than for male.

In addition, not only are female participation rates significantly lower than for men but there has been a decline in the female participation rates in the 1990s.

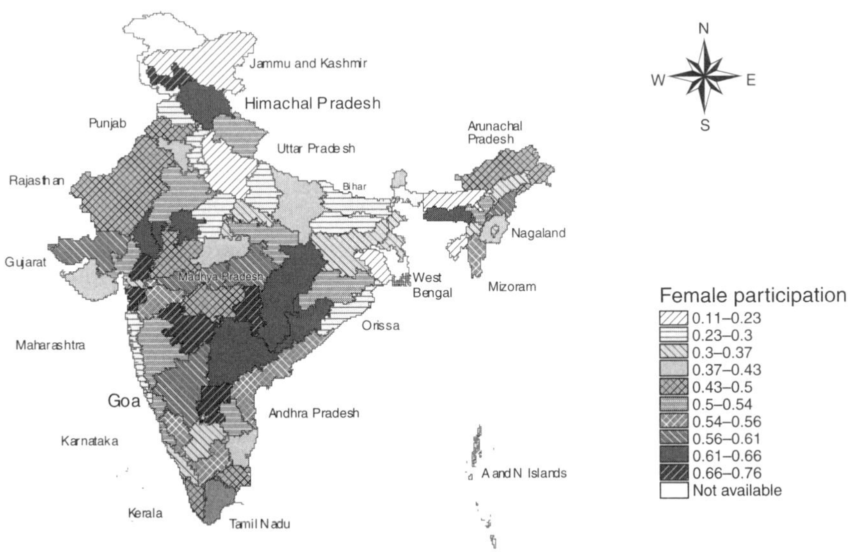

Map 5.2 Participation rates for females, 1999–2000, NSS 55th round (source: Based on author's estimates from the NSS rounds).

Table 5.6 Participation rates for men and women for prime age and 25 to 59 group

Participation rates	*1* *Male 15–59*	*2* *Female 15–59*	*3* *Male 25–59*	*4* *Female 25–59*
Dummy for 1987–1988	–0.011	–0.024	0.003	–0.022
	(1.61)	(0.42)	(1.48)	(0.41)
Dummy for 1993–1994	–0.021	–0.011	0.005	0.009
	(3.05)**	(0.19)	(2.58)*	(0.16)
Dummy for 1999–2000	–0.033	–0.118	–0.002	–0.084
	(4.91)**	(1.97)*	–0.83	(1.46)
Constant	–0.091	–1.102	–0.01	–1.019
	(10.49)**	(7.95)**	(3.96)**	(7.34)**
Observations	610	611	610	611
R^2	0.38	0.26	0.33	0.27
Adj R^2	0.34	0.22	0.29	0.23

Notes

Robust t statistics in absolute value in parentheses; + significant at 10%; * significant at 5%; ** significant at 1%.

Several authors (Vaidiyanathan 2001; Mazumdar 2005, Sundaram and Tendulkar 2005a) have suggested that much of the decline in participation is explained by the rise in school attendance by females. Further, marriage at the age of 15 to 24 may also account for women dropping out of the labor force. These points are generally confirmed in Table 5.6 which shows that while participation rates markedly declined in the 1990s for females in the prime age group (15 to 59 years), this decline was not significant for females in the 25 to 59 age group.

However, it is clear from the coefficients of variation presented in Table 5.7 that the regional variation among the 25–59 age group is also high and not very different from the variation for females. Understanding the regional variation among females in the 25–59 age group would help us better understand the determinants of female labor-force participation. We now turn to estimates of the determinants of participation of this group.

Table 5.7 Participation rates for male and female groups

Variable	*Rural*		*Urban*	
	Mean	*CV*	*Mean*	*CV*
Prime-Age male 15–59	0.892591	0.053957	0.823559	0.060779
Male (without schooling effects) 25–59	0.976455	0.019959	0.963766	0.019026
Prime-Age female 15–59	0.548692	0.368957	0.253506	0.358385
Female (without schooling effects) 25–59	0.588716	0.351426	0.288471	0.356256

The key issue that we take up is what role do income and substitution effects play in explaining differences in participation rates for females? Income effect refers to the effect of rise in income of the household from increasing earnings of the spouse or due to other sources of household income due to which female workers can opt out of the labor force to do housework or enjoy leisure. Substitution effect refers to the greater incentives for females to work due to higher wages or better employment opportunities for women. Conversely, substitution effects will lead to lower female participation if opportunities for gainful work decline. If substitution effects are present, then the scope for bringing more women to the labor force increases by providing them with greater opportunities.

We approach this issue from two different sides. In the first approach, presented in Table 5A.3, we estimate the determinants of participation rates for females 25 years or older by using *both female wages and spouses' wages* to capture substitution and income effects. The unemployment rate is taken to measure the absence of opportunities in the labor market. Our results suggest that urban unemployment and overall high unemployment rates for females tend to discourage participation. Higher wages encourage participation in rural casual work for females, denoting the presence of substitution effects. Men's wages appear to have little impact indicating the weak role of income effects in this approach.

In our second approach to estimating income and substitution effects, we construct variables to represent *expected earnings by female and male workers* by multiplying wages by the probability of employment (or 1 minus the unemployment rate). Female expected earnings represent substitution effects and also capture opportunities available. Men's expected earnings capture income effects. The results shown in Table 5A.4 consistently indicate that higher expected female earnings in rural areas robustly increase female participation. The same effects are found in urban areas, but the coefficients are not statistically reliable. Still, the overall indication is that raising opportunities for female employment increases female participation across regions, particularly in rural areas. This association is also observed within regions across time (see first row of Table 5A.4 columns 4 and 6, and 7 and 9). Thus, in periods when women enjoy higher work opportunities (measured by higher expected earnings), female participation increases. Conversely, increase in male casual wages in rural areas and salaried wages in urban areas reduce female participation, a sign of income effects working. We estimate that substitution effects would have led to a 25 percent increase in female participation, while income effects would have reduced participation by 16 percent between the early and the late nineties. The net result, assuming no other effects were at play and that expected earnings by male and female would increase by the same proportion, would have been an increase in female participation of 9 percent.[13]

Summing up

In this chapter we have characterized labor-market outcomes across Indian states and regions over a period spanning the last four thick rounds, from 1983 to

2000. We have shown how regional differences in labor-market outcomes are striking in India, and have persisted over the last two decades. The exception is wages which show signs of converging across regions and across rural and urban areas. The latter fact combined with unemployment in states may help to explain why economic migration rates and urbanization rates are unusually low in India. Some interesting implications can be drawn.

Foremost among these is economic growth and activity levels have been important in causing good labor-market outcomes, though in a somewhat nuanced way. When regional differences are taken into account, growth has not been jobless. In the short run though, growth has a muted effect on employment. Increasing labor productivity, which has led to growth, is associated with lower employment growth as an immediate effect. But in the medium term, increasing productivity does not adversely affect employment growth. Over the longer term, however, the relationship with growth and employment is clearer. States with higher levels of GSDP are also states which have created more urban employment and rural earnings in the case of males. Given that male-unemployment rates are negligible in rural areas this result is understandable. Significantly, the effect of differences in GSDP levels is more striking for female employment, which tend to vary much more than male employment. Higher GSDP levels lead to higher female employment in rural and urban areas.

Our analysis also suggests that increasing employment opportunities for females will also help to arrest the decline in female-participation rates. Although there is some evidence of income effects that lead females to drop out of the labor force, economic opportunities are the strongest factor affecting female participation.

The analysis in this chapter also highlights the importance of urbanization and domestic migration. The narrowing of the wage gap between rural and urban areas in each region and higher unemployment rates has lowered urbanization rates. Seen from the opposite direction, impediments to urbanization lower the growth of employment and higher wages. At present slow urban development also slows down manufacturing growth – with about half of new manufacturing jobs being created in rural areas. A complementary approach would also be to facilitate economic migration both to regions that are more dynamic and also to urban areas. Policies that can mitigate obstacles to domestic migration, through better safety nets and insurance for migrants, will also improve labor-market outcomes by allowing workers to work in areas where there are more opportunities and higher return.

Given that poor employment outcomes are persistently clustered in Northern, North-eastern and some coastal regions a regional focus on growth and employment is called for. Investment in infrastructure - power, road, and irrigation and credit facilities, which are found to affect GSDP positively, can lead to higher employment prospects. Related to this is the need to improve investment climate in these regions - a key aspect of which are labor-market-related regulatory reforms.

Appendix

Table 5A.1 Instrumental variable estimates of the effect of GSDP on employment levels for male and female workers

	Without state dummies			*With state dummies*			*Without state dummies*			*With state dummies*		
	1 Male rural	*2 Male urban*	*3 Male all*	*4 Male rural*	*5 Male urban*	*6 Male all*	*7 Female rural*	*8 Female urban*	*9 Female all*	*10 Female rural*	*11 Female urban*	*12 Female all*
GSDP	0.21 [1.73]+	0.817 [4.73]**	0.423 [4.99]**	−0.155 [0.22]	0.452 [1.05]	−0.453 [0.26]	0.515 [4.41]**	0.77 [3.63]**	0.677 [4.02]**	1.089 [1.20]	0.188 [0.14]	2.115 [1.28]
Rural casual-wage male	0.146 [0.31]		0.242 [0.52]	−0.223 [0.26]		0.968 [0.67]						
Urban salaried-wage male		−8.368 [2.90]**	−3.835 [2.15]**		−0.493 [0.54]	0.145 [0.08]						
Rural casual-wage female							0.287 [0.83]		1.249 [2.11]*	0.014 [0.03]		−0.723 [0.89]
Urban salaried-wage female								5 [1.22]	−2.201 [0.90]		0.48 [0.39]	1.544 [0.91]
1987–1988 dummy	0.054 [0.30]	1.095 [2.17]*	0.422 [1.25]	0.142 [1.51]	−0.105 [0.60]	−0.179 [0.55]	−0.052 [0.39]	−0.775 [1.15]	0.176 [0.43]	−0.123 [0.86]	−0.19 [0.62]	−0.554 [1.23]
1993–1994 dummy	−0.03 [0.14]	2.913 [2.74]**	1.213 [1.67]+	0.295 [1.76]+	0.112 [0.24]	0.1 [0.09]	−0.225 [1.20]	−1.933 [1.25]	0.456 [0.45]	−0.386 [0.95]	−0.013 [0.01]	−1.287 [1.02]
1999–2000 dummy	−0.229 [0.75]	4.954 [2.65]**	2.023 [1.59]	0.326 [1.13]	0.038 [0.05]	−0.052 [0.03]	−0.648 [2.31]*	−4.137 [1.40]	0.368 [0.22]	−0.929 [1.35]	−0.407 [0.24]	−2.502 [1.17]
Urban dummy			−1.262 [24.02]**			−1.262 [24.02]**			−2.063 [39.42]**			−2.063 [26.90]**
Constant	11.311 [5.53]**	38.175 [3.21]**	24.39 [2.91]**	16.653 [3.26]**	10.058 [1.44]	15.326 [0.77]	7.554 [5.20]**	−15.334 [1.05]	11.713 [1.48]	1.822 [0.20]	7.397 [0.46]	−12.847 [0.62]
Observations	247	277	492	270	253	492	235	253	462	233	251	462

Test for validity of instruments

Overidentification test of all instruments (P-val=)		0.29779	0.20501	0.22334	0.73552	0.1719	0.40246	0.50153	0.49159	0.18463	0.47135	0.40425	0.8337
1st stage centered R^2 for instrumented variables	IGSDP	0.341	0.2407	0.3395	0.9971	0.9968	0.9965	0.2838	0.4053	0.3121	0.9959	0.9968	0.9959
	Urban salaried wage, male		0.761	0.7736		0.8426	0.8553						
	Rural casual wage, male	0.3231		0.3201	0.5754		0.5792						
	Urban salaried wage, female								0.4177	0.4916		0.5315	0.6218
	Rural casual wage, female							0.1864		0.1931	0.3726		0.3723
Excluded instruments	Share of industry in GSDP	x		x		x	x	x	x	x	x	x	x
	Road density	x	x	x	x	x	x	x	x	x	x	x	x
	Percentage of villages electrified	x		x	x	x	x	x	x	x	x	x	x
	Industrial credit Rs. per capita	x	x	x	x	x	x			x	x	x	x
	Agricultural credit Rs. per capita	x	x	x	x	x	x	x	x	x	x	x	x

Notes
1 Absolute value of z statistics in brackets. Robust z is reported where heteroskedasticity exists.
2 + significant at 10%; * significant at 5%; ** significant at 1%.
3 x excluded instruments used in the specification.

Table 5A.2 Estimates of the effect of GSDP on earnings for male workers

	Without state dummies				*With state dummies*			
	1 *Rural*	*2*	*3* *Urban*	*4*	*5* *Rural*	*6*	*7* *Urban*	*8*
	Casual non-agriculture	*Casual agriculture*	*Casual*	*Salaried*	*Casual non-agriculture*	*Casual agriculture*	*Casual*	*Salaried*
GSDP	0.018	−0.202	−0.021	−0.045	1.934	1.381	−0.368	−1.181
	[0.27]	[2.64]**	[0.38]	[0.93]	[2.23]*	[2.44]*	[0.55]	[2.17]*
Schedule tribe	−0.043	−0.075	0.009	0.059	−0.048	−0.068	0.026	0.063
(share in 25 plus)	[1.43]	[2.36]*	[0.27]	[2.17]*	[1.13]	[1.70]+	[0.57]	[1.63]
Schedule caste	−0.121	−0.029	0.005	0.092	−0.153	−0.141	0.023	0.057
	[2.14]*	[0.51]	[0.10]	[2.35]*	[2.40]*	[2.22]*	[0.51]	[1.50]
Primary educated	0.062	0.193	0.108	0.002	0.172	0.221	0.068	0.07
	[0.55]	[2.29]*	[1.03]	[0.03]	[0.93]	[1.30]	[1.10]	[1.37]
Post primary	0.085	−0.067	0.659	0.465	−0.148	−0.177	0.08	0.027
educated	[0.79]	[0.58]	[2.69]**	[2.73]**	[0.80]	[1.08]	[0.53]	[0.21]
1987–1988 round	0.487	0.532	0.359	0.438	0.301	0.343	0.436	0.619
	[5.91]**	[6.14]**	[4.61]**	[7.40]**	[2.15]*	[3.73]**	[4.19]**	[7.46]**
1993–1994 round	1.081	1.26	1.017	1.274	0.256	0.533	1.273	1.903
	[11.44]**	[11.25]**	[9.84]**	[15.48]**	[0.62]	[1.89]+	[4.03]**	[7.24]**
1999–2000 round	1.73	1.973	1.554	1.903	0.297	0.73	1.95	2.951
	[14.04]**	[14.51]**	[11.53]**	[17.31]**	[0.41]	[1.51]	[3.60]**	[6.46]**
Constant	3.954	5.83	5.323	6.361	−16.377	−10.394	8.58	18.07
	[4.85]**	[7.11]**	[8.36]**	[11.48]**	[1.80]+	[1.84]+	[1.22]	[3.16]**
Observations	245	245	244	246	245	243	246	248
Adj R^2	0.6	0.61	0.56	0.68	0.57	0.6	0.57	0.69

Test for validity of instruments

Overidentification test of all instruments (P-val=)		0.6053	0.63297	0.899	0.22666	0.13694	0.26443	0.19339	0.15474
1st state centered R^2 for instrumented variables	GSDP	0.5734	0.5265	0.5328	0.5655	0.9963	0.9964	0.996	0.9963
Excluded instruments	Road density	x	x	x	x	x	x	x	x
	Share of industry in the state economy	x	x	x	x	x	x	x	x
	Percentage of villages electrified	x	x	x	x	x	x	x	x
	credit to industry per capita	x		x	x	x	x		
	credit to agriculture per capita	x	x	x	x	x	x	x	x

Notes
1 State fixed effects is not reported in this table.
2 Robust z statistics in brackets.
3 + significant at 10%; * significant at 5%; ** significant at 1%.
4 x excluded instruments used in the specification.

Table 5A.3 Estimates of determinants of female participation rates: female and male wages, household earnings and unemployment rates

Dependent variable: female participation rates	*OLS*			*Female wages and unemployment rate instrumented*			*Household per capita expenditures, unemployment instrumented*		
	1 Rural	*2 Urban*	*3 All*	*4 Rural*	*5 Urban*	*6 All*	*7 Rural*	*8 Urban*	*9 All*
Rate of unemployment	–0.098	0.001	–0.05	–0.778	0.092	–0.338	–0.475	–0.235	–0.325
	[3.68]**	[0.05]	[2.74]**	[2.70]**	[0.22]	[3.91]**	[2.72]**	[0.40]	[1.45]
Real household per capita expenditure							–1.812	3.381	1.685
							[0.93]	[0.47]	[0.52]
Rural (non-agr) casual wages, female	0.133		0.119	0.734		1.491	1.547		1.359
	[2.20]*		[3.35]**	[1.06]		[2.59]**	[1.69]+		[1.50]
Urban casual wages, female		–0.019			–2.069	0.155		2.855	–1.596
		[0.29]			[0.94]	[0.19]		[0.53]	[0.68]
Urban salaried wages, female		–0.114	–0.126		5.651				
		[1.10]	[1.44]		[0.97]				
Urban casual wages, male		0.211							
		[1.92]+							
Rural casual wages, male	–0.187		–0.051	0.046		–0.617			
	[2.01]*		[0.79]	[0.10]		[1.57]			
Urban salaried wages, male		–0.169	–0.071		–4.35	–1.412			
		[0.77]	[0.40]		[0.98]	[1.91]+			
Urban dummy			–0.573			–0.182			–0.71
			[10.85]**			[1.18]			[0.57]
1987–1988 round	0.217	0.016	0.097	0.624	0.199	0.405	0.889	–2.226	–0.229
	[2.16]*	[0.20]	[1.40]	[2.16]*	[0.49]	[2.42]*	[1.29]	[0.49]	[0.24]
1993–1994 round	–0.012	0.162	0.105	–0.486	–0.026	0.144	1.072	–4.339	–1.636
	[0.11]	[1.70]+	[1.28]	[1.44]	[0.05]	[0.77]	[0.67]	[0.48]	[0.63]

1999–2000 round	−0.032	0.122	0.066	−0.724	−0.112	0.152	1.217	−6.719	−2.494
	[0.26]	[0.89]	[0.56]	[1.48]	[0.13]	[0.56]	[0.57]	[0.50]	[0.70]
Constant	−0.946	−0.87	−0.316	−6.757	0.668	1.034	2.006	−27.422	−9.869
	[2.48]*	[1.14]	[0.48]	[2.55]*	[0.12]	[0.53]	[0.26]	[0.53]	[1.03]
heteroskedasticity test (P-val=)	0.0981	0.8393	0.0459	0.9498	1	0.9828	0.999	1	0.9995
R^2	0.14	0.04	0.45						
Adj. R^2	0.11	0.01	0.43						
Observations	177	210	371	159	170	322	161	177	324

Test for validity of instruments

Overidentification test of all instruments (P-val)=		0.81588	0.88074	0.15068	0.543	0.84699	0.39977
1st state centered partial R^2 for instrumented variables	Rate of unemployment	0.1884	0.1247	0.4474	0.3931	0.236	0.4387
	Rural (non-agr) casual wages, female	0.2989		0.3332	0.292		0.2699
	Urban salaried wages, female		0.6647				
	Urban casual wages, female		0.4212	0.3408		0.2027	0.267
	Real household per capita expenditure				0.4962	0.5121	0.5342
Excluded instruments	Share of industry in GSDP	x	x	x	x	x	x
	Share of sch tribe 25–59; female	x	x	x	x	x	x

continued

Table 5A.3 continued

Test for validity of instruments

Overidentification test of all instruments (P-val)=	0.81588	0.88074	0.15068	0.543	0.84699	0.39977
Share of sch caste 25–59; female	x	x	x	x	x	
Share of primary educated female 25–59			x	x	x	x
Share of second educated female 25–59			x	x		x
Industrial Credit Rs. Per Capita		x				
Agricultural Credit Rs. Per Capita		x	x	x	x	x
Gini–real daily wage count no salaried 15–59	x	x	x			

Notes
1 t statistics in brackets. Robust is reported where heteroskedasticity exists.
2 + signigficant at 10%; * significant at 5%; ** significant at 1%.
3 x scheduled instruments used in the specification.

Table 5A.4 Determinants of female participation rates: expected earnings of male and females

Female participation rate	*OLS without state dummies*			*OLS with state dummies*			*Expected earnins instrumented with state dummies*		
	1 *Rural*	*2* *Urban*	*3* *All*	*4* *Rural*	*5* *Urban*	*6* *All*	*7* *Rural*	*8* *Urban*	*9* *All*
Expected earnings for females in rural casual work	0.083 [1.68]+		0.045 [1.31]	0.1 [3.96]**		0.074 [3.47]**	0.926 [3.26]**		0.352 [2.19]**
Expected earnings for females in urban casual work		−0.06 [1.03]	−0.045 [0.94]		−0.069 [1.50]	−0.055 [1.62]		−0.021 [0.10]	−0.649 [3.43]**
Expected earnings for males in rural casual work	−0.318 [3.40]**		−0.228 [3.19]**	−0.183 [2.13]*		0.149 [2.28]*	−0.685 [3.24]**		
Expected earnings for males in urban casual work		0.222 [2.43]*	0.233 [2.55]*		0 [0.00]	−0.075 [0.75]		−0.086 [0.78]	−0.128 [0.71]
Expected earnings for males in urban salaried work									0.19 [0.85]
Urban dummy			−0.708 [20.59]**			−0.716 [29.08]**			−0.749 [23.21]**
1987–1988 round	0.05 [0.66]	0.003 [0.04]	−0.003 [0.07]	0.051 [1.14]	0.026 [0.55]	0.046 [1.26]	0.106 [1.24]	0.033 [0.51]	0.11 [1.67]+
1993–1994 round	0.042 [0.54]	0.053 [0.80]	0.009 [0.17]	0.041 [0.88]	0.094 [1.57]	0.083 [1.87]+	−0.093 [0.96]	0.083 [1.14]	0.076 [0.80]
1999–2000 round	0.042 [0.51]	−0.06 [0.85]	−0.047 [0.82]	−0.01 [0.17]	0.006 [0.10]	0.028 [0.54]	−0.248 [1.98]*	−0.01 [0.10]	0.022 [0.15]
Constant	0.214 [0.78]	−1.911 [6.69]**	−0.624 [2.56]**	−0.809 [3.10]**	−1.314 [3.32]**	−0.298 [0.99]	−1.235 [2.86]**	−1.167 [3.11]**	−0.546 [0.63]

continued

Table 5A.4 continued

Female participation rate	*OLS without state dummies*			*OLS with state dummies*			*Expected earnins instrumented with state dummies*		
	1 *Rural*	*2* *Urban*	*3* *All*	*4* *Rural*	*5* *Urban*	*6* *All*	*7* *Rural*	*8* *Urban*	*9* *All*
Heteroskedasticity test (P-val=)	0.7878	0.4838	0.1421	0	0		1	0	0.006
Observations	263	277	498	263	277	498	258	232	432
R^2	0.05	0.03	0.48	0.71	0.55	0.74			
Adj R^2	*0.03*	*0.01*	*0.47*	*0.67*	*0.48*	*0.71*			
Test for validity of instruments									
Overidentification test of all instruments (P-val=)							0.21917	0.3455	0.60499
1st stage centered R2 for instrumented variables	Expected earnings for females in rural casual work						0.4564	0.4703	0.60499
	Expected earnings for females in urban casual work								0.5021
Excluded instruments	Share of sch tribe 25–59; female						x	x	x
	Share of sch caste 25–59; female						x	x	x
	Share of primary educated female 25–59						x		
	Share of secondary educated female 25–59						x		
	Gini–real daily wage								x
	Industrial Credit Rs. Per Capita							x	x
	Agricultural Credit Rs. Per Capita								x
	share of industry in GSDP							x	x
	count no salaried 15–59								x

Notes
1 State fixed effect is not reported in this table.
2 Absolute value of t statistics in brackets. Robust is reported where heteroskedasticity exists.
3 + significant at 10%; * significant at 5%; ** significant at 1%.
4 x excluded instruments used in the specification.

6 Trends in the regional disparities in poverty incidence

An analysis based on NSS regions

In this chapter we work on the basis of the 59 NSS regions in the 38th, 50th and 55th rounds rather than the 16-odd major states of India. Our focus is the rural sector and the inter-regional variations in rural poverty. Work using time series from successive NSS surveys has firmly established the connection between poverty reduction and agricultural productivity growth (Ahluwalia 2002). Ravallion and Datt (2002) use state-level cross-section and time-series data pooled together to re-establish the connection. The contrary view of Beasley and Burgess (2004) is probably due to a dubious fixed-effect model which has been rightly criticized by Peter Timmer (2005). Few studies have used the cross section data available for the NSS regions. One exception is Palmer-Jones and Sen (2003). This chapter attempts to push the work based on NSS regions further.

Poverty map for NSS regions

Jain and Tendulkar (1988) had studied the regional variation in poverty incidence based on the unit-level data for 1973–1974 NSS regions available to them. The number of regions used was 56. They had divided the regions into four quartiles using the headcount ratios calculated for each region. This enabled them to draw the "poverty map" for India which is reproduced in Map 6.1 The basic data on the different regions – the upper terminal value of the headcount ratio for each quartile, along with the shares of the population involved – are given in Table 6.1.

The overwhelming impression from the map of 1972–1973 (Map 6.1) is that the regions with varying incidence of poverty form reasonably clear blocks of contiguous areas. The high poverty NSS regions (in the fourth quartile), numbering fourteen, form a continuous East–West belt stretching all the way from West Bengal to Rajasthan in the west. Similarly the regions with the lowest headcount ratio (in the first quartile) are concentrated in the North-West of the country. The other regions, constituting the second and third quartile ranges of the headcount ratio, are not so compactly placed but they are not distributed geographically in a random way either. Both groups are represented in fairly large blocks both in North and South India.

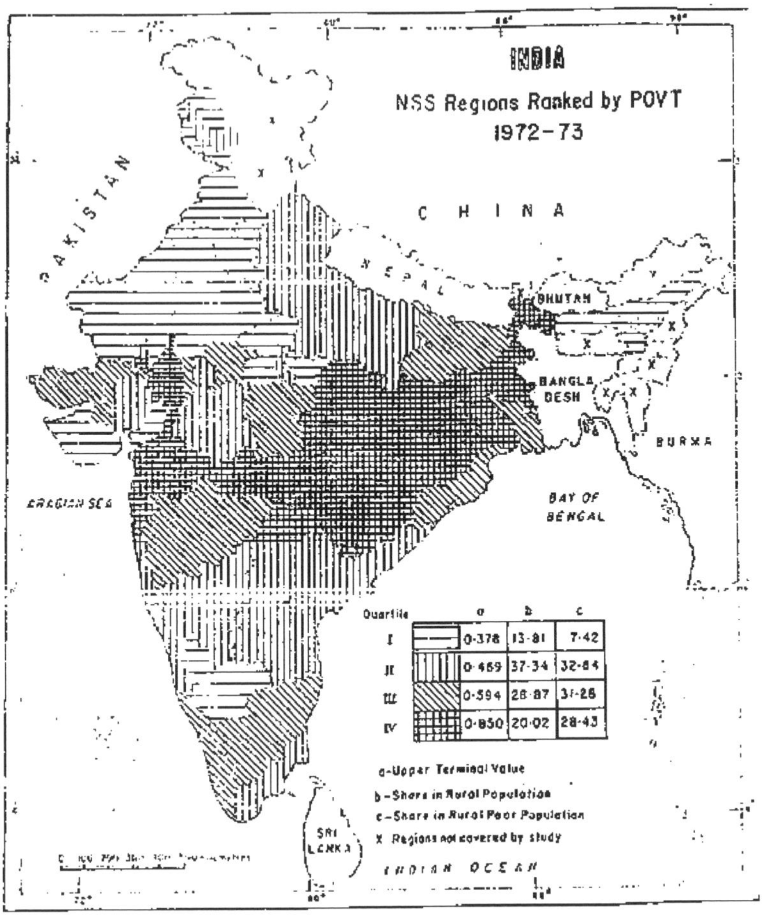

Map 6.1 NSS regions ranked by rural poverty 1972–1973 (source: Jain and Tendulkar (1988)).

We wanted to see how a similar poverty map looked from the NSS data of the 55th round in 1999–2000. The regions now numbering 58 as against 56 in 1972–1973 and were again broken down into four groups by the quartile values of the headcount ratio. The poverty map for 1999–2000 is presented in Map 6.2. The statistics comparable to these two years are presented in Table 6.1.[1]

When we compare the two maps the first strong points which impress us are the very slight changes which have taken place in the spatial distribution of poverty incidence over the 30-year period. In particular the high-poverty region stretches from the East to the West across the heart of India, as it did in the early seventies, but it stops at the border of West Bengal. The low-poverty region is confined as before to the North-West. Assam (north-eastern India), which used to be a low-poverty region, now falls in a mid-poverty region. However, unlike

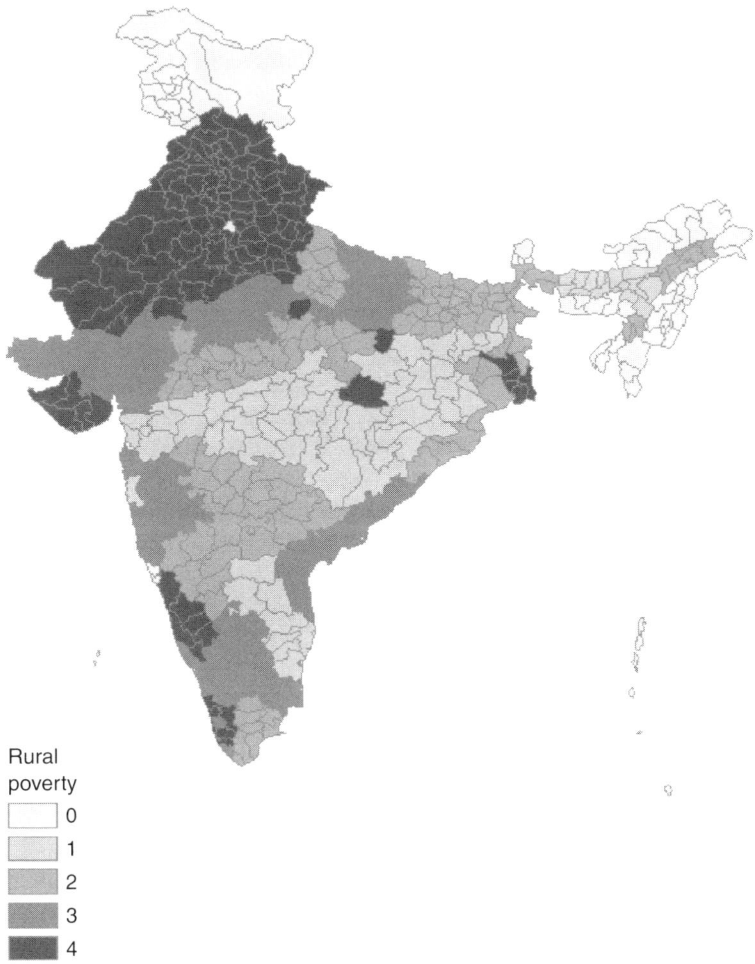

Map 6.2 NSS Regions ranked by rural poverty 1999–2000 (source: Generated from unit level data of consumption schedule of 55th round).

Note
NSS regions are ranked in descending order in terms of rural poverty. The '0' shows regions not covered. Codes 1 to 4 reflect high to low level of poverty (HCR) in four quartiles.

in the early 1970s, in the late nineties one can discern low-poverty regions in patches spreading over northern and eastern India. The Table 6.1 does show the substantial decline in the headcount ratios that has taken place in the country over this period but the impact on the relative variations by regions is minor. The comparative stability of the inter-regional differences in poverty is surprising, because the period has seen some important changes in the rural economy – in particular the spread of the second wave of the green revolution to the rice-growing states.

Table 6.1 Poverty characteristics of four groups of NSS regions for 1972–1973 and 1999–2000

	Quartiles of regions			
	I	*II*	*III*	*IV*
Year 1972–1973				
Upper terminal value of POVT	0.3777	0.4693	0.5939	0.8500
Percentage of total rural population in quartile	13.81	37.34	28.83	20.02
Percentage of total rural poor population in quartile	7.42	32.84	31.31	28.43
Year 1999–2000				
Upper terminal value of POVT	0.1080	0.1926	0.3043	0.4329
Percentage of total rural population in quartile	22.72	25.82	30.14	21.32
Percentage of total rural poor population in quartile	7.42	19.67	36.78	36.13

Source: Jain and Tendulkar (1988) and NSS unit level data of 55th round.

Relationship between the growth of rural household incomes and poverty incidence

An econometric analysis of the cross-section data from the 1972–3 survey had revealed two points: (i) the incidence of rural poverty was explained mostly by the level of household income (as measured in the NSS by RAPCE-the rural per capita expenditure of households; (ii) the contribution of the inequality measure in household expenditure was significant but added only a small amount to the explanation of the variance (Mazumdar 1990). We wanted to see if this relationship held in the data set for 1999–2000, thirty years later.

The relationship between poverty incidence (as measured by the headcount ratio) and APCE in the rural areas is indeed close and non-linear. The non-linearity is to be expected. It shows that as rural income levels increase across regions its marginal impact on the headcount ratio diminishes as fewer people are below the poverty line.

We fitted a non-linear model to the two variables, and also added a measure of the inequality of the distribution of APCE in a second model. The model specification was as follows:

$$HCR = a^*[\exp(bRAPCE + cRAPCE^2 + dGINI)]$$

The estimated results are given in Box 6.1. It is seen that adding inequality variable GINI to the equation improves the fit, but the R^2 increases only slightly by 8 percentage points. Evidently the degree of inequality matters but is of minor importance compared to RAPCE in explaining the inter-regional variation in poverty incidence. This result may come as a surprise since the NSS regions in our sample of observations vary a good deal in the structure of land distribution and off-farm activities, as well as other sociological factors (like caste composition, the proportion of agricultural laborers, etc.) which have an impact on the degree of inequality in the distribution of RAPCE. We conclude that the

$$\text{LN (RPOV99)} = \underset{(8.77)}{7.39} - \underset{(-3.38)}{0.017}\ \text{RAPCE99} + \underset{(1.01)}{0.00001}\ (\text{RAPCE99})^2,\ R^2 = 0.896$$

$$\text{LN (RPOV99)} = \underset{(50.68)}{5.99} - \underset{(-38.00)}{0.01305}\ \text{RAPCE99} + \underset{(10.23)}{9.51253}\ \text{GE(0)},\ R^2 = 0.963$$

$$\text{LN (RPOV99)} = \underset{(13.62)}{6.15} - \underset{(-7.71)}{0.021}\ \text{RAPCE99} + \underset{(2.77)}{0.00001}\ (\text{RAPCE99}^2) + \underset{(12.15)}{8.39}\ \text{GINI},\ R^2 = 0.982$$

Box 6.1 Regression estimates of rural poverty ratio in 1999–2000 across NSS regions.

evidence shows that the variation in mean expenditure across regions is much more than that of the degree of inequality – and it is the former which is the more significant determinant of rural poverty. It should also be emphasized that as indicated the situation in rural India in this respect has not changed over the thirty years.

The close relationship between RAPCE and poverty incidence means that in studying inter-regional variations in poverty we can concentrate on the determinants of the former. This is what we do in succeeding sections of this chapter.

The Palmer-Jones–Sen model

A paper by Richard Palmer-Jones and Kunal Sen (2003) attempts to explain the spatial stability of poverty incidence in rural India in terms of initial ecological conditions in the 80-odd NSS regions. They used the 43rd and the 50th rounds of the NSS to calculate the *average* headcount ratio (HCR) for each of the NSS regions for 1987–1988 and 1993–1994. The authors then used a simple linear relationship to explain the inter-regional variation in HCR by the agricultural growth rates (measured by gross output per hectare – aggregated from available district level data into NSS regions). An initial level of HCR for the only year available 1973 is used as a control variable, and some socio-economic factors are added to ‘allow for social factors and agrarian structure’ (Equation 1). The strong negative effect of agricultural growth on poverty incidence remains even after allowing for the other variables (Table 3), and vindicates the importance of the relationship between poverty reduction and agricultural growth at a fairly disaggregated cross-section level.

The authors then work out in some detail the proximate determinates of agricultural growth. Their empirical results are based on two propositions: (i) a positive relationship between irrigation and agricultural growth – worked out in a time series production function form (equation 2 and table 4); and (ii) a positive relationship between initial agro-ecological conditions and irrigation – worked out in an empirical relationship between the level of irrigation in the district and the proportion of the district included in each one of 15 ‘agro-ecological’ zones, the latter capturing the best conditions for irrigation (equation 3 and table 5).

The message seems to be that *initial agro-climatic* conditions have driven the process of agricultural growth and poverty reduction in India. These are the conditions which have defined the potential for irrigation, the 'fundamental variable' for growth in land productivity in South Asian conditions. They have been "conducive to agricultural growth given the emerging technologies and public investment, and which once set off, induces through political administrative pathways, further investments, growth and poverty reduction" (ibid., p. 5). The model is then in the genre of 'ecological fundamentalism'. 'The initial conditions are unchangeable and unmodifiable and hence truly exogenous to policy, while variables such as irrigation, literacy, and rural infrastructure would be regarded as outcomes of "policies", past and present, and, of course, private actions through markets' (ibid.).

In the empirical work the authors use the relatively homogeneous agro-ecological zones (AEZs) defined by National Bureau of Soil Sciences and Land Use Planning sponsored by the Indian Council of Agricultural Research (ICAR 1992) (see Palmer-Jones and Sen Map 1, p. 14). Each AEZ would comprise NSS regions (or States or districts) in different proportions – the proportions could be ascertained by overlying the map of the unit of analysis (state, NSS region or district) over the AEZ map.

The amount of detailed work in piecing together different sources of data is impressive. But at the end of it one is left with some points of enquiry:

1 The role of factors other than agricultural productivity growth, e.g., the role of the non-farm sector, is not addressed in the exercise.
2 Any change in the process, e.g., in the post-reform period, is not discussed.
3 The analysis speaks to the determinants of poverty for the country as a whole. It does not throw much light on possible differences in the trajectories of development in different regions. Dividing the whole of India just into two groups of the ecologically 'favored' and 'non-favored' regions is' illuminating for a limited purpose only. Even then the authors were unable to evaluate the marginal returns to public investment in the two regions in terms of the limited objective of poverty reduction. The only strong result was about region 13 which 'seems to have favorable agro-ecological conditions and moderate irrigation levels but has the highest poverty ratio in India'. Evidently this region was an outlier in the model and cried out for better attention to its potential for poverty reduction through agricultural productivity growth. But as we shall see even for this region more recent developments point to better conditions than what was diagnosed in the P–S analysis.

Broad regions

We decided to divide the country up into a limited number of 'broad regions', grouped from the available 60-odd NSS regions, on the basis of three

Table 6.2 Broad regions of India

Regions	*Region description*	*Agro-climatic regions*
1	North-western prosperous regions	2, 4, 14 and part of 9
2	West-central high-poverty regions	11, 12 and part of 6 & 10
3	Central-eastern medium-poverty regions	5, 13 and part of 9 & 10
4	East-coast and north-eastern regions	15 to 19
5	West-coast low poverty regions	20
6	West–southern medium-poverty regions	3, and part of 6 and 8
7	Southern high-poverty regions	7 and part of 8

Source: Classification of agro-ecological zones from Palmer-Jones and Sen and our classification of broad region.

principles: (i) the *average* incidence of poverty (as measured by the headcount ratio over the three rounds of the NSS – 83, 93 and 99; (ii) the agro-climatic zones into which the NSS regions fell; and (iii) geographical contiguity. After some experimentation 7 (seven) regions were distinguished. They are reported in Table 6.2.

(See Palmer-Jones and Sen, Map 2 and Table 2, for the definition of the agro-clmatic zones.)

Map 6.3 should be read with the representation of poverty incidence in Map 6.2 above to get a fix on the demarcation of the broad regions in our analysis. It should be noted that in Map 6.3 we have divided the medium-poverty zones into two sub-groups – medium low and medium high. We have also distinguished geographically between sub-regions in the Northern and Southern parts of the country with similar incidence of poverty. Thus we end up with seven 'broad regions' in our subsequent analysis.

Defining the broad regions

Region 1 is the most clearly demarcated – not only did it have the lowest incidence of poverty in 1999 (less than 6 percent) but also the steepest decline over the period considered. It stretches from the Western Plain, Kutch and part of Kathiwaar peninsular into the Northern Plain and central highlands, and further into the fertile irrigated areas of Punjab and Haryana.

Region 2 is the 'heart' of the poverty belt, which had been identified as early as the early 1970s (Jain and Tendulkar) accounting for substantial part of the rural poor in 1999. It covers the area of the Eastern (Chattisgarh) plateau and Eastern Ghats and extending into the central highlands and part of the Deccan plateau. This is a hot semi-arid region with limited scope for irrigation.

Region 3 is the medium-poverty region extending over Eastern UP, Bihar and into the Central Highlands. It had more potential for irrigation than Region 2 though the soil is less favorable for staple agriculture.

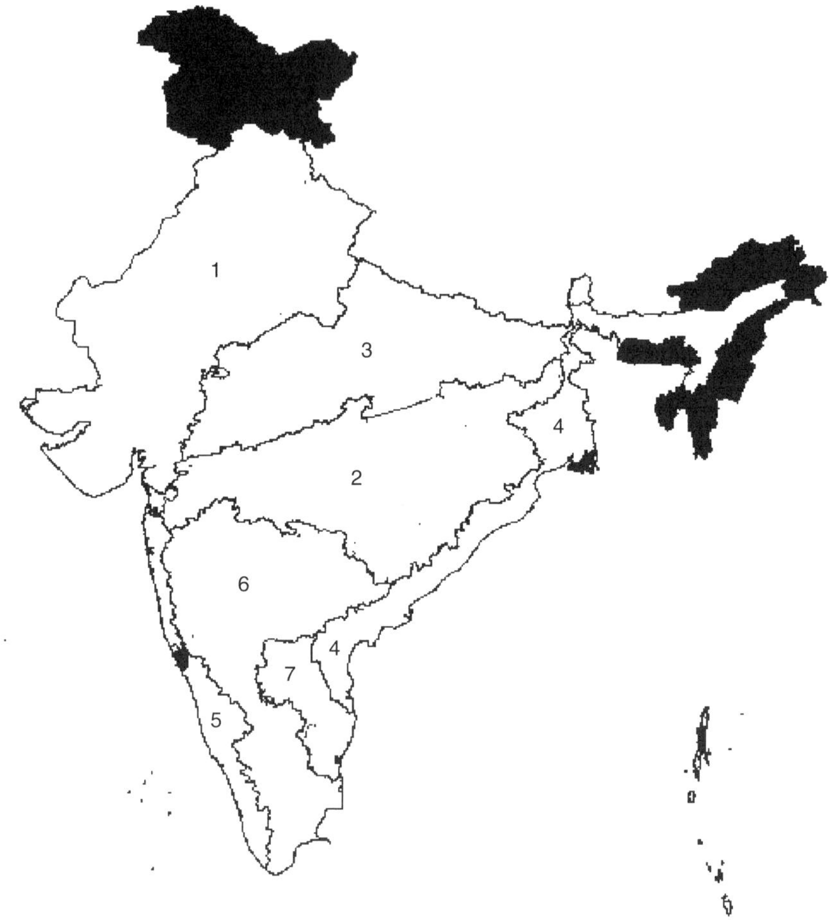

Map 6.3 Broad regions of India (source: Generated through GIS software).

Region 4 is a more heterogeneous one stretching along the east coast of India. It includes the hot sub-humid to humid plains of Bengal and Assam and stretches north-east to include the area of the Eastern Himalayas, and further south into the semi-arid perhumid area of the Eastern coastal plain.

Region 5 is the Western Gnats and Coastal Plain with red laterite and alluvium derived soils and humid to perhumid ecological conditions.

Region 6 is the arid region of the Deccan, including parts of Telengana and the Eastern Ghats with red and black soil.

Region 7 is the Eastern Ghats and Tamil Nadu uplands the Karnataka Deccan plateau with red loamy soil.

Table 6.3 presents the cropping pattern in seven broad regions. In terms of cropping pattern broad region 5 clearly stands out.

Table 6.3 Main crops grown during 1997–1999

Broad region	*Main crops grown*
1	Wheat, Bajra, Paddy and Cotton
2	Paddy, Jowar, Wheat and Cotton
3	Wheat, Paddy, Soya bean and Maize
4	Paddy and Jute
5	Rubber, Spices and Paddy
6	Small Millets, Jowar, Paddy and Bajra
7	Groundnut, Small Millets and Paddy

Source: Computed from district-wise crop-wise data of all India for the years 1997–1998 and 1998–1999.

Note
Crops in descending order of importance.

Characteristics of broad regions

Incidence of poverty

Table 6.4 gives the headcount ratio (% poor) by broad regions for different NSS rounds. The method of calculating the HCR is as follows:

1 The HCR is calculated by using a state-specific poverty line built up by Deaton for all the three years. Therefore, the portion of each broad region falling in different state would have different poverty line.
2 rpov87 and rpov93u are based on APCE (average per capita consumption expenditure) of uniform reference period (URP), given in the NSS unit-level data of the year 1987–1988 and 1993–1994. The rpov99 was based on APCE of mixed reference period (MRP). To make 1993 poverty estimate comparable with that of 1999, we have converted APCE (URP) of 1993–1994 to APCE (MRP) by following the procedure of Sundaram and Tendulkar (2003a). Note that given the comparability problems posed by the change in reference periods, it is pertinent to compare poverty incidence between 1987 and 1993 on the basis of the URP, and the change between 1993 and 1999 on the basis of the MRP estimates.

Figure 6.1 graphs the HCR by broad regions for the different NSS rounds. It is seen that the reduction in poverty is more uniform across regions in the first period 1983–1993 than in the subsequent post-reform years. The second line from the top in the graph (showing poverty incidence in 1993) has shifted down in a roughly parallel way, except for region 2 (slightly less poverty reduction) and region 7 (slightly larger poverty reduction). The change in the incidence of poverty in the post-reform years 1993–1999 varies more as between the broad regions. The three regions 3, 4 and 6 have rather similar incidence of poverty in the 1999–2000 round but regions 3 and 6 had substantially higher poverty incidence than region 4 in earlier years. That is to say 3 and 6 had a steeper decline in poverty than region 4. Region 2 – the high poverty region of the North,

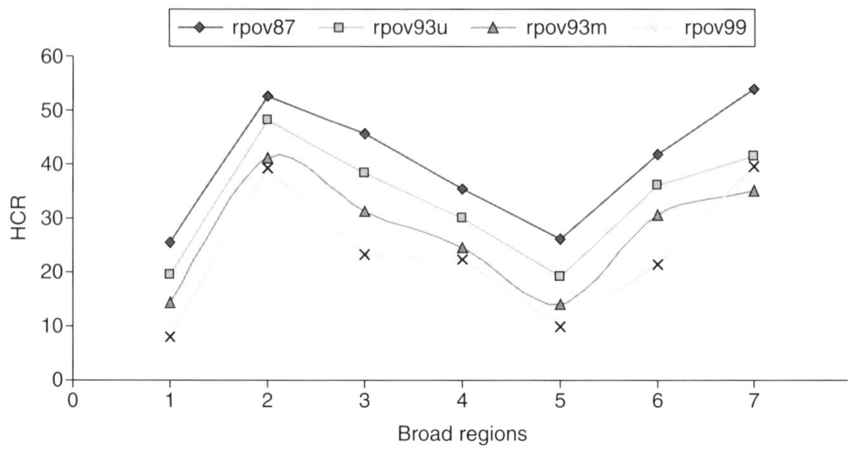

Figure 6.1 Trends of HCR across broad regions.

managed little poverty reduction in the second period, while region 7, the high poverty region of the South, actually saw an increase in the headcount ratio. The two low-poverty regions, 1 in the North and 5 in the South, continued to reduce the incidence of poverty at much the same rate.

We now turn to the relative importance behind the inter-regional difference in the headcount ratio. The major elements are: i) the levels of land productivity relative to the pressure of population of land (the land-man ratio); (ii) the relative importance of off-farm rural employment; and (iii) the relative importance of urban development. We discuss each of these elements in the equation individually before bringing them together in the last two sub-sections.

Land productivity

Land productivity is obtained by dividing Value of output (at constant 1993–1994 all-India prices) by net sown area.[2] Its variations across the broad regions and over the three years 1980, 1990 and 1999 are portrayed in Figure 6.2.

The two low poverty regions, 1 and 5, have consistently maintained and improved upon their land productivity. But high land productivity had been achieved by region 4 as well, particularly in the last period after the second green revolution, and by regions 3 and 6 to a smaller extent. Evidently, in the case of these other regions greater pressure of population on land has depressed household welfare.

Land–man ratio and land productivity

Figure 6.3 maps the position of the seven broad regions at two dates – 1983 and 1999 in the land–man ratio and land-productivity space.

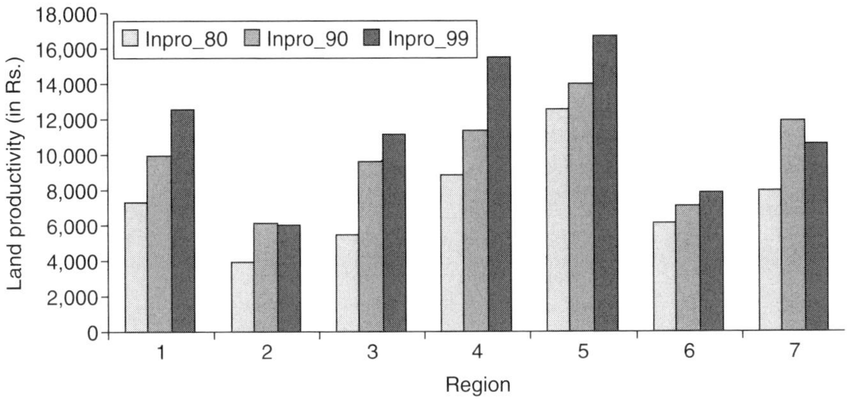

Figure 6.2 Land productivity across region.

Ishikawa (1978) suggested that in Asian peasant agriculture, as the land–man ratio deteriorates due to the pressure of population on land, the agricultural economy adjusts by increasing land productivity – that is the movement in the space of Figure 6.3 would be in the direction of the south-east or the fourth quadrant. A second part of the Ishikawa hypothesis was that the points in the graph will lie along a rectangular hyperbola. The area under this hyperbola remains constant, signifying that the productivity per man remains roughly constant. In other words more intensive cultivation increases land productivity but only just compensates for the deterioration of the land–man ratio. Technical progress or the availability of co-operant inputs like capital can of course shift the curve upwards and to the right, thus increasing land productivity by more than the hypothetical level.

The following points can be made by looking at the scatter in Figure 6.3:

1 The movement of *all regions* over time has been in the Ishikawa direction – to the South East.
2 Region 1 – the low poverty region of the north-west have a position all of its own lying above and to the right of the other regions. It shows the importance of the higher level of technology – based presumably on irrigation – which enable it to attain a higher level of land productivity for all levels of land–man ratio relative to the other regions. Note that both in 1983 and 1999 it had a lower land–man ratio than region 2 and only slightly higher than region 6, but substantially higher land productivity.
3 Regions 2 and 6 are distinguished by having a steep slope of the curve connecting the two variables. It signifies a sharper decline in land–man ratio, relative to the increase in land productivity, than the other regions, The increase in the pressure of population on land for these regions has been of critical importance in depressing household welfare.

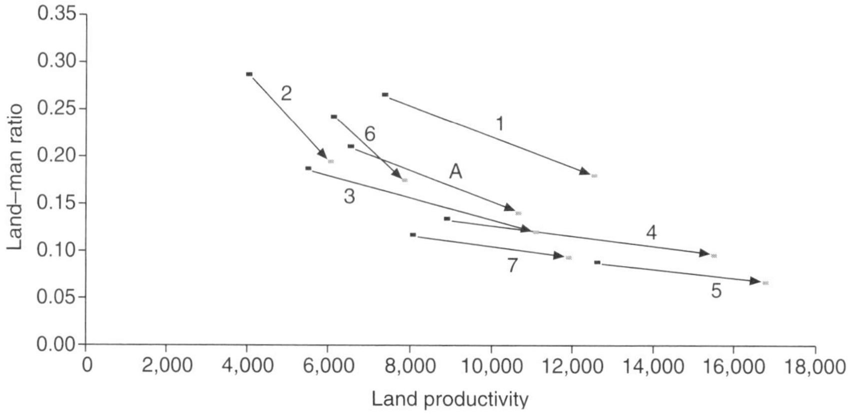

Figure 6.3 Land–man ratio and land productivity in agriculture: 1983 data points connected to 1999 points by arrows, across broad NSS region.

Notes
Land Productivity is Value of Output per hectare of Land (in Rs.) at 1993–1994 constant prices. Land–Man Ratio – Hectare of land per person.
1 to 7 show changes in broad regions 1 to 7 and A is the figure for all-India (combined 1 to 7). Y-axis is land–man ratio.

4 All the other regions lie close together along a downward sloping non-linear curve. But it should be apparent that at most points of this hypothetical curve the elasticity would seem to be more than *unity* That is to say these regions over time have been able to increase its land-productivity at a higher rate than what would just compensate for the deterioration of the land–man ratio. This is the basis for the increase of productivity per man in these regions – though obviously at different rates (This point is pursued further below.)

5 Turning now to inter-regional comparisons it is interesting to note that outside of region 1, as we move down the scale of the land–man, each region, at both dates, lies to the south-east of the one before it. The only exception would seem to be region 7 – whose position at both dates is left or south-west of the region. Evidently this southern high-poverty region is burdened by particularly low potential for raising land productivity to compensate for its relatively low land–man ratio.

Rural non-farm sector

EMPLOYMENT

The welfare levels of rural households depend on the development of the non-farm sector along with the level of land productivity. Regions with low land productivity or unfavorable land–man ratio might be able to pull up their income levels with active participation in either the rural off-farm sector or employment

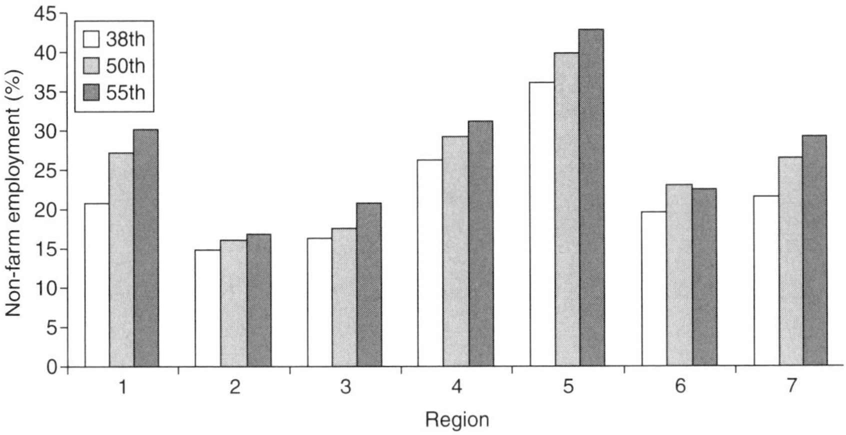

Figure 6.4 Share of non-farm employment across region.

in the urban areas. The role of the urban sector is portrayed in the next sub-section. Figure 6.4 presents the percentage employment in rural non-farm activities in the seven regions of our study.

Employment in the rural non-farm sector (NFS) can respond to two different types of developments. High growth in the farm sector creates demand for non-farm products (including services) and 'pulls' labor into it. On the other hand, limited opportunity for increase in land productivity together with pressure of population on land could 'push' labor into the off-farm sector.

The 'pull' effect seems to have been important in the prosperous low poverty region 1 – particularly in the development over time. The percentage of employment in NFS was relatively low in 1983 (NSS 38th round) but grew 30 percent over the period until 1999 as the farm economy prospered. Although NFS has increased somewhat over time in other regions, the rate of growth has been quite limited in all the regions – with the possible exception of region 7.

Looking across the seven regions it is clear that it is the pressure of population on land (as represented by the land–man ratio) that seems to be critical in determining the relative size of NFS. It is striking that the *lowest* levels of NFS outside region 1 are to be found in the regions with a relatively high land–man ratio: regions 2, 3 and 6 (see Figure 6.4). Since the regions differ a lot in terms of their incidence of poverty and hence levels of income, the conclusion suggested by this evidence is that it is the pressure of population on land, rather than the level of income, that is the dominant influence on the size of the NFS.

Both regions 5 and 7 are low land–man regions. The NFS sector in region 5 has been at the highest level in India for the entire period of our study, while the sector in region 7 has had a growth rate almost as high as that of the low-poverty region 1. But the two regions differ in terms of poverty incidence. Region 5 can clearly point to the successful development of its NFS sector as an instrument in its achievement of a low incidence of poverty in spite of the unfavorable land–man ratio. But region 7 continues to be a high-poverty region despite its relatively high growth rate of NFS.

LABOR PRODUCTIVITY

The proportion of rural income generated in the non-farm sector does not depend only on the proportion of employment in this sector. The other variable is the relative level of labor productivity. It is not possible to determine *a priori* how the latter will vary with the prosperity of the region. On the one hand, we would expect that in a relatively poor region there will be good deal of labor 'pushed' into off-farm activity for lack of opportunities in cultivation and related activities – and this will tend to depress the relative productivity in non-farm sectors. On the other hand, we would expect the agricultural sector to be less integrated with the non-farm economy in poorer regions. The enhanced 'dualism' in such regions would tend to make the productivity in non-farm to be relatively higher. We do not know which of these two influences would prevail in an inter-regional comparison. The empirical data presented in Table 6.4 suggests that in fact the latter is the more dominant influence. High-income regions (like 1, 3 and 5) have a *lower* productivity gap, while the highest productivity gap is found in the poorest regions 2 and 7.

Rate of urban-employment growth

How far does creation of employment outside the rural sector provide an additional element to the pattern of inter-regional differences? The data for the different rounds on this point are portrayed in Figure 6.5. There is a clear correlation between the incidence of poverty and the rate of urbanization across

Table 6.4 Income per rural UPS worker in agricultural and non-agricultural sector

Broad region	*lp_ag55*	*lp_nag55*	*lp_ag50*	*lp_nag50*	*y_gap55*	*y_gap50*	*gr_yag*	*gr_ynag*
1	1,224	1,276	1,030	1,073	104	104	2.92	2.93
2	542	812	510	774	150	152	1.03	0.79
3	923	925	777	872	100	112	2.91	0.98
4	807	909	764	878	113	115	0.91	0.59
5	946	1,090	895	965	115	108	0.93	2.05
6	598	882	520	764	147	147	2.37	2.41
7	474	708	466	797	149	171	0.28	–1.94

Notes

lp_ag – consumption expenditure of agricultural households divided by total agricultural UPS worker.

lp_nag – consumption expenditure of non-agricultural households divided by total non-agricultural UPS worker.

y_gap – ratio of lp_nag to lp_ag.

Gr_yag and Gr_yanag are annual growth rates of lp_ag and lp_nag.

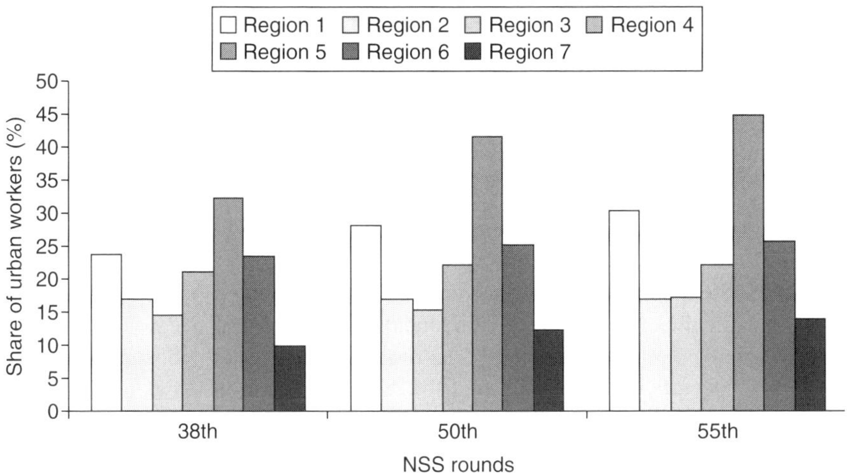

Figure 6.5 Share of urban UPS workers in All UPS workers.

regions. As with NFS, region 1 again stands apart from the others in not only having a higher than average proportion of employment in the urban areas all along, but also in experiencing a faster growth of this sector than the other regions. The low poverty region 5 shows the highest urban rate, which increases by a third between the 38th and the 55th rounds. Clearly urban employment played as much of a role in poverty reduction as the NFS in this region. The lowest urban rates are found in the two high-poverty regions of the Central-West and the South (regions 2 and 7). The medium poverty regions 3, 4 and 6 have intermediate levels of urbanization and show only small gains over the period.

Components of RAPCE across broad regions

There is a close relationship between the rural household welfare levels as measured by the average rural household expenditure per capita (RAPCE) and the incidence of poverty as measured by the headcount ratio (see section 1). We therefore tried to look at the different components of RAPCE which contribute to its differences across regions.

We make use of the identity:

$$Yr/Pr = Ya/N. \; N/P. Yr/Ya. \; P/Pr \qquad (1)$$

Where Yr = total rural household income (expenditure)
P = total (rural + urban) population in region
Pr = rural population
Ya = total income (expenditure) of agriculture households
N = net sown area
Then Yr/Pr is RAPCE

Ya/N is land productivity
N/P is the land–man ratio
Yr/Ya is the ratio of total rural income to agricultural income (an index of the relative importance of the rural non-farm sector)
P/Pr is the inverse of the proportion of the population in the rural sector

Note that the Yr/Pr as given in the identity will not correspond exactly to the actual RAPCE obtained from the unit level data of the NSS. There is the issue of missing crops, and there is also the problem of the difference between household income and expenditure due to household savings among other things. Furthermore, a critical element missing from equation (1) is that of net value added per unit of gross output since detailed data on this point for the NSS regions is not available. Nevertheless, we can treat the Yr/Pr in equation (1) as a reasonably close index of the actual RAPCE.

Taking logs of all the terms equation (1) the percentage difference of all the variables in any region with respect to the base region – say region 1 – can be calculated. Thus the percentage difference in Yr/Pr between region 1 and every other region can be expressed as a sum of the percentage differences of the variables included in the RHS of equation (1). We can then form some notion about the relative quantitative importance of the latter in accounting for the difference in the hypothetical Yr/Pr.

Table 6.5 sets out the calculations for the 55th round of the NSS. We also include in the second column the actual value of RAPCE for this round (at 1993–1994 prices). It is seen that the signs of the differences of the actual values agree fully with those of the hypothetical values entered in the last column as the sum of the components in columns 3 through 6. It is, however, seen that the differences in the hypothetical values are exaggerated in all the regions except 4 and 7.

The following interesting conclusions emerge from the values of the components in relation to the sum:

1 Difference in land productivity is of overwhelming importance in the lower value of Yr/Pr in regions 2 and 6. It is also a significant factor in the lower

Table 6.5 Change (in %) from broad region 1 in the year 1999–2000

Regions	*Yr/Pr*	*lnpro*	*N/P*	*Yr/Ya*	*P/Pr*	*Sum*
(1)	(2)	(3)	(4)	(5)	(6)	(7)
1	0	0	0	0	0	0
2	−36	−52	8	−10	−8	−62
3	−30	−11	−32	−13	−16	−72
4	−27	24	−47	4	−8	−28
5	9	34	−63	31	26	29
6	−17	−37	−3	−1	8	−33
7	−32	−15	−48	13	15	−35

level of rural income in regions 3 and 7. Only in two regions 4 and 5 land productivity seems to be higher than that of region 1, but in both these regions the adverse land–man ratio overwhelms the land-productivity advantage.

2 The more unfavorable land–man ratio plays a bigger role in the regions 3–5 and 7.

3 The important role played by the rural off-farm sector and urbanization (columns 5 and 6) in the southern regions 5 and 7 are striking. Region 5 is able to lift itself to a low-poverty region, in spite of a very unfavorable land–man ratio, through major developments in these activities, while region 7 mitigates its unfavorable land productivity and land–man ratio to some extent.

4 Off-farm activity and urban development are much less important in the more northern regions where the pressure of population on land is not as great (regions 1, 2 and 6). Regions 2 and 3 are in fact poorer because of the lower level of performance of these sectors compared with region 1, but the dominant factor behind the difference is lower land productivity – as indeed it is so in region 6 as well.

Dynamics of the broad regions

Using equation (1) the growth rate of RAPCE can be decomposed into the algebraic sum of the growth rates of the variables on the RHS. Note it is expected that N/P will all be negative. Yr/Ya is an index of the growth of the non-farm sector in the rural areas, and as we have seen will be positive. P/Pr shows the effect of urbanization and also will be positive. The decomposition exercise helps us to quantify the relative importance of the different variables in the identity in the growth rate of RAPCE in the seven regions. The results are given in Table 6.6.

The data presented in Table 6.6 help us to throw some light on the question: does the difference in land productivity – which was seen to be of such importance in the lower level of rural welfare in most of the regions relative to region 1 – a result of differential growth over the 1983–1999 period? Considering the period as a whole the growth rate of land productivity (Lnpro) was indeed higher in region 1 – with the exception of regions 3 and 4. But looking at the two shorter periods 1983–1993 and 1993–1999 separately, the striking fact emerges that the differential growth rate is largely due to developments in the 1993–1999 period. Over the 1983–1993 period, the growth rate of land productivity was significantly *lower* than that of three of the other region and exceeded the growth rate only in regions 4 to 6. This changed in the post-reform period 1993–1999. The growth rate of land productivity in region 1 shot up, while it became low or negative in three of the other regions. Even the four regions which had positive growth rate – the growth rates fell far short of the one attained by land productivity in region 1 with sole exception of region 4. The point underlines the problem of uneven regional development in agriculture in

Table 6.6 Decompostion of growth of RAPCE in period 1983–1999 and in sub-periods 1983–1999 and 1993–1999

	Regions	*Lnpro*	*N/P*	*Yr/Ya*	*P/Pr*	*Sum*
For 1983–1999						
	1	3.43	–2.37	0.63	0.45	2.15
	2	2.66	–2.36	0.31	0.17	0.78
	3	4.54	–2.60	0.10	0.13	2.17
	4	3.55	–2.16	0.92	0.19	2.49
	5	1.81	–1.67	0.85	1.05	2.03
	6	1.56	–1.97	0.55	0.77	0.91
	7	1.79	–1.38	1.09	0.53	2.02
For 1983–1993						
	1	3.18	–2.27	0.65	0.41	1.96
	2	4.42	–2.24	0.40	0.07	2.65
	3	5.81	–2.17	0.00	0.14	3.78
	4	2.50	–1.70	1.21	0.22	2.23
	5	1.09	–0.97	0.40	1.13	1.65
	6	1.53	–0.98	0.94	0.48	1.97
	7	4.03	–0.93	1.64	0.29	5.03
For 1993–1999						
	1	3.85	–2.55	0.61	0.54	2.45
	2	–0.20	–2.56	0.14	0.35	–2.27
	3	2.45	–3.35	0.28	0.11	–0.51
	4	5.32	–2.96	0.41	0.13	2.90
	5	3.01	–2.88	1.63	0.90	2.66
	6	1.61	–3.69	–0.12	1.28	–0.92
	7	–1.85	–2.17	0.12	0.96	–2.94

the immediate post-reform years which have been emphasized by many commentators.

The second point pertains to the role of the rural non-farm and the urban sectors. We had noticed the difference in 1999–2000 between region 1 and the other northern regions on the one hand, and the southern regions as a group, on the other. It is now seen that theses differences had indeed gathered momentum over the 1983–1999 period. It was the result of the differential patterns of growth over the entire period. The low-poverty region of the North (region 1) has maintained its difference in RAPCE (and poverty incidence) or pulled away from the others partly because of its high growth rate of land productivity, but also partly (with respect to the northern regions 2 and 3 in particular) because of higher growth rate of the rural non-farm and the urban sectors.

The importance of the rural non-farm and urban sectors were seen to be more important in the Southern regions in the 55th round. It is now seen that this is due to the relatively high growth rates of these sectors over the preceding twenty years. They grew at a relatively high rate not because of, but to compensate for, the low growth of land productivity.

Conclusions

The spatial stability in the inter-regional variation in rural poverty is impressive, The Palmer-Jones–Sen model is a very useful contribution in suggesting that the stability can be traced to the *initial* agro-ecological conditions of different regions of India which determined the effectiveness of infrastructure investments, particularly irrigation, and the subsequent growth of land-augmenting technical progress in agriculture. In this chapter we have tried to see if this broad interpretation is too restrictive, and if the aggregate picture might not hide important variations in poverty incidence and of factors other than land productivity in explaining the inter-regional variations.

A first attempt has been made to divide India into 'broad regions', grouping the NSS regions into seven clusters determined partly by agro-ecological conditions. Since it was shown that the relationship between RAPCE and the head-count ratio is very close in rural areas, we tried to concentrate on the determinants of the variations in RAPCE across our broad regions. It was seen that while the variations in land productivity is indeed of major importance, we need to take account of other factors to have a fuller explanation. Most important are: (i) the variations in land–man ratio; (ii) the relative importance of rural off-farm employment; and (iii) the degree of urban development. The decomposition model given in this chapter seeks to highlight the comparative importance of these factors in accounting for the variations in RAPCE across the broad regions. To mention one result in particular: the more important role played by the latter two factors in the southern regions of 5 and 7 is striking. The dynamic extension of the decomposition model helped us to unravel some of the interesting differences in trends across the regions. It was seen that the low poverty region of the North-West (region 1) was in fact losing in advantage over the other regions in terms of the growth of land productivity in the period 1983–1993, but that this equalizing trend has been reversed in the post-reform years of 1993–1999. Over the entire 1983–1999 period the maintenance of the leading role of region 1 in poverty reduction has not been entirely due to differential growth in land productivity (relative to the offsetting trend in land-man ratio). The growth of off-farm employment, both in the rural and the urban areas of this region, has contributed at least half of the differential growth in RAPCE relative to regions 2 and 3. The rural non-farm and urban sectors played a larger role in determining the level of RAPCE in the southern regions in the 55th round. These sectors grew at a relatively high rate over our period not because of, but to compensate for, the low growth of land productivity.

Part III

Employment and earnings in the major sectors

7 Agricultural productivity, off-farm employment and rural poverty

The problem of labor absorption in agriculture

Background

The growth of agricultural output decelerated in the post-reform period. According to the National Account Statistics the trend rate of growth of GDP at factor cost in agriculture, which was 3.3 percent in the period 1981/1982 to 1990/1991 and 3.1 percent over the years 1991/1992 to 1995/1996, decelerated to 2.4 percent during 1996/1997 to 2000/2001. Much higher growth rates were registered by manufacturing and particularly the services sector. Since agriculture is still the largest labor-intensive sector in the Indian economy, the slow-down in output growth in this sector has raised concerns if the possibility of economically viable labor absorption is reaching its limits in agriculture. It should be noted that a slow-down in output growth can also be expected to reduce the employment elasticity in this sector. As the returns to labor fall it will move out into alternative occupations, including schooling and off-farm employment, even if it does not significantly increase open unemployment. We shall now briefly review the various difficulties – both at the external and internal margins – which might have led to a marked slow-down in output and employment. We will see that problems in policy making might have had their share in the causes of the slowdown.

The external margin

The net sown area in agriculture marginally declined in India in the 1990s – from 143 million hectares in 1990–1991 to 141.23 million hectares in 1999–2000 (Statistical Abstract: India 2002). It can be seen from the data on 'patterns of land utilisation' that in the same period 'land not available for cultivation' increased from 40.48 million hectares to 42.41 million hectares. It indicates an increase of two million hectares of land for non-agricultural uses – not an insignificant shrinkage of the external margin for cultivation, at the annual rate of about 1.5 percent per decade. However, gross cropped area has increased from 185.78 million hectares to 189.74 million hectares in the same period. It appears that there exists little scope for labor absorption through extensive cultivation. We will now discuss why the possibility through intensive cultivation (raising cropping intensity) also appears to be limited.

Increasing labor absorption through irrigation

It is well known that in Indian agriculture, as in many other Asian economies, controlled water supply is the critical input which not only enhances land productivity but also increases opportunity for increasing the input of labor. In fact we have discussed in Chapter 6 that the Palmer-Jones–Sen model has made irrigation the centre of their interpretation of the pattern of rural growth in India. In recent years, however, there has been much discussion in the literature of the increasing difficulties and costs of providing controlled water supply to agriculture.

At the end of the nineties the total gross irrigated area (GIA) reached 39 percent of gross cropped area. In the last two decades of the century ground-water irrigation (through wells) increased much more rapidly. By the triennium ending 1998/1999 ground water accounted for 56.7 percent, canals for 31.2 percent and tanks for 5.5 percent of net irrigated area (World Bank 2005, p. 30).

It has been maintained that ground-water extraction through private pumps has reached its limit in most parts of India except eastern India. The subsidized power for agricultural use is an important factor that led to the decline of ground water resources. The remaining potential of ground-water resources largely lies in eastern India where it is hampered by the inadequate spread of electric power (Hanumantha Rao, 2004). However, as the World Bank reports: 'Capital Expenditure on major and medium surface irrigation schemes and flood control continue to account for the largest share of public expenditures in the agricultural sector… But future expansion of surface irrigation infrastructure will come at increasing cost'. (2005, p. 31).

Under-pricing of canal water is extensively practiced by state governments, who are responsible for the administration in this sector. The consequent financial crunch leads to a vicious circle of deterioration of the irrigation infrastructure, diminished water supply to farmers and their reduced capacity to meet even the subsidized costs. Further, the system is regressive. 'Small and marginal farmers who comprise about 82 percent of the farmers *who use canal irrigation*, cultivate about half of the area that is irrigated by canals' (ibid., p. 33, italics ours).

The impact of fertilizer price policy

Fertilizer subsidy has been one of the crucial elements in the package of policies introduced in the seventies to support the green revolution in agriculture. Domestic producers of urea are given a designated retention price, calculated on a cost-plus basis. The difference between this price and the administered farm-gate price, minus the distribution margin, is paid as subsidy to the producers. The amount of the subsidy increased continuously through the eighties and the nineties reaching a peak of 0.7 percent of GDP at the end of the century (ibid., Figure 4.1, p. 28).

At the state level the main beneficiaries of this large volume of subsidies have been the richer states, in which irrigation is also more extensive. Gulati and

Naryanan (2002) estimated that between 1981/1982 and 1999/2000 the subsidy shares of farmers was 66.5 percent of the total, the remaining 33.4 percent accruing to the fertilizer industry.

Another important by product has been that, together with the other subsidies in the overall agricultural package of policies, this expenditure has been a major factor reducing the availability of finance for agriculture extension and research and development. The longer-run impact of this policy on the growth of the sector has been substantial though difficult to quantify.

Diversification of output

Diversification of the product mix is an important way of increasing markets, including exports and also of increasing the labor use in the sector. Figure 7.1 reproduces the chart for labor use in selected agricultural products from the World Bank Report.

The substantially higher use of labor per unit of land in non-cereal products is striking. Sectors outside vegetables, like livestock and fisheries, have also been important in providing both extra employment and high value added to agriculture in many developing countries.

Recent growth in Indian agriculture has indeed seen evidence of significant development of the non-cereal sector. The share of food grains in total value of output in the crop sector declined from 48 percent at the beginning of the 1980s to 40 percent at the end of the 1990s (ibid., Table 2.5, p. 7). There has also been significant growth in meat and fish output, including exports. But some aspects of agricultural sector policies have been a drag on the process of diversification.

India has liberalized the regime of controls in agricultural pricing and trade,

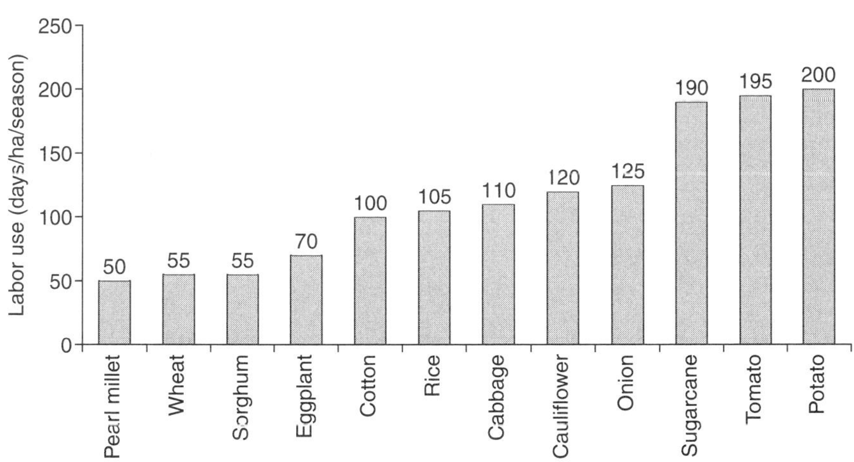

Figure 7.1 Average labor use for selected crops (days/ha/season) (source: World Bank (2005)).

Table 7.1 Comparison of average yields of major crops in India (1998–2000) with other major producing countries

Crops	*India*	*Brazil*	*China*	*Indonesia*	*Pakistan*	*Thailand*	*Vietnam*
Rice	1,938	2,875	6,317	4,283	3,000	2,501	4,101
Wheat	2,619	1,713	3,790		2,299	639	
Maize	1,768	2,767	4,938	2,693	1,730	3,523	
Soybean	1,106	2,375	1,743	1,209	1,240	1,445	1,159
Sugarcane	71,514	68,340	68,902	64,783	47,981	54,831	50,094
Potatoes	17,053	16,375	14,212	14,480	15,690	12,505	10,970
Cotton	640	1,995	3,130	1,281	1,776	1,396	994

Source: World Bank (2005).

both in the wake of the reform process of the nineties and in response to the responsibilities under the WTO agreements. But the late nineties saw an increase in the nominal protection coefficients (NPCs – the ratios of domestic to world prices). Of most significance in the present context is the increase in NPCS for rice and wheat. This increase was driven by the maintenance of minimum support prices in the domestic market in the face of a rapidly declining world prices.

The government's food-grain policy was meant to achieve two objectives: provide adequate income to farmers, and to ensure an adequate supply of food grain at reasonable prices. The major elements of the policies are: procurement of grains at the minimum support price from the farmers; distribution through the public system at subsidized prices; and a variety of restrictions on private trade in these commodities. With the downward trend in the world prices of rice and wheat since the mid-nineties, and the limited opportunity for exports, the volume and cost of buffer stocks in the government distribution system have increased. The effective subsidies associated with this system have benefited disproportionately the states growing the bulk of these commodities – which happen to be the richer states – and the richer farmers within them. Along with the regressive nature of the subsidies, this price policy has been a major element in slowing down diversification to non-cereals in the agricultural sector.

Investment in agriculture

A persistent criticism of the agricultural policies in India has been that the financial burden of the elaborate system of subsidies, quite apart from the impact on efficiency and equity, has produced a financial crunch which has inevitably reduced the funds potentially available to support public investment and research on R&D. Even India's elaborate extension services, which had played such a crucial role in the green revolution, is said to be starved of funds. The lack of productive research has meant that there is no major breakthrough in agricultural technology on the scale of the green revolution insight. The prospect for a high rate of growth of output and consequent growth in labor absorption on this sector does not look all that good at the beginning of the new century.

Land productivity continues to be at a low level in India relative to comparator countries (Table 7.1).The low level of land productivity is a major reason for the low incomes of households' dependent on the sector – both in absolute and relative terms. Increase in land productivity creates the virtuous circle of higher agricultural income, higher off-farm employment, and further income growth per worker in agriculture as 'surplus' labor pulled away from the sector (see 'Diversity of activities in agriculture' section below).

Employment elasticity in agriculture

We now turn to a discussion of employment elasticity in agriculture. Tables 7.2 and 7.3 combine the NSS data on employment in this sector with our own estimates of the index of agricultural; output used in Chapter 6 to provide

Table 7.2 Employment and output growth in agriculture, 1983/1984–1993/1994

Region	*Gr_UPS_80s*	*Gr_op_80s*	*elas_ups80*	*Gr_UPSS_80s*	*elas_upss80*
1	0.15	3.15	0.05	0.40	0.13
2	1.29	4.49	0.29	1.41	0.31
3	1.74	5.86	0.30	1.83	0.31
4	1.79	2.75	0.65	2.15	0.78
5	–0.09	1.70	–0.05	0.02	0.01
6	1.40	2.78	0.50	1.55	0.56
7	1.89	4.88	0.39	1.98	0.41
All	1.26	3.66	0.34	1.44	0.39

Source: Unit-Level NSS data on all three rounds of NSS and district-level value of output data on agriculture.

Table 7.3 Employment and output growth in agriculture, 1993/1994–1999/2000

Region	*Gr_UPS_90s*	*Gr_op_90s*	*elas_ups90*	*Gr_UPSS_90s*	*elas_upss90*
1	–0.19	5.06	–0.04	–0.44	–0.09
2	1.58	0.17	9.29	1.10	6.50
3	0.89	3.00	0.30	0.72	0.24
4	0.97	4.86	0.20	0.48	0.10
5	1.25	2.55	0.49	1.39	0.54
6	1.67	0.44	3.78	1.25	2.83
7	–1.70	–1.30	1.28	–1.78	1.34
All	0.92	3.06	0.30	0.60	0.19

Source: Unit-Level NSS data on all three rounds of NSS and district-level value of output data on agriculture.

Notes

Gr_op is the annual percentage rate of growth of agricultural output; Gr_UPS and Gr_UPSS refers to employment growth rates for these categories of workers; elas is employment elasticity (for the relevant count of workers) for the 83–93 and the 93–99 periods.

estimates of employment elasticity over the two NSS periods – the 1980s covering the period between the 38th and the 50th rounds (1983/1984 to 1993/1994) and the 50th and the 55th rounds (1993/1994 to 1999/2000).

It should be noted that the estimates of employment elasticity presented in the tables above are different from the ones given in Chapter 3. The earlier estimates are based on NSS employment data combined with National Account estimates of agricultural growth. The latter of course are not available for the broad regions given in Tables 7.2 and 7.3.

The overall figures for employment elasticity for all-India confirm its decline in this sector which has been mentioned in Chapter 3. We have discussed earlier the problems on the supply side of labor. The withdrawal of labor for education in the younger age-groups for example pulls down the numbers reported to be employed in the NSS counts. To minimize this problem we have defined employment as comprising only those reported in the prime 15–59 age group. Agriculture of course has a high incidence of self-employment. Thus the problems mentioned in Chapter 3 about the count of employment would be particularly strong in this sector – and would affect the UPSS estimates more than the UPS ones. It is seen that the decline in employment elasticity in the 1990s is only marginal based on the UPS estimates and is substantial for the UPSS count. This is as it should be. The upsurge in the demand for secondary female labor during the second green revolution in Eastern India, and its decline in the subsequent period, has already been discussed in Chapter 4.

The results for the broad regions show some large variations. But before we can discuss the possible reasons for these differences we need to have a digression on a conceptual issue about the value of employment elasticity in agrarian economies.

The determinants of employment elasticity in peasant agriculture

What determines the volume of employment in an agricultural economy of the Indian type – in which self-employed farmers provide the majority of labor input, and hired wage labor is only a part of the labor force? There are two different approaches to the question. These might be called the 'production function approach' and the 'disguised unemployment approach'. In the production function model the amount of labor used is determined by a profit-maximizing farmer much like in an industrial firm. The level of employment is then determined by the volume of output, the use of co-operant factors like capital, and the relative price of labor (wage rate). The labor used in this model is of standard efficiency. If the supply of workers in the region is larger than the demand the excess moves away to other occupations or regions or is openly unemployed.

In peasant agriculture dominated by family farms employment is determined more by work sharing than profit maximization. If supply of labor exceeds demand, and the opportunities of off-farm employment are limited, workers are not wholly unemployed but are absorbed in farm activities at a lower level of work intensity.

The disguised unemployment model has two important predictions for the level of employment per unit of land (or output), and hence on the value of the elasticity of employment with respect to output over time. First, poorer regions with low land productivity can be expected to be beyond the point of labor absorption at which a reservoir of 'disguised unemployment' has begun to accumulate. If then the labor-force growth exceeds the growth of agricultural output we can expect to see a further accumulation of surplus labor. The resultant high elasticity of employment would then just be reflecting the growing volume of 'disguised unemployment'. Second, the elasticity of employment in agriculture will be higher in regions in which the opportunities for non-farm employment are less. If we find (as will be discussed in the next section) there is a positive relationship between off-farm employment and land productivity, the two conclusions will reinforce each other.

Differences between 'broad regions' in employment elasticity

It will be recalled from the material presented in Chapter 6 that of the seven broad regions distinguished in our classification, regions 1 and 5 are the ones with high land productivity and low incidence of poverty. Regions 2 and 7 are the high-poverty regions, while the other three occupy intermediate positions on terms of income levels and poverty incidence.

The contrast in employment elasticity between the low-poverty region 1 and the high-poverty region 2 is striking (see Table 7.3). The former had a high rate of growth of agricultural output in both periods, actually increasing to the highest among all regions in the 1990s. But labor absorption in agriculture was quite low, turning negative in the 1990s. Most of the growing labor force was absorbed outside agriculture, partly due to rising wages and mechanization, and partly due to the high growth of off-farm employment. In region 2, on the other hand, the labor force had to be absorbed in the agricultural sector itself. When output growth declined in the 1990s to a very low rate, the increase in 'disguised unemployment' in the sector was reflected in a massive increase in employment elasticity.

Region 5 is the other low-poverty region which has succeeded in finding productive employment for its growing labor force with the highest rate of growth of *urban* employment in the 1983–1993 period. In the post-reform period the growth rate of urban employment slowed down significantly (see Chapter 5). Agriculture was called upon to absorb a larger proportion of the growth in the labor force – well in excess of the moderate growth in farm output. It is likely that this is the major reason for the jump in the value of employment elasticity in agriculture in this region in the 1993–1999 period.

Two conclusions follow from these examples. First, relatively high employment elasticity in agriculture could result, not so much from a higher rate of demand for labor with agricultural growth (as the production function approach would suggest), but rather from the fact that this sector serves as the reservoir for labor unable to find more productivity employment in other sectors (as the disguised unemployment hypothesis stresses). Second, there is some suggestion from the inter-regional variations given in Tables 7.2 and 7.3 that relatively higher employment elasticities are found in low-income regions in which opportunities for non-agricultural development have been small or has grown weaker over time.

It is not, however, possible to prove this suggestion conclusively with regression models using unit level data because our observations are for three single years separated by time, and as such subject to large variations caused by random factors.

Our tentative conclusion is that, with the existing pattern of development of the agricultural sector, the prospects for gainful absorption of labor in agriculture is not all that great. In fact increase in land productivity, and the resulting increase in income per worker in agriculture, is more likely to increase labor absorption through non-farm development which might be induced. It is to this topic that we turn in the next section.

Diversity of activities in agriculture

We have so far discussed employment in agriculture on the basis of the UPS and UPSS classifications of the employed workers in agriculture. These concepts are used by the survey to classify the employed respondents to allocate the latter to different occupations/industry on the basis of their major activity. The data collected this way pays no attention to the time spent by the workers in different activities. The CDS concept attempts a partial accounting of the time budget. It gives the distribution of *person-days* in different types of work undertaken by members of rural households.

All activities relating to production of crops are included in "cultivation". They comprise six manual and one non-manual activity (Table 7.4a). However, in all rounds of the NSS *a little more than 40 percent* of all person-days are classified in 'other cultivation activities' and this proportion does not show any definite change over time. The next in importance is harvesting which accounts 21–22 percent of cultivation activities, followed by ploughing and weeding (10–12 percent each). Note that 'other cultivation' is different from 'other agriculture'. The latter as seen in Table 7.4b account for a sizable proportion of the total rural households' activities: the most important of this type is 'animal husbandry'. Nevertheless a substantial part of this type of activity is also not definitely specified in the NSS codes.[1]

It will be seen from Table 7.4c that rather more than a quarter of the rural person-days of work are spent in 'non-agricultural activities'. This fraction does not change much over time (not presented here), but there are interesting variations over the broad regions – which also do not vary much over time. The more prosperous regions 1, 4 and 5 have a larger share of time devoted to these activities. So has broad region 7 – a high-poverty region which has a high man–land ratio and limited opportunities in agriculture (see Chapter 6). The regions of relatively high poverty incidence – regions 2, 3 and 6 have a relatively smaller proportion of time devoted to non-agriculture. We conclude that for rural households, diversification to non-agriculture is significant, and, across the 'broad

Table 7.4a Distribution of CDS person days in cultivation across various operations (55th round, 15–59 years)

Broad region	*Ploughing*	*Sowing*	*Transplanting*	*Weeding*	*Harvesting*	*Other cultivation activities*	*Non-manual work in cultivation*	*Total*
1	6.3	4.8	2.9	10.6	20.7	53.2	1.4	100
2	9.1	3.6	6.2	13.1	21.3	45.9	0.8	100
3	8.7	5.8	4.4	9.5	27.5	41.3	2.9	100
4	11.2	4.3	8.6	9.3	20.5	43.7	2.4	100
5	11.0	4.2	7.7	10.3	19.9	41.9	4.9	100
6	10.1	4.7	3.6	18.3	19.3	42.4	1.5	100
7	10.1	2.5	4.4	14.7	20.4	46.0	1.9	100
Total	9.1	4.7	5.0	12.3	22.3	44.9	1.9	100

Source: Calculated from NSS unit-level data of 38th, 50th and 55th rounds of employment schedule.

Table 7.4b Distribution of other agricultural activities across various operations (55th round, 15–59 years)

Broad region	*Other agricultural activities operation code*						
	Forestry	*Plantation*	*Animal husbandry*	*Fisheries*	*Other agricultural activities*	*Non-manual work in activities other than cultivation*	*Total*
1	0.8	0.2	**65.8**	0.1	28.2	4.9	100
2	**9.2**	0.2	10.9	1.0	69.2	9.5	100
3	0.9	0.7	35.3	0.6	54.5	7.9	100
4	2.0	18.1	11.6	**4.2**	57.1	7.0	100
5	3.7	**36.2**	8.6	2.3	44.1	5.2	100
6	2.2	1.9	18.0	1.0	**71.3**	5.6	100
7	3.6	1.4	22.6	1.4	66.6	4.4	100
Total	2.5	6.3	31.2	1.3	52.3	6.4	100

Source: Calculated from NSS unit-level data of 38th, 50th and 55th rounds of employment schedule.

Note
Bold figures show maximum values in different activities in specific broad region.

Table 7.4c Distribution of CDS employment across various activities (55th round, 15–59 years)

Broad region	*Cultivation*	*Other agricultural activities*	*Non-agricultural activities*	*Total*
1	48.1	25.9	25.9	100
2	68.1	14.0	17.9	100
3	63.7	17.2	19.1	100
4	49.3	19.0	31.7	100
5	26.2	32.4	41.3	100
6	56.6	19.6	23.8	100
7	51.3	16.7	31.9	100
Total	55.3	19.9	24.7	100

Source: Calculated from NSS unit-level data of 38th, 50th and 55th rounds of employment schedule.

regions', its relative importance in terms of labor time spent on such activities is inversely related to the incidence of poverty.

One would like to know what levels of income are generated by the labor time spent on such activities, and how they compare with income originating in agriculture. Unfortunately the 'thick' rounds of the NSS (on which much of the work on this book is based) do not collect data on the components of household income. But there was special survey of the NSS, the so-called 59th round which collected data on this topic as part of a general survey of farmers' economic conditions. The share of household income of farmers derived from off-farm activities is given in Table 7.5.

Table 7.5 Share of off-farm income in household income of farmers' households (2003)

Broad region	*Micro (<0.1 hectare)*	*Marginal (0.1–1 hectare)*	*Small (1–2 hectare)*	*Medium (2–4 hectare)*	*Large (>4 hectare)*	*Total*
1	44.8	22.8	8.6	4.5	3.1	10.7
2	26.6	20.9	9.0	4.9	4.9	10.6
3	33.9	14.3	5.5	4.8	1.2	8.2
4	50.0	20.6	7.5	4.5	3.8	14.1
5	18.9	31.6	10.1	5.8	5.3	21.2
6	40.1	21.1	10.3	6.8	3.1	10.1
7	57.0	25.0	12.2	4.3	2.6	11.2
Total	40.6	20.6	8.1	5.0	3.0	11.0
Distribution of farmers' households across land- size groups	1.4	64.5	18.0	10.5	5.6	100.0

Source: Unit-Level data of NSS 59th round (2003), schedule 3.3.

Note

Farmer's household is defined as any rural household possessing some land and any member of household should be engaged in some agricultural activities on that land. On-farm activities include crop cultivation, plantation activities and farming of animal.

It is seen that the relative income in off-farm activities of farmers' households is quite low. This is as one expects since the off-farm activities recorded in this survey are *marginal* for the households concerned. Nevertheless, the substantive point remains that, in contrast to some other Asian agricultural economies, most notable Taiwan from its early stage of development, both the total income and income per unit of labor time generated in off-farm activities of farming households have been quite low in India. Even the more prosperous regions in India like regions 1 and 5 do not seem to have higher relative labor productivity in off-farm activities.

In the next section we consider the role of non-farm activities who 'specialize' in the non-farm sector in the rural economy. The 'thick' rounds of the NSS distinguish such households on the basis of occupation/industry of the principal earner in the household. We do not have income data but the welfare level of households can be approximated by the statistic of household expenditure per capita.

We need to be aware of the limitations of the main source of our data, the NSS, before proceeding further. First, a large share of employment in India is in the 'self-employed' category. There is an inherent difficulty of allocating income accruing from self-employment when more than one earner from the same household is in income-earning activity. Households from different self-employed activities by different members of the household would be typically pooled together. There is no way of distinguishing the individual contributions of individual earners. Hence the income we can deal with is household income, and we can normalize for the size of the household. Further, it is generally accepted that figures on expenditure given by the respondent in the household is more reliable than that of income. Thus we use the measure of household welfare as given by mean expenditure per capita.

When we are comparing levels of household welfare across sectors we need to identify the *principal occupation of the household.* This poses problems both conceptually and in terms of execution. The conceptual problem arises from the fact that a significant number of households will have more than one earner, and not all earners will be in the same category of occupation. The secondary earners might not be all wage earners. If they are working in the self-employed sector, they will be pooling their earnings with other earners of the household to create the household's pot of earnings. By assigning all the household income effectively to the principal occupation of the household we might be exaggerating the income – and the expenditure which it sustains – originating from this occupation.

Rural off-farm employment

It might appear at first sight that the pressure of excess labor supply on land and the incidence of 'disguised unemployment' in poor regions would be partly relieved if off-farm employment were to develop in a significant way in theses areas. We saw in the last chapter that while in the northern 'broad regions' off-farm growth seemed to add to the process of regional difference in growth over time, there was some suggestion that the southern regions, particularly in the

1983–1993 period, were able to compensate for the slow growth in land productivity through a more vigorous growth of the off-farm (and urban) sectors. What is the evidence on this point from the pattern of development of off-farm employment in rural India, taking all 75-odd NSS regions together?

Off-farm rural employment is a heterogeneous sector. Kijima and Lanjouw (2004), drawing on the evidence from a host of village studies, distinguish three major categories of NFS: (i) regular employment (generally salaried); (ii) casual employment (daily wages); and self-employed enterprise activities. The first category, often related to public-sector jobs created by rural development programs, are generally the most sought after as it not only offers higher earnings but more importantly stability of employment. 'Casual non-farm employment is generally thought to be less demeaning to a worker than agricultural wage labor, but returns may be only marginally higher'. Finally, the self-employed consist both a group of low income earners who are pushed into the sector, and higher-income workers with business activity. Kijima and Lanjouw report that analysis of the NSS for the last three 'thick' rounds shows that the overall employment share of the non-farm sector as a whole has hovered around 25–30 percent for all-India, with no evidence of any growth over time. Casual labor has been in the neighborhood of 6 percent, regular wage workers constituted 7–8 percent and 12–14 percent was the self-employed. The three components obviously have different distributional impact – regular workers and a portion of the self-employed in particular would tend to be recruited from the better-off economic classes.

The significant question about off-farm employment relieving the pressure of population on land is its relationship to the level of productivity (or income) in agriculture. There are two different hypotheses in the literature about this relationship.

The Johnston–Mellor hypothesis

In the traditional view, associated with the work of Johnston and Mellor, off-farm activity develops in response to the prior development of agriculture. High land productivity, such as was achieved in selected regions due to the green revolution, increases demand for off-farm goods and services, both in the rural areas and smaller towns. The growth of farm productivity and off-farm activity constitute a virtuous cycle of mutually supported development.

This model has also an important implication for relative productivities in the farm and non-farm sectors at different levels of rural welfare across regions. As already mentioned, the existence of an excess supply of labor in traditional agriculture is not compensated adequately by off-farm employment, and does not take the form of open unemployment. Agriculture is the 'residual' sector for the population which cannot move to other occupations or regions. Since there is no floor to self-employed income in this sector one sees a fall in the income of households' dependent on agriculture. In off-farm employment on the other hand, the level of wage earnings or business income will have a floor determined either by the reservation price of labor or the opportunity cost of capital. Thus we would expect to see regions with a low absolute level of income in agricultural households would also show a relatively lower ratio of agricultural to non-agricultural incomes. That is to say, the hypothesis is that in a cross-section sample of NSS regions the relative income in agriculture would be *positively* related to the absolute level of agricultural income.

The Foster–Rosensweig hypothesis

The contrary view has been most elaborately developed by Foster and Rosensweig (2004). They distinguish between 'traded' and 'non-traded' types of off-farm activities. While the latter could be a function of the development of the local rural economy and hence would be sensitive to the growth of agricultural income in the region, the 'traded' part is not necessarily tied to local development. Further, Foster and Rosensweig suggest that writers have over-emphasized the self-employed part of off-farm employment to the exclusion of wage earners. The development of business activity in the rural economy is expected to be a function of the growth of capital from outside the local economy seeking out labor at affordable cost. Thus low-wage regions with low land productivity would have a preferential pull on such investments. The proportion of employment in off-farm activities in such regions would accordingly be higher. Clearly this interpretation of the development processes in the rural economy outside agriculture emphasizes the importance of outside capital rather than capital generated by internal savings of rich farmers.

It is useful to note that the Foster–Rosenweig hypothesis has no particular prediction about the relative incomes in the farm and off-farm sectors. While we do have the scenario of capital migrating to less prosperous regions, presumably with lower agricultural incomes, we cannot expect to see any particular changes in the wage or income differences between the two sectors in the regions concerned without more specific indication about labor market dynamics.

Testing with NSS data

The analysis in Chapter 6 for broad regions revealed that the evidence on the basis of the seven regions distinguished leaned towards supporting the predictions of the Johnston–Mellor rather than the Foster–Rosensweig model. It was the pressure of population of land which seemed to be critical in the determination of the share of employment in the non-farm rural sector. Since a higher man–land ratio was generally associated with a lower level of per capita income and higher incidence of poverty, there was some positive relationship between income levels and the share of non-farm employment. Also the poorer regions tended to have a larger gap between the income per worker in the non-farm sector relative to the farm sector. It is the purpose of this section to go beyond the level of aggregation involved in the discussion of Chapter 6. We shall try to test the hypotheses in a more detailed and rigorous way with the help of all the observations available from the 70-odd NSS regions.

The partial correlation of RAPCE with selected variables

We first examine the relative importance of different variables affecting rural incomes (approximated by RAPCE), taking one variable at a time. The correlation matrices for the variables enable us to do so. The definitions of the key variables are as follows:

rapce_ci – Rural average monthly per capita consumption expenditure at constant prices adjusted for inter-state difference in prices.
uapce_ci – Urban average monthly per capita consumption expenditure at constant prices adjusted for inter-state difference in prices.
Rapce – Rural average monthly per capita consumption expenditure at current prices.
lnpro – Land productivity obtained by dividing value of output of crops at constant 1993–1994 prices divided by net sown area.
hn_ag – Ratio of income in the non-farm relative to the farm sectors. It is proxied by ratio of average monthly household mean consumption expenditure per capita of non-farm to farm households.
tur – urbanization ratio obtained as the share of urban UPS workers to total UPS workers.
tnfups – share of UPS non-farm labor to rural labor.
cul_nsa – net sown area per UPS worker involved in cultivation.

We define the variables in logs so that it is easy to examine the relative elasticity of RAPCE with respect to each of the variables from the regression models to follow. The correlation matrix is given in Table 7.6.

The more important conclusions are as follows:

1 The correlation of RAPCE with land productivity is quite high, showing an elasticity of 0.48. In fact it increased quite dramatically between 1983 and 1993, before falling off somewhat in 1999 (not shown in the table). Some of the reason for the low correlation in the 1983 round is the problem with

Table 7.6 Correlation matrix, Year: 1999–2000

	rapce_ci	*lnpro99*	*hn_ag55*	*t55ur*	*t55nfups*	*uapce99_ci*	*cul_nsa99*
rapce_ci	1.0000						
lnpro99	0.4797	1.0000					
hn_ag55	–0.3203	–0.2372	1.0000				
t55ur	0.5578	0.2190	–0.0150	1.0000			
t55nfups	0.4963	0.5667	–0.2269	0.3166	1.0000		
uapce99_ci	0.4743	0.3028	–0.0373	0.5357	0.4532	1.0000	
cul_nsa99	0.4206	–0.0640	–0.4177	0.3570	0.0073	–0.0158	1.0000

Source: Unit-Level NSS data on all three rounds of NSS and district-level value of output data on agriculture.

inter-region price conversions in that round in particular. But even when we look at the results without these price corrections, the correlation coefficient of these two variables for 1983 at 0.39 is much lower than for the later dates. Evidently the importance of land productivity in the determination of the inter-regional variation in rural household welfare becomes substantially stronger after the second green revolution of the 1980s.

2 Non-farm employment is positively correlated with land productivity – supporting the Johnston–Mellor rather than the Foster–Rosensweig hypothesis. In fact the correlation co-efficient between tnfus and lnpro is at 0.5667 the highest in the matrix of Table 7.6.

3 As is to be expected from the last two results, the non-farm employment variable tnfups is positively correlated with RAPCE and the correlation value increased as much as that of yield between 1983 and 1993 and continued to increase somewhat in 1999. But the ratio of income per capita (as proxied by household expenditure) of non-farm to farm households is negatively correlated with RAPCE. The obvious inference is that in higher RAPCE areas the productivity per worker in non-agriculture falls relative to that in agriculture. A plausible interpretation is that in a cross-section view of the rural NSS regions, as non-farm employment becomes a source of increasing importance, the 'dualism' between farm and non-farm activities decreases.

This is a second important finding of relevance to the Foster–Rosensweig thesis. Part of the reason why non-farm employment seems to be of more importance in poorer, low land-productivity regions is now seen to be because its relative productivity is higher in such regions due to a stronger incidence of 'dualism' – and not because a greater proportion of non-farm employment is found in them.

4 Both the urbanization variables tur and uapce increased their correlation coefficients with RAPCE dramatically between 1983 and 1993, specially the former. The former in fact increased marginally also between 1993 and 1999, while the latter fell slightly. All this can be interpreted in terms of a greater integration of the urban and rural economies, particularly the development of small towns which has been noticed as an important aspect of development since 1983.

5 The correlation of cul_nsa (the net sown area per cultivator) with RAPCE also increased steeply from 1983 to 1993 and further to 1999. Thus the impact of the farm sector on the rural expenditure also increased along with the bigger role of urbanization. All this contributed to a very large increase in the explanatory power of these variables in the regression to determine RAPCE.

The elasticity of RAPCE with respect to the key variables

What are the relative strengths of the variables studied above – particularly land productivity and non-farm employment on rural income levels? Regression

Table 7.7 Elasticities of RAPCE with respect to selected variables

Variable	*38th round*	*50th round*	*55th round*
Tnfs	0.156 (1.53)	0.081 (2.08)	0.120 (2.24)
Lnpro	0.159 (1.91)	0.142 (3.73)	0.112 (2.62)
Cul_nsa	0.132 (1.97)	0.111 (3.47)	0.144 (3.91)

Source: Unit-Level NSS data on all three rounds of NSS and district-level value of output data on agriculture.

Note
Figures in parentheses are corresponding t-values of estimated regression coefficients.

models with the relevant variables put together were tried in order to decipher their joint impact on RAPCE. We tried the regressions both with the dependent variables rapce and rapce_ci (that is to say, both without and with price deflation at the regional level). While the values of the coefficients are not that different, slightly better fits were obtained for the former set. We therefore report and discuss the results from only this set.

The more important conclusions are summarized below.

1 The elasticities of RAPCE with respect to tnfs for the different rounds are given in Table 7.7. The elasticities with respect to land productivity and the cultivated area per worker are also included in the table. It is apparent that the elasticity of RAPCE with respect to farm income is much more than that of non-farm employment. (Note that the elasticity of farm income would be the *sum* of elasticities of land productivity and cultivated area per worker.)
2 The elasticity of RAPCE with respect to *income generated* in the non-farm sector is probably a more relevant variable to compare with the elasticity with respect to farm income. As already indicated the labor productivity gap between the non-farm and farm sectors narrows with increase in RAPCE.

The elasticity of RAPCE with this variable hn_ag is highest in the 50th round at –.213 in the multiple regression framework. Since this value is well below unity, it can be easily be demonstrated algebraically that the elasticity of the income ratio of non-farm to farm with respect to RAPCE will be positive but below the value of the employment ratio (tnfs). In other words the positive association of the proportion of employment in non-farm and the rural APCE is moderated to some extent by the narrowing of the productivity gap between the two sub-sectors because of the diminishing 'dualism' between them as regional rural income increases.

A surprising finding of our regressions is that the elasticity of RAPCE is very high with respect to the urbanization variables, particularly UAPCE. Table 7.8 reports the elasticity value for the two such variables used in our regressions. The relationship seems to be especially strong in the 50th and the 55th rounds and the value of the elasticities well exceed those of farm income and rural non-farm

Table 7.8 Elasticities of RAPCE with respect to selected variables

Variable	*38th round*	*50th round*	*55th round*
Tu_r	–0.132 (–1.76)	0.052 (1.44)	0.041 (0.84)
Uapce	0.163 (0.89)	0.427 (3.97)	0.435 (3.15)

Source: Unit-Level NSS data on all three rounds of NSS and district-level value of output data on agriculture.

Note
Figures in parentheses are corresponding t-values of estimated regression coefficients.

employment. The importance of urban development – particularly the development of small towns – for rural incomes in recent decades is evidently an important part of the changing rural economic scenario.

The results give unequivocal support to the model of a 'cumulative' process of development in the rural sector. Rural incomes are propelled by increased land productivity, and off-farm employment adds to the virtuous circle by responding to it positively. The gap in labor productivity between farm and off-farm sectors is reduced in this process.

The impact of liberalization on marginal farmers

We have seen that liberalization in the agricultural sector has been more on the external front in the post-reform years with limited effort to dismantle the regime of controls and subsidies in the internal economy. The impact on agricultural output growth has not been very impressive. At the same time several authors have raised the issue of adverse effect of post-reform developments on equity in this sector (see, for example, Chandrasekhar and Jayati Ghosh 1999; Sheila Bhalla 2005). Some evidence emerged in the analysis presented in Chapter 6 above that the post-reform growth process in the rural sector favored the more prosperous regions. There has also been an undercurrent of concern that important changes are taking place – which affect particular sections of the population adversely – and which are not captured by aggregate statistics. One of the issues is the impact of changes introduced by liberalization on small and marginal farmers.

'Distress inducing' growth

Liberalization has allowed competition from foreign countries even as world prices of some key agricultural commodities had a substantial downward trend in the nineties. The impact of these developments on distribution in the agricultural sector has been significant in some areas. A notable example is the case of Telengana in Andhra Pradesh. This case study has been analyzed by Vakulbrahmanam (2005) who has sought to generalize the case of Telengana as an instance of 'distress' of small farmers in the growth process fueled by liberalization.

Two crops, rice and cotton, account for almost 50 percent of the gross cropped area in Telengana. World prices of both have taken a dive while the domestic prices in Telengana have remained stagnant (ibid., Figures 2 and 3, p. 977). Indian manufacturers have begun to import cotton lint in response to its downward trend. In spite of this increased competition the area under cotton has continued to increase at a high rate. Between 1985 and 2001 the area under cotton in Andhra Pradesh increased at an annual rate of 17.2 percent, while the area under rice increased at only 3.3 percent, and the area under a number of coarse grains actually decreased (ibid., Table 16). This is because cotton is a high-value crop and also provides a higher level of employment per acre.

It is possible to provide a dynamic model in which with a large enough differential in output per acre between the commercial and food-crop sectors, the rate of shift of acreage to the former would be continuing even if the gap is reduced over time. But a reading of the article by Vakulbrahmanam reveals that there might be several supplementary factors at work. First, marginal farmers are more specialized in *non-food crops* because they do not have access to irrigated fields which is necessary for cultivation of rice. They are net buyers of food. So with the increase in the relative price of food their welfare declines and the response is to increase work on crop cultivation at the expense of leisure – a process emphasized by Chaynov (1966). Second, the reform process saw an increase in input prices – of power, credit and fertilizer, in particular, which squeezes the "net surplus" further. This effect is likely to be more important for marginal farmers, both absolutely and relatively, and might elicit the Chaynov type of response even further.

Vakulbrahmanam's data from the NSS showed that the average per capita expenditure for large and medium farmers increased significantly in the pre-liberalization decade of 1983–1993 but was nearly stagnant in the post-liberalization period of 1993/1994–1999/2000. The contrast was much sharper for marginal farmers and agricultural laborers – who actually suffered a significant decline in welfare in the second period. Consistent with this poverty decline was arrested in the post-liberalization period, and the agricultural growth rate in real terms was stagnant contrasted with its robust growth in excess of 4 percent per annum in the eighties. (ibid., Tables 2, 4 and 6).

The scenario presented above is for one region or district and is consistent with qualitative evidence about distress among farmers including suicide due to economic pressures. Part of the pressures arises from the fluctuations in market prices for non-food crops and is clearly related to liberalization not accompanied by adequate measures for crop insurance. How does the experience generalize to the all-India picture?

The trends for all-India

A significant point emphasized by Vakulbrahmanam is that while agricultural output in Telengana had grown over the 15 years of the last century at the healthy rate of 4.7 percent per annum, the growth in the real wage rate for agricultural

Table 7.9 Growth rates of agricultural output and daily wage 1993/1994–1999/2000 (1993/1994 prices)

Variable	*1st Quartile*	*Median*	*3rd Quartile*	*Mean*	*St deviation*
Real output	0.34	3.24	6.05	2.905	–2.255
Real wage	1.56	2.44	4.20	2.829	2.122

Source: Unit-Level NSS data on all three rounds of NSS and district-level value of output data on agriculture.

Table 7.10 Household expenditure per capita (APCE) for different classes 1993/1994–1999/2000 (at 1993/1994 prices)

Household type	*1st Quartile*	*Median*	*3rd Quartile*	*Mean*	*St. deviation*
Large Farmers	–1.26	3.13	5.43	2.558	4.433
Medium	–0.37	1.57	4.69	2.040	3.636
Small	0.05	1.82	3.49	1.640	3.052
Marginal	0.41	2.08	4.16	2.189	3.326
Agriculture laborers	0.87	2.12	3.64	2.217	2.225

Source: Unit-level data of consumption expenditure schedule of 50th and 55th rounds.

labor had slowed down over this period, becoming virtually stagnant over the period of 1994–2000 (ibid., Table 6). We analyzed the data on output growth in agriculture and the wage rate (daily average earnings) of agricultural worker for 57 NSS regions between the 50th and the 55th rounds. The statistics are set out in Table 7.9. The much higher inter-quartile range for output growth implies that the means of the two variables are fairly close, but the median growth rate of the wage rate is much lower.

We also studied the growth rates of household welfare as measured by the household expenditure per capita for the different classes of agricultural households as distinguished by Vakulabrahmann. Table 7.10 gives the statistics of growth rates calculated.

It is seen that, unlike in the Telengana case, there is no monotonically decreasing growth rate of household welfare as we go down the landholding classes. There is, however, a difference between large farmers on the one hand, and the marginal farmers and the agricultural laborers on the other. In spite of the bottom quarter of the large farmers having negative growth, the overall growth rate of this class – either in terms of the median or the mean – was substantially above that of marginal farmers or agricultural laborers. There is some evidence supporting the Telengana phenomenon for all-India.

Region-specific evidence

Doubts remain nevertheless about the validity of the above analysis of central tendencies based on all-India figures averaged over many regions when the

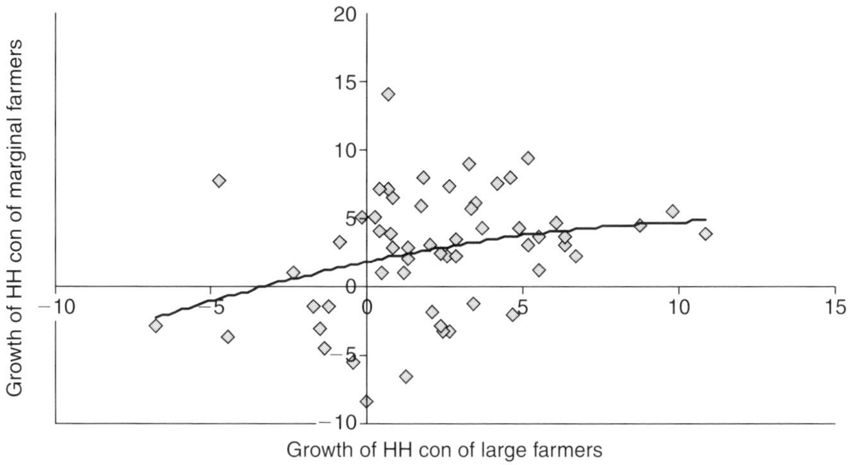

Figure 7.2 Growth rate of consumption of marginal farmers vis-à-vis large farmers.

inter-regional variance is so high. In an alternative exercise we looked at the question if any significant trends could be found in the period studied by looking at region-specific growth rates for the household welfare of different classes of farmers. This was done by taking each of the lower farming classes in turn and then regressing the region-specific growth rate of per capita expenditure (measuring household welfare) of each class on the same variable for large farmers. As an example, the graph showing the scatter is given for one pair of the classes distinguished in Figure 7.2 – namely the growth rate of APCE for the 'marginal' farmers. plotted against the growth rate for 'large farmers'. The variance is large but a regression line could nevertheless be fitted to the scatter with a significant slope. Similar scatters for the growth rate of each of the other three classes plotted against the growth rate of large farmers also show a significant positive relationship (not shown here).

Table 7.11 presents the linear equations of the growth rates of each of four classes in the agricultural sector regressed on the growth rates of large farmers. Agricultural labor households are defined as those whose main source of earnings is wage labor in agriculture, whether or not they are landless or cultivate a small piece of land. The other landholding classes are distinguished on the basis of the size of their operational holdings.[2]

In spite of the relatively low value of R^2 (suggesting there are many other factors behind the large inter-regional variance in growth rates of APCE), all the coefficients of 'b' are significant at an acceptable level. We find that even for medium farmers the growth rate is only a third of the rate achieved by the large farmers. Further, there is indeed a gradual reduction in the slope co-efficient as we move from medium to marginal farmers and to agricultural laborers. There does not, however, seem to be any difference between the coefficients for small and marginal farmers.

Table 7.11 Results of growth regressions for different classes 1993/1994–1999/2000

Class	*Intercept*	*Value of b*	*t-value (P)*	*R^2 (F)*
Medium	1.131	0.353	2.221 (0.001)	0.170 (0.001)
Small	1.066	0.222	2.524 (0.015)	0.088 (0.015)
Marginal	1.611	0.223	2.311 (0.025)	0.088 (0.025)
Agriculture laborers	1.884	0.129	1.942 (0.057)	0.047 (0.057)

Source: Unit-level data of consumption expenditure schedule of 50th and 55th rounds.

Notes

All equations are of the form: $Y= a+bX_i$, where Y is the growth rate of HH per capita expenditure of large farmers; X_i is the growth rate of HH per capita expenditure of the ith class: (P) in parenthesis is the significance level of 'b' and F in parenthesis is the significance of F-value for the equation.

The results give credence to an aspect of the hypothesis that post-reform developments in the agricultural sector have helped larger farmers more than the marginal ones. But it should be remembered that the period between 1993/1994 and 1999/2000 which we have considered has not been a particularly prosperous one for agriculture. We would like to see developments in subsequent periods when relevant data are available from further rounds of the NSS.

Conclusions

In conclusion we can recount the more important results from the detailed discussions in this chapter:

1 Policies affecting the agricultural sector continue to favor the more prosperous regions.
2 The objective of policy should not be viewed as maximizing employment elasticity in agriculture. There is some evidence to suggest that employment elasticity is higher in low-productivity regions simply because agriculture, as the residual sector dominated by family farms, is best able to absorb 'surplus' labor.
3 Off-farm employment, both in the rural and the urban sectors, seem to be more important in regions with higher agricultural income – supporting the hypothesis of 'cumulative causation'.
4 There is disturbing evidence of post-reform developments favoring larger farmers more than the marginal ones and the landless.

8 Employment elasticity in organized manufacturing in India

This and the following chapter are devoted to the manufacturing sector of India. The center of attention in the current chapter is the organized (or formal) manufacturing sector in India. It is identified with the sector covered by the *Annual Survey of Industries* (ASI) conducted by the Central Statistical Organization of the Government of India – which in its turn covers all manufacturing establishments which come under the purview of the Factories Act. They comprise units employing ten or more workers using power or units with 20 or more workers not using power. Our analysis of the employment trends in the formal manufacturing sector is focused on the issue of its low employment elasticity. In spite of a healthy rate of growth of output or value added, the absorption of labor has been very low.

The problem of low employment elasticity in manufacturing – that is, the feeling that employment growth has been lagging seriously behind output growth – has been a serious issue in development economics since the sixties, when concerns about the employment problem in Third World countries began to be discussed (see, for example, Morawetz, 1974). It has been a particularly important matter of concern in India which has had a dismal record on employment generation in 'organized (formal) manufacturings' in recent years. The concern is a serious one for two basic reasons: first, formal manufacturing has been traditionally expected to take the lead in the generation of new productive employment and have large multiplier effects on the other sectors; and second, because of the huge labor productivity differential between the organized and the unorganized sectors, wage levels are at a much lower level in informal manufacturing, and so the dependence on the latter for manufacturing growth does not do much for raising living standards at the lower part of the distribution.

In this chapter we undertake a systematic analysis of the determinants of employment elasticity in Indian formal manufacturing based on the unit-level data available from the *Annual Survey of Industry*. The plan of the chapter is as follows. In the first section we give an overview of the behavior over time in employment elasticity in this sector over the last four decades. We are able to classify the entire period into four sub-periods which reveal a cyclical pattern of the value of employment elasticity. The political economy of the four periods are explained. The second section sets out the outline of the decomposition model, used elsewhere by Mazumdar (2003), which seeks to break down the different factors affecting the growth rate of employment given the growth rate of output (value added in constant prices). This section also goes beyond the earlier paper in setting out a model of the equilibrium of the firm which illuminates the economic process behind the decomposition model. The three factors shaping the value of employment elasticity are (i) the trend in the share of wages; (ii) the wage–employment trade-off; and (iii) the movement in the 'domestic real exchange rate' (DRER) or the ratio of the producer price index to the consumer price index. While the third is more a product of macro-economic factors, the first two are primarily labor-market variables. The mechanics underlying the movements in the three variables are explained. The determinant of the wage-share variable is explained in terms of a model which gives primacy to the firm's investment rate and its financing. In order to preserve the flow of the argument in the body of the paper, a full exposition of the model, and its testing with data from the ASI, is relegated to the Appendix. The results spelled out in the third section for the four periods distinguished show the relative importance of the three factors over the cycles. In the fourth section we turn to some analysis with disaggregated sectors of formal manufacturing. In particular we discuss the experience of different sub-groups of industry distinguished by the dual criteria to exposure to world markets, and level of technology. Other topics include the private–public classification and disaggregation by size groups of firms. The final section summarizes some of the more important results.

Classifying the periods of manufacturing growth in terms of employment elasticity

The organized manufacturing sector in India has grown at different rates in different periods of its development in the last thirty years. At the same time employment elasticity – the rate of growth of employment relative to output growth has also varied enormously over these phases of growth. Figure 8.1 plots volume of employment against the real value added in manufacturing (at constant 1981–2 prices) in logarithmic scale, so that the slope of the curve gives an idea of the changing value of employment elasticity in different periods.

We are able to distinguish between four periods in terms of distinct breaks in the value of employment elasticity (i) 1974–1980 when employment elasticity had a high positive value of 0.99 (ii) the 1980–1986 period of "jobless growth" when employment elasticity actually turned negative (with an average value of –0.16); (iii) the reform period of 1986–1996 which saw a recovery of the employment elasticity to positive values (increasing to 0.33), although significantly lower than the value attained in the first period (iv) the post reform period 1996–2001. These periods also witnessed widely differing growth rates of value added. The data are given in Table 8.1.

The periods distinguished above are, as it happens, reasonably separate in terms of the politics of Indian economic policy. The beginning of the eighties

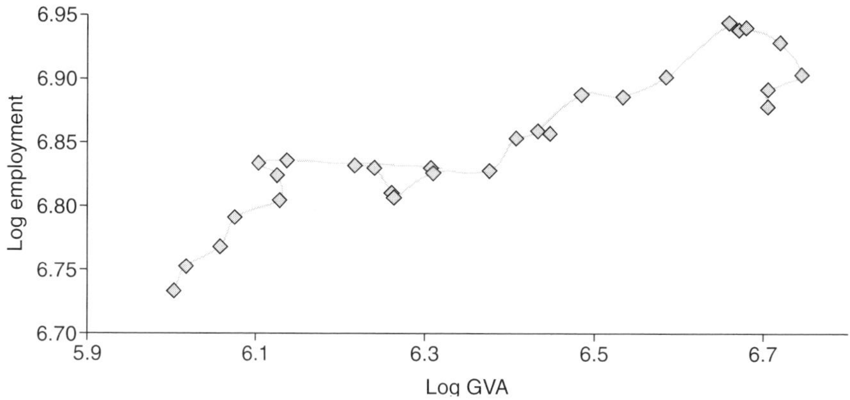

Figure 8.1 Employment and real GVA (1974–1975 to 2001–2002).

has been identified by some researchers as an "attitudinal shift" towards private business on the part of the government (Rodrik and Subramanaian 2004).

> The change was inaugurated with the return of a much-chastened Indira Gandhi to political power in the 1980s after a three-year rule by the Janata Party ... But the attitudinal change was grounded primarily in political calculation, and not in a desire to enhance the efficiency of the economic regime.
>
> (Ibid., p.15)

The motivation has been ascribed to Indira Gandhi's desire to undercut one prong of the support of the Janata Party coming from organized business groups. "This shift had more to do with currying favor with existing business interests (essentially large, politically influential firms in the formal manufacturing sector) than with liberalizing the system" (ibid.). Rodrik and Subramanain had identified in a more detailed way the significant increase in growth rate – of organized manufacturing in particular – evident in the data of Figure 8.1 They also pointed out that when the industrial firms were operating so far below the production possibility frontier small changes in

Table 8.1 Growth rate of value-added and employment elasticity

Period	*Value-added growth*	*Employment elasticity*
I 1974–1980	3.99	0.99
II 1980–1986	6.21	–0.17
III 1986–1996	10.65	0.33
IV 1996–2002	1.75	–1.39

Source: Various years' data of Annual Survey of Industries (ASI), CSO, Government of India.

government policy – even of the 'attitudinal shift' kind could bring about a substantial response.

Indira Gandhi herself was not able to go through much substantial reform program even if she had planned to do so. After her assassination, it was left to Rajiv Gandhi to start on some pieces of substantive reform. It is customary to date the coming of reforms from 1991. This is because liberalization on the external and trade accounts was only seriously addressed as part of the package agreed with the IMF after the serious balance of payments crisis of 1991. But as indicated above, the reform process had started earlier in a substantive way. The decade spanning the period stretching from the mid-eighties to the mid-nineties could be legitimately regarded as the reform period. This was the period that saw an upsurge of business optimism in the organized manufacturing sector, leading not only to a still higher growth rate of output, but also, as we shall see, a large lift in the investment ratio as manufacturing firms sought to build up their capacity. The overhang of the excess capacity of the controlled era of low efficiency had presumably been run down by the surge in output growth, starting at the beginning of the eighties.

The most recent decade has seen a post-reform recession. The windfall gains form the initial liberalization of the economy had been realized, and the manufacturing sector had to adjust to the more difficult problems of market growth in competitive environment. The reform process itself might have slowed down as policy makers and the various interest groups started to grapple with the thorny issues of continuing on the reform path.

The determinants of employment elasticity: a conceptual framework

This section discusses the conceptual framework for analyzing the significant factors determining employment elasticity which has been used for the analysis of the Indian data. It will hopefully identify the quantitative importance of some of the critical variables which have affected the growth of employment in Indian manufacturing, and the way they have varied over the four periods distinguished in the last section. The empirical results are presented in the next section following the discussion of the analytical framework.

Employment growth in manufacturing is obviously limited by the rate of growth of output or value added. But given the growth rate of output there are three important elements determining the value of the employment elasticity:

1 the trend in the share of wages, i.e., the rate of growth of the wage bill relative to value added in current prices facing the producer (α);
2 the relative rates of increase in the producer and consumer price indices (sometimes called the domestic real exchange rate DRER) – which determines the value of the wage bill for the workers in terms of the prices facing them; and
3 the trade-off between employment increase and real wage increase.

Output growth ⇒ Wage-bill growth ⇒ DRER ⇒ Wage-bill growth ⇒ Emp.–Wage trade-off
(producer prices) α (producer prices) P_p/P_c (consumer prices)

Figure 8.2 Determination of employment elasticity.

The process is shown in Figure 8.2.

We can use an algebraic decomposition, explained elsewhere (Mazumdar 2003) to quantify the different elements:

$$\dot{L} = \alpha\,\dot{v} + \alpha\,\dot{P}_p - \dot{P}_c - \dot{w} \tag{1}$$

where w is the real wage (average earnings per worker); v is value added (in constant producer prices); L is employment; P_p is the index of producer prices and P_c index of consumer prices; and α is a technological and behavioral parameter which is assumed to remain constant over the period under consideration. A variable written with a dot on top (˙) represents the *proportionate* rate of change of the variable concerned. α defines the rate of growth of the wage bill related to the growth rate of output and hence determines the trend of the share of wages over the time-period being considered. The relative movements of the producer price and the consumer price indices, sometimes called the ‘domestic real exchange rate’ (DRER), translates the wage bill growth into real terms (in terms of consumer prices. The negative relationship between $\dot{w}$ and $\dot{L}$ clearly shows the wage-employment trade-off, i.e., the way the growing wage-bill cake is divided between wage increase and employment increase.

If the firm has no external source of finance, and cannot either accumulate or draw down financial reserves, then it must balance its books in every period, and equation (1) is an identity. But no firm can be expected to behave in this way. Generally it would have means of external borrowing, but in order not to face bankruptcy, it will aim at achieving a target gearing ratio. This target has to be reached, not on a day-to-day basis, but over a period of time – usually determined by its accounting period of consequence. Equation (1) then becomes a condition of equilibrium of the firm which enables it to maintain a stable gearing ratio over time. The model then has to be completed by a theory of the equilibrium of the firm in which the interconnected variables would force the firm towards this equilibrium.

The formal model and its testing with Indian data are to be found in Appendix 2. Here we present an overview of the relationships.

The model of the firm and its equilibrium

We have assumed that one of the key determinants of employment elasticity – the DRER – is an exogenously determined variable. Prices of both producer goods and consumer goods are given to the firm. This of course means that our firm is a competitive one and a price-taker in the goods market. It does not have the ability to influence either the price of its product or the price of the wage goods. In a more general framework these assumptions, particularly the first one might be dropped, but this issue is not addressed here.

The other two, the share of wages and the wage–employment trade-off, are both labor-market variables. They are tied together in neo-classical economics by the supply functions of labor and of capital working through the production function. Together they determine the share of wages, the level of employment and the wage per worker.

Economists have in more recent discussions recognized the importance of *expectations* both in the determination of the wage per worker and the share of wages. Thus the difference between the neo-classical tradition, stressing the dominance of factor-supply functions, and the post-Keynesian tradition, emphasizing the importance of decisions originating on the employers' side, have been reduced.

In post-Keynesian models the independence of the investment function from the general savings function is stressed. There is a long tradition in economics which has worked with the idea that firms finance investment principally from the internal surpluses generated by the firm. Even though we have external financing the need to achieve the target-gearing ratio effectively makes internal sources the principal source of investment. Thus the share of profits in value added is the crucial variable here. In fact it can be postulated that it is the investment rate which determines the share of profits (and hence wages).[1]

This does not mean that firms are able to fix their investment arbitrarily so that any share of wages will do. For any investment rate there is a determined level of the wage bill corresponding to the wage share. The firm must make sure that this level of the wage bill is sufficient to elicit the supply of labor needed to work with the investment which is achieved.

There is another decision-making involved in the firm. The supply of work (in efficiency units) is a function of two variables: the number of workers and the supply of efficiency units per worker. The latter is a function of the wage rate. Thus for the profit-maximizing firm, for a given wage bill, the optimum labor supply will be achieved where the marginal cost of hiring an extra body of worker is exactly equal to the marginal cost of increasing the same number of labor units by increasing the wage rate of the existing workforce. This formal condition, of course, hides a number of factors which will affect the employer's choice. This includes institutional factors like job-security legislation, union pressures, etc., as well as economic variables affecting the relationship between the decision makers in the firm and their employees.[2]

The employer's decision about the wage per man (determined within the constraints just mentioned) yields both the supply of work units per man and the wage cost per work unit. For the overall general equilibrium of the firm the total supply of work units (the product of the number of workers hired and the supply of work units per man at the wage offered) must be sufficient to produce the level of output (value added) which in fact supports the investment ratio. If the wage bill corresponding to the equilibrium wage share falls short of the amount required, the investment rate and profit share must fall, and hence the wage bill increases. In the contrary case the investment rate might increase with an attendant fall in the wage bill.

Needless to say the production function determining the productivity of capital (and of labor) is an essential part of the system of general equilibrium.

The cyclical predictions of the model

It is generally accepted in the economic literature that the rate of investment of the firm is very sensitive to *expectations* of market trends. This sensitivity to the *perception* of the future by entrepreneurs makes the investment ratio follow a typically cyclical pattern. Since the share of wages in our theory is ultimately determined by the investment ratio, it will have a cyclical pattern – though it would be anti-cyclical. The investment ratio increases in periods of optimism and thus the share of wages (and in our model α) falls. This has the effect *ceteris paribus* of *reducing* the value of employment elasticity.

Consider now the second labor-market variable: the wage–employment trade-off. It has been recognized increasingly in modern labor economics that labor is also a *quasi-fixed* factor. We have discussed above that entrepreneurs have the option of increasing the flow of labor units either by hiring more workers, or by eliciting more work-units from the existing workforce by increasing the wage per worker. In many economies including India, a distinction has to be made between the permanent core of workers and contract labor of various types. The firm operates with at least a core body of tenured workers whose size is slow to respond to changes in the current demand for labor. This is because the cost of hiring-and-firing of 'permanent' workers is significant. Like the stock of fixed investment the firm's stock of the 'permanent' workers is built up more on their perception of *expected* demand. If current demand deviates from the expected demand, firms adjust the labor input for the period in question by varying the flow of labor units per worker rather than the stock of labor. They are able to do so principally because of the wage-efficiency mechanism making the flow of labor per worker an (increasing) function of the wage per worker. If expectations are buoyant firms would build up the stock of labor, and there would be less concern with an increase in wage per worker to elicit a larger inflow of labor units per worker. This will *ceteris paribus* tilt the wage–employment trade-off towards employment increase. Conversely, when there is a downward trend in expected growth, firms would tend to be more inclined to reduce the size of their labor force (through normal attrition of the quasi-fixed part and retrenchment of the non-tenured component) and meet their demand for labor input by increasing the wage per worker. Thus the trade-off would show a bias to wage growth.

It should be noted that wage increase in this kind of model is fuelled by three separate factors: (i) the inelasticity of supply of quasi-fixed labor of the requisite type to the individual firm; (ii) the upward institutional pressure on wages exerted by the firm-specific labor; and (iii) the increase in wage needed to elicit a larger flow of labor per worker. In a recessionary period, with pessimistic expectations, presumably the factors (i) and (ii) will be weak or totally absent.

But we can expect an increase in wage per worker due to the third factor. Taking all factors into account the net effect is more likely to be a slowdown in the rate of growth wages, but the wage–employment trade-off might still see a significant swing to wage growth if the relative fall in employment growth is high.

It is then seen that the cyclical behavior of the wage–employment trade-off is *pro-cyclical* – the tilt to employment tends to increase in periods of optimistic expectations and decrease in times of gloomy prospects. Thus as far as the impact on employment elasticity is concerned the two elements of our decomposition model works in opposite directions with respect to economic cycles. In the upswing the wage share tends to fall leaving a smaller pie of value added to be taken in the form of either employment or wage increase, but the trade-off leans towards a larger share for employment growth. The net result on employment elasticity depends on the relative strength of these two effects.

Decomposition of the factors determining employment elasticity: empirical results

The methodology of decomposition expounded in the last section is now applied to the time series for the organized manufacturing sector as given in the Annual Survey of Industry data set. The equation (1) is applied to growth rates separately for the four periods, which has been distinguished in the previous section. The results are presented below in Table 8.2. Note that for each period the compound growth rates of the variables in the first five columns are calculated, and the value of the last variable *alpha* is calculated as a residual using equation (1). This is because, as explained, the equation (1) must hold over a discrete period of time (in our case over the years covered by each of the four cycles). The value of α tends to adjust itself in each period to secure the equilibrium of the firm.

We can see at once the enormous differences in employment elasticities – just about unity in the first period, turning strongly negative in the second period, and recovering to a value of just over 0.3 in the last period. In the last period post-reform years the employment elasticity has turned negative in a more substantial way than before, even as the output growth has faltered.

Period I can be considered to be the period of 'benign' growth in terms of the variables treated in our analysis. The economy experienced a moderately high rate of output growth at around 4 percent per annum. This was, however, supplemented by a favorable trend in the producer prices relative to consumer prices. Since the value of α was just over unity, the share of wages in gross value added grew at the same rate as output, so that in terms of real wage bill the growth rate was over 6 percent per annum, including the real output growth plus the relative increase in producer prices. It is seen from Table 8.2 that this growing cake was shared between wage growth and employment growth, with the latter taking the lead with the more substantial sharc of the wage bill growth.

The subsequent periods register major deviations from this standard. Of the non-labor market variables the trend in the DRER over all the three succeeding periods is a significant difference. The trend turned negative after the 'benign' first

Table 8.2 Proportionate growth rates of selected variables for three periods

Period	$\dot{w}$	$\dot{v}$	$\dot{L}$	$\dot{P}_p$	$\dot{P}_c$	α	*Output effect*	*Price effect*	*Employment elasticity*
I (1974–1980)	2.63	3.99	3.95	7.10	4.72	1.02	4.07	2.52	0.99
II (1980–1986)	3.51	6.31	–1.01	6.32	8.91	0.90	5.68	–3.20	–0.16
III (1986–1996)	1.83	10.65	3.54	9.10	9.56	0.76	8.10	–2.68	0.33
IV (1996–2002)	0.88	1.75	–2.74	3.07	6.92	1.11	1.93	–3.53	–1.42

Source: Various years' data of Annual Survey of Industries (ASI), CSO, Government of India.

Notes

The values of growth rates are compound rates. Alpha is calculated as a residual using the decomposition equation. The output and price effects are also calculated from the equation as defined.

period, and quantitatively it was in all periods a significant 'leakage' from the growth in the real output. This can be seen by comparing the magnitudes in the column of the 'price effect' with those in the column headed 'ν'. This adverse trend in the domestic terms of trade against manufactured products must be considered to be a major factor tending to dampen the value of employment elasticity after the first period of our study. The macro-economic factors causing this shift in the trend of this variable will be considered further in our subsequent discussion.

While this factor was a persistent negative influence on all the three periods, the cyclical swings in employment elasticity were the net result of the way the actual magnitudes of the two labor-market variables worked out in these periods. *Period II* has been called the period of 'jobless growth' in India. In spite of a healthy rate of growth of output the employment elasticity turned negative (employment actually fell). It can be seen from Table 8.2 that this was largely because of the large shift to wage growth in the wage–employment trade-off. The period of benign growth preceding it had seen an accumulation of excess labor in manufacturing, driven in part by the policies of government in alliance with a trade-union movement biased to the policy of expanding and protecting employment in the formal sector. When the dominance of this institutional support in favor of those already in employment eased, employers responded by policies which met the demand for labor by eking out more efficiency units of labor from a reduced stock.

The succeeding two periods of boom and slump saw working out of the labor-market variables much as had been predicted in our theoretical discussion in the last section. In the upswing of the post-reform years of *Period III* the uplift in the investment ratio resulted in a sharp reduction of the share of wages (a drastic reduction of α). This would have pushed employment elasticity to further lower levels. But it was overshadowed by a tilt in the wage–employment trade-off to employment growth, as employers buoyed up by optimistic expectations and an erosion of the excess stock of labor from the last period, sought to build up their labor complement. The net result was a positive if low value of employment elasticity. The downswing of *Period IV* saw a large recovery of the value α and the wage share as the investment ratio slumped, but again it was swamped by the drastic shift in the wage–employment trade-off, this time against employment growth in line with our a priori expectations, and we see significant negative employment elasticity for the period.

We shall now add short notes on each of the three periods II–IV, elaborating on the economic and institutional factors influencing the value of employment elasticity as outlined in the last paragraph. The trend decrease in the domestic terms of trade will be discussed at the end of this section, together with its policy implications.

The period of jobless growth 1980–1986

The spectacular fall in employment elasticity in the second period, extending from the end of the 1970s to 1985–1986, is to a major extent due to the tilt in the trade-off to wage growth. It has been ascribed to institutional factors emanating from trade unions pushing up wage rates (Hanson and Lieberman, World Bank Country Report 1989). But it can be seen from Table 8.2 that although there was some increase in the rate of real wage growth (in constant consumer prices) in period II, a much larger part of the increase of product wage (in constant producer prices) was because of the sharp increase of the rate of growth of consumer prices relative to producer prices (or the domestic real exchange rate, DRER). Ajit Ghose (1994), in fact, pointed to the increase in the DRER as the crucial factor in the rise in capital intensity in industry, which slowed down employment increase. The increase of DRER was in turn a consequence of the abandoning of government policies to fix the price of food at low levels.

The impact of relative price changes meant was that, although the real output growth increased somewhat in period II, the growth rate of the real wage bill which could support wage and employment growth was drastically reduced below the level of period I (from 6.59 to 2.46). The fact that the real wage growth (in constant consumer prices) did not fall but actually increased somewhat in response is prima facie evidence of the wage–employment trade-off being tilted in favor of the wage of those already in employment. Detailed examination of labor-market institutions in this period, however, casts serious doubt on the hypothesis if this tilt was mostly or even primarily due to enhanced trade union power.

Reshaping of labor institutions

As already mentioned, this period saw the 'attitudinal' change to private business in Indian policy making. One aspect of this was the withdrawal of virtually automatic state support from the large all-India trade unions which had been dominating industrial relations in the organized sector with the help of the major political parties. This attitudinal change was nowhere more prominently seen than in the textile strikes of Bombay and Ahmedabad at the beginning of the eighties.

The power exerted by large-scale industry wide unions, often backed by political parties, and sometimes supported by the government in power, was seriously challenged in the early 1980s by the owners of large factories in the older industries – which were rapidly becoming uncompetitive. The confrontation led to a large-scale closure of the mills, and after a long period of lock-out, job loss without compensation on a fairly extensive scale. This major event saw a turning point in industrial relations in the large-scale manufacturing sector. Uchikkawa (2002, p. 38) writes:

> The phenomenon reduced the incentive of workers to join labor unions. Membership of workers' unions including the service sector decreased from 8.18 million in 1986–1987 to 5.61 million in 1996–1997. Closure of many mills did big damage to the labor union movement because labor unions failed to protect job security.

Uchikawa has produced a graph of the time series of job losses due to strikes and those due to lock-outs over the eighties and the nineties. His graph demonstrates that man-days lost by labor disputes dropped sharply during our second period, and for the first time fell below the level of jobs lost due to lock-outs. This altered relationship continued into the third period in the nineties (ibid., Figure 2, p. 39).

Moreover, as pointed out by Tirthankar Roy (2002), there was shift in the nature of bargaining institutions. It began to be much more plant based than industry based. Industry-wide unions were in decline throughout the eighties, making way for firm-specific bargaining. There is evidence for continued disputes at the plant level, sometimes spilling over into closures of factories. But such closures ceased to be industry-wide. It has been pointed out by several commentators that one of the major causes of the decline of the large industry-wide unions has been their de-linking with public-sector undertakings, and the budgetary support they received from non-profit making firms financed by state budget deficits.

> Indian labor regime is decisively changing. It seems to be changing from a pluralist regime, where unions can play a role in national politics via their dependent relationship with political groups, to a truly decentralized regime where unions have little or no relationship with political groups.
>
> (Roy 2002, p. 117)

It might seem odd that along with the decline in centralized union power which the last paragraphs suggest, there should have been an attempt by the government to strengthen job-security legislation by the 1982 amendment to the Industrial Disputes Act which extended the protection to workers already in employment. The lower limit for the employment size of establishments beyond which permission had to be sought from the quasi-judicial authorities for any retrenchment was in fact reduced from 300 workers enunciated in the 1976 Industrial Disputes Act to 100 workers in the amendment of 1982. Fallon and Lucas (1993) used this amendment to 'explain' the reduction in employment elasticity in the eighties in their estimated labor-demand function. The conflicting trends can be reconciled in terms of the hypothesis that the government in the initial period of 'attitudinal' change was in effect pursuing a carrot-and-stick policy. The withdrawal of automatic support for the all-India unions during large industry-wide strikes was accompanied by the promise of extended support for job security if militancy were avoided.

Consistent with this stick-and-carrot policy employers seemed to have pursued a two-prong strategy of cutting down the size of a large union-supported labor force but instead developing a core of smaller committed body of workers who could enjoy guaranteed employment. Moreover, the employment structure started to shift to the industry groups with lower labor intensity – electrical machinery, chemicals, transport equipment, rubber, plastic and petroleum products, non-electrical machinery, etc.

As far as the wage growth reported in Table 8.2 is concerned several researchers, including Nagaraj (1994). Papola (1992), Bhalotra (1998) and Uchikawa (2002), have all pointed out the weakness in the analysis which refers only to *number of workers* rather than person-days worked. According to Uchikawa's latest research average annual working days in all manufacturing rose from 273 during the first period, to 300 days in the second period to 309 days during the third period. (Uchikawa's periods are fairly close to our first three periods distinguished in Table 8.2.) Thus the wage cost per man-hour of work did not increase at nearly the same rate as average earnings or average product wage person.

Why did the number of person-hours per worker start to increase at the beginning of the second period? Uchikawa's explanation is that "the manufacturing sector had redundant workers in the late 1970s. Although growth rates of GVA (gross value added) declined, man-days increased during the recession period between 1978–1979 and 1982–1983" (ibid., p. 38). Strong labor unions, still powerful at the end of the second period, prevented retrenchment of redundant workers. Thus when industry recovered at the beginning of the eighties, there was enough 'surplus' labor available to increase the flow of labor in terms of hours of work required. The employer response to the changed climate of labor deployment in Indian manufacturing was to increase the flow of labor per worker from a reduced rationalized labor force.

The reform period (1986–1996)

It has already been mentioned in our summary of the developments of period III that the reform decade saw a jump in output growth to around 10 percent. Another feature of the period was a sharp fall in the share of the wage as wages grew at only three-quarters of the rate of growth of output. But the rate of output growth was very high, and, furthermore, was augmented by the DRER swinging in favor of producer goods, so that the growth rate of the real wage bill – which could support either wage or employment growth – was high at 5.37, up from 2.50 of the jobless growth period. The change in the wage–employment trade-off was also drastic, swinging substantially to employment rather wage growth. It might be tempting to suggest that both the tilt in the wage–employment trade-off towards employment growth and the decline in the share of wages in value added are due to the weakening of union power in the last period, which was discussed above.

As far as the bias towards employment growth is concerned one of the elements in the story is quite clearly that the excess capacity of the labor force, which might have been a legacy of the previous years, had been largely eliminated during the period of 'jobless growth'. With the strong output growth registered in this period it was necessary to increase the size of employment over time. Nevertheless, the relatively low employment elasticity suggests that employers might have been wary of the critical role of job security legislation. Not only was labor used more efficiently, employers in this period are widely reported to have used a variety of other methods of organizing production which helped to moderate the increase in 'permanent' employment. A major development discussed in the literature was the increasing use of subcontracting. Ramaswami (2006) constructed an index of subcontracting by taking 'the value of goods sold in the same condition as purchased *plus* the value of work done by concerns on material supplied" – both sets of information given for the registered factories surveyed in the ASI. Although not covering all types of subcontracting, the data showed that 'subcontracting intensity' rose from 10.0 in 1989–1990 to 12.3 percent in 1994–1995, and the real value of subcontracting grew at a compound growth rate of 10.9 percent – at a faster rate than total output in manufacturing (ibid., Table 4, p. 135).

The investment rate–wage share nexus

A major factor which influenced employment elasticity – albeit in a downward direction – was the increased investment rate. Careful work by Uchikawa (2001) has shown that there was a sharp acceleration in gross investment in the first half of the nineties. The gross fixed capital stock in ASI industries increased at the rate of 10.1 percent per annum at 1980–1981 prices. A regression equation estimated for the time-series of capital stock showed that a multiplicative dummy for the post-1990 period was significant at the 5 percent level, confirming the acceleration of investment after the economic reforms. The rate of growth of the capital stock was about *three times* the rate of growth of employment. There are several reasons for this spurt in investment, some of them having to do with the easing of control over the stock market which encouraged the corporate sector to shift their sources of finance from term lending to paid-up capital. The share of the latter suddenly rose from 7.1 percent in 1992–1993 to 29.6 in 1993–1994 (Uchikawa 2001).

The spurt in capital growth was clearly expectations of continued market expansion. This was the reason for the build-up of both capital stock and permanent labor by the manufacturing firms. The fact that the capital build-up was so much faster than the increase in the stock of labor shows that employers were still wary of labor as a potentially costly quasi-fixed factor, although improving the quality of production through more mechanized techniques might have been an additional motivation. This meant that although the trade-off shifted to employment growth, employment elasticity was lower than it might have been.

There is another way that the spurt in investment rate depressed employment growth. As indicated, the financing of investment shifted to retained profits to a considerable degree in this period. It has been suggested that a significant factor in the fall in the share of wages was the need to finance the increased investment rate form internal 'surplus' (see Appendix 2) for an elaboration and testing of this 'Kalecki-type' model. In terms of our decomposition equation the fall in the share of wages (or α in the equation) meant that a smaller chunk of the growing cake was available to support the wage bill growth. Thus employment growth was lower than otherwise.

Decline in the growth rates of output and employment (1995–1996 to 2001–2002)

The upswing in manufacture output tapered off in the second half of the 1990s. From a highpoint of 14 percent growth rate in 1995–1996 the real value added (as well as the production index) has showed a steady decline. Over the period until 2001–2002 the compound rate of growth has been a modest 1.75 per annum.

For manufacturing as a whole the rate of growth of real value added slumped to 1.75 percent compared with 10.65 in the previous period. But the response of employment to the slump was even more drastic. Employment growth turned substantially negative: falling at the rate of 2.74 percent per annum compared with the mere 1 percent per annum during the earlier period of jobless growth in the eighties. This, in spite of the rather sharp recovery of α to above unity, signify an increase in wage share (and hence in wage-bill growth) as the rate of investment slumped.

The drastic fall in employment elasticity was due to both factors isolated in our decomposition exercise: (i) the DRER turning against manufacture further as the producer-price index increased at a much slower rate than the consumer-price index; and (ii) the tilt in the wage–employment trade-off towards, once again, wage growth at the expense of employment growth. Both these factors were important as indeed they were in the period of jobless growth. But looking at the magnitudes involved the quantitative importance of the DRER (price) factor was more important than the wage–employment trade-off.

The relative importance of the wage–employment trade-off can be quantified by noting the difference between $\dot{L}$ and $\dot{w}$. A negative sign of the value signifies that there is a tilt towards wage growth, while a positive value indicates that employment growth is preferred. Thus, other things being equal, a positive value of the first term would favor an increase in employment elasticity, while a negative value would signify that the bias towards wage growth reduces employment elasticity. The DRER effect is the difference between $\dot{P}_p$ and $\dot{P}_c$. Given real output growth, $\dot{v}$ a negative value of the DRER indicates a leakage from the growing cake, which has to be shared between wage growth and employment growth. *ceteris paribus* it depresses employment elasticity. The quantitative importance of the two effects can be studied by comparing the *difference* $[\dot{L} - \dot{w}]$ with the *difference* $[\dot{P}_p - \dot{P}_c]$. The way these relative magnitudes varied as between the four periods of our study is given in Table 8.3.

It should be emphasized, however, that although the negative trend in the DRER was strong, the tilt in the wage–employment trade-off towards wage growth was also substantial – in fact a more important *relative* change compared with the previous period.

The shift in the wage–employment trade-off: labor-market behavior

An interpretation in terms of a strictly dynamic neo-classical model is very problematic. It will be recalled that in period III for all-India, while employment

Table 8.3 The relative importance of the wage-employment trade-off and the DRER effect

Period	$\dot{L} - \dot{w}$	$\dot{P}_p - \dot{P}_c$	Employment elasticity
I (1974–1980)	1.32	2.38	0.99
II (1980–1986)	–4.84	–2.59	–0.16
III (1986–1996)	1.71	–0.46	0.33
IV (1996–2002)	–3.62	–3.85	–1.42

Source: Various years' data of Annual Survey of Industries (ASI), CSO, Government of India.

grew at 3.54 percent per annum, the real wage increased at the rate of 1.83. In the post-reform period IV when employment growth was significantly negative at –2.74 percent per annum, real wage still increased at 0.88 percent. The fall in the rate of growth of real wage with the decrease in employment growth might at first sight seem to be consistent with a neo-classical model in which the dynamic supply curve of labor is gently upward sloping. But the fact that wage growth still grows at nearly 1 percent per annum even when employment is falling at the annual rate of 2.74 percent is inherently implausible in strictly supply-and-demand terms. It is necessary to invoke one of several labor-market forces which pushes the wage level upwards at a significant rate even when employment growth is zero or negative. Such factors include the following, which might operate singly or in combination: (i) an upgrading of labor might be going on with skill formation due to technological change; (ii) the efficiency–wage function, so that the flow of labor units supplied per worker increases; and (iii) 'insider' power which keeps the wage increasing through time even when employment growth is negative.

All these types of wage behavior imply the existence of a firm-specific labor force which is a 'quasi-fixed' factor in the firm's production function. As already mentioned, the firm operates with at least a core body of tenured workers whose size is slow to respond to changes in the current demand for labor. Like the stock of fixed investment the firm's stock of the 'permanent' workers is built up more on their perception of *expected* demand. If current demand deviates from the expected demand, firms adjust the labor input for the period in question by varying the flow of labor units per worker rather than the stock of labor. They are able to do so principally because of the wage–efficiency mechanism making the flow of labor per worker an (increasing) function of the wage per worker.

This hypothesis would seem to fit the different scenarios witnessed in the Indian manufacturing sector for the periods of reforms and the post-reform years – the periods III and IV respectively of the analysis presented above. In the reform decade there was a general euphoria about the expansion of business in which the entrepreneurs participated with enthusiasm. It seems to have led to a rebuilding of the stock of labor which had been drawn down during the preceding decade of 'jobless growth'. The recession of the second half of the nineties, along with the adverse movement of the producer prices facing manufacturers, led to a revision of these expectations. It might have prompted a hurried attempt to reduce the permanent workforce, and possibly a greater use made of out-sourcing, which led to the substantial negative employment elasticity. The increase in wages slowed down relative to period III but it was positive. Thus the wage–employment trade-off swung to wage growth.

The downward trend in the domestic terms of trade[3]

We have seen that the adverse movements of producer prices to consumer prices had a significant role in depressing the value of employment elasticity in manufacturing, and in fact producing negative values for this variable in periods II and IV. The relative movement of prices, however, depends not only on labor-market conditions but also on overall macroeconomic factors. For instance if real effective exchange rates appreciate or do not depreciate to maintain manufacturing competitiveness, the domestic terms of trade can be adversely affected. As Figure 8.3 (top panel) shows, this indeed happened since the mid-1990s: real effective exchange rates stabilized and even appreciated slightly since then. This was associated with an adverse movement of produce prices relative to consumer prices. Econometric estimates show that, after controlling for time trends, there is a robust relationship between real exchange-rate appreciation and adverse movements in the domestic real exchange-rates (Figure 8.3, bottom panel), which in turn lowers employment elasticity. Thus, one policy implication will be to keep exchange rates competitive through guarding against inflation, especially of consumer goods. This in turn has implications for fiscal policy. Higher deficits, government borrowing and inflation tend to appreciate real exchange rates. If government expenditure growth is directed disproportionately towards consumption – as has been the trend in India in the 1990s – that will also turn the domestic real exchange rate against producers and discourage the growth of jobs. If government policy raises food prices in an artificial manner, that would also lower manufacturing elasticity.

Desegregation: some selected issues

We have so far dealt with the whole of organized (formal) manufacturing as a single entity. It is now important to extend the story to cover some critical issues involving a more disaggregated view of this sector. These are: (i) the difference between the publicly and privately owned units in manufacturing; (ii) individual sub-sectors distinguished by key characteristics like technology and trade-orientation: and (iii) manufacturing establishments of different size-groups.

Public and private sub-sectors[4]

The public sector was a significant part of organized manufacturing in period I. The high employment elasticity observed in this period was at least partly due to the influence exerted by the all-India unions, with strong affiliation to political parties, in favor of expanding "good jobs" in the formal sector. Since the

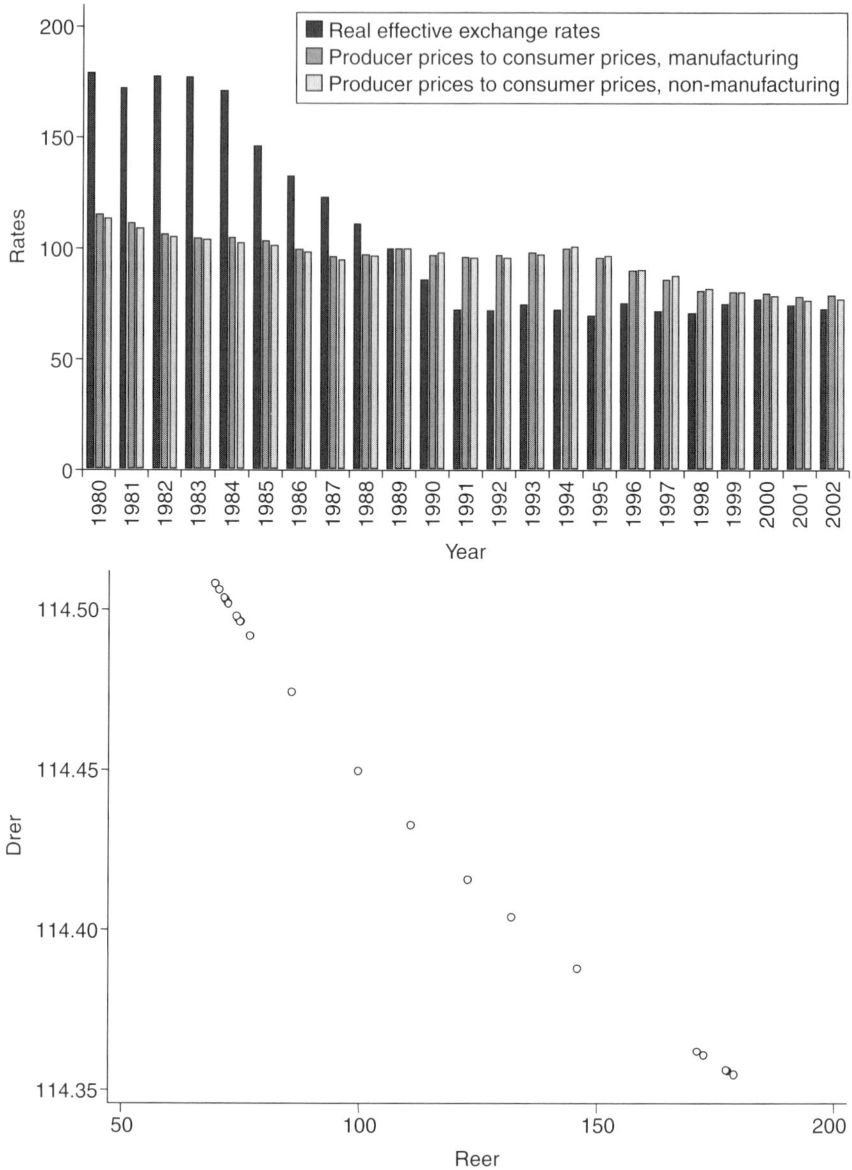

Figure 8.3 Changes in real effect exchange rates and domestic real exchange rates (producer prices to consumer prices) (source: Estimated from data on prices given in the Annual Abstract of Statistics (GOI and RBI data on real exchange rates).

wage-gap was already very high in favor of the formal sector, the interest of unions was more in the direction of increasing its membership of the privileged workers – rather than the OECD type of bias towards the wage increase of 'insiders'.

The reform period saw a decline in the public sector as the state-controlled pattern of manufacturing growth was gradually whittled down. Table 8.4 gives the results of the decomposition analysis separately for the public-and private-sector establishments in the ASI time series.

The data in Table 8.4 show the slower growth rate of output in the public sector undertakings, as well as the attempt to reduce over-manning. The relatively high growth rate of wages in this sub-sector probably is partly an attempt to reduce the excess capacity built up among the workers. As pointed out earlier, the increase in wage per person-hour would probably be not as much. However, the broad conclusions arrived at above for all manufacturing, without making the public–private distinction, are not altered.

The composition of industry

New technology and greater openness are the two characteristics of the reform period. Accordingly it is useful to classify the industries at the two-digit level of the NIC classification in term of the dual characteristics of the level of technology, and exposure to the world markets. The latter in turn involves the degree of import penetration and/or the proportion of output exported. We used the input–output table for the Indian economy constructed by the Planning Commission for 1991 to undertake such a classification. The results are given in Table 8.5.

It is seen that in 1991 the high technology sub-sectors had not yet started to play a significant role in exports. Rather, trade liberalization measures allowed some of these groups to establish themselves with a sizable 'import penetration' ratio (sector 1 in Table 8.5). The industries classified as using medium-low technology were of two types: NIC groups 31–34 (code 2a) was domestically oriented, although making use of a not insignificant proportion of imports. But a group had emerged (group 38), consisting a variety of new 'other manufacturing' which exported a substantial proportion of its output, and also had a high import penetration. This was then the sub-sector with the highest degree of globalization (our 'exposure ratio'). However, its overall importance in terms of the total share in value added in all manufacturing was only around 5 percent in 1991. Low-technology manufacturing, as is to be expected, had very low import penetration. But one sub-group (3b) had a significant export ratio, and indeed accounted for nearly a quarter of the total output of manufacturing. These included textiles and textile products, paper and leather products. Industry groups 20, 22 and 27 – food and beverages and wood products – were the truly domestic industries at this date, with a share of 15 percent of total manufacturing.

It might be of some interest to look at the trends in the key variables studied above for all variables, separately for the industry groups just distinguished. The data are reproduced in Table 8.6.

Table 8.4 Proportionate growth rates for the public and the private sectors, 1986–1987 to 1994–1995

Sub-sector	$\dot{w}$	$\dot{v}$	$\dot{L}$	$\dot{P}_p$	$\dot{P}_c$	α	*Output effect*	*Price effect*	*Employment elasticity*
Public	2.38	5.58	–0.11	9.28	9,43	0.79	4.40	–2.12	–0.02
Private	1.60	10.97	3.55	9.28	9.43	0.72	7.90	–2.75	0.32
All manufacturing	1.50	9.68	2.77	9.28	9.43	0.72	7.00	–2.73	0.29

Source: Various years' data of Annual Survey of Industries (ASI), CSO, Government of India.

Notes

1 The figures for all manufacturing differ from those given in Table 8.1 because we could not include the high growth year of 1995–1996 because our data period ends on 1994–1995.

2 'Public' includes establishments wholly owned by state and/or local governments as well as those owned or owned jointly with the private sector. Employment in joint sector establishments was around 10 percent of the total in all public manufacturing in 1987–1988. The private-sector variables are calculated as residuals and therefore include 'unspecified' units.

Table 8.5 Classification of industries by technology level and exposure to trade 1991

Technology level plus exposed ratio	*NIC code*	*Import penetration*	*Export ratio*	*Exposed ratio*	*Size of sector (%)*	*Sector code*
High exposed	30+35 to 37	29.5	6.1	33.8	31.8	1
Medium domestic	31 to 34	11.1	3.8	14.5	23.9	2a
Medium exposed	38	25.3	28.4	46.5	5.5	2b
Low domestic	20, 22, 27	1.4	3.0	4.3	15.6	3a
Low exposed	23 to 26; 28+29	2.7	15.8	18.1	23.4	3b
	All	14.3	8.5	21.6	100.0	

Source: Planning Commission 60×60 input–output table, 1991.

Notes

Import penetration = (Value of Import)/(Value of Output – Value of Export)*100

Export ratio = (Value of Export)/(Value of Output)*100

Exposed ratio = (Value of Import + Value of Export)/(Value of Output)*100

NIC codes: 30: Basic Chemicals and chemical products.
35–36: Machinery and Equipment other than transport equipment
37: Transport equipments and parts.

31: Rubber, plastic, petroleum and coal products.
32: Non-metallic mineral products.
33: Basic metals and alloys industries.
34: Metal products and parts except machinery.

38: Other manufacturing Industries.

23: Cotton textiles.
24: Wool, silk and man-made fiber textiles.
25: Manufacture of jute and other vegetable fiber.
26: Textile products including wearing apparel.
28: Paper and paper products.

20–21: Food products.
22: Beverages, tobacco and related products.
27: Wood and wood products.

Table 8.6 Trends in selected variables by industry groups, 1986–1987 to 1996–1997

Period III	*Industry group*	$\dot{w}$	$\dot{v}$	$\dot{L}$	$\dot{P}_p$	$\dot{P}_c$	α
	1	1.58	12.83	4.73	8.49	9.56	0.74
	2a	2.38	11.22	3.01	8.71	9.56	0.75
	2b	0.44	16.57	7.54	5.27	9.56	0.80
	3a	2.51	7.58	3.27	9.79	9.56	0.88
	3b	0.66	6.86	2.75	10.40	9.56	0.75

Source: Various years' data of Annual Survey of Industries (ASI), CSO, Government of India.

The first point to note is that there is a clear difference in the rates of growth in industry groups of different levels of technology. The higher technology sub-groups 1, 2a and 2b had a significantly higher rate of output growth. The group of "new" industries identified above (2b) as leading the charge in export markets suffered from a relatively lower trend in producer prices (compared with the trend in consumer prices), so that some of its growth was 'lost' in the declining terms of trade. Both the low-technology industry groups – the more 'exposed' as well as the less so – had a decidedly lower rate of growth.

Turning to labor-market outcomes, domestically oriented low-technology sub-group (3a) seems to have suffered the least from the adverse price (DRER) effect, and labor's share declined the least in this industry group. Thus the wage-bill growth was nearly on a par with output growth. But the tilt to employment growth as against wage growth was the least pronounced in this group. A reasonable hypothesis is that these older domestically oriented industries continued to experience some of the old power of 'insiders'. Thus in spite of the rate of output growth being the second lowest, the growth rate of real wages was highest in this group.

It is, however, remarkable that all three sub-groups with the highest 'exposure ratios' – groups 1, 2b and 3b – had the lowest rate of growth of real wages. In the two exports-oriented groups, 2b and 3b, in fact, the growth rate of real wages was barely positive. The wage–employment trade-off had in fact swung heavily in favor of employment growth even as the share of wages declined significantly. We can conclude with some confidence that, if the aim of liberalization had been to promote labor-intensive growth and reduce the power of those already in employment, our first cut at the evidence shows that the policy certainly succeeded in its objectives to some extent.

The experience during the post-reform slowdown

The upswing in manufacture output tapered off in the second half of the nineties. From a highpoint of 14 percent growth rate in 1995–1996, the real value added (as well as the production index) has showed a steady decline. Over the period until 2001–2002 the compound rate of growth has been a modest 1.75 per annum.

What has been the experience of different industry groups during this slowdown?

Looking at the industry groups (Table 8.7), as classified by us, this slump is significantly due to a *negative rate of growth* in group 1 – the sector with the most import penetration (chemicals and machinery). The two other large groups (in terms of employment share in 1991) are the medium domestic (2a) and the low exposed (3b). Both had their growth rates cut but continued to have above-average positive growth rates. The newly emerging group 2b with high export ratio – miscellaneous manufacturing – continued to have a high, though reduced, rate of growth, but presumably it was still too small a sector to have a substantial effect on the overall ratio of growth. Generally the more export-oriented sub-sectors reduced their rates of growth by a smaller amount than the domestically oriented or import competing groups. This suggests that the slowdown was more due to domestic market conditions than to recession in the export markets.

We have already seen that for industry as a whole, although the negative trend in the DRER was strong, the tilt in the wage–employment trade-off towards wage growth was also substantial – in fact, quantitatively more important. The data are now presented by industry groups (Table 8.8).

It is seen that, comparing the two periods, the shift in the DRER against manufactured producer prices was pretty widespread across product groups. But it seemed to have been particularly strong the domestically oriented groups – 2a and 3a. In fact for the newly emerging group of export-oriented industries (3b) the fall in DRER is relatively small. The importance of the slackness of the domestic market is again brought out: we had seen earlier that the slow-down in output growth was more prominent for these groups.

The tilt in the wage–employment trade-off towards wage growth was also as widespread as the shift in DRER, and reduced the rate of employment growth significantly in all sectors. The largest shift seems to have been in group 1 – the high-technology import-competing sector – where the tilt to wage growth was nearly 9 percentage points. Otherwise the domestically oriented groups were as much affected by this phenomenon as the export-oriented ones. The evidence suggests that there is some general labor-market phenomenon causing this tilt to wage growth in the post reform period when the output growth slowed down.

Changes in the size structure of industry[5]

A major development in the reform period has been that, along with the change in labor institutions mentioned in the last paragraph, there has been a distinct shift of production and employment to small-medium enterprises (SMEs), reducing the role of large factories in the manufacturing sector. It will be recalled from our analysis in the second section that this development has important implications for economic welfare generally, and on employment elasticity in particular. Table 8.9 gives the relevant data documenting the change.

These figures show that size groups with 500–999 employees increased their share in employment and gross value added while the size group of 1,000 and

Table 8.7 Output and employment growth rates by industry groups: periods III and IV compared

Industry group	*1986–1987 to 1995–1996*			*1995–1996 to 2001–2002*		
	$\dot{v}$	$\dot{L}$	*Employment elasticity*	$\dot{v}$	$\dot{L}$	*Employment elasticity*
1 High exposed	12.83	4.73	0.37	–0.57	–4.56	8.05*
2a Medium domestic	11.22	3.01	0.27	2.28	–2.25	–0.98
2b Medium exposed	16.57	7.54	0.46	10.77	1.42	0.13
3a Low domestic	7.58	3.27	0.43	5.15	–0.19	–0.04
3b Low exposed	6.86	2.75	0.40	3.01	–3.03	–1.01
All	10.65	3.54	0.33	1.75	–2.47	–1.42

Source: Various years' data of Annual Survey of Industries (ASI), CSO, Government of India.

Note
* Both output growth and employment growth are negative.

Table 8.8 Relative importance of wage–employment trade-off and DRER in employment elasticity

Sub-group	*1986–1987 to 1995–1996*			*1995–1996 to 2001–2002*		
	$\dot{L}-\dot{w}$	$\dot{P}_p-\dot{P}_c$	*Employment elasticity*	$\dot{L}-\dot{w}$	$\dot{P}_p-\dot{P}_c$	*Employment elasticity*
1	3.83	–1.07	0.37	–5.72	–2.36	8.05*
2a	1.38	–0.85	0.27	–3.88	–4.69	–0.98
2b	6.16	–4.29	0.46	0.42	–4.55	0.13
3a	0.51	0.84	0.40	–3.29	–6.34	–1.01
3b	1.30	0.21	0.43	–2.25	–1.28	–0.04
All	1.94	–0.46	0.33	–3.35	–3.85	–1.42

Source: Various years' data of Annual Survey of Industries (ASI), CSO, Government of India.

Note
* Both output growth and employment growth are negative.

above employees reduced their share. In the late eighties the SMEs in the size groups 50–199 and 200–499 were the most dynamic groups, and in the nineties the group 500–999 joined them in having a relatively high rate of growth. Employment in the largest size was particularly affected, *falling* at the rate of 4.68 percent per annum in 1984–1989, and of 1.16 percent in the first half of the nineties, while the other groups had significant positive rates of growth.

How much was this change in the size-structure related to the change in the composition of industry noted in the paragraphs above? We crossed the five-group classification of industries given in Table 8.8 above with the five size groups of Table 8.9 and noted the cells showing substantial increase or decrease (more than 5 percent) in its share. The results are given in Table 8.10.

It is seen that the reduction in the relative importance of the very large firms was generally across the board, although the low-tech, somewhat export-oriented group (3a) seems to have had the most spectacular loss in this size group. Only the group of miscellaneous industries rapidly expanding in the export markets (2b) might have increased its average employment size as the share of 50–199 enterprises increased at the expense of the very small ones. Were there significant differences in labor-market outcomes in different size classes of enterprises? The decomposition analysis, used above for all manufacturing, was applied separately for the five size groups distinguished. The results are set out in Table 8.11.

The rate of growth of real output was somewhat low in the smallest size group though not so low as the largest size-group (1,000+), but all the other three SME groups with employment size ranging from 50 to 500 workers registered a remarkably high rate of output growth. It is seen that, with the sole exception of the smallest size group 10–49, the employment elasticity ($\dot{L}$ divided by $\dot{v}$) decreases as the size-class increases. It is then clear that the redistribution of output to small and medium enterprises from the largest size-group (though

Table 8.9 Employment and gross value added by size classes of factories

Size group	*Distribution of employment (%)*			*Annual growth rate (%)*	
	1984–1985	*1989–1990*	*1994–1995*	*1984–1989*	*1989–1994*
10–49	15.1	18.1	17.4	4.4	1.3
50–199	19.8	24.3	26.2	4.7	3.7
200–499	14.0	15.7	16.4	2.9	3.1
500–999	13.0	12.9	15.3	0.5	5.8
1,000 and above	38.2	29.1	24.7	–4.7	–1.2
Total	100.0	100.0	100.0	0.6	2.1
Size group	*Distribution of GVA (%)*			*Annual growth rate (%)*	
	1984–1985	*1989–1990*	*1994–1995*	*1984–1989*	*1989–1994*
10–49	8.3	9.1	9.1	9.4	8.6
50–199	13.2	16.0	17.7	12.0	10.6
200–499	14.9	16.8	18.7	10.4	11.1
500–999	17.2	17.4	21.3	8.5	13.5
1,000 and above	46.4	40.6	33.2	4.8	5.2
Total	100.0	100.0	100.0	7.8	9.0

Source: Various years' data of Annual Survey of Industries (ASI), CSO, Government of India.

Note
The total mentioned here is total of five size groups mentioned above. But it excludes factories in the 0–9 employment size group. So growth rates of the total will not match with manufacturing sector's growth rates.

not to the smallest) was one of the factors which help bump up the overall employment elasticity in the reform period.

The DRER effect in terms of the differences in the rates of growth of producer and consumer prices is of minor importance in the overall differences in the wage–employment outcome by size-groups. It should be apparent that the

Table 8.10 Size classes with substantial change in the share of total employment by industry groups, 1984–1985 to 1994–1995

Industry group code	*Substantial gain*	*Substantial fall*
1	50–199; 200–499	1,000+ (13%)
2a	10–49	1,000+ (8%)
2b	50–199	10–49 (7%)
3a	50–199; 200–499	1,000+ (24%)
3b	50–199	1,000+ (6%)

Source: Various years' data of Annual Survey of Industries (ASI), CSO, Government of India.

Note
Industry codes as defined in Table 8.5.

Table 8.11 Decomposition results by size-classes of factories, 1984–1985 to 1994–1995

Size groups	$\dot{w}$	$\dot{v}$	$\dot{\underline{i}}$	$\dot{P}_p$	$\dot{P}_c$	α	*Price effect*	*Output effect*	*Employment elasticity*
10–49	3.18	8.89	2.53	8.78	9.35	0.85	–1.89	7.60	0.29
50–199	2.91	11.47	6.64	8.78	9.29	0.84	–1.92	9.63	0.58
200–499	2.34	11.55	3.49	8.78	9.30	0.75	–2.72	8.67	0.30
500–999	1.34	10.94	2.97	8.24	9.30	0.71	–3.44	7.77	0.27
1,000 and above	1.88	5.03	–1.55	8.32	9.30	0.71	–3.39	3.57	–0.31

Source: Own calculations from data tapes of ASI.

differences in employment elasticity by size-groups are the joint outcome of different values of α *and* the wage-employment trade-off.

a The most striking result in Table 8.11 is the inverse relationship of α with the size classes – with the exception of the largest size-class, for which α stayed at the same value as the next lower size-group. The major conclusion reached earlier about the third period for manufacturing as a whole was that the reduction in wage elasticity with respect to value added – which implies a fall in the share of wages – was due to the increase in investment rate. In the extended econometric exercise reported in Appendix.2 we get the result that the inverse relationship of α with the investment rate is confirmed (after allowing for variations in capital productivity) – but α still falls monotonically with the firm-size groups. This is most likely due to capital intensity increasing with firm size.

b The wage–employment trade-off did not have such a clear pattern. But we can read from the table it favored wage growth for the smallest (10–49) and the largest (1000+) groups, employment growth actually being negative in the latter case. In all other size-groups the employment growth rate was substantially higher than wage growth. The bias to wage growth relative to employment growth in the smallest and the largest size-groups have probably different explanations. The wage growth in the 10–49 size-group is likely to have been a supply-side phenomenon as the period saw a faster increase in the alternative earnings of labor in the unorganized (informal) sector. For the very large firms (1,000+) the tilt to wage growth reflects the continued effort on the part of employers to trim the number of permanent workers and increase the efficiency of the smaller body of the workforce through higher wages per worker.

Conclusions

The review of the Indian experience in formal manufacturing over the last quarter of the century revealed the enormous fluctuation in employment elasticity from period to period. Starting with the period of 'benign' growth in the last half of the 1970s, when employment elasticity was nearly unity, employment growth turned somewhat *negative* in the period of 'jobless growth' in the 1980s. It picked up to a reasonable, but not unduly high, value of 0.33 during the reform period, when output growth was also high. But it slumped badly to a substantial negative figure in the latest post-reform years of 1996–2001 when output growth also stumbled.

We have learnt from the decomposition model that there are three sets of factors affecting employment elasticity, given the rate of growth of real value added: (i) the trend in the share of wages as measured by our α; (ii) the wage–employment trade-off; and (iii) the trend in the domestic real exchange rate or the relative movement over time of the producer-price index relative to the consumer-price index. The last variable is, for the present analysis, more in the nature of an exogenous factor which defines the rate of growth of the wage bill in consumer prices (which is of relevance to the workers' welfare). The first two are labor-market variables. At first sight they might both seem be related to the strength or weakness of workers' organization like trade unions, but this would be overlooking the different decision-making processes at the firm level which affect the two variables.

The model has a strong suggestion that the employment elasticity resulting from the interaction of these factors will have a cyclical pattern. This is because expectations about future market conditions play a critical role in the model with two factors – capital and labor, which are both, quasi-fixed. The model enables us to decompose the determinants of employment elasticity into these three key factors. It is applied to the case of formal manufacturing in India over the period 1974–1975 to 2001–2002.

As predicted the employment elasticity does show the cyclical pattern – and four phases are distinguished. They correspond reasonably way to different periods of the recent political economy of Indian development culminating in the reform period (1986–1996) and the immediate post-reform period of 1996–2002. The relative importance of the three key factors in the fluctuating trend of the employment elasticity over the four periods is discussed – particularly in terms of the changes in labor-market institutions.

While the illustrative case of India is interesting in itself, some of the findings are of general importance for many economies in the globalizing world.

First, a strong finding was that the downward trend in the DRER has been persistent for the last two decades of the past century. The DRER is of course closely related to the terms of trade of manufactured products to that of primary commodities (particularly cereals). This turning of the terms of trade against the latter has been noted in the literature (cf. Kaplinsky 2006 for a recent contribution). In the Indian case desegregation of the manufacturing sector shows that the competitive pressure facing manufacturing producers in the domestic market after liberalization might have as much to do with downward trend of the DRER (which seemed to have gathered momentum in the post-reform period) as the trend in prices of the growing manufactured exports.

Second, the close relationship between the investment rate and the share of wages (or with α) is established in the Indian case and we have provided independent evidence of the importance of growing importance of internal finance to the boom in investment in the reform period. Although economies would differ in the importance of this connection, it is probably of general importance, and would indeed be found to be of importance in the determination of employment elasticity in most economies.

Third, wage–employment trade-off is a key determinant. It is influenced partly by employer perception of the expected demand for labor relative to the perceived cost of altering the complement of permanent workers. On the other hand, institutions on the labor side will play an important role the decisions about this trade-off. Some of the theoretical issues as well as possible empirical differences between regions of the world were discussed in Mazumdar (2003).

In this chapter, the Indian case illustrates how difficult it might be to reduce the perception of labor as a quasi-fixed factor of perception once it has been established in the industrial culture. Our discussion of the reform period in India showed that important changes have been made in the direction of slackening the rigidity in the labor market of the formal sector, both in the way labor unions operated and the way job-security legislation was being implemented. But the results do suggest that employers continue to be wary of the fixed costs of increasing their complement of permanent labor, and the downward revision of expectations in the post-reform years of 1996–2002 is seen to have had a strong effect in tilting the trade-off to wage growth relative to employment growth.

In the previous section of the chapter we looked at some selected issues for disaggregated sub-sectors of formal manufacturing. The analysis was applied, for example, separately to groups of industry classified by trade exposure and technology. An important result is that while the elasticity of employment fell in all categories in the post-liberalization period (period IV) compared with the previous one, revealingly it fell most in the low-technology exposed industries and the least in high-technology domestic industry. Sectors more exposed to trade have tended to have higher employment elasticity in both periods but it also suffered a decline in elasticity in the post-reform years. However, while employment elasticity declined across the board, the reasons for the decline differ according to the degree of exposure to trade. In the more exposed industries, the choice of techniques that tilted towards higher wages instead of employment – which is consistent with firms adjusting to raise skills and productivity of workers – has been the more important factor behind reducing elasticity. In the less exposed domestic industries, the domestic real exchange rate effect – the increase in consumer prices relative to producer prices – has been more important one.

Appendix 1

The decomposition model used in the paper

The following are the variables used:

w = real wage (average earnings per worker)
S_w = wage bill (in current prices)
V = value added (in current prices)
v = value added (in constant prices)
L = employment
P_p = index of producer prices
P_c = index of consumer prices

The relationship defining the movement of the wage bill with respect to value added over time is specified by the following equation:

$$S_w = A\,V^{\alpha} \qquad (1)$$

A is a positive constant less than unity, determined by the base-year share of wages; α is a technological and behavioral parameter which is assumed to remain constant over the period under consideration. However, it can take any positive value and would generally vary from one economy to another depending on the factors determining the share of wages over time. If it has a value of unity, the share of wages remains constant. A variable written with a dot on top ($\dot{}$) represents the *proportionate* rate of change of the variable concerned.

Note that from (1)

$$\dot{S}_w = \alpha \dot{v}$$

where A is a positive constant less than unity, determined by the base-year share of wages.

We can then write the equation for the real wage growth as:

$$\dot{w} = \dot{S}_w - \dot{L} - \dot{P}_c \qquad (2)$$

$$= \alpha(\dot{v} + \dot{P}_p) - \dot{L} - \dot{P}_c$$

$$= \alpha\dot{v} - \dot{L} + \alpha P_p - \dot{P}_c \qquad (2a)$$

(Output Effect – Employment Effect + Price Effect)

The trend rate of growth of real wages is thus seen in equation (2a) to be the sum of three effects: the output effect is the first term of the right-hand side; the employment effect is the second term; and the sum of the third and fourth is the price effect. The equation focuses our attention on employment elasticity as being an outcome of the trade-off between employment growth and wage growth. But it is seen that the borders of this trade off are governed by three variables: output growth; the value of the α parameter determining the trend in the share of wages; and the price effect. The equation shows that real wage growth is higher the lower is employment growth. But two other factors have an impact upon it: the output effect, which is the part of the real wage increase ascribed to real growth in value added, given the value of α; and the last two terms, showing the impact of changes in the price levels facing producers and consumers over time.

The price effect is really composed of two distinct elements. The last two terms in equation (2a) could be re-written as:

$$(\alpha - 1)\dot{P}_p + \dot{P}_p - \dot{P}_c \qquad (3)$$

The first term in (3) could be called the wage-share effect of price changes over time. If $\alpha < 1$, the share of wages in net output falls over time in current prices in accordance with equation (1). In this case the first term in (3) is negative, showing that a certain part of the real output growth, as measured by this term, is not available for the growth of the real wage bill. It is clear that the higher the inflation rate the greater will be the leakage from the available wage bill in real terms to support wage and/or employment growth. As mentioned in the second section of this chapter, this effect can be traced to the lag in the adjustment of wage to the inflationary increase in prices. The second term is the rate of change in the ratio of producer to consumer prices or the so-called domestic real exchange rate (DRER). One can intuitively grasp its importance by considering the case of an inflationary economy in which the exchange-rate depreciation lags behind the rate of inflation – a common enough scenario in developing countries. In this case the consumer-price level that affects the real value of workers' wages increases faster than producer prices that are tied to international prices of traded goods. Thus the second term in (3) is also negative implying that a portion of the real output growth is used to keep the wage bill growing at the same real rate. Both these price effects, if negative, can be thought of as leakages from the real output growth, which decrease the rate of growth of the portion available for supporting either employment or real wage growth.

Appendix 2

A model of investment rate and the share of wages

The following definitions apply:

P = profits of the firm in the period in question
I = investment Planned for the period
V = Value Added produced by the investment
σ = productivity of the capital investment
S_p = propensity to save of entrepreneurs out of profits

In the equilibrium portrayed in Figure 8A2.1 it is assumed that the wage per man has been determined within the constraints of institutional factors mentioned in the text. Thus the both the supply of work units per worker and the wage cost per work unit is determined, and it is assumed it is constant for the range of work units needed. For any share of profits in value added P/V (and hence the wage bill) we then have a supply of work units forthcoming as the product of number of workers and the supply of work units per worker. The curve in the fourth quadrant is the result of the production function – combining the capital used (as determined by the investment ratio corresponding to the profit share) with the quantity of work units available. It shows diminishing return to the use of capital per work unit (for a given technology and economic environment of the period in question). As K/L increase with I/V along the y-axis of this quadrant, the productivity of capital σ falls.

The curve in quadrant I on the other hand shows the *feasibility* of sustaining different values of profit share. The profit share is the residual from the value added after the pre-determined wage bill is deducted. Obviously it increases with

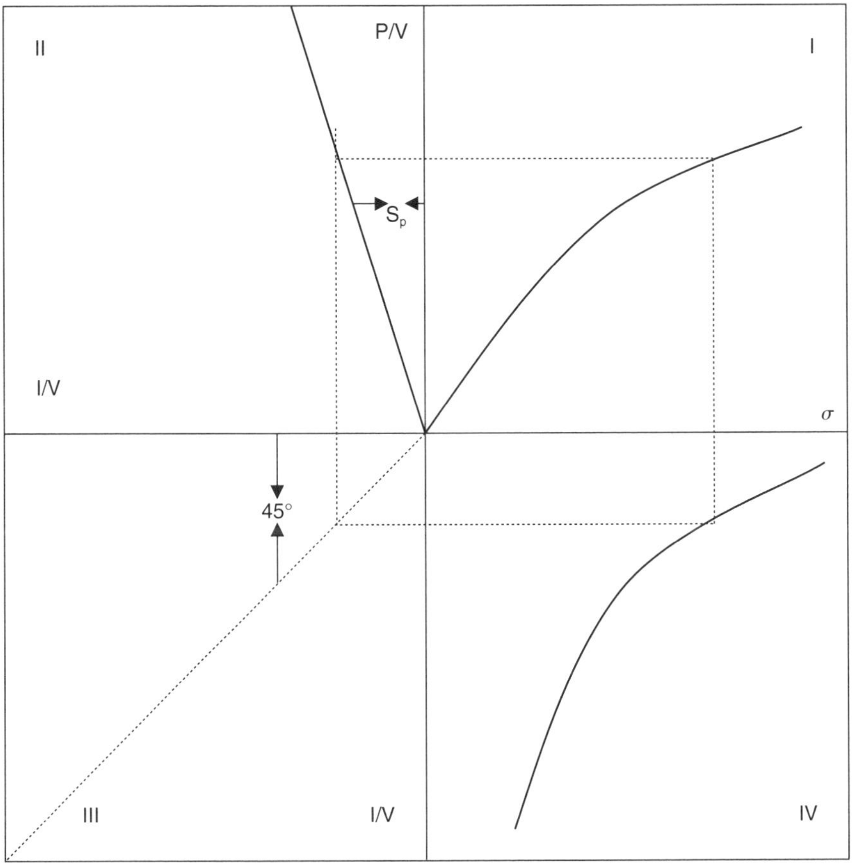

Figure 8A2.1 The equilibrium with capital productivity (σ) profit share (P/V) and investment share (I/V).

the productivity of capital σ (some non-linearity in the function is allowed in the diagram to allow for increase in marketing costs but this detail is unimportant).

In equilibrium the share of profits which is attained in any period must satisfy both σ and the share of investment (I/V) which is desired. But given the production function, σ varies with the amount of investment and hence with I/V. If the system is to stay in equilibrium the σ yielded by the production function has to be consistent with that yielded by the function of Proposition 1. The full equilibrium can be described in the diagram shown as Figure 8A2.1.

Quadrant 2 depicts the relationship between the Investment ratio (I/V) on the x-axis and the profit share on the vertical. Following Kaldor (but not invoking the aggregate demand or macro-economic aspects of his analysis), the relationship is a straight line at an angle less than 45 degree to the vertical axis, i.e., a slope of S_p (less than one) where $I/V=S_p(P/V)$, S_p being the propensity to save of the profit earners. The straight line in quadrant 3 copies the investment ratio from quadrant 3 to the vertical axis of quadrant 4. The relationship between I/V and σ (negative assuming diminishing returns and a given production function) is portrayed in Quadrant 4.

The dotted lines show the full equilibrium of the system in any period. The planned I/V ratio at the beginning of the period must be sustained by a level of σ *and* a share of profits as shown in quadrants 4 and 2 respectively, and both must be consistent with each other as per the relationship shown in quadrant 1. Any attempt, given the production function and market conditions, to increase I/V leads to a lower σ and a hence lower P/V than what is required to finance the investment. The wage–price nexus required to support the increased I/V fails as it comes up against the inflation barrier posed by workers' wage demands and/or the loss of competitiveness in the product market.

The reform process, by relaxing the constraints on the markets for inputs and outputs, can be expected to shift the production function upwards, as discussed above, and thus the schedule in quadrant 4 relating I/V to capital productivity shifts outwards. Firms can then sustain a higher I/V ratio relative to the pre-reform situation with a higher σ and a higher profit ratio.

Firms differ in their levels of capital productivity. Thus comparing equilibrium positions across firms or groups of firms (or industries), we get a testable hypothesis:

> *Hypothesis 1: The share of profits (wages) will be higher (lower) the higher (lower) the I/V ratio and the level of capital productivity.*

Disequilibrium situations

In any period, it would be unusual for the system to be in complete equilibrium. But any deviation from it would tend to be corrected in the next period. Thus suppose entrepreneurs plan a certain I/V ratio on the basis of information about the profit share and capital productivity in period t-1. They would expect the system to be in equilibrium with these values of the three variables in period t. But suppose capital productivity falls short of the expected value in period t. Then P/V is not large enough to sustain the planned I/V, and in planning for the next period entrepreneurs would aim at a lower I/V unless they have reason to believe that the shortfall was due to exceptional events. Considering that the observed points of different combinations of the three variables are likely to be a series of disequilibrium points, we have a hypothesis much like *Hypothesis 1* above. In other words:

> *Hypothesis 2: Even if we do not have firms differing in their levels of capital productivity in equilibrium, we would expect to see that the observed share of profits (wages) is directly (indirectly) related to the investment ratio and capital productivity.*

Testing the hypotheses

We tested the hypotheses emerging in the discussion of the last section by regressing the value of α, the elasticity of the wage bill with respect to value added (and hence determining the trend in the share of wages) on the investment ratio and capital productivity. The data for the years from 1986–1987 to 1994–1995 by the five size-classes of firms were pooled together. Since we get only nine observations for each size class, it was decided to test a fixed-effect model (i.e., a pooled regression model with size-group dummies). The results are presented in Table 8A2.1.

The result shows that both investment ratio and capital productivity are negatively related to dependent variable α. The coefficients of size dummies are also negative relative to the smallest size class of 10–49 workers, showing that the effect of size on alpha is negative. All the independent variables are significant.

In the regression model of Table 8A2.1 the absolute value of capital productivity has been used. We have also tried an alternative specification of capital productivity, viz. taking capital productivity of each size class for the year 1986–1987 as 100 and then calculating the capital productivity separately for each class for successive years. Such a specification neutralizes the initial disparity in capital productivity as between different size-classes. The estimated coefficient of capital productivity in this specification also turned out to be significantly negative.

The results lend support to the conclusions from the Kalecki (1971) model outlined above. The increased rate of investment induces the dynamic firm to plough back the surplus above material and wage costs into the financing for investment. The decrease in the share of wages, which this process involves, is

Table 8A2.1 Regression results for alpha (α)

Dependent variable	α		
Model: Fixed-effect model with size dummies			
R^2 = 0.715 F-values = 13.724			
Variables	*Estd. coeff.*	*t-values*	*Significance*
Constant	1.55415	9.03	0.000
Investment ratio	–0.00190	–3.76	0.001
Capital productivity	–0.00001	–3.65	0.001
Size dummies			
1 50–199	–0.246	–5.43	0.000
2 200–499	–0.295	–5.40	0.000
3 500–999	–0.434	–6.71	0.000
4 1,000 and above	–0.449	–5.84	0.000

Note
The constant term absorbs the effect of excluded dummy variable size-group 10–49. The estimated values of other size dummies are with respect to the excluded size-group.

possible because of the increase in total-factor productivity. The higher rate of surplus can be generated without a decrease in the rate of growth of real wages and of employment below a threshold, which might have triggered worker resistance, or a potential shortage of labor of requisite skills. As we have seen, the fall in the share of wages in value added in the third period was accompanied by a much reduced rate of real wage growth, but it continued to be positive, and the rate of employment growth actually increased substantially.

9 Dualism in Indian manufacturing

Causes and consequences

The evidence presented in Chapter 8 of the generally low employment elasticity in organized manufacturing suggests that much of the growing labor force outside agriculture has been absorbed either in the tertiary sector or in unorganized manufacturing. Since the gap in labor productivity and earnings between the unorganized and the organized sectors is large, this leads to the phenomenon of 'dualism' in the manufacturing sector – which is alleged to be the source of welfare loss both from the efficiency and equity angles. There are in fact two aspects to 'dualism'. The first has its origin in the productivity gap and distribution of employment between the 'formal and the 'informal' sectors, where the demarcation line between the two is fixed by the internationally comparable definition of the use of more than five workers in the establishment. Second dualism would be accentuated if, within the formal sector, distribution of employment is skewed heavily to large firms, with relatively small representation of small and medium enterprises. In other cases the distribution of employment, even within the 'formal' sector, might be strongly bi-polar, with two peaks of employment at the low and the high end of the size spectrum, and a wide range of size groups with a relatively small number of workers. This is the phenomenon of the 'missing middle'.

Categories in the 'unorganized' manufacturing sector

Before embarking on a detailed analysis of the problem it is important to be clear about the sub-groups within informal manufacturing (or the unorganized sector, as it is called in India), and which sub-sector we are considering in our comparison with the formal (organized) sector.

The data on the sub-sectors in manufacturing outside the ASI sector (analyzed in the last chapter) as well as trade and services come from the sample surveys organized by the National Sample Survey. The surveys used the sample frame of Economic Censuses conducted by the Central Statistical Organization (CSO) of the Government of India in selected years. The Unorganized Sector Surveys define three categories of enterprises, classified by the size of enterprise and the type of labor used:

1 Own-account manufacturing enterprises (OAME). These units make use of only of family labor, and most of them are on the household premises.
2 Non-directory establishments (NDME) which have at least one hired worker, but the total size of all workers (including family labor) do not exceed five.
3 Directory manufacturing establishments[1] (DME) which have at least one worker hired more or less on a regular basis and their total complement of workers is six but less than ten. If it is more than ten then the enterprise is under the purview of the Factory Act and is part of the formal sector covered by the *Annual Survey of Industries.*

> Within the unorganized manufacturing sector nearly 67 percent of the workers were in own account enterprises in 2001 (Table 2). The proportion of workers in own account units was even larger in rural areas 79 percent, compared to urban, 43 percent. Less than 20 percent of workers were in the larger unorganized enterprises with 6–10 workers (DME) and about 14 percent were in the NDME, less than 6 workers. Overall workers were engaged in larger enterprises in urban areas, 30 percent in DMEs and about 26 percent in NDMEs. Over the period 1983 to 2001, the share of employment in the larger units increased marginally.
>
> (Unni 2006, p. 219)

The OAME units represent the 'pure' informal sector, based on households and in most cases in the same premises. They generally pursue the traditional or craft activities. A great deal of the NDMEs also fall into this type of activity, although they make use of 'at least one' hired worker (who indeed might be partly a house servant). For our purposes we will use the DME sector as representing a part of the formal sector – the other component of the latter being the sector covered by the ASI including units with ten or more workers. Admittedly this demarcation is to some extent arbitrary, determined by the practices of the National Sample Survey. But it stands to reason that the establishment has entered a more 'modern' economic relationship when it has graduated to a six-worker employment size. This size group is also a highly convenient one because it permits comparison with other countries in the region (see below).

The DME sector is then be distinguished, at the lower end, from the informal sector on the one hand – comprising the very large household sector – and the smaller non-household units. At the upper end it is demarcated from the larger-scale component of the 'organized' manufacturing sector covered by the ASI (which was discussed in the last chapter). Table 9A.1 gives the size distribution of the entire spectrum of enterprises, including the sub-sectors of the unorganized as well as the formal sector in manufacturing.

Distribution by size-groups in manufacturing could be considered with respect to either value added or employment. In fact, the former is the more basic of the two and is the product of two separate variables: first, the distribution of employment by size groups; and second, the differences in productivity or value added per worker as between size groups. In what follows we will work with these two variables to shed more light on the economic processes involved. Wages generally increase proportionately with labor productivity. Thus the extent of productivity differentials between small and large units would reflect differences in wage levels between them. In so far as informal sector undertakings would have wage and productivity near to the levels found in the smallest size-group in the formal sector, the large-small productivity differential in the formal sector would also be a measure of the economic distance between the informal and the formal sector firms in the economy concerned.

The size distribution and labor productivity differentials by size-group: India relative to selected Asian countries

This section seeks to present a snapshot of the Indian pattern of size distribution and productivity differential by size in manufacturing relative to selected Asian countries. It should be noted that we are confining ourselves to the size-distribution *within* the 'modern' sector. That is to say, our international comparison refers to the second aspect of 'dualism' mentioned above: the establishments employing five or more workers. Data could be assembled for only a few Asian countries, for various years in the late 1980s.

Table 9.1 presents data on the distribution of employment by size groups, while Table 9.2 sets out the data on relative labor productivity for the various size groups. The data reported in Tables 9.1 and 9.2 for other Asian countries also have a similar cut-off points at the lower end based on employment size they are comparable to the Indian statistics.

Basically three 'types' can be distinguished within this small sample:

1 a fairly even-size distribution in which small, medium and large firms plays more or less equally important roles and the productivity difference between the size classes is small;
2 the pattern in which the distribution of employment by size groups is distinctly skewed to the large firms. Typically in this pattern the productivity difference between large and small firms tends to be substantial; and
3 the 'dualistic' pattern in which there is a strong mode at both ends of the distribution – a relatively large proportion of employment is found both in the small and the large size groups. Within this 'type' two sub-types can be distinguished depending on the extent of the productivity differential between small and large firms.

(i) The first group is classically represented by the case of Hong Kong. As can be seen in Table 9.1 employment was fairly evenly distributed among the various size-groups, with the small enterprises playing as much a role in the island's manufacturing structure as medium and large enterprises. At the same

Table 9.1 Percentage distribution of employment by size-groups in manufacturing, selected Asian countries (various years in the 1980s)

Size-groups	*India 1989–1990*	*Korea 1986*	*Japan 1987*	*Hong-Kong 1982*	*Malaysia 1981*	*Philippines 1988*	*Taiwan 1986*
5–9[1]	41.8	3.8	13.2	12.2[2]	4.3	21.5	10.4
10–49	10.1	20.6	29.2	27.4	20.5	13.6	24.0
50–99	5.9	12.9	12.9	15.6	13.5	6.5	13.5
100–199	6.2	12.7	11.6	14.5	15.4	8.9	28.1
200–499	7.7	14.8	12.4	13.8	16.6		
500 and over	28.0	35.0	20.8	16.5	29.7	49.5	24.1

Size-groups	*Indonesia 1985*	*Size-groups*	*Thailand 1989*
5–19	29.5	1–4	3.7 (0.7)
20–49	9.3	5–9	4.9 (1.2)
50–199	13.3	10–49	17.3 (8.4)
200–995	25.2	50–99	9.3 (9.1)
1,000 and over	22.8	100–299	17.9 (20.7)
		300–499	10.2 (16.1)
		500 and over	36.6 (43.7)

Sources: India: Directory of Manufacturing Establishments (6–9 workers) and Annual Survey of Industries (10+)
Korea: *Statistical Yearbook*
Japan: *Statistical Yearbook*
Hong Kong: *Annual Digest of Statistics*
Malaysia: Onn Fong Chan (1990, p. 161)
Indonesia: Hal Hill (1983, Table 19, p. 91)
Taiwan: Abe and Kawakami (1997, Table 1, p. 386)
Philippines: National Statistical Office
Thailand: *Yearbook of Labor Statistics*. The figures in parentheses are for the provinces surrounding Bangkok which saw the fastest growth of manufacturing in the last two decades.

Notes
1 6–9 for India. The sources for India are fully documented in Mazumdar 1997b.
2 1–9 for Hong Kong.

time, the difference in labor productivity between the largest and the smallest size-group is the smallest in the sample (Table 9.2).

The pattern of distribution in Hong Kong could be usefully compared with that in the Japanese economy which has been characterized by the strong role of small establishments. It will be seen from Table 9.1 that although the modal size group for both Hong Kong and Japan is the small enterprises of 10–49 workers, the proportion of employment in large enterprises of 500+ workers is significantly larger in Japan. Further, the data in Table 9.2 show that productivity differences between small and large firms were much less in Hong Kong. The wage differential between small and large units was accordingly much smaller. Average earnings in Hong Kong in 1982 were only 55 percent higher in establishments with more than 1,000 workers than in those with 1–9 workers. In Japan the wage differential was twice as much.[2]

Table 9.2 Relative productivity (value added per worker) by size-groups of enterprises in manufacturing, selected Asian countries [around 1985]

Size-groups	*India 1989–1990*	*Korea 1986*	*Japan 1987*	*Hong Kong 1982*	*Malaysia 1981*	*Philippines 1988*	*Taiwan 1986*
5–9	12[3]	31	32	54[4]	54	9[4]	34
10–49	39	42	39	61	58	30	35
50–99	45	59	50	66	73	56	38
100–199	60	56	59	71	94	74	49
200–499	74	81	76	82	93		
500 and over	100	100	100	100	100	100	100

Size-groups	*Indonesia 1985*
5–19	21
20–49	44
50–199	84
200–999	95
1,000 and over	100

Source: India: Directory of Manufacturing Establishments (6–9 workers) and Annual Survey of Industries (10+)
Korea: *Statistical Yearbook*
Japan: *Statistical Yearbook*
Hong Kong: *Annual Digest of Statistics*
Malaysia: Onn Fong Chan (1990, p. 161)
Indonesia: Hal Hill (1983, Table 19, p. 91)
Taiwan: Abe and Kawakami (1997, Table 1, p. 386)
Philippines: National Statistical Office
Thailand: *Yearbook of Labor Statistics*. The figures in parentheses are for the provinces surrounding Bangkok which saw the fastest growth of manufacturing in the last two decades.

Notes
3 6–9 for India.
4 1–9 for Hong Kong.
4 1–9 for the Philippines.

Hong Kong comes closest to a free-market model of development in Asia. Beng (1988) observes that 'within the proclaimed *laissez faire* environment in Hong Kong the government does not seem to have a policy towards manufacturing not to mention any policy towards the SSIs' (p. 88). An obvious hypothesis emerging from the Hong Kong case is that left to itself modern industry makes efficient use of small enterprises in a striking way. Also, in the absence of the usual set of policy biases which protect both capital and labor in large firms, labor productivity and wage differentials are kept within fairly narrow bounds.

Of the other countries represented in the sample, Taiwan comes close to the Hong Kong pattern. The size distribution is very similar. While the productivity difference in Taiwan would seem to be larger if we compare the lowest and the highest size-groups, closer examination shows that this appearance is largely due to the high relative productivity of the largest (500+) size-group in Taiwan.

Value added per worker rises very gently up to the level of the large firms of 500 plus workers, and then seems to take a big jump.

Differences in wage levels, as measured by average earnings of the workers between the smallest and the largest size-groups, are almost the same for Taiwan and Hong Kong.[3]

(ii) The second pattern in our sample is a size distribution of employment which is skewed to the right, with the modal size-group employing 500+ workers.

The countries in our sample which show this distribution are Korea and Thailand, although, as of 1986, Korea had a larger presence of smaller firms than Thailand, particularly in the 20–50 size-group. But Korea had been consciously trying to develop its small and medium sectors since about a decade earlier. In 1976, when the proportion of employment in the largest size-group peaked at 45 percent, the Korean distribution was much more skewed – almost at par with Thailand's.

Malaysia is another country which, in 1981, showed a pattern of distribution skewed to the large size-group. But it can be seen from Table 9.2 that the productivity differential between small and large firms is much smaller than in the case of Korea. Thus we would expect different economic forces operating on the size distribution in the case of these two countries.

(iii) The 'dualistic pattern' is characterized by, first, the strong presence of both small establishments and large firms, and second, the substantial economic distance between small and large firms. The classic case of this type is Japan. The 'dualistic' pattern of Japanese industrialization has a long history. It has its roots in the initial surplus-labor conditions prevailing in Japan during its initial industrialization (which contributed to labor-market segmentation) and the simultaneous development of a complex tying large industry, the state and financial conglomerates which accentuated capital market dualism.

The other less developed countries in Asia – the Philippines, Indonesia and India – all share with Japan the dualistic pattern in their modern (formal) manufacturing sector.[4] There is, however, a big difference with Japan, which is brought out in Table 9.2. The productivity difference between the small and the large size-groups of firms is much larger in these Asian countries than in Japan. Thus while the 'surplus labor' situation in Asian countries makes the 'dualistic pattern' emerge in a wide variety of Asian economies, Japan had, by the middle 1980s, succeeded in narrowing the gap in productivity between small and large firms which typically characterizes the dualistic development. We will return to this point later.

In South Asia, the extreme peculiarity of the Indian structure is immediately apparent. India has an exceptionally large proportion of employment in the lowest size-group of 6–9 workers and an exceptionally low relative value added per worker in this group. Furthermore, the size distribution is characterized by a large presence of the 500+ group of firms with a conspicuous 'missing middle'. This pattern resembles that of Japan in terms of a 'dualistic' development, but is wildly exaggerated in the Indian case. There can be little doubt that this outcome

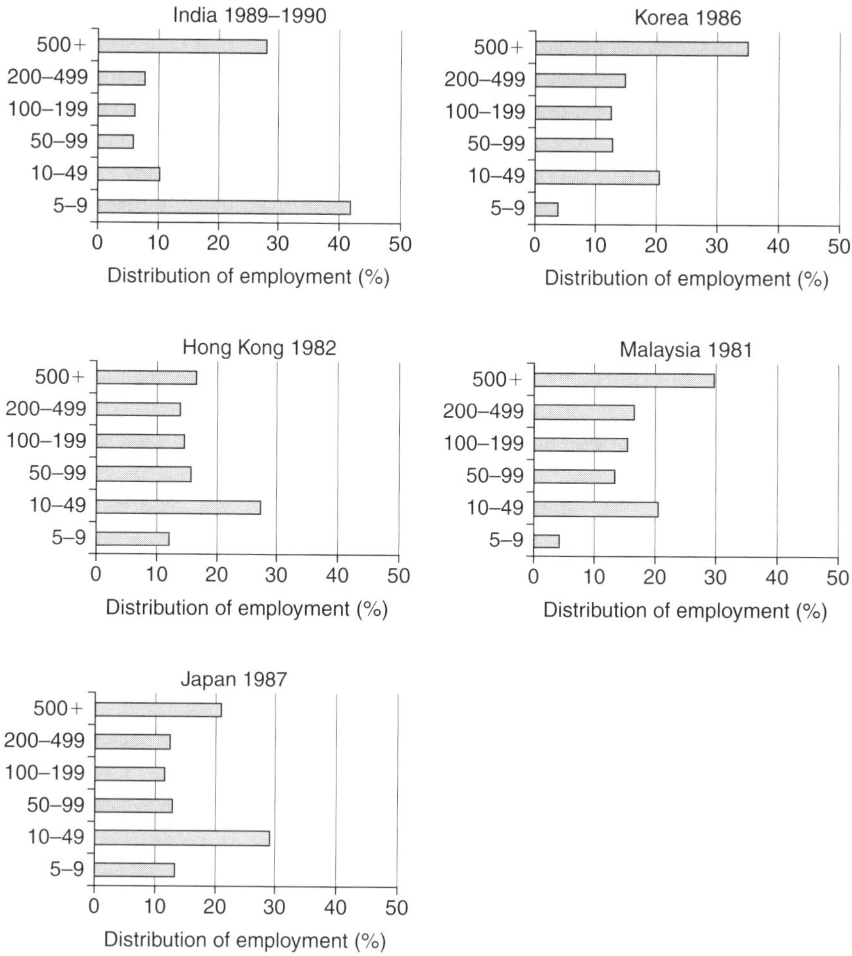

Figure 9.1 The missing middle manufacturing firms: India compared to other countries (source: Figures are taken from Table 9.1).

is basically due to the protectionist policy adopted by the government since 1950 which favored the small scale.

The problem of the missing middle

Figure 9.1 shows the extreme case of the formal manufacturing sector in India – how employment was concentrated in the two extreme size-groups compared with the other Asian countries.

It would seem in the Indian case there are formidable obstacles to the small units growing beyond a threshold size into middle-sized ones. This is a serious barrier in so far the middle-sized entrepreneur is often the most dynamic, and the competitiveness (and hence efficiency) of the manufacturing sector depends a good deal on the buoyancy of such units.

The productivity gap between the informal and the formal sectors in manufacturing

The second problem distinguishing the Indian case from the other Asian countries is the much larger productivity gap noticed in India. In Japan, Korea and Taiwan the labor productivity in the largest units (employing more than 500 workers) was around three times that in the smallest units. In India it was *eight* times as large. Even in less developed Asian country like Indonesia the larger units had labor productivity no more than *five* times that in the smaller units.

The policy of SME development in India

Both the two exceptional characteristics of the Indian case can be traced to have its origins in the peculiar policy of industrial controls practiced in the first 40 years or so after independence. In India a dual system of protection has been in effect since the beginning of independence. On the one hand, the policy has been to protect the small-scale from the competition of the large – the policy of 'reservation', under which a long list of items has been designated as the exclusive preserve of the small-scale (defined in terms of the value of capital assets). The capacity of production of these items by large-scale units has been frozen at the level at the time of the legislation. At the same time, the import substituting industrialization has protected all domestic units – small and large – from the competition of foreign firms. The result has been that small and large firms have developed their own niches of markets in different lines of production without too much competition between them or from foreign firms.

This method of fostering the growth of SMEs was first introduced in 1967 and the list of items "reserved" for the small-scale have been progressively increased and in the mid-nineties it comprised a total of around 830.[5] The value of the limit in plant and machinery has been increased over time in nominal terms, but the increase in value of this limit after allowing for inflation has been small.

Initially, this approach encouraged the establishment of large numbers of new SE units which were protected from competition from the large-scale sector. But the problem with the continuation of such policies is two-fold: (i) in attempting to select *labor-intensive products or industries*, it misses the point that labor-intensive enterprises are found in many, nearly all industries, not just a limited set which can be easily identified; and (ii) it is not sufficiently biased towards small enterprises which show potential for growth.[6]

(i) Industry-based policies of reservation overlook the fact that small enterprises are not confined to specific product lines, and that their importance in different product groups is constantly changing. What is needed is for policies to have a *pervasive* effect so that all small enterprises, no matter in what product groups, could potentially take advantage of the assistance measures available.

Small enterprises are generally more labor-intensive than large ones, especially if size is defined in terms of fixed investment rather than employment. But it does not mean that they are concentrated in industries where the *mean* capital–labor ratio is particularly low. SMEs are found in many industries. There is no reason that in any economy the number employed (or the proportion of total output or investment) in SEs would be larger in those industries which have a less than average K/L ratio than in those in which the ratio is above the average. This is because there is a spectrum of techniques within each industry, and enterprises of different sizes and capital intensities will be found in most of them.

(ii) Turning to the second point of criticism, it is important that SE support policies do not discourage the growth of small into medium enterprises. Here the approach of the Indian package of polices has been the opposite of what is desired. Along with the reservation policy, there have been a number of fiscal subsidy programs and other forms of support which provide benefits to enterprises below a certain size. Thus there is a built-in disincentive for enterprises to go beyond this size limit. Labor laws on wages, benefits and job security are applied to units *above* the critical size. Enterprises graduating out of the protected small sector are thus faced with extra costs even as they are denied the benefits of fiscal subsidies and other programs.

The effect has been a polarization of the industrial structure. The small-scale and large enterprises have increasingly occupied different niches of the market in the same industry. Even when industries are defined narrowly in terms of specific product lines, there is generally a great deal of difference in the quality of the product. Small enterprises with low wages and less mechanized techniques occupy the lower end of the spectrum, catering to the demand of low-income consumers, while larger mechanized firms serve the high price segment of the market. The classic example is the textile industry. Small units with non-automatic, often reconditioned, looms ('powerlooms', as they are called in India) produce cheap cloth, while the large factories with automatic looms produce more durable cloth for the upper-class domestic and export markets. This type of polarization accentuates dualism and increases the productivity and wage gap between the small and large sectors.

Post-reform developments

The package of reforms in the last decade could be expected to have made a serious dent to the traditional policy of protection for the small scale. On the one hand, liberalization of import controls, particularly on a range of consumer goods, should have reduced the strength of the protective umbrella. At the same time the relaxation of the licensing system for large-scale industrial units could be expected to have reduced the effectiveness of the policy of 'reservation' for small enterprises. What is the evidence on the effect of these developments on the size structure of manufacturing?

Table 9.3 Percentage distribution of employment in different size classes

Type and size	*1984–1985*	*1994–1995*	*2000–2001*
6–9	40.27	44.91	41.52
10–49	9.47	10.34	10.42
50–199	11.83	13.31	15.34
200–499	8.27	8.56	9.49
500–999	7.65	7.02	8.87
1,000 and above	22.52	15.85	14.35
All	100.00	100.00	100.00

Source: Unorganized manufacturing survey 40th, 51st and 56th rounds of NSS and ASI, various years.

Table 9.4 Indices of labor productivity by size groups (500+ = 1.00)

Type & Size	*1984–1985*	*1994–1995*	*2000–2001*
6–9	0.19	0.12	0.10
10–49	0.42	0.35	0.37
50–199	0.53	0.47	0.49
200–499	0.86	0.77	0.84
500–999	1.06	0.98	1.02
1,000 and above	0.98	1.01	0.99

Source: Unorganized manufacturing survey 40th, 51st and 56th rounds of NSS and ASI, various years.

Note
Growth of labor productivity is given in Table 9A.2.

The relevant data culled from the NSS Establishment Surveys and ASI for the various dates are given in Tables 9.3 and 9.4. They are graphed in Figure 9.2.

As far as the distribution of employment is concerned the only change over the period covered seems to have been a significant reduction in the number employed in very large firms (1,000 and above). The distribution is, however, still bi-polar with strong modes at the employment size groups at the two extremes (6–9 and 500+).

The productivity differentials by size-groups seem to have changed even less. If anything the extreme 'dualism' noticed in India compared with other Asian countries seems to have worsened since 1984–1985, though much of the deterioration occurred in the first half of the nineties.

Size structure of enterprises in the ASI sector

The problem of the 'missing middle' carries over into the large-scale or ASI sector of manufacturing. The inability or unwillingness of smaller non-ASI units to grow is reflected in the paucity of small-scale establishments in the latter. Little *et al.* (1987) pointed out the peculiarly biased structure of employment

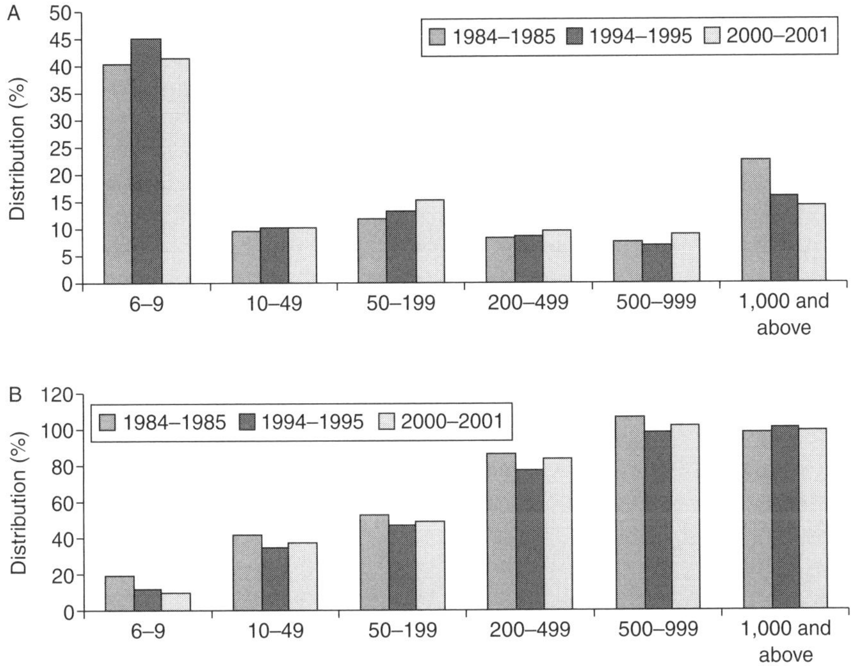

Figure 9.2 India – distribution of employment and productivity by size groups. Panel A: Distribution of employment (in %) in manufacturing firms by employment size groups. Panel B: Index of labor productivity by different size of firms (source: ASI data).

Note
The slabs have been adjusted to take care of the varying length of the size groups (see Little *et al.* p. 88).

in the ASI sector for the early year of 1977. The proportion of total employment in size-groups increased progressively as one went from the smaller to the larger groups. In other words, the dualism one noticed in formal manufacturing as a whole, taking the ASI and the DME sectors together, was not apparent when one looked at the ASI sector by itself. Rather, the distribution was heavily skewed to the largest size-group. This picture contrasted starkly, not only with the experience of Japan, which had a 'cascading' employment structure with the proportion of employment falling as the size category increased, but also with the United States, Korea and Taiwan. All three of these had an employment distribution more or less resembling the 'normal' curve and had the highest proportion of employment in the 100–500 size-group (or what might typically be called the 'medium-scale' units). The dominance of the very large firms in India had been whittled down somewhat between 1956 and 1977, but even so in 1977 the establishments with more than 1,000 workers accounted for no less than 45 percent of the total employment in the ASI sector.

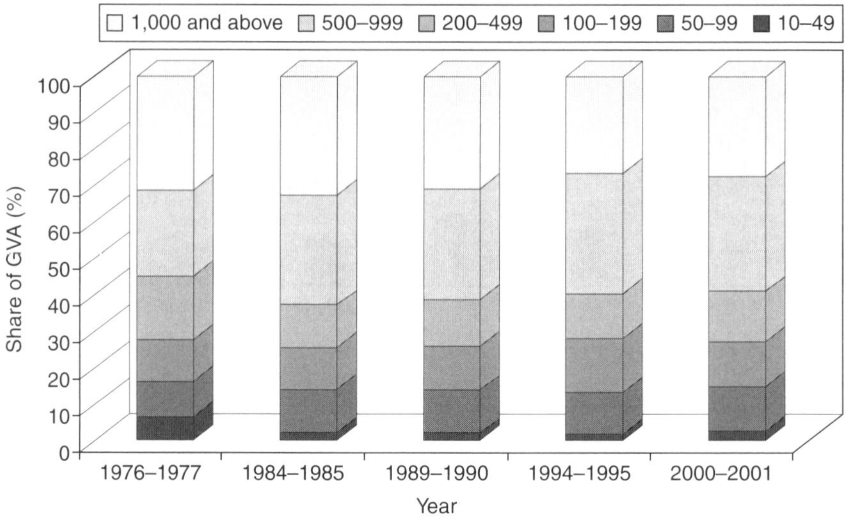

Figure 9.3a Size structure of ASI GVA.

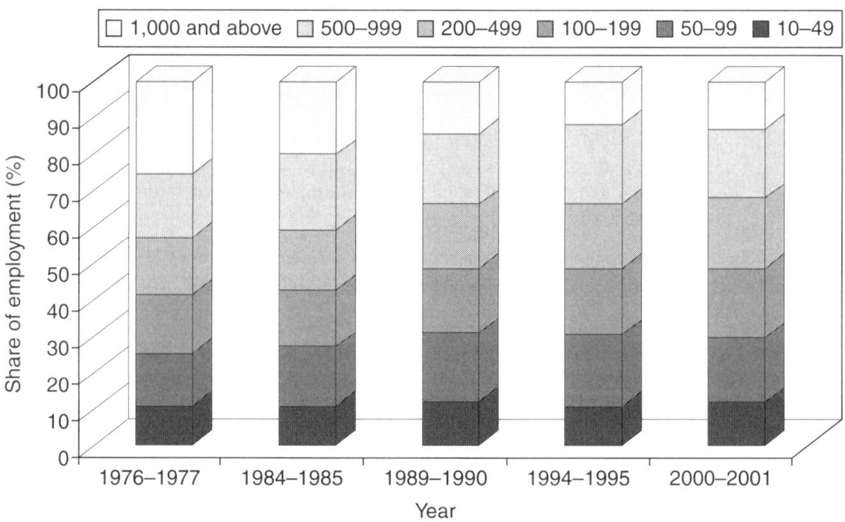

Figure 9.3b Size structure of ASI employment.

Note
The slabs have been adjusted to take care of the varying length of the size groups (see Little *et al.* 1987: p. 88).

How does the size structure look in more recent years? The package of reforms in the last decade could be expected to have made a serious dent to the traditional policy of protection for the small scale. On the one hand, liberalization of import controls, particularly on a range of consumer goods, should have reduced the strength of the protective umbrella. At the same time the relaxation of the licensing system for large-scale industrial units could be expected to have reduced the effectiveness of the policy of 'reservation' for small enterprises. What is the evidence on the effect of these developments on the size structure of manufacturing?

The evolving picture in the last 25 years of the last century is presented in Figures 9.3 which give the distributions of value added and employment respectively for different years. It is clear that the whittling down of the largest size-groups, which had been noticed earlier between 1956 and 1977, continued in the recent decades. But it is also clear that much of this change took place before the post-reform period. In fact the biggest reduction in the importance of the size-groups of 1,000 and above had taken place in the early eighties and was associated with the closure of many cotton and jute mills.

Uchikawa (2002, p. 46) found that the

> average gross profit ratio between 1979–1980 and 1997–1998 was highest in units employing 50–99, second in units employing 100 to 199 and lowest in units employing 1,000 and above. Medium scale units were (therefore) dynamic sector to gain employment and investment. That is a reason why medium scale units increased employment.

He emphasized that this did not mean that medium-scale units were more profitable than large–scale ones in the same industry. In fact, many of the large units were in the depressed textile industries which were suffering from gross inefficiency and had to be closed down or retooled. These industries pulled down the gross profit ratio for large units in the manufacturing sector as a whole.

Nevertheless, there were some new industries which had a growth rate of value added in excess of 10 percent per annum (between 1979–1980 and 1997–1998) and were also home to many of the medium-scale units. These industries were chiefly NIC 26 (textile products or wearing apparel), NIC 29 (leather and leather products) and NIC 30 (chemicals and chemical products). Firms in these industries contributed to the improvement of average gross profits in the medium-scale units. There was a good deal of churning of establishments in these industries. Many medium-scale units failed, but others merged to take their place.

We can use the ASI to present a disaggregated picture of the industrial structure, and its changes in the post-reform years. It is worth emphasizing that the persistence of dualism in India appears to cut across most manufacturing sub-sectors. Data disaggregated by sectors show that in 14 of the 18 two-digit industries the largest shares of workers are found in the *smallest* of the ASI groups (10–99 group). Comparing 2000–2001 figures with those of 1994–1995, it is seen that the loss in the share of employment was found in the 100–199 class for as many as 13 out of 18 industries (Table 9.5). It is likely that both these developments are due to the barrier imposed by the job-security legislation which comes into play for units with 100 or more workers. There is a distinct disincentive for establishments to cross this threshold. One way industrial units could deal with the difficulty of crossing the employment barrier of 100 workers is to resort to subcontracting of some of their product lines or components. This topic is discussed in the next sub-section.

Table 9.5 Change in employment shares by factory size 1994–2000: gainers and losers

Industry	*Employment-size class of factories*					
	10–99	*100–199*	*200–499*	*500–999*	*1,000–1,999*	*Above 2,000*
Food	3.5	–4.7	–2.0	–5.6	2.3	5.4
Beverage and tobacco	–48.9	–3.4	–4.7	–11.5	2.4	63.0
Cotton textiles	5.0	–6.5	–4.3	–3.1	–5.4	–1.0
Other textiles	0.1	–1.6	7.2	–3.0	–6.7	–1.4
Jute	0.6	–0.1	–0.5	0.9	–4.4	3.3
Textile products	–11.3	–9.4	18.8	5.8	4.3	4.7
Wood	–12.8	1.9	4.9	1.7	2.3	0.0
Paper	13.0	–3.4	1.5	–5.5	–4.9	–0.2
Leather	–4.1	–11.7	16.7	0.9	5.3	–4.3
Chemicals	–11.8	4.9	5.7	0.1	–2.5	1.5
Rubber	19.0	–8.7	0.2	–4.0	1.6	–5.8
Non-metallic minerals	3.0	–3.5	0.9	–0.5	3.0	–1.7
Basic metals	5.3	–4.0	–4.3	–7.2	–0.5	3.0
Metal products	1.9	0.2	7.4	–1.9	1.3	–6.4
Machinery	4.4	–4.5	6.7	–0.4	1.4	–9.0
Transport equipment	7.4	1.4	1.3	2.5	0.1	–15.7
Miscellaneous	–5.7	–7.3	7.8	–3.8	–6.2	15.5
Repairs	50.9	–0.2	–1.5	–5.9	–4.7	–27.4

Source: Calculations by Ramaswami (2006) based on ASI data.

To sum up, the size structure of industry in the organized sector, as in the manufacturing sector as a whole, showed only limited change in the post-reform years. There was one clear change: the relative decline of very large units of 1,000 and above. But this was mainly due to the sickness and decline of old industries – chiefly cotton and jute. There is some indication of medium-scale units emerging. But the trend is not a particularly striking one. The ASI sector is still skewed to large-scale establishments. At the same time dualism in manufacturing continues to be striking because of the large employment in very small units outside the ASI sector (even if we leave out of consideration the non-directory establishments and household units).

The role of subcontracting in Indian manufacturing

The fall in the share of 100–199 size-group in a large number of industries, which we infer from the data in Table 9.5 has its counterpart in the rising practice of contract labor. Contract intensity (the percentage of contract labor used to the total labor force in the establishment) in export-oriented or import-competing industries peaks in the 100–199 group when we look at disaggregated groups of industries (Ramaswamy 2006, Table 9.5). This happens probably in response to firms searching for more flexible ways to respond to changing market conditions facing the firms more exposed to global competition.

Use of contract labor is of course not the only form of devolution of activity by larger firms to smaller units. Much the more important method is that of outsourcing – getting smaller firms to produce some components of the final product or producing inputs used in the manufacture of the final product. Subcontracting in this sense has been historically a very important part of the dual structure of the Japanese manufacturing economy, and it has been praised as an ideal system of ensuring the co-existence of small and large firms without sacrificing the efficiency and competitiveness of the sector. But this favorable outcome depended crucially on the subcontracting system graduating from a dependant to a technologically advanced system. It has been noted in the literature that, with advanced technology spreading rapidly, the quality of subcontractors' output became increasingly important, along with their costs. Accordingly, large primary enterprises came increasingly to monitor and upgrade the quality of subcontractors as well as select them carefully (Kaneda 1980, p. 43). This type of *keiretsu* or 'vertical inter-firm hierarchy' spread rapidly in the fast growing industries like machinery, automobile, metal working and electrical appliance industries. A 1981 survey conducted by the Central Bank for the Ministry of Commerce and Industry revealed that 51.5 percent of the more than 1500 subcontracting firms surveyed claimed that their technology was equal to or even superior to their parent companies (Koshiro 1990, p. 202). The traditional subordination of the subcontractors faded away over a large area of the SME sector with this increasing technological independence. In matters of pricing, negotiated rates for the products supplied by the subcontractors increasingly replaced the old system of dictated rates.

What is the evidence of subcontracting in India developing in the direction of the Japanese model? Ramasawmy (2006) has used data on this point from the ASI and classified them by size-groups of enterprises and the type of industry. His results are reproduced in Table 9.6.

It is clear that in India the largest incidence of product outsourcing takes place, not in larger firms, but in the smallest size groups. This would suggest that the motivation for outsourcing is rather different in India than in the Japanese model. It would seem that small firms are anxious not to grow beyond the employment

Table 9.6 Product outsourcing intensity by employment size of factories: 2000–2001

Employment size	*Export oriented*	*Import competing*	*Auto*	*Food*	*Others*
0–9	22.1	26.2	–	36.2	11.2
10–99	8.8	11.4	27.6	12.5	11.8
100–199	6.1	9.1	7.7	7.4	4.7
200–299	7.7	6.2	–	10.5	5.6
Above 300	6.3	3.4	4.0	8.6	4.2
Total	6.3	4.0	6.0	10.0	5.1

Source: Calculations by Ramaswami (2006) based on ASI data.

size of nine workers as it would make them come under the purview of labor laws. This is an altogether different scenario from the Japanese model where outsourcing was perceived more as a policy of vertical disintegration by large firms.

Further evidence on this point is provided in the evidence collected by the 'Unorganized Sector Survey of the NSS. Using this source, Unni (2006) reports that 30 percent of firms in this sector undertook subcontracting work for other firms. The industries in which this percentage was particularly high were: tobacco products (89 percent), textiles (56 percent), chemical products (67 percent) and office accounting and computing. Consistent with the small size of the typical firm which outsourced work, the firms catering to the demand for such work were even smaller. The distribution of subcontracting firms by place of work showed that the overwhelming portion of them (81.2 percent) operate at home, and only 15 percent in business premises. It seems that much of this activity was non-mechanized. While 88 percent of the firms reported receiving raw materials from the contractor, and 93 percent reported working to design specified by the latter, only 7 percent were supplied with any equipment for the work.

One is left with a strong impression that the subcontractors in Indian manufacturing are yet to graduate from the dependent status vis-à-vis the parent firm with a low level of technology. It is a far cry from the Japanese model in which many of the subcontractors were dynamic small firms actively seeking out large producers anxious to collaborate in the production of finished products, and were often at the technological frontier, with a high grade of specialized workforce.

The problem of 'dualism' in Indian manufacturing

We have, in the material provided so far in this chapter, discussed the size distribution in Indian manufacturing and brought the peculiarity of the Indian size structure compared with other Asian countries. "Dualism" and the problem of the 'missing middle' were identified as a dominating characteristic of the Indian structure. Why is this a problem, and in what sense can we consider this phenomenon to be a major factor retarding manufacturing growth in India? We turn to a discussion of this group of questions in this part. Following a discussion of the impact of 'dualism' we discuss the proximate causes of its origin. This discussion leads us to an analysis of the persistence of this phenomenon even when some of the policy distortions seem to have been removed in the post-reform years.

Why is dualism a problem for manufacturing growth?

Why should we regard the phenomenon of 'dualism' in manufacturing as drag on the growth and performance of the manufacturing sector? Of the many points relevant here the more important are the following:

1 the impact on allocative efficiency and wage inequality;
2 the dynamic impact on the growth of skilled labor and entrepreneurship;
3 the stagnation in the growth of markets for manufactured goods.

Allocative efficiency and inequality

The large gap in productivity between the firms in the two extreme size-groups, as described in the data on manufacturing presented above, suggests the existence of a large gap in the marginal products of labor and capital between the two classes of firms. We know from independent evidence that large firms have access to capital supplied by the formal financial institutions, while small firms mostly have to depend on local informal sources of finance and the interest-rate differential between these sources can be huge (Little *et al.* 1987, Chapter 15). It is also well known that wage levels follow differences in labor productivity and large firms have a wage per worker which, even after we have controlled for measurable human capital attributes, are much higher in the large firms. Again the detailed study in a specific labor market (Bombay City) reported in Little *et al.* (1987, Chapter 14) revealed that, after allowing for the effect of education, training, occupation and knowledge of English, wage per person of *manual* workers in the largest-size-class of factories employing 1,000+ workers was almost twice the level in 'small' enterprises with less than ten workers. Two conclusions are suggested by this evidence of size-related factor price differentials: first, the larger the differential the larger is the loss in welfare in terms of static allocative efficiency theory; second, since employment in the 'dualistic' is concentrated in the smallest and the largest size-groups, inequality in the distribution of wage per person is very unequal.

Impact on dynamic efficiency

In a more dynamic sense the missing middle implies a weak process of graduation of small firms and the development of entrepreneurship. It is arguable that the dispersion of entrepreneurship as well as industrial technology over a wide spectrum of spatially and economically distributed regions is dependent on the mushrooming of medium-scale enterprises, into which the small units are able to graduate.

Similarly dualism slows down the growth of the labor force with industrial skills. This is particularly true in developing economies in which many of the skill requirements of modern industry (including discipline in the workplace) are acquired by on-the-job-training rather than education in schools. The slow growth of the skilled workforce in its turn has an impact on the choice of technology. It has been established that capital-intensive techniques have been adopted in economies or sectors more in response to a shortage of skilled rather than unskilled labor. Thus a potential shortage of skilled labor of the type needed by modern manufacturing could dampen the value of employment elasticity and slow the rate of growth of employment in the industrial sector. An important result in our research work on Indian manufacturing in the preceding chapter was the evidence that although employment elasticity varied with the economic cycles it did not exceed 0.33 in the best period of the post-reform upswing. As analyzed in the research there are several important reasons for the low employment elasticity, but a perceived shortage of labor of the requisite skill and efficiency is one of them.

Dampening the growth of markets

While the last two points emphasize problems created on the supply side, 'dualism' might also affect the growth of manufacturing through its impact on the demand side – on the expansion of markets for industrial goods. The medium-sized establishments have been lauded in the literature for having the desired amount of flexibility and enterprise to seek out new export markets in new industries. But their importance in the expansion of domestic markets also needs to be emphasized. Dualism strengthens and perpetuates product market segmentation. The market for industrial products is split into low-quality products catering to the need of low-income consumers, and supplied by small-scale local producers on the one hand, and the higher-quality segments which the large establishments supply to a limited number of high-income consumers. The lack of integration of markets could be a bottleneck in the development of mass markets for manufactured consumer goods.

Causes of the emergence and persistence of dualism

What are the major factors causing the emergence of dualism in its two aspects, the phenomenon of the 'missing middle' and the unusual productivity gap between the small and the large units? What are the reasons for its persistence over time, even when the reform process reducing some of the strength of the proximate causes of dualism has been eroded?

The more important reasons behind the origin and persistence of 'dualism' will be now be discussed under the following heads:

1 segmentation in the factor markets – of (i) labor and (ii) capital;
2 education policies affecting the relative price of skilled labor;
3 the policy of protection of the small scale;
4 hysteresis causing persistence of critical causal factors.

Segmentation of factor markets

LABOR MARKETS

An important factor which cements labor-market segmentation and discourages the upward mobility of small establishments is labor legislation. The aspect of this type of legislation which is most relevant to the problem of the missing middle in India pertains to job security laws rather than those impacting on wage levels. Wage differential between small and large firms are known to have preceded the era of wage legislation and could be traced to some extent to differences in the quality of labor. Wage cost per efficiency unit of labor was probably never as large as the difference in wage per worker in small and large firms (Little *et al.* 1987, Chapter 13 and the literature cited). Job-security legislation, such as those embodied in the Industrial Disputes Act of 1947, however, is critical since it places enormous costs on factories in so far as they have to obtain permission from the state designated authorities before *permanent* workers can be laid off. It is not so much the actual compensation that has to be paid to workers who are laid off which is important as the fact that the process of obtaining permission takes a long time and has considerable uncertainty. Even if the number of workers sought to be laid of in a particular period of time is small, the law creates a fixed overhead cost (of, for example, maintaining legal officers who can pursue the long process through the labor courts), which is only mildly variant to the size of the workforce in the factory. Thus over a considerable range of size, the overhead costs would be significantly higher for smaller firms than the larger ones. Labor legislation of this type bites for factories employing more than 100 workers. Other types of labor laws involving inspection and supervision over conditions of work are applicable to units covered by the Annual Survey of Industries (employing ten or more workers). Both sets of legislation add to the fixed cost of labor for units employing more than the respective threshold.

Employers have various means of working round these legislative requirements. For instance, a common practice is to employ part of the workforce as 'casual' labor: although they work regularly in the unit they are kept in the books as non-permanent labor as long as inspectors can be kept off the practice by bribes or other means. Similarly, in some states of India employers wanting to close down factories have deliberately refrained from paying electricity bills which have led to the effective closure of the units. But all these ways of finding ways of adjusting the labor force to avoid confrontation with the law imply the incurring of transaction costs. The possibility of bearing such costs is a clear discouragement to small employers to expand vertically in size. There is an incentive to expand horizontally with a multiplication of small units rather expanding into larger size groups.

CAPITAL MARKETS

It is well known that modern financial institutions find it much easier to lend to larger establishments than to smaller ones The high transaction costs of dealing with small units, as well as the relative scarcity of collaterals, operate against the latter, The result is the interest cost of finance – even when it is available – typically tends to be significantly higher for small units. Financial liberalization and globalization have, if anything, increased the effective bias on the part of largely urban-based financial institution to lend to large-scale establishments.

State policies in India have sought to counter this bias by creating institutions like the Small Industries Development Organization (SIDO) which have reached out specifically to the units under their purview (whether defined in terms of employment or capital size). Units which expand beyond this size tend to lose both ways – deprived of the special opportunities provided under SIDO and not large enough to avail of the low-cost finance potentially available in the modern large-scale sector. This type of segmentation in the capital market strongly discourages the growth of small firms into middle-sized ones.

Education polices

Policies that have been implemented in India over the years have been biased towards the promotion of tertiary education and have neglected basic primary and low secondary education.[7] It has been maintained in the literature (e.g., by Adrian Wood among others) that modern manufacturing requires a minimum of basic education for a workforce to be able to perform up to minimum standards in modern manufacturing. Small- and medium-sized units – adopting comparatively labor-intensive technology – benefits from an ample supply of such labor. They are contrasted with tiny units which could use nearly unskilled labor with less than primary education for low-grade production, but would find it difficult to grow beyond a certain scale with such labor. The relatively plentiful supply of skilled labor with higher education biases production to less labor-intensive industry and modes of production. Large units have a comparative advantage in using such labor which smaller units cannot afford.

Recently researchers in the IMF (2006) have explored the question if the organized manufacturing sector in India has specialized more in industries using less unskilled labor compared with other countries. The authors use the cross-country data sets for the formal manufacturing sector prepared by the United Nations Industrial Development Organization (UNIDO) to identify industries (at the 3-digit level) which are 'labor-intensive'. For labor intensity the proxy is

> the share of wages in value added for the industry in a country averaged across a broad group of developing countries – examples of industries that score highest on labor intensity are clothing, printing and publishing and non – electrical machinery while those which are lowest are beverages, tobacco and petroleum refineries.

Labor-intensive industries are identified as those below the median on the range of scores thus calculated. The authors then examine the pattern of manufacturing in each of the countries in their sample to determine the share of output/employment in labor-intensive industries. They regressed the shares of each country on per capita GDP, its square and a dummy for India. It was found that even for as early a date as 1981 the Indian dummy was negative and significant in the value-added regression, signifing that it was specializing exceptionally in less labor-intensive industries. For employment the Indian scenario was in the same direction but less significant.

In the next exercise the authors analyzed skill-intensity, using the input – output matrix for South Africa – which enables them to classify industries by the share of remuneration of highly skilled and skilled workers. As with labor intensity the industries in each country were divided into above and below median skill-intensive ones and then the ratios of value added of the two subgroups (in the cross-country sample) in 1981 were regressed against GDP per capita, its square, country size and the dummy for India. The dummy was strongly significant and positive, showing that in 1981 India was abnormally specializing in skill-intensive industries.

In order to see what has been happening since the early eighties, the authors plot the evolution in the share of output generated in labor-intensive industries for India and a select group of comparer countries – which include China, Indonesia, Korea and Malaysia. India contrasts dramatically with Indonesia which shows a rising share of labor-intensive industries. Korea and Malaysia – at much higher income levels – also show mildly increasing shares. China, on the other hand, has a declining share of such industries but from a much higher level of this share (see ibid., Figure 2, p. 48). Turning to the topic of skill intensity, the graphs for the evolution in comparator countries also show that

> India's share which was already high in 1980 despite its lower level of per capita income, has been increasing and is at levels reached by Malaysia or Korea at much higher levels of per capita income. There is also a striking contrast with China. China's share of output in skill-intensive industries is lower than India's and has been virtually flat.
>
> (Ibid., p. 22 and Figure 4, p. 52)

The tilt towards skill-intensive industries in India is also reflected in exports: the share of India's exports in skill-intensive goods has increased from 25 percent in 1970 to 65 percent in 2004.

The protection of small-scale units

The policy of protecting small-scale enterprises (SSEs) has been an important aspect of Indian industrial policy since independence. It has taken the form of reservation of large number of items for production in exclusively small units and the provision of incentives – fiscal, financial and legislative – as long as the units stayed below a certain size. The threshold size was first defined in terms of the traditional employment size of five workers. It was in later years changed to a definition based on capital size and it was also increased somewhat over the years. Nevertheless, the policies have always provided an incentive for entrepreneurs to expand horizontally with more small units, rather vertically with larger middle-sized units.[8]

Hysteresis

The policy of reservation for the small scale was largely ended in the post-1991 reform process. But we have seen that the impact on the size structure of establishments in manufacturing has been minimal. This limited impact might be due to widely recognized processes in which a socio-economic system established over a long period of time tends to persist even after the original causes have disappeared. This persistence is not just due to inertia. Economic agents and institutions acquire characteristics which sustain the system. For example, entrepreneurs develop with ambitions to think in terms of horizontal rather than vertical growth. Marketing channels, financial institutions and infrastructure are geared more to supporting small units with limited market rather than dynamic units growing into larger sizes and different markets.

It is not easy to determine how much of the inertia of the industrial structure can be ascribed to 'hysteresis'. It should be remembered that there are institutional factors, particularly labor legislation and the segmentation in the capital market, which continue to reinforce the dualism in this sector, with the attendant problems discussed in this chapter.

Conclusions

This chapter has dwelt on the peculiarities of the size structure in Indian manufacturing, relative to the experience of other comparator Asian countries. The employment size distribution is pronouncedly bi-modal. This is not just the usual phenomenon, often witnessed in developing countries when we put the household enterprises in the informal sector together with the modern enterprises in the formal sector. Rather the Indian scenario is peculiar when we take the 'organized' – or what is internationally accepted as the 'formal' – sector employing five or more workers. The size distribution in this subset of organized sector firms shows two strong modes in India, in the 5–9 and 500+ size-groups. There is a very large productivity differential between these groups, and a conspicuous feature of the size distribution is the low proportion of workers in its middle part. We have discussed the analytical and empirical reasons as to why this phenomenon of the 'missing middle' could be considered to be a significant drag on the healthy development of a dynamic manufacturing sector. While the problem of the 'missing middle' might have had its origins in past policies it has shown a remarkable persistence in the post-reform era. We refer to some possible reasons for this persistence in the previous section of the chapter.

Appendix

Table 9A.1 Number of workers (in millions)

	1984–1985	*1989–1990*	*1994–1995*	*2000–2001*
OAME	25.4	22.8	20.5	25.1
Establishments	15.6	17.0	17.3	19.8
NDME	4.3	4.4	4.1	5.6
DME	4.5	5.7	5.5	6.5
ASI (Organized)	6.7	6.9	7.7	7.8
Gross value added (in Rs. billion)				
OAME	118	119	104	174
Establishments	563	773	1,086	1,511
NDME	63	61	60	103
DME	71	83	95	134
ASI (Organized)	429	628	932	1,274
Productivity (Rs. Per worker)				
OAME	4,662	5,222	5,057	6,929
Establishments	36,116	45,456	62,736	76,328
NDME	14,610	13,901	14,573	18,479
DME	15,583	14,709	17,318	20,800
ASI (Organized)	63,790	90,547	120,723	163,775

Sources: Unorganized Manufacturing Enterprise Survey (NSS) various years and ASI, various years.

Table 9A.2 Growth of labor productivity (in % per annum)

Type and size	*1984–1985 to 1989–1990*	*1989–1990 to 1994–1995*	*1994–1995 to 2000–2001*
OAME	2.30	–0.64	5.39
Establishments	4.71	6.66	3.32
NDME	–0.99	0.95	4.04
DME	–1.15	3.32	3.10
ASI (Organized)	7.26	5.92	5.21

Sources: Unorganized Manufacturing Enterprise Survey (NSS) various years and ASI, various years.

10 Growth of employment and earnings in the tertiary sector

The growth of the tertiary sector in India seems to be somewhat out of line with international experience of recent decades. Table 10.1 brings together the data for sectoral changes in the *shares* of employment for several Asian countries over the last three decades of the twentieth century. The newly industrializing countries of Asia – Korea and Taiwan – had their share of employment in manufacturing increasing much faster than that of the tertiary sector during their initial period of growth in the 1970s. In the next decade tertiary-sector employment grew faster, but the magnitude of the increase relative to manufacturing was not nearly as high as was observed in India during this decade. Only in the 1990s, after Taiwan and Korea had developed into mature industrialized economies, did their tertiary sector become the dominant provider of employment outside agriculture. By contrast India's share of employment growth in the tertiary sector in the seventies was already 60 percent *higher than in manufacturing*. Since then, the decades of 1980s and the 1990s have seen a virtual stagnation in the share of employment in manufacturing, with the tertiary sector absorbing virtually the entire loss of employment share by the agriculture. The figures also show that other developing countries of Asia – Thailand, Malaysia and Indonesia – do have their larger shares of employment created in the tertiary sector, but the contrast with India is that none of them have a stagnant share in manufacturing in any decade. On the contrary, something between a third and one half of the often large decline in the share of employment in agriculture was taken up by manufacturing. The only country in the sample with an experience close to that of India is the Philippines.

The tertiary sector has been the leading sector of growth in the Indian economy in recent decades, both in terms of output and employment (Table 10.4). The employment elasticity in the sector as a whole in the post-reform period (1993–2000) has been 50 percent higher than in manufacturing sector. Is this growth due to labor being pushed into the sector because of limited growth of jobs in the productive sector or due to labor being pulled into it because of increasing earnings? Are there different trends in different components of the tertiary sector, and between the formal and informal segments of it? What light do the trends in the tertiary sector throw on the process of equitable growth in India?

Table 10.1 Change in the sectoral shares of employment

Country	*1971–1980*			*1980–1991*			*1990–2000*		
	Agriculture	*Manufacturing*	*Tertiary*	*Agriculture*	*Manufacturing*	*Tertiary*	*Agriculture*	*Manufacturing*	*Tertiary*
Rep. of Korea	–14.4	8.3	6.0	–17.3	5.0	12.9	–7.6	–6.7	14.5
Taiwan, China[1]	–15.6	11.1	3.7	–6.6	1.7	8.9	–5.0	–4.1	9.2
Thailand	–1.4	0.3	1.7	–10.5	3.2	7.3	–15.3	4.3	10.2
Malaysia	–14.8	6.1	9.9	–10.4	4.6	6.6	–7.9	2.9	3.0
Philippines[2]	–1.4	–0.7	2.1	–6.2	–0.6	6.7	–7.8	0.3	7.6
Indonesia				–2.7	1.3	1.1	–10.9	2.8	7.1
India[3]	–5.5	1.8	3.0	–4.6	0.0	3.4	–3.6	0.3	2.4

Sources: For the last period calculated from ILO Year Book data.
1 Figures for first two periods are obtained from Mazumdar and Basu (1997, Table 3.2, p. 38).
2 For all periods calculated from ADB *Key Indicators*, 2001.
3 For all periods calculated from NSS adjusted by population from decadal census. The periods refer to 1973–1983, 1983–1993 and 1993–2000.

We should mention at the outset that the Indian statistical series do not allow for the construction of time series of employment and output by formal and informal sectors, however defined. Hence the substance of our analysis in this part will be based on the study of trends in the tertiary sector as whole. We will address the question of absorption of labor in this sector at low- and high-income levels, as well as the earnings gap between 'good jobs' and 'bad jobs' in the sector by looking at the entire distribution of earnings in the sector. But before we come to this analysis it would be useful to give an overview of the structure of employment in the tertiary sector at one time period, i.e., 1999–2000. The 55th round of the NSS, however, included some questions which provide criteria for distinguishing the formal and the informal sub-sectors within the tertiary activities. The broad structure of tertiary employment will be clear from these data.

Formal and informal sub-sectors within the tertiary sector

The 55th round questionnaire obtained information on the type of establishment in which a worker was employed. We grouped workers in all public and semi-public establishments as being in the formal sector. This round of the NSS also reported for the first time the employment size of the establishment in which a worker was employed. We take ten workers as the cut-off point, with those in establishments with ten or more workers being in the formal sector. For the large group of self-employed workers we adopt the usual classification in terms of the workers' education. Those with lower secondary education or less are in the informal sector, and the more highly educated (which would include the professionals) are in the formal sector. These criteria help us to give a rough picture of the composition of tertiary-sector employment for the year 1999–2000 across formal and informal sectors (Table 10.2).

The following points emerge from Table 10.2:

1 The formal sector accounts for a quarter of tertiary employment in the rural areas and rather more than a third in the urban economy. Overall it accounts for 30 percent of all tertiary-sector employment.
2 Even after the decline of public-sector employment in the post-reform period, this sector still accounts for more than half of *formal* tertiary employment in the urban areas, and more than two-thirds in the rural.
3 Females account for a small part of tertiary employment in the formal sector, and surprisingly no more than 10 percent of informal tertiary employment, both in the rural and the urban areas. It should, however, be remembered that we included only UPS workers (principal workers).
4 The share of the self-employed in the non-public part of the tertiary employment is high, but contrary to expectations it is higher in the formal sector of both the rural and urban economies.

It will be interesting to know how the levels of employment in the formal and informal segments of the tertiary sector compare with those in manufacturing.

Table 10.2 Distribution of employment in the tertiary sector: formal and informal (in percentages)

Category	*Formal*			*Informal*		
	Males	*Females*	*Total*	*Males*	*Females*	*Total*
Rural						
Public	64.1	82.8	66.8	–	–	–
Private regular wage	10.8	11.2	10.9	16.1	15.4	16.0
Casual wage	–	–	–	32.3	27.6	31.7
Self-employed	25.0	6.0	22.4	51.5	57.0	52.3
Total	100.0	100.0	100.0	100.0	100.0	100.0
% of rural tertiary	19.1	3.1	22.2	67.6	10.1	77.8
% of all tertiary	7.7	1.3	9.0	27.4	4.1	31.5
Urban						
Public	52.7	64.3	54.5	–	–	–
Private regular wage	15.8	22.3	16.8	26.6	33.2	27.6
Casual wage	–	–	–	23.5	26.7	24.0
Self-employed	31.5	13.4	28.7	49.9	40.1	48.4
Total	100.0	100.0	100.0	100.0	100.0	100.0
% of urban tertiary	30.6	5.6	36.1	54.2	9.7	63.9
% of all tertiary	18.2	3.3	21.5	32.3	5.8	38.0

Source: Estimated from NSS unit-level Data of 55th round.

Table 10.3 throws light on this question. It is seen that three-quarters of all employment outside agriculture and construction are in the tertiary sector and this percentage is only slightly more in the urban areas. As is to be expected, a larger proportion of tertiary employment is in the formal sector in urban areas. But the rural areas still have a good deal of formal-sector presence.

Employment elasticites by broad sectors

We presented the basic tables in Chapter 3 on employment trends by broad sectors of the economy (Table 3.1) Table 3.1 combined output trends calculated from the National Accounts Statistics with employment trends obtained from the NSS which provides an overview of employment elasticities over a time period for sectors at 1-digit National Industrial Classification (NIC 1987). The employment estimates are based on Usual Principal Status Workers (UPS).

The major points to emphasize from these tables are:

1 Tertiary-sector employment grew faster than manufacturing in all three periods. The differential in the growth rates was much higher with respect to agriculture, particularly between the 50th and the 55th rounds. However, we should remember that the employment growth in the last period was disproportionately affected by the fall in employment-growth rate in the agricultural sector.

Table 10.3 Tertiary employment as a percentage of the total in manufacturing plus tertiary 1999–2000

Area	*Formal*			*Informal*		
	Male	*Female*	*Total*	*Male*	*Female*	*Total*
Rural	13.6	2.3	16.0	46.8	6.9	53.7
All urban	22.4	4.1	26.4	41.1	7.3	48.4
Metro	23.5	4.6	28.1	37.5	7.6	45.1
Non-metro	21.9	3.9	25.8	42.6	7.3	49.8

Source: Estimated from NSS unit-level Data of 55th round.

Note
Total employment in manufacturing plus tertiary in each area = 100.0.

2 Employment growth in the tertiary sector fell in the second half of the nineties relative both to the 1987–1993 period and even the longer 1983–1993 decade. But this was entirely because of the decline in employment in the community and social services. The table shows that compared with the 1983–1993 decade, the decline in employment growth was marginal in financial services. The rate of growth of employment increased in all other groups, particularly strongly in trade.

3 Employment elasticity mirrored the story of employment growth. The employment elasticity fell slightly in all the other tertiary sectors but was in the last period well above that in manufacturing.

Productivity differentials between sectors

Is the employment growth in the tertiary sector being driven by high demand for labor or is labor entering this sector because of lack of jobs in other production sectors. In other words, is labor being pulled or pushed into this sector? A first cut at this question is to see if there are major productivity differentials or if the productivity differential increasing vis-à-vis the production sectors as revealed by sectoral GDP figures. The data given in Table 10.4 gives an initial answer to this question.

1 The average productivity in the tertiary sector as a whole is pulled up by the high value in the financial sub-sector, but seems to be above the level of manufacturing (in 2000) in most sectors except trade (where it is 20 percent lower). There is a suggestion that the trade–manufacturing differential might have slipped over time. Between 1983 and 2000 productivity in trade relative to its base (agriculture) remained practically constant (in real terms) but went up by more than 40 percent in manufacturing. This allowed manufacturing productivity to go significantly above trade, but it is interesting to see that this differential was established only recently – between the 50th and the 55th rounds.

Table 10.4 Labor productivity by broad sectors 1983–2000

NIC 1987 classification	*Labor productivity (UPS)*				*Labor productivity index (UPS)*			
	55th	*50th*	*43rd*	*38th*	*55th*	*50th*	*43rd*	*38th*
Agriculture (0)	13,349	11,752	10,116	10,223	100	100	100	100
Mining (1)	129,579	73,754	64,802	62,920	971	628	641	615
Manufacturing (2–3)	46,999	34,444	27,547	24,801	352	293	272	243
Electricity, gas, etc. (4)	239,870	139,433	111,410	93,247	1,797	1,186	1,101	912
Construction (5)	34,406	34,492	25,551	37,543	258	294	253	367
Trade, hotel, etc. (6)	42,838	36,593	32,298	31,866	321	311	319	312
Transport, etc. (7)	60,537	48,310	42,871	38,468	453	411	424	376
Finance, insurance, etc. (8)	303,895	259,820	184,626	171,029	2,276	2,211	1,825	1,673
Community, social and other services (9)	47,729	27,137	26,387	22,588	358	231	261	221
Tertiary sector (6–9)	61,216	44,144	37,985	33,950	459	376	375	332

Source: Calculated from several years data of National Accounts Statistics (NAS) and data from four rounds of NSS.

2 Not all sub-sectors of tertiary, however, suffered the fate of NIC sub-group 6, i.e., trade. Both finance (group 8) and community and social services (group 9) improved their relative productivity vis-à-vis manufacturing. In the transport services (group 7) the relative improvement of productivity seems to have been under way since the 43rd round. But in the community and social services (group 9) the relative improvement was prominent only between the 50th and the 55th rounds. The surge in salaries in the public sector is reflected in the large increase in productivity between these two rounds in this group.

3 The above pattern suggests that there is indeed some evidence to support the general perception that some sub-groups, like the trade (group 6), have had a relatively large influx of labor pushing down its relative productivity to some extent, while others, like business services in group 7, have improved their position due to demand factors.

However, a study of trends in average relative productivity can carry us only so far in our understanding about the trends in relative earnings at which labor is being absorbed in the tertiary sector. For a more complete understanding we need to look at the way the entire distribution of earnings (or incomes) have been changing in the tertiary sector in response to the high rate of growth of employment in this sector.

Before getting into further analysis of the tertiary sector on the basis of unit-level data it will be worthwhile to discuss the limitations of the database that we have used.

Limitations of the NSS data

We need to be aware of the limitations of the main source of our data, the NSS, before proceeding further. First, a large share of employment in India is in the 'self-employed' category. There is an inherent difficulty of allocating income accruing from self-employment when more than one earner from the same household is in income-earning activity. Households from different self-employed activities by different members of the household would be typically pooled together. There is no way of distinguishing the individual contributions of individual earners. Hence the income we can deal with is household income, and we can normalize for the size of the household. Further, it is generally accepted that figures on expenditure given by the respondent in the household is more reliable than that of income. Thus we use the measure of household welfare as given by mean expenditure per capita.

When we are comparing levels of household welfare across sectors we need to identify the *principal occupation of the household.* This poses problem both conceptually and in terms of execution. The conceptual problem arises from the fact that a significant number of households will have more than one earner, and not all earners will be in the same category of occupation. The secondary earners might not be all wage earners. If they are working in the self-employed

Table 10.5 Proportion in tertiary sector for different categories of workforce

Category	*Rural*			*Urban*		
	38th round	*50th round*	*55th round*	*38th round*	*50th round*	*55th round*
Household	12.90	15.15	16.72	57.31	59.54	61.55
UPSS workers	10.75	11.48	12.51	54.57	55.40	59.17
UPS workers	11.48	12.46	13.23	54.58	56.01	59.79

Source: Estimated from unit-level data of several NSS rounds.

sector, they will be pooling their earnings with other earners of the household to create the household's pot of earnings. By assigning all the household income effectively to the principal occupation of the household we might be exaggerating the income – and the expenditure which it sustains – originating from this occupation.

In terms of execution, one of the major problems faced in the 55th round of the NSS is that, unlike in the earlier rounds, households were not classified in terms of their detailed occupational or industrial code of their main source of earnings. We first have to match household type (given in household file) to the individual workers' file which provides the code for occupation, industry, work status, etc. We generated household type for each individual worker. Thus through an arduous process we could identify main earners in most of the household and then assign main earners' industry–occupation code to the household's main earning source. The occupation–industry distribution of households will differ somewhat from that of individual earners to the extent that our matching has been unsuccessful particularly in households where more than one principal earner belongs to a different industry–occupation. The difference in the proportions of employment in the tertiary sector obtained on the basis of households and two definitions of the individual worker (usually principal and usually principal-cum-secondary status) are given in Table 10.5.

Evidence on the marginal absorption of labor

We can get some idea about the question posed – how far labor is being pulled rather pushed into the tertiary sector – by looking at the share of labor in the tertiary sector at different parts of the distribution of income. Specifically, we can look at the proportion of the main earners working in the tertiary sector in different quintiles of the distribution of household expenditure per capita for successive rounds.

Table 10.6 gives the share of household employment across different rounds. It shows that the share of tertiary sector in household employment increased over the successive rounds. Table 10.7 seeks to throw light on the question as to where the jobs were created – at the low end or uniformly across household

Table 10.6 Structure of household employment (in different NSS rounds)

Sector	*38th*	*50th*	*55th*
Primary	61.43	57.99	54.33
Secondary	14.95	15.58	16.95
Tertiary	23.62	26.42	28.72
All	100.00	100.00	100.00

Source: Estimated from unit-level data of several NSS rounds.

Table 10.7 Share of tertiary sector in different quintiles of household APCE (different NSS rounds)

Rural			
Quintiles	*38th*	*50th*	*55th*
1	8.17	7.91	10.17
2	10.41	10.77	12.50
3	11.87	14.00	14.93
4	13.84	17.21	18.31
5	20.23	25.83	27.69
All	12.90	15.15	16.72
Urban			
Quintiles	*38th*	*50th*	*55th*
1	49.80	50.46	52.34
2	53.84	56.15	60.00
3	58.71	61.05	63.24
4	60.48	64.53	64.12
5	63.72	65.52	69.04
All	57.31	59.54	61.55

Source: Estimated from unit-level data of several NSS rounds.

quintile ranges.[1] The data are presented in Figure 10.1 which shows the changes in the distribution more clearly, separately for the rural and the urban areas.

A major change seems to have taken place in the post-liberalization period (between 50th and 55th rounds) both in the rural and the urban areas, compared with the movement in the pre-liberalization period (between the 38th and the 50th rounds). In the earlier pre-liberalization years more jobs in the tertiary sector seem to have been created in the higher quintiles. The slopes of the graphs increased with the quintile groups between 1983 and 1993 (the 38th and the 50th rounds) – more prominently in the rural areas, and except for the highest quintile in the urban economy. But between 1993 and 2000 (the 50th and the 55th rounds), the graph for the rural sector shows a more or less parallel movement outwards, with some suggestion that the movement was larger in the 1–2, as well as the 5th quintiles. In the urban sector the differential movement

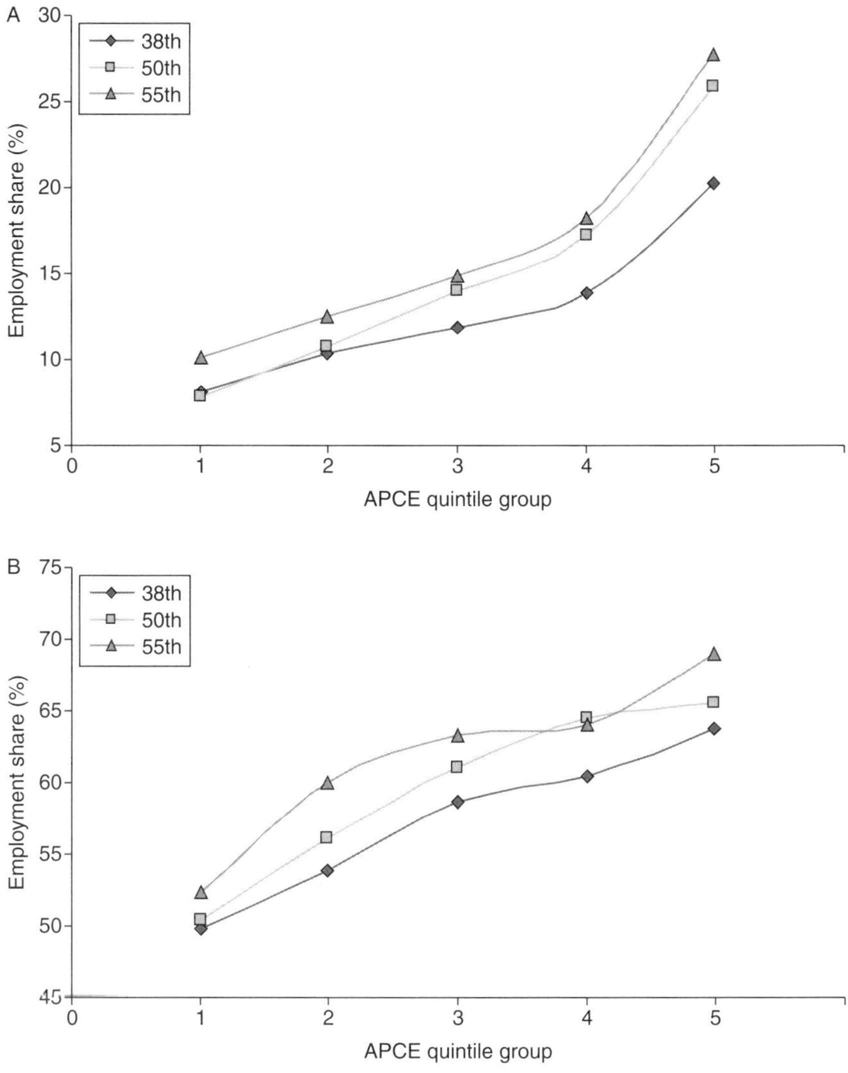

Figure 10.1 Employment share of the tertiary sector by quintile groups, different rounds.

Note

Panel A is rural and panel B is urban.

by quintile groups was quite striking at the two ends of the distribution. There is a sharp increase in the share of tertiary earners both at the lower (2nd) and the highest (5th) quintiles at the expense of the middle (3rd and 4th) quintiles.

The fact that more tertiary-sector employment has been created at the lower quintiles does not mean that there has been immiserizing growth of the tertiary sector in the sense that labor pushed into this sector has depressed earnings in the sector absolutely. The mean of the distribution might have increased over the period. There is a suggestion that the distribution of incomes in the sector might have deteriorated, particularly in the urban areas, with the incomes of the low earners falling *relative* to the high earners. But to shed more light on this specific question we need to look directly into the changes in the distribution of income (or household welfare in our case). This we do in the next section.

Evidence on the distribution of average per capita consumption expenditure (APCE) in the tertiary sector

The Kernel density functions for the three rounds have been graphed, separately for the rural and the urban areas in Figure 10.2. Both the distributions have shifted to the right in the post-liberalization years – much more perceptibly so in the post-liberalization years than between the previous two rounds. Further the outward movement is more striking in the urban economy. This is our first important conclusion: in spite of tertiary-sector jobs being created disproportionately in the lower quintiles, particularly in the urban areas, the evidence suggests that levels of earnings have gone up significantly including at the lower part of the distribution.

The graph also confirms what has been suggested by the evidence discussed in the last sub-section: that there has been some increase in the inequality in the distribution in the urban sector – perhaps not at all in the rural economy. Further information on the changes in distribution can be found from the decile and quartile ratios reported in Table 10.8.

The conclusions emerging from two tables are as follows:

1 As far as the rural areas are concerned there has been a decided improvement in the distribution. Inequality decreased in magnitude in the lower half

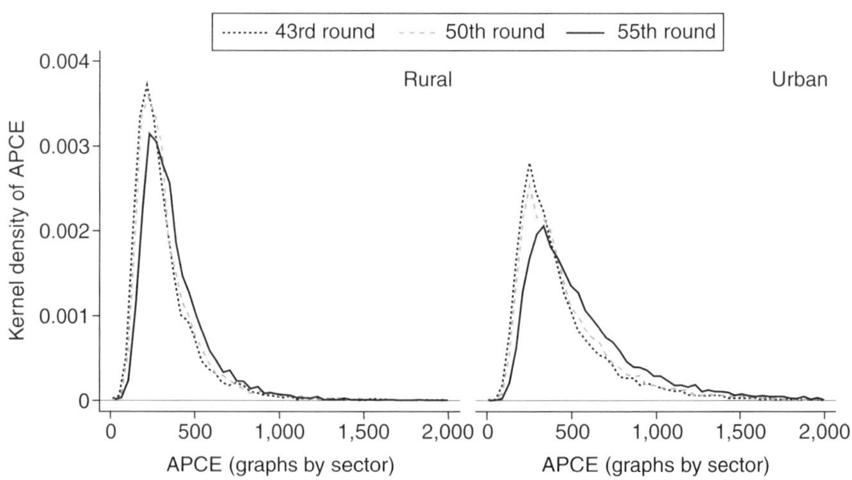

Figure 10.2 Kernel density functions of APCE in the tertiary sector, different rounds.

Table 10.8 Decile and quartile ratios for the distributions of APCE in the tertiary sector

A Rural areas

Round	*P90/P10*	*P90/P50*	*P10/P50*	*P75/P25*	*P75/P50*	*P25/P50*
43rd	3.660	2.068	0.565	1.938	1.432	0.739
50th	3.442	1.989	0.578	1.883	1.401	0.744
55th	3.265	1.919	0.588	1.869	1.408	0.754

B Urban areas

R	*P90/P10*	*P90/P50*	*P10/P50*	*P75/P25*	*P75/P50*	*P25/P50*
43rd	4.054	2.174	0.536	2.090	1.482	0.709
50th	4.107	2.191	0.533	2.118	1.496	0.706
55th	4.067	2.116	0.520	2.118	1.476	0.797

Source: Estimated from unit-level data of several NSS rounds.

of the distribution – judged both by the decile and the quartile ratios. There has been a smaller improvement in the top half; both the P90/P50 and the P75/P50 ratio moved down a bit.

2 In the urban economy, there is an evidence of the deterioration in the distribution at the lower part of the distribution. The P10/P50 ratio deteriorated particularly between the 50th and the 55th rounds – when we saw there was such a pronounced increase in the absorption of labor in low-income tertiary jobs. But the deterioration is not by any means large.

Trends in poverty and inequality in the post-liberalization years

It has been noted in the earlier chapters in Part I that, while the incidence in poverty has fallen both in the rural and the urban areas in the post-liberalization years, the reduction in poverty in the urban economy has been accompanied by a perceptible increase in inequality (see Chapter 2). The graphs of APCE given in Chapter 3 (Figures 3.4a and 3.4b) clearly bring out the change between the successive NSS rounds in the urban and rural sector.

The material presented in the two previous sections above suggests that the increase in inequality in the urban sector (and not so much in the rural) has been driven by the trends in the distribution of incomes in the tertiary sector. The point has relevance to the wider literature on the impact of liberalization in inequality.

It has been expected on the basis of standard trade theory of the Heckscher–Ohlin type that greater openness of an economy would tend to increase the relative returns to those factors of production which are in abundance in the economy concerned. Thus a less developed economy, where labor rather than capital is the more abundant factor, will see an increase in the relative return to labor – leading to a more equitable trend in the distribution of income. The experience of many developing countries after the recent spate of liberalization has, however, belied this expectation. Economists have tried to explain the observed increase in inequality in less developed economies by modifying the Heckscher–Ohlin model to allow for the inclusion of two types of labor – skilled and unskilled. Liberalization in this extended model leads to an increase in demand, not of unskilled labor but of more skilled labor which is demanded by the manufactured products in the sector open to international markets. In other words the industries which have a spurt in growth following liberalization demands labor of a type which might be less skilled than labor in manufactured goods produced by advanced countries, but they are more skilled than the general mass of unskilled labor which is in abundant supply in less developed countries. Thus the increase in skill differential in the latter drives the observed increase in inequality (Acmogolu, 2002).

The discussion in this chapter suggests that the mechanism described in the literature would be more pertinent if we incorporate the tertiary sector in the discussion. In other words the relative increase in demand for more skilled labor after liberalization comes as much, if not more, from the growth of some parts of the tertiary sector, as from the traded manufacturing sector. Clearly this effect can come only from the sub-sectors of the tertiary activities which deal with services to the globalized part of the economy. These contrast with those branches of the tertiary sector which are 'non-traded' catering to the needs of the domestic economy. As far as the latter are concerned, we would like to know if they show any evidence of 'immiserizing growth' which the aggregate view of the tertiary sector does not reveal – i.e., is labor being 'pushed' into the sector with falling incomes because of lack of opportunities in the production sectors.

The next section, therefore, goes into a discussion of trends in income distribution in different branches of the tertiary sector.

Shifts in the KDF distribution in different sub-sectors of tertiary activity

How do the shifts in the APCE distribution compare in different sub-sectors of the tertiary activities? We can go a fair distance by looking at the picture for the four major one-digit sectors distinguished in the National Industrial Classification (NIC). This is done in Figure 10.3.

The NIC Group 8 (business services) would contain the bulk of the services catering to the traded part of the economy, while group 6 (trade, hotels and restaurants) would comprise the bulk of the *private* non-traded services. Group 9 includes community, social and personal services, but is also heavily represented by government activities, including administration.

Two points stand out in the picture presented in Figure 10.3. First, the shift in the distribution between the two rounds is more pronounced for the urban areas than the rural ones even when we look at the disaggregated tertiary sub-groups.

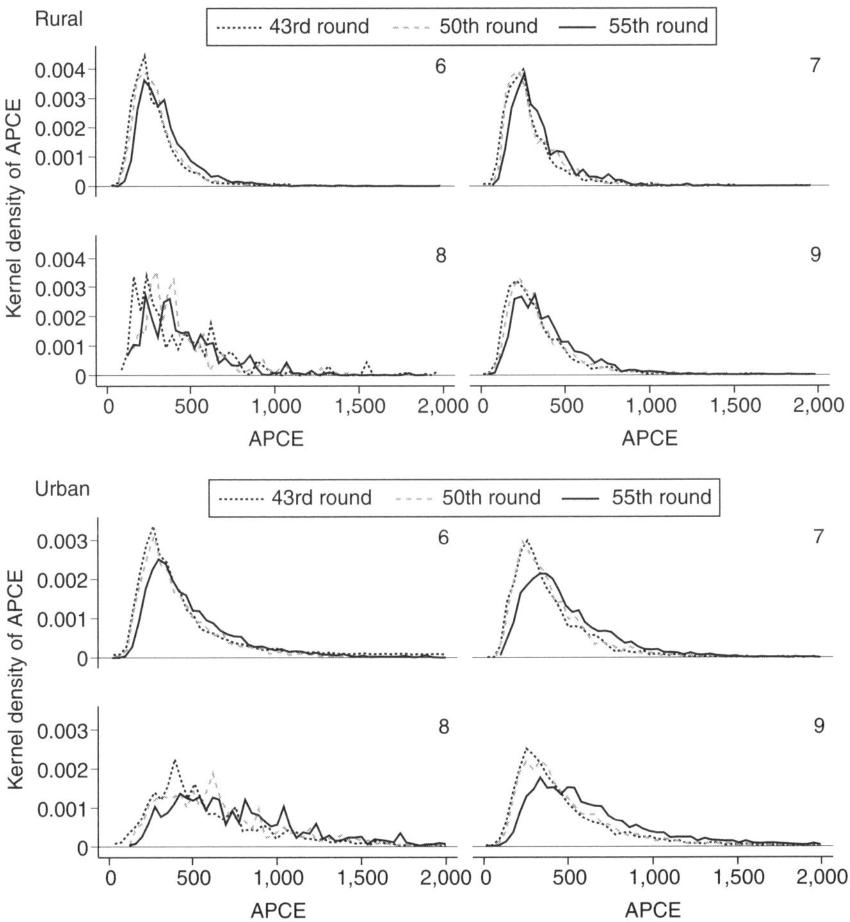

Figure 10.3 Kernel density functions by major sub-groups of the tertiary sector.

Note
6: Trade, hotels and restaurants; 7: transport, storage and communication; 8: finance, real estate and business activities; 9: community, social and personal services.

Second, the shift is least for the NIC group 6 (trade, hotels and restaurants) in both the rural and the urban areas, and the most striking for groups 8 (business services) and 9 (community, social and personal services). Further, in the groups showing the larger outward shifts, the shift in the urban areas is more prominent. Nowhere is there any evidence of any increase in the incidence of low-income groups.

KDF distributions for regular wage earners in the tertiary and other sectors

It might be useful to look at the KDF functions for the three rounds exclusively for regular wage earners (see Figure 10.4). The incomes of these respondents are

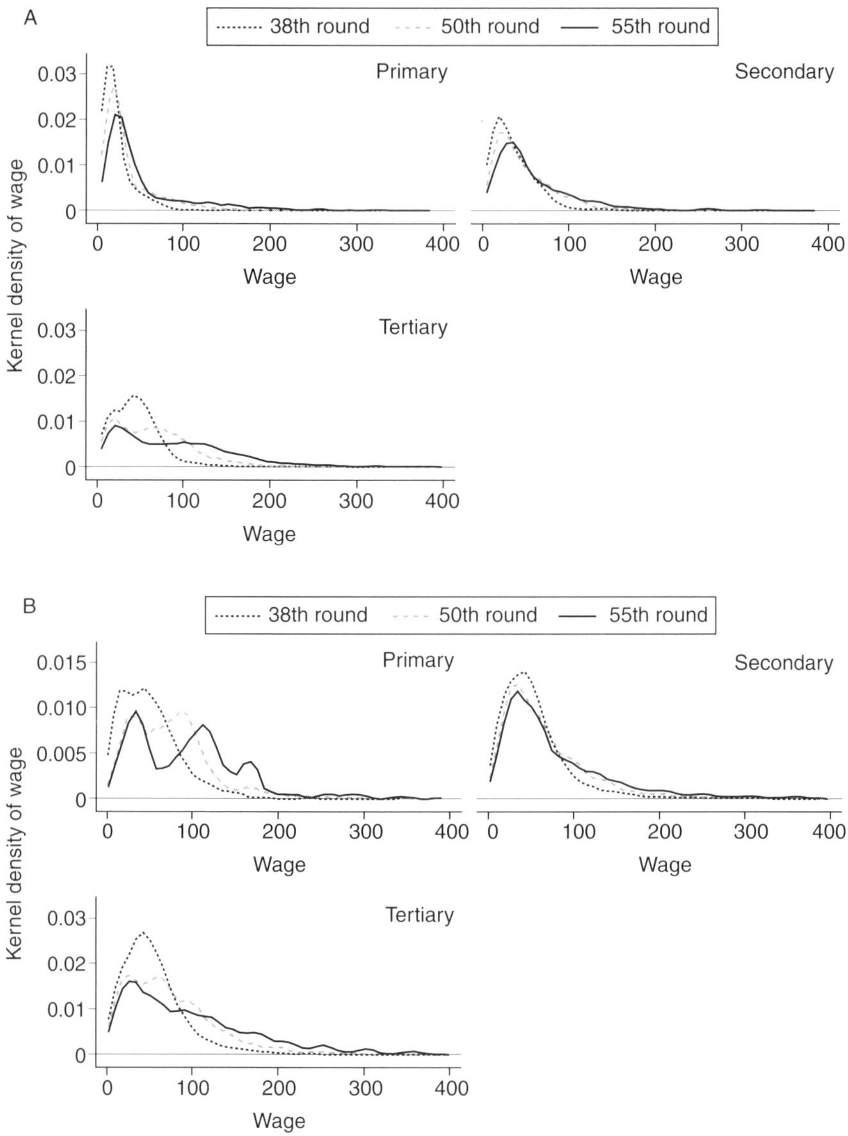

Figure 10.4 KDF distributions for regular wage regions by major sector, and rural and urban areas: three rounds.

Note
Panel A is rural and panel B is urban.

more easily obtained in the NSS survey. A study of the change in the distribution of their earnings over the three rounds of the survey is a useful supplement to the changes in the household welfare by the classification of 'main earners' presented above.

Two points need to be emphasized:

1 There is a rightward shift in the KDF in the successive rounds for both the rural and the urban areas, but it is clear that the shift is largest for the tertiary-sector regular wage earners. The ordering of the primary and secondary sectors are, however, rather different for the rural and urban areas. In the urban areas the shift seems to be larger for the primary rather than the secondary sector, presumably because of the development of different types of high-value primary activities. In the rural areas, however, the outward shift in the secondary sector is more pronounced relative to the primary sector.
2 The shape of the KDF in the tertiary sector is altered in rather the same way in the rural and the urban areas in the later rounds, even though the movement is stronger for the urban economy. There is marked *flattening* of the curve suggesting a wider dispersion of earnings and larger proportions of workers with higher earnings. There is a clear reduction of the proportion of people with low earnings, but interestingly both in the rural and urban sectors, the mode seems to have moved to the left (even though much reduced in its density). This might suggest that there is a sizable influx of low wage workers – earning rather less than in the 38th round in real terms. However, this phenomenon might really mean that there is a larger influx of younger or less educated workers along with others who earn much more.

The last point carries with it an implication that "dualism' has increased in the tertiary sector, and might indeed be stronger in the tertiary than in the secondary or manufacturing sectors. We cannot be sure about this hypothesis unless we control for the quality – in particular the human-capital attributes – of the workers entering these sectors.

Is 'dualism' higher in the tertiary sector? Earnings differentials (net) as between sectors in different points of the distribution

Our purpose is to know how the earnings in the tertiary sector relative to the earnings in the other two sectors, in particular manufacturing, vary in different parts of the distribution. 'Dualism' in terms of the gap between low and high earners in manufacturing is high in the Indian economy and has also been discussed in Chapter 9. If the dualism is stronger in the tertiary sector, then we would expect to find the 'net' tertiary-manufacturing differential, after controlling for the other major determinants of earnings (like human-capital attributes) to increase as we move up the scale in the earnings distribution. We ran quantile regressions for the 55th round of the NSS to estimate the net differential at the five quintiles of the distribution. Dummies for the sectors (with primary sector as base) were used in the regressions along with a set of other explanatory variables. The latter included education, age, sex, urban–rural location and regions.

Table 10.9 Values of dummies of quantile regressions: 55th round

Quantiles	*q5*	*q25*	*q50*	*q75*	*q95*
APCE					
Tertiary	0.048	0.08	0.108	0.128	0.172
Secondary	0.024	0.05	0.064	0.079	0.145
Wage of Regular Workers					
Tertiary	0.171	0.211	0.222	0.192	0.142
Secondary	0.039	–0.03	–0.13	–0.096	–0.038

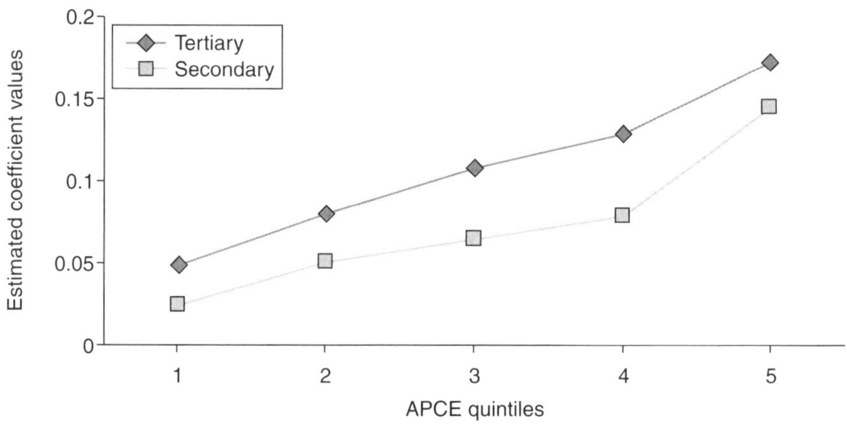

Figure 10.5 Estimated coefficients of (dummy) variables from quantile regressions: APCE.

The exercise was done separately for the APCE of households (for in which the characteristics of the 'main earner' were used for the explanatory variables) and for the daily earnings of regular wage earners. There were some differences in the sets of explanatory variables used in each case. (Model description is given in the Appendix.)

The coefficients of the tertiary and manufacturing sector dummies at the different quintiles are given in Table 10.9, and they are graphed in Figures 10.5 and 10.6. There are apparent differences in the shapes of the distribution. This is primarily because for the wage sector secondary wages are *below* tertiary wages (remembering that the base in each case is primary sector earners), while for the APCE of households the values for the tertiary and the secondary sectors are all above the primary. This rather intriguing difference is probably because secondary wage earners in the middle range of the distribution (q25 to q75) earn less than those in regular primary employment. The relatively high wages observed in the latter are due to public-sector and similar government employment in the primary sector.

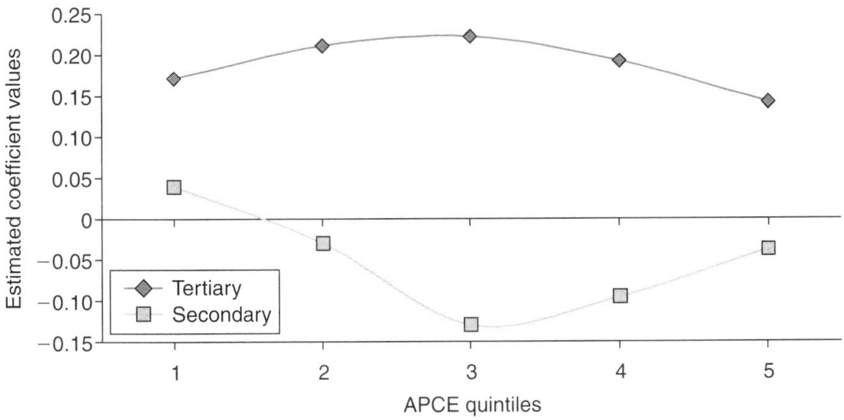

Figure 10.6 Estimated coefficients of (dummy) variables from quantile regressions: regular wage earners.

But as far as the tertiary–secondary differential is concerned the results are the same for APCE and daily wages. The differential is all along higher for the tertiary-sector workers. The gap between the two sectors increases in the middle range and diminishes somewhat only at the highest quarter of the distribution.

We conclude that *dualism is quantitatively more important in the tertiary sector when we compare the earnings of the lowest quintile with those in the higher quintile – except that the difference is reduced for the highest quintile.* There is then some support for the popular perception that the tertiary sector is home to a body of low earners more so than the secondary sector.

Conclusion

The structure of employment observed in the NSS survey year of 1999–2000 (the 55th round) shows that the *formal* sector accounted for a quarter of tertiary employment in the rural areas and one third in the urban areas. Even after the decline in public-sector employment in the post-reform period this sub-sector still accounts for more than half of formal tertiary employment in the urban areas and more than two-thirds in the rural. Around one-half of employment in the informal segment of the tertiary sector is accounted for by the self-employed in both the areas. Regular wage earners are more important in the urban sector, the rest (25 percent in the urban, and 33 percent in the rural) being casual wage-workers.

In the absence of time-series data for the formal and the informal sectors we are obliged to analyze the trends in the low- and high-paid employment in the tertiary sector by looking at the changes in the entire distribution of earnings in this sector over time. We have looked at the issue from several angles and for different variables representing income levels. As mentioned the self-employed constitute a very large part of the tertiary sector. By definition the individual earnings of the self-employed are not recorded for each worker. All the earnings of the household members are pooled together. The variable most relevant to look at, then, is a measure of household welfare – which in the simplest formulation is mean household per capita expenditure (APCE). The industry affiliation of the household is given by the occupation of the main earner. This may create some errors for multiple-earner households whose earners follow different occupations.

The movement of the distribution of APCE for the successive rounds brings out two important points: (i) there is an outward shift in the distribution in the tertiary sector, so that earnings at all levels have increased; and (ii) there has been proportionately larger increase in the number in the first and the fifth quintiles of the distribution – with relatively less absorption of labor in the middle range. This implies an increase in inequality in the bottom half of the distribution – a trend more prominent in the urban economy. Disaggregating the tertiary sector by its 1-digit components, it is seen that these effects are mild in trade (group 6) but much more striking in business services and in the community and social services,

We looked specifically at regular wage earners whose individual earnings are recorded. The outward movement of the earnings distribution over successive rounds (and particularly during the 1987–1993 and 1993–1999 periods), as well as the 'flattening' of the curve, is more striking for the tertiary sector than either the primary or the secondary. It is also more prominent for the wage-earners than the welfare index for all tertiary households (APCE) which we had used. Thus we conclude that while there is no evidence for the incidence of low incomes in the tertiary sector to increase in any absolute sense, more jobs are being created in the bottom and the topmost part of the distribution.

This last point suggests an increase in 'dualism' in the tertiary sector. We have seen in the last chapter that dualism was particularly striking in Indian manufacturing compared with other Asian economies, and it had most likely increased in recent years. Our quintile regression analysis was meant to see how the earnings differentia between tertiary and the manufacturing sectors compare at different parts of the earnings distribution. The results for the 1999–2000 round of the NSS show that the differential, after controlling for human-capital attributes and location of the labor, increases from the lowest quintile to the fourth – and only in the highest is there some reduction in the 'net' differential. This is true for both the APCE measure and for regular wages. We conclude that dualism has become higher in the tertiary sector than in manufacturing.

Appendix

In the last section, both sets of regressions were simultaneous quantile regression with bootstrapping standard errors. The quantile regressions were simultaneously run at five quantile points namely 5, 25, 50, 75 and 95.

Both regressions were based on NSS unit level data of 55th round. The regression with APCE as dependent variable was estimated at household level and it had 92,282 observations. The regression with wage of the regular workers as dependent variable was estimated at individual level and it had 52,439 observations.

In the following tables, we present variable descriptions of both regression models.

Table 10A.1 Description of independent variables: set A

Variable	*Description of independent variables*
Sec	dummy for households with secondary sector as principal industry
tert	dummy for households with tertiary sector as principal industry
edu	average years of education of main workers
age	average age of main workers in the household
east	dummy for eastern region
south	dummy for southern region
cent	dummy for central region
nw	dummy for north-western region
empl	dummy for self-employed
urban	dummy for urban

In addition, all independent variables were interacted with urban to control urban influence on them.

Dependent Variable: ln (APCE).

Table 10A.2 Description of independent variables: set B

Variable	*Description of independent variables*
ind2	dummy for workers in secondary sector
ind3	dummy for workers in tertiary sector
Edu	years of education of regular workers
East	dummy for eastern region
South	dummy for southern region
Cent	dummy for central region
Nw	dummy for north-western region
Male	dummy for male
Urban	dummy for urban
occ2	dummy for workers with occupation codes – 2
occ3	dummy for workers with occupation codes – 3
occ4	dummy for workers with occupation codes – 4
occ5	dummy for workers with occupation codes – 5
occ6	dummy for workers with occupation codes – 6
occ7	dummy for workers with occupation codes – 7, 8 and 9

In addition, all independent variables were interacted with urban to control urban influence on them.

Dependent Variable: ln (Wages of Regular Workers).

Table 10A.3 Description of occupational codes

NCO divisions	*Description of the occupation code*
0–1	Professional, technical and related workers
2	Administrative, executive and managerial workers
3	Clerical and related workers
4	Sales workers
5	Service workers
6	Farmers, fishermen, hunters, loggers and related workers
7, 8 and 9	Production and related workers, transport equipment operators and labourers

Part IV

Labor-market institutions

11 Legislation, enforcement and adjudication in Indian labor markets

Origins, consequences and the way forward

Ahmad Ahsan, Carmen Pages and Tirthankar Roy[1]

Introduction

Throughout the world, governments have enacted laws to protect the interests of the workers. India is no exception. In fact, in India, laws are often perceived to be too restrictive on employers. International comparisons show that the problem is not one of laws relating to conditions of work, but one of laws on hiring and, especially, dismissals. Laws in India on these matters are restrictive compared with other emerging economies, other nations in Asia and even developed countries.

While some regulations are necessary, excessive controls are not necessarily better for workers and society. Indeed, whereas the particularly restrictive provisions were created to protect jobs, many studies show that the effects of job security on growth of employment in large enterprises have been adverse (Fallon and Lucas, 1993; Anant *et al.* 2003; Besley and Burgess 2004; Dutta Roy 2004; Saha 2005; Ahsan and Pagés 2006). Nor have these provisions been helpful to the cause of industrial peace. In 2004, 482 major cases of work-stoppage cost industry 15 million person-days. It is obvious that little *de jure* liberalization in the regulatory framework has been allowed to happen since the reforms began despite demand from industry, economists and media. That being said, others have noted several areas of de facto and indirect liberalization (Roy 2003). For example, incidence of voluntary retirement, fixed-term and contractual employment has increased. Some degree of *de jure* rationalization, therefore, is needed.

Why did legislation take the particular form that it did in India? What are the problem areas? What are the economic impacts of such legislation? What changes have occurred? What is the way forward? These are some of the questions addressed in this chapter.

The conclusion of this chapter is that the current dispute and retrenchment-related laws do not preserve existing jobs and prevent the creation of new ones. In terms of reforms, it is found that while no significant change has occurred in legislation and formal union presence, weakening law enforcement, increasing recourse to contract employment, judicial decisions upholding the legality of temporary and contract employment, and increasing decentralization in the legislation initiative are some of the ways that flexibility has increased. Nonetheless, this chapter argues that substantial transformations are still needed. To create a new institutional infrastructure that can truly advance the cause of workers and promote job growth it is necessary to expand the reform debate beyond chapter Vb of the Industrial Disputes Act to areas such as dispute resolution, adjudication, labor inspections and labor policy.

The chapter has five main sections. The first three deal with labor regulations, law enforcement and the adjudication process, respectively. The following section examines the economic impact of this legal and institutional system. A final section concludes and provides some suggestions to move forward.

Regulatory framework

Labor laws

Seeds of over-regulation were present in the history of labor laws before independence (1947). A broad coalition between nationalists and mill workers in the interwar period encouraged legislation that created a role for elected provincial governments in collective bargaining and firm-level negotiation. After independence, labor laws continued to be influenced more by the desire to protect labor, which had originated in nationalism, than by considerations of efficiency in labor markets and dispute settlement. The principle of protection was subsumed under the pursuit of 'social justice', and employment security was enhanced in the formal sector by a range of new laws and case laws. Removing or changing laws became politically difficult, with the result that new demand for laws led to proliferation. Big business implicitly traded off labor-market flexibility for a trade regime that offered them a high degree of import protection. After the economic reforms started in the 1990s and protection was reduced, the lack of flexibility became a serious issue.

The present legal framework consists of major acts, and a number of minor, usually state-level acts. Industrial relations are governed by the Trade Unions Act, 1926, which specifies the conditions that a trade union needs to satisfy in order to be recognized under the act, and the Industrial Disputes Act, 1947, (IDA), which sets out the institutions for adjudication of disputes.

The IDA specifies a multi-tier conciliation-cum-adjudication system. The tiers are created and maintained by the state governments. The lowest and the immediate tier consist of Conciliation Officers and Boards appointed by the government. The Conciliation Officer either settles the dispute, or sends a 'failure report'. The dispute then goes to Labor Courts, and further to Industrial Tribunals. The Labor Courts deal with disputes that affect workers. The Industrial Tribunals, apart from working as appellate bodies, deal with cases that affect all workers in an industry. In rarer cases, disputes go to National Tribunals, which are centrally administered bodies, empowered to deal with cases that have potentially national significance. The IDA imposes significant restrictions on employers regarding retrenchment and exit. It gives power to labor courts and Tribunals to set aside any discharge or dismissal that has been referred to them as not justified and direct reinstatement of the worker in any terms it sees fit. In units employing more than 100 workers, retrenchment requires seeking authorization from the government. Such authorization is rarely granted. In the event of retrenchment, longer tenure workers are given priority to stay. In addition, retrenched workers receive priority in case of new recruitment. Closure also requires prior authorization.

Working conditions are governed principally by the Factories Act, 1948; the Industrial Employment (Standing Orders) Act, 1946, which specifies the form of the employment contract; and the Contract Labor (Regulation and Abolition) Act, 1970. The Factories Act governs the health, safety and welfare of workers in factories. The Industrial Employment (Standing Orders) Act, 1946, requires employers of industrial units with 100 or more workers (excluding management and supervision) to specify working conditions more or less in line with a 'model standing orders'. The Contract Labor (Regulation and Abolition) Act, 1971 (CLA), was created with the objective of gradual abolition of casual labor hiring, and where permitted, to regulate the working conditions of casual labor. Although it is now being used extensively as the principal means available to employers and state governments to increase flexibility within the existing legal regime, the original purpose of the Act was quite the opposite. Section 10 of the act prevents firms from outsourcing most core functions or hiring workers on temporary contracts for more than 120 days. Anyone so employed can demand permanent employment from the company.

The principal laws relating to wages are the Payment of Wages Act, 1937 and the Minimum Wages Act, 1948. The Payment of Wages Act, 1937, is a central act, the enforcement of which is a state responsibility, except in mines, railways, oilfields, ports and air transport. The Act specifies the standard wage period (a month or less), payment day, permissible deductions, mode of payment and inspection. It applies to workers below a certain salary range. The Minimum Wages Act, 1948 specifies minimum wages (and is empowered to specify also the length of the working day) in 'scheduled' employment.

Social Security and Insurance are governed by, first, the Workmen's Compensation Act, 1923, which specifies compensation that the employers need to pay on account of injury by accident at work-site or occupational diseases. An important provision of the Act is the liability of the principal employer in case of contract labor employment. Other important acts in this class include the Employees State Insurance Act, 1948, which extends to all factories under the Factories Act, and other commercial establishments employing 20 or more persons, and to workers earning less than a certain salary limit within these, and requires contributions from both employers and employees to be paid for insurance against sickness, maternity, funeral and disablement. The Employees Provident Funds Act, 1952, which applies primarily to factories and specifies deposit-linked provident fund or pension scheme, is also relevant.

Since the early 1990s, demands have been raised to reform the IDA and the CLA, the two most disputative acts. However, little success has been achieved on this front. Important changes have been introduced in the Trade Unions and Factories acts. Somewhat more bold initiatives have occurred at the state level. In June 2000, the Government of Maharashtra announced a fairly broad-based labor law-reform package. The National Labor Commission cited the Government of Punjab's fast-track courts, called Labor Lok Adalats, which cleared more than 11,000, or two-thirds of, the pending cases in the Labor Courts and Tribunals in three rounds of hearing since 2000. The Andhra Pradesh government announced its intention to introduce liberalized labor laws for designated Special Economic Zones.

International comparison

Is the Indian legal framework especially restrictive by comparison with other developing countries? *Doing Business*, 2004, a publicly available database based on a detailed study of employment laws across the world (see http://rru.worldbank.org/DoingBusiness), provides information on legal provisions related to hiring, hours of work and retrenchment of workers across a large number of countries in the world. Such provisions are then ranked with scores that are higher the more protective of workers the labor laws.

A first index (*restrictions on hiring*) measures how difficult it is for employers to hire workers other than with indefinite, permanent contracts. A higher score indicates higher difficulty to hire through alternative contracts. A second index (*restrictions on hours of work*) measures legal provisions pertaining to hours of work. It compares overtime, restrictions to night work and length of the work-day and work-week. Countries where employers face more restrictions on hours of work are given a higher score. A third index (*restrictions on retrenchment*) measures legal and administrative constraints on dismissals. A fourth index measures the *cost of dismissal* measures in weeks of pay. Such costs are related to the compensation that workers obtain in that event although not one to one, as often times legislation imposes costs on firms that are not transferred to workers (for example, the cost of legal fees). Finally, the *rigidity of employment* index provides a summary indicator of different aspects of labor legislation across countries.

According to the latter, Indian laws are more protective of workers than the international average or the average of a group of comparator countries, composed by large developing economies and countries in East and South Asia (see Table 11.1, column 5). On paper, Indian laws are also much more protective of workers than in developed countries. Disaggregating among different indicators, it emerges that this more protective stand of the law in India comes from the higher restrictions on dismissal. In comparison, other aspects of the labor law are closer or below the international norm.

Thus, for example, Indian laws concerning the ability to hire workers with alternative contracts are in line with international standards, although they impose somewhat higher constraints on employers than in the sample of

Table 11.1 International comparison of labor legislation in India and comparator countries

Country	*Difficulty of hiring (1)*	*Rigid hours (2)*	*Restrictions to retrenchment (3)*	*Compensation for dismissal (4)*	*Rigidity of employment (5)*
India	33	20	90	79	48
Bangladesh	11	40	20	47	24
Brazil	67	80	70	165	72
Cambodia	33	80	30	39	48
China	11	40	40	90	30
Indonesia	61	40	70	157	57
Korea Rep.	11	60	30	90	34
Malaysia	0	0	10	74	3
Nepal	22	20	90	90	44
Pakistan	78	40	30	90	49
Philippines	22	60	40	90	41
Russian Federation	0	60	20	17	27
Sri Lanka	0	40	80	108	40
Thailand	67	40	20	47	42
Vietnam	44	40	70	98	51
Comparators' average	27	45	48	87	40
High-income countries					
Average	22	49	24	41	32
World average	35	516	38	56	41
World median	31	60	40	46	41

Source: Doing Business 2004: http://rru.worldbank.org/DoingBusiness/.

comparator countries. Similarly, Indian labor laws exert little restrictions on hours of work, compared either with the international standard or the median of the group of comparator countries. Indian labor laws also impose lower monetary costs to employers in the event they dismiss a worker relative to comparator countries (although higher than the international average and way above the average for developed countries). Instead, Indian labor laws impose more administrative hurdles to initiate a dismissal than almost anywhere else in the world. Only in a few countries firms need to obtain authorization to retrench from the government. Moreover, in India, authorization to retrench is hardly granted, which leads to a few requests for authorization in the first place. In a scale of 1 to 100, India scores 90 in the *restrictions of dismissals* index, well above the international norm, the average of the group of comparators, or the average in developed economies.

Law enforcement

While labor laws have remained largely unchanged, their effects may be changing depending on the application and enforcement of such laws, the capability of unions to monitor application, as well as the strategies firms are following to avoid them. We find that little has changed in the formal presence of unions, either in terms of affiliation or the number of disputes. Yet, there are signs of weakening law enforcement, ineffective and corrupted inspections, and rising recourse to contract labor. A shift in the stand of the judiciary might be also contributing to a more flexible application of the law.

Union membership and labor disputes

Data on union membership is sketchy and incomplete. Data for few states that have more complete information suggest that union membership has not declined. A regression of such measures against state and a time trend for data covering the period 1985–1997 yields a positive although not statistically significant coefficient on the trend variable. Data by state (Figure 11.1) indicates that in a number of states union membership increased (Assam, Orissa, Punjab, Gujarat), although in the latter state, union membership suffered a decline in the second half of the nineties. In other states, most notably Karnataka and Kerala, union membership declined. The lack of significant overall trends is also evident when union membership is measured in relation to population (Figure 11.2). There has been a *decline in disputes* during the nineties, although disputes were high in some years at the end of the decade. The time trend is statistically significant, and it indicates a decline in

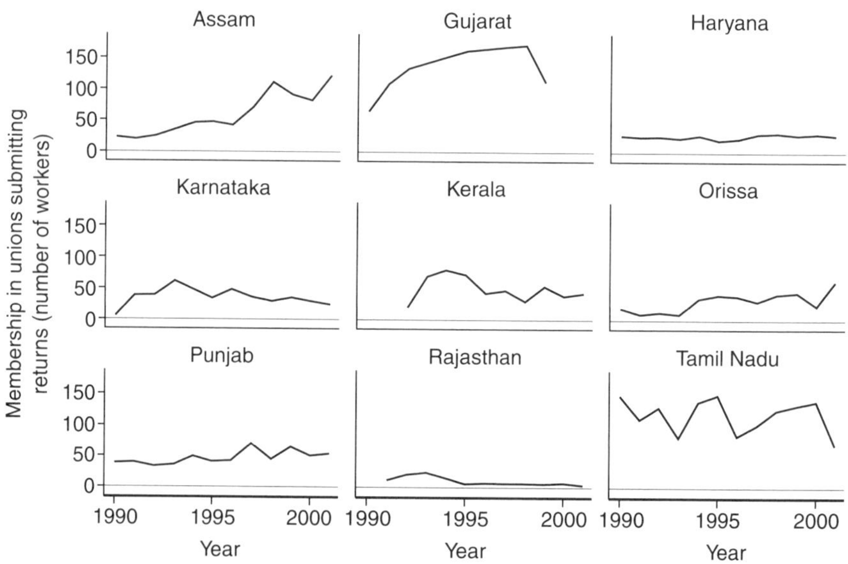

Figure 11.1 Evolution of union membership by state (in '0000s) (source: Labor Bureau).

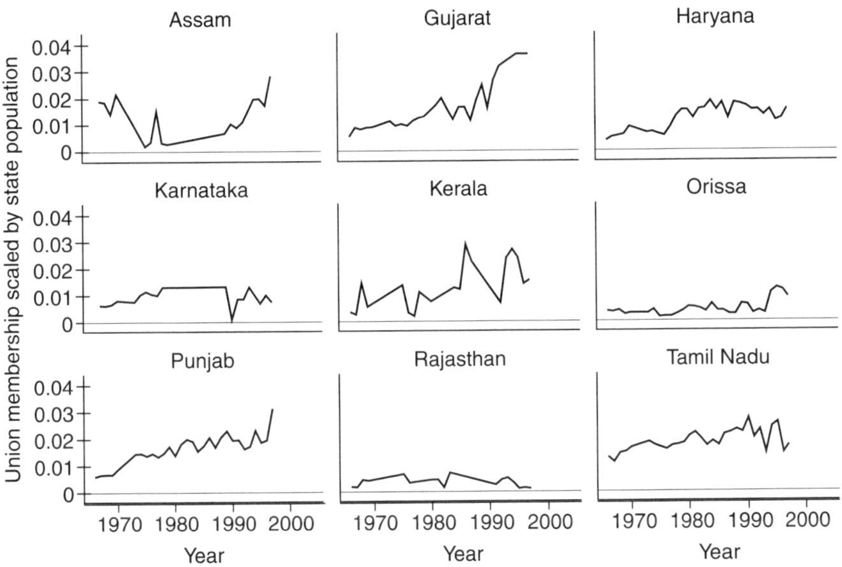

Figure 11.2 Evolution of union membership (scaled by state population) by state (source: Labor Bureau).

Figure 11.3 Number of disputes per 10,000 manufacturing workers (source: Author's computations based on Labor Bureau and ASI data).

disputes at a rate of 2.2 disputes per ten thousand workers a year within states (Figure 11.3). It should be noticed, however, that while on average the number of disputes have declined the *number of person-days lost in such disputes has increased since 1997* after a sustained decline throughout the first part of the nineties (Figure 11.4).

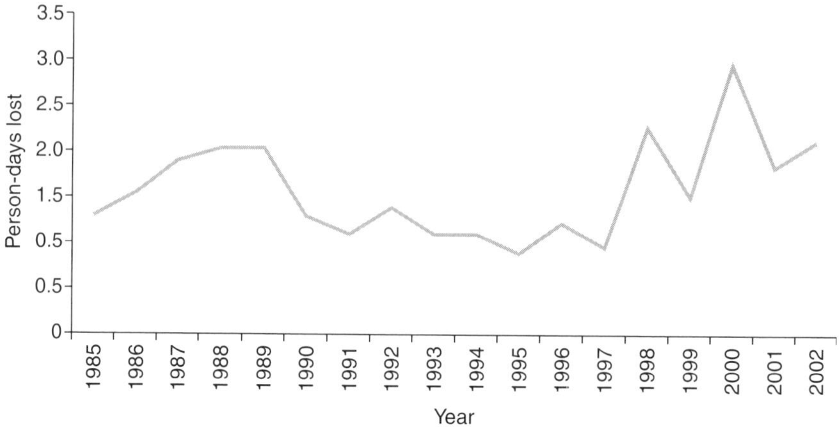

Figure 11.4 Person-days lost to disputes per manufacturing worker (source: Author's computations based on Labor Bureau and ASI data).

Labor inspections

All governments inspect business for compliance with their regulations. Yet, law enforcement becomes particularly difficult when the legal framework is overly complex and outdated, and when reforms in other markets are increasing the demand for flexibility and adaptability.

Inspectors in India have certain duties and powers. Among their duties, they are supposed to inquire into the correctness of any of the particulars appearing in any statement, or return. They have also to find out whether the provisions of the laws have been complied with. To do that they are awarded the power of requiring any employer or contractor to furnish the appropriate information and of entering at any reasonable time in a establishment, factory or office, examining the employer or contractor, and making copies of any documents maintained by the premises.

There has been a large decline in the number of factories inspected relative to the number of registered factories in the post-reform period (Figure 11.5).[2] In principle, it is possible that the trend reflects a changed inspection strategy that subjects a smaller set of firms to stricter inspection. Some evidence documented below, however, suggest an increasingly inefficient system of inspections. There are also significant differences in the share of factories inspected across states in 1991–2001 (Figure 11.6). State differences explain 73 percent in the total variance of the share of factories inspected, suggesting important differences in enforcement policies across states.

India's 2002 Investment climate survey (ICS) provides a more detailed picture of labor inspections obtained from the responses of a large sample of firms. On average, firms report 0.4 labor inspections from the Central labor

Figure 11.5 Share of factories inspected (as % of factories registered) (source: Labor Bureau).

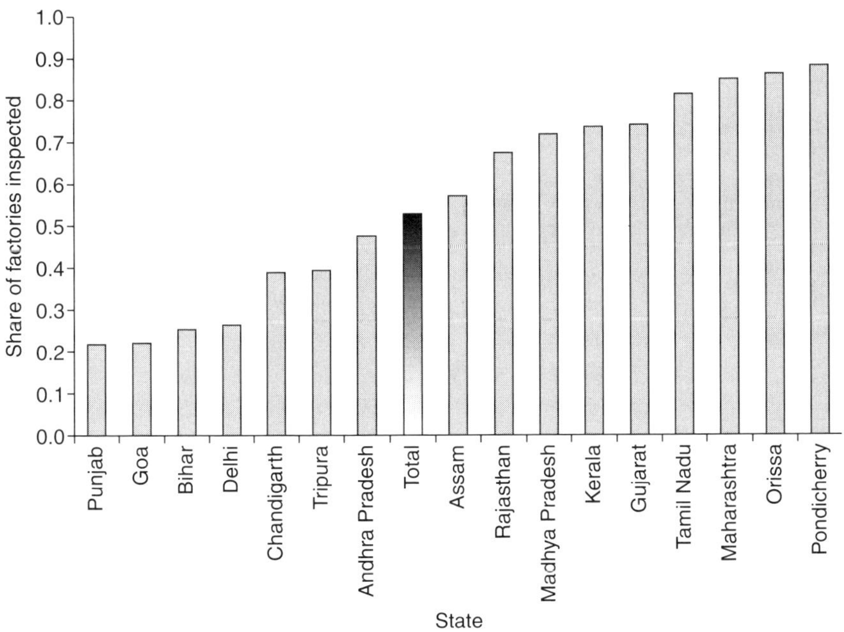

Figure 11.6 Share of factories inspected by state (source: Labor Bureau).

administration and 1.76 State labor inspections per year (Table 11.2). It is noticeable that at the state level, labor inspections are more frequent than any other type of inspections. The breakdown by states indicates that states such as Tamil Nadu, Gujarat or Kerala, which according to the labor bureau data are states with a large share of firms inspected, are also the states with the highest number of inspections per firm (Table 11.3). The ICS data also suggests important differences in law enforcement policies across states.

There are numerous accounts that suggest the presence of irregularities. For example, there are accounts that many inspectors collect bribes in exchange for reduced enforcement. Firms rarely know about the rules and inspectors are seen as unwilling to provide this information since that could endanger their future bribes (Rastogi 2002). The ICS data provides some information about the incidence of

Table 11.2 Average inspector visits to establishments per year (different agencies)

	Central government	*State government*
Sale tax	0.59	1.61
Income tax	0.51	0.42
Customs duty	0.89	0.21
Excise duty	2.13	1.24
Labor and Social Security inspectors	0.40	1.76
Fire and building safety	0.21	0.66
Environment	0.19	1.26
All others	0.12	1.46

Source: ICS, World Bank.

Table 11.3 Average state labor inspections and incidence of irregularities

	State inspections per establishment	*% of respondents acknowledging that unofficial payments reduce number of visits*
AP	1.76	0.27
Chandigarh	0.78	0.22
Delhi	0.32	0.21
Gujarat	2.54	0.10
Haryana	1.59	0.07
Karnataka	1.53	0.23
Kerala	2.13	0.20
MP	0.61	0.20
Maharashtra	0.84	0.29
Punjab	4.65	0.17
Tamil Nadu	3.06	0.33
UP	1.74	0.19
W. Bengal	0.80	0.10

Source: Authors' elaboration from ICS data.

Table 11.4 Average reduction in inspector visits and time spent if unofficial payments are made, by government agency

	Number of firms reporting incidents	*Reduction in number of visits (percent)*	*% reduction in time spent*
Tax	57	33.49	NA
Labor and social security	157	53.25	49.66
Environment	92	42.52	37.06
Fire and safety	100	42.43	41.62
All others	73	38.97	36.31

Source: Authors' elaboration from ICS data.

these accounts. This Survey asks firms' managers if inspectors respond to unofficial payments by reducing the number of visits to their establishments. On average, a positive answer is confirmed for 20 percent of the respondents, although in states such as Maharashtra and Tamil Nadu this percentage increases to around 30 percent (Table 11.3). While this question refers to inspectors from all government agencies, additional evidence suggests that labor and social-security inspectors are among the ones that are more responsive to unofficial payments. Not only there were more instances of irregularities involving labor inspectors, but also the response in terms of the reduction in the number of visits was higher than for officials of other state administrations (see Table 11.4).

The ICS data also allows examining whether inspectors target their inspections to particular firms. Table 11.5 reports the results of a regression of the number of inspections against firm characteristics such as size, age of the firm, whether the firm is public, whether the firm is owned by foreigners or has foreign participation, whether it dominates a substantial share of the market for its main product, and finally whether (at least some) workers employed in that firm belong to a union. The regression also includes state and industry dummies. Both the reported number of inspections (column 1) and the adjusted number of inspections (column 2) are used. The adjusted number is computed by adding to the reported inspections the ones that did not happen because unofficial payments were made.[3]

Notably, results are very different depending on whether the adjusted or the reported number of visits is used as dependent variable, indicating that irregularities tend to be concentrated in certain types of firms. Thus, reported inspections do not exhibit any systematic pattern other than the fact that exporting firms tend to experience more state labor inspections per year than firms that sell in domestic markets. Instead, the adjusted number of inspections indicates that large firms, firms that sell abroad and firms that dominate a large share of the market (more than 20 percent of the market share of their main product) would experience more labor inspections than the ones that actually take place after making unofficial payments to inspectors. Once such payments are made, they experience the same intensity of inspections than other firms. This difference

Table 11.5 Patterns of inspections and effect of inspections on compliance

	Number of inspections – observed	*Number of inspections – adjusted?*	*Labor laws as an obstacle?*	*Labor laws as an obstacle?*	*Labor laws as an obstacle?*	*Labor laws as an obstacle?*
	(1)	*(2)*	*(3)*	*(4)*	*(5)*	*(6)*
Medium	0.161	0.222	0.229	0.25	0.252	0.257
	(0.28)	(0.3)	(2.93)**	(2.57)*	(2.56)*	(2.62)**
Large	1.115	3.059	0.306	0.243	0.226	0.206
	(1.24)	(2.72)**	(2.56)*	(1.65)	(1.49)	(1.36)
Age	0.027	0.012	0.002	0.002	0.002	0.002
	(1.76)	(0.62)	(1.06)	(0.75)	(0.82)	(0.58)
Public	−1.138	−2.357	−0.303	−0.654	−0.533	−0.524
	(0.49)	(0.68)	(0.97)	(1.53)	(1.15)	(1.14)
Foreign participation (20–49%)	−0.758	−2.864	−0.591	−0.707	−0.701	−0.675
	(0.33)	(0.93)	(1.89)	(1.74)	(1.71)	(1.65)
Foreign (>49%)	0.575	1.852	−0.156	0.259	0.187	0.183
	(0.24)	(0.57)	(0.47)	(0.61)	(0.43)	(0.42)
Export	1.461	2.092	0.115	0.091	0.091	0.077
	(2.58)**	(3.06)**	(1.48)	(0.98)	(0.98)	(0.83)
Market share>20%	0.159	1.381	−0.017	0.057	0.065	0.075
	(0.31)	(2.10)*	(0.24)	(0.65)	(0.73)	(0.85)

Presence of unions	−0.55	−1.639			0.068	
	(0.69)	(1.68)			(0.51)	
% of LF in union						0.002
						(1.04)
# inspections – observed			0.003			
			(0.93)			
# inspections – adjusted				0.015	0.015	0.016
				(3.64)**	(3.62)**	(3.64)**
Constant	1.644	−0.197	0.502	0.501	0.471	0.483
	(1.41)	(0.13)	(3.13)**	(2.49)*	(2.32)*	(2.37)*
Observations	1497	1016	1498	1016	1006	998
R^2	0.04	0.06	0.12	0.16	0.16	0.16
Industry effects	Yes	Yes	Yes	Yes	Yes	Yes
State effects	Yes	Yes	Yes	Yes	Yes	Yes

Notes
'Labor laws as an obstacle'. The answer to this question ranges from 0 to 4, where 4 corresponds to labor laws are a major obstacle for growth, while 0 is no obstacle.
Absolute value of t-statistics in parentheses * significant at 5%; ** significant at 1%.

between adjusted and actual number of visits suggests that inspectors target and respond to the unofficial payments of firms with higher profits and rents (which presumably can offer higher payments).

Quite surprisingly the presence of unions in a firm does not increase the number of inspections it experiences, as it would be expected if inspectors responded to unions' calls of unfair labor practices or breaches with labor laws. Instead, the negative sign in the adjusted visits suggests two alternative hypotheses. The first one is that employers of unionized firms are more compliant with labor laws; the second is that unions could expose irregular inspection practices and therefore inspectors stay away from such firms.

ICS data provide information on whether employers perceive labor laws to be an obstacle to their growth. The answer to this question ranges from zero to four where four indicates that a firm perceives labor laws as a major obstacle and zero as no obstacle. If inspections induce compliance with labor laws, then firms' perceptions on the stringency of labor laws are expected to increase with the number of inspections.[4] Table 11.5, columns (3)-(6) report the results of regressing individual firms perceptions against the number of inspections, controlling for industry and state dummies, firm characteristics such as size, age and export status, and whether the firm is publicly owned, foreign controlled or foreign participated or whether it dominates more than 20 percent of the market of its main product.

Interestingly, once again results are different depending on whether inspections are measured according to the reported or the adjusted number. While the reported number of inspections is not related to firms' perceptions on the stringency of regulations, the adjusted number – that is, the number of inspections that would have taken place if inspectors had not responded to unofficial payments – is positively related. This suggest that firms that are engaged in payments in exchange of a reduction in inspections perceive labor laws to be more binding, which in turn leads to two alternative hypotheses: Either paying to inspectors is perceived to be the *problem with labor laws* or, perhaps more likely, inspectors target firms for which labor laws are more binding and therefore are more interested in evading the law.

Unions can also contribute to law enforcement if they are vigilant for infractions and alert inspectors of breaches in the law. The results presented in Table 11.5 however, suggest that the presence of unions in a firm does not affect managers' views regarding the stringency of labor-market laws. This result is consistent with the estimated lack of effect of unions in bringing about inspections. It also suggests that the fact that inspectors target firms without unions for irregular payments is not related to a higher compliance of unionized firms. Instead, the results suggest that it is the fear of being exposed by unions, or a lower profitability of unionized firms, that deters inspectors from soliciting payments from such firms.

Overall the results indicate that labor inspectors do little to enforce labor laws. If anything, the evidence points to the opposite, that is, to a coalition between employers and inspectors to evade the law. Unions may prevent some of these exchanges from taking place but seemingly cannot bring about more inspections. This in turn, reduces their effectiveness to enforce the law. The conclusion is an ineffective system plagued with irregularities that seemingly does little to promote compliance or advance the cause of workers while increasing the costs of doing business for firms.

Firms' strategies to cope with strict labor legislation

While labor-law enforcement is in general weak, laws that force firms to seek and obtain permission from the government prior to retrenchment are well enforced. Thus, still today, few firms seek permission to retrench, and for those who do, permission is rarely granted.[5] Hiring labor to contractors and subcontracting non-core activities to other companies provides flexibility to firms that seek to manage their labor force in an uncertain and volatile context. Perhaps not surprisingly the use of contract labor has increased substantially during the nineties climbing from 15 to 25 percent of manufacturing labor force (Table 11.6).[6] This rise, however, has not occurred in all states. In a number of large states, the use of contract labor has remained low and stable. This is the case in Delhi, Karnataka, Kerala, Tamil Nadu and West Bengal. In contrast there has been a large increase in contract labor in states like Orissa or Andhra Pradesh. State differences explain as much as 74 percent of the total variance in the use of contract labor suggesting the importance of state policies in determining firms' hiring decisions.

Table 11.6 Percentage of contract labor by state and period

State	*1985*	*1990*	*1995*	*2002*
Kerala	1.6	1.8	1.5	2.33
Assam	8.2	6.4	7.9	3.95
Tamil Nadu	6.9	5.2	4.4	7.21
West Bengal	4.6	5.1	5.3	7.63
Delhi	7.5	7.4	4.8	7.64
Karnataka	11.5	10.4	8.1	9.33
Punjab	19.1	8.8	10.8	14.32
Maharashtra	5.7	6.4	12.8	16.34
Bihar	9.8	8	7.8	22.08
Rajasthan	8.8	13.2	14.1	22.25
Madhya Pradesh	13.6	23.1	21.5	23.94
Uttar Pradesh	14.2	12.6	13.5	25.92
Haryana	19	9.9	14.8	28.07
Gujarat	14.5	19.9	23.5	31.27
Jammu & Kashmir	25.4	8	16.1	31.55
Orissa	30	26	28.7	40.14
Andhra Pradesh	33.8	39.9	49.2	62.08
Total	12.1	13.5	16.8	23.22

Source: Annual Survey of Industries.

A recent study on contractual employment in Karnataka (Rajeev and RoyChowdhuri 2005) documents that the main reason mentioned by principal employers to hire contract labor is flexibility, along with lower cost, higher efficiency and lower dispute-propensity. A field survey in that state indicated that contract workers' wages were substantially lower than those of regular workers, very few contract workers received bonuses or wage raises, many worked longer hours, and few received any training from employers. The survey also reveals a burgeoning growth of contract employment agencies and a decline in the commissions charged to workers. And while higher competition among contractors should be welcomed by workers, in this context higher competition has seemingly resulted in corruption, in particular, collusion between primary employers and contractors to pay wages below the minimum wage.

Another loophole actively exploited by employers is that voluntary retirements (VR) require no permission from the State. Fallon and Lucas (1991) reported that offers of one month pay per year of work in exchange of retirement were not unusual. While there are no reported data on the number of VR, or the median payments, casual evidence suggest that such payments are still widespread and that offers of one month or six weeks per year of work are still the norm. The Industrial Employment (Standing Orders) Act allows employment for a fixed term, which, under certain conditions, does not involve a commitment on the part of the employers to offer job security. This clause has been reportedly used by a number of large employers in manufacturing.

Adjudication

The IDA makes provisions for dispute settlement in three stages: negotiation, mediation and adjudication. The first stage involves voluntary communication between the disputants. The Act makes provisions for the constitution of Works Committees for the purpose. If such negotiations fail, the Act allows for outside conciliation, for example, settlement of industrial disputes by Labor Courts, Industrial Tribunals or National Tribunals. Collective bargaining is the accepted means to negotiate terms of employment, especially in larger organizations. However, there is a widely held opinion that both collective bargaining and conciliation systems are rather ineffective mechanisms in settling disputes on retrenchment, and are not much more than a necessary formality, before an industrial dispute case goes to adjudication (see, for example, Malhotra 2001).

Legal experts suggest that there is a built-in bias for judicial reference. The majority of cases of dispute concern discharge, dismissal and retrenchment. The legal provisions under the IDA are so protective that the worker expects to gain more from the court-room than from conciliation efforts. 'The easy accessibility of adjudication on these cases encourages the parties to take rigid stands' (Mukhopadhyay 2005). Khan (2005) states that 'Trade Unions prefer the adjudication process because the ministries and the labor judiciary, as well as the appellate courts are expected to be sympathetic to the cause of workers'.

Table 11.9 confirms the impression that conciliation is not very effective. Labor Bureau statistics suggest that conciliation is more effective at the state level, but the percentage of disputes sent for adjudication is increasing in the 1990s.

In sources of data on disputes, the word 'dispute' is employed in two senses. The *Indian Labor Statistics* refers to strikes and lockouts alone, the legal literature refers to cases that fall under specific labor laws, and are heard in courts of law as 'disputes'. The total number of strikes and lockouts has fallen somewhat in the early 2000s compared with the 1990s, even though the average duration and person-days lost has increased. 'In other words, though we are having fewer disputes the cost of a given dispute has substantially risen' (Saha 2005, p.89). There is some statistics that suggest a rather poor rate of disposal of cases, about 10 percent in 1997, by the Labor Courts, which implies an average duration of proceedings in Labor Courts of ten years.

With the judiciary, however, the situation is complex. While the legal framework has changed rather little in the 15 years since the economic reforms began, observers and experts have noted a significant shift in the axis of judicial interpretation of the most restrictive of the labor laws. In order to examine what has happened in the sphere of judgments, we decided to use case data compiled from the legal literature, instead of the less readable labor statistics. Table 11.7, prepared from case data, shows that:

Table 11.7 Industrial Disputes Act and Contract Labor Act cases heard in the Supreme Court and/or High Courts

	Number of cases under the Contract Labor Act and under Sections 11-A and 25 of IDA, which resulted in a definite verdict	*Of these cases, those decided in favor of employers*	*2 ÷ 1 (%)*	*Cases with a clear verdict as a ratio of total IDA and CLA cases*
	(1)	*(2)*	*(3)*	*(4)*
1990	23	4	17	45
1991	22	7	32	44
1992	3	1	33	3
1993	20	5	25	14
1994	18	11	61	9
1995	16	8	50	14
1996	16	3	19	12
1997	26	10	38	27
1998	16	9	56	10
1999	12	5	42	9
2000	23	9	39	14
2001	37	16	43	19
2002	34	19	56	29

Sources: *Labor Law Reporter*; *Labor Law Journal*; *Awards Digest*, various issues.

a The number of labor cases that find their way to the High Courts and the Supreme Court has increased since the economic reforms began in India. A large increase has happened with the Contract Labor Act cases, that is, cases concerning dismissal of a contract worker. The disputant worker makes the case that the worker deserved to be regularized and, therefore, the case should fall under 'retrenchment' rules of IDA.

b Unambiguous decisions in favor of or against the worker occur only in a minority of cases. Of the 165 cases in 2001, 37 had an unambiguous verdict.

c Of those cases unambiguously decided, a larger share of decisions goes in favor of the worker.

d However, the employer is faring better in the later period, the percentage of cases settled for the employer is higher in more recent times than before. A regression of the logarithm of these percentages on time yields a significantly positive trend, and suggests that time accounts of about 30 percent of the increase in pro-employer decisions.

The most disputative individual laws in IDA are the Sections 11-A, 25-O, 25F and 25G. Many cases of retrenchment under Section 11A end up before the judiciary. The section permits the Labor Courts to modify the retrenchment order dealt to an employee. This is also true in the case a worker is retrenched on disciplinary grounds. In nearly every case that reached the judiciary the aggrieved employee had filed an industrial dispute case with the Labor Court, received a judgment in his or her favor, and the employer challenged the judgment. What about the cases that were not challenged by the employer? In principle it is possible that in those cases the Labor Court gave an award in favor of the employer. But that is highly unlikely, for the cases that did go to the judiciary consisted of many in which the Labor Court condoned grave misconduct. In many cases, the order to take an errant worker back was passed in 'humanitarian interest'.

Section 25-O of the IDA makes it mandatory for employers to refer cases of closure to the state government. This clause has been in the eye of a legal storm for nearly 50 years, during which legislative intent and judicial interpretation of individual freedom came into conflict on several occasions. Legislative intent has been driven by the idea that unemployment through retrenchment or closure in any context was against the public interest. On the other hand, the idea that a bankrupt employer could be forced to keep a firm open at serious cost to personal well-being and finances seemed to contradict constitutional rights. The section 25-O has been a perennial source of anxiety for the judiciary. The historic amendment in 1982 that seriously restrained the rights of the employer was the response of the legislature to a generally adverse judicial opinion about the constitutionality of 25-O. In the more politically charged contexts, 25-O has been misused by the powers that rule the state governments. In *Jay Engineering Works Ltd.* v. *State of West Bengal*, Calcutta High Court, 1991, for example, it was observed by the judge that 25-O was invoked by the state government refusing permission to close a sick unit based on consultations with the workers alone.

The Section 25-G imposes on the employer the 'last-come-first-go' principle when carrying out retrenchment. As in many other pieces of legislation, this one too loads the job-security provisions for the insider by making the jobs of the older employees more secure than the younger ones. In effect, it violates the employer's right to select among the best workers, and neutralizes the right to retain the younger and better-trained workers in favor of the older and less well-trained ones. The clause arises out of a mindset that sees experience to be more valuable than formal training, measures experience by years rather than quality of service, and that sees technology as static during the lifetime of a worker, a world of the public-sector engineering firm at 1980. It is clearly incompatible and dangerous in activities that must keep up with rapid growth of knowledge.

Section 25F states that any employee working in a firm for 240 days or more in the previous 12 months can in principle claim retrenchment compensation. Other sections in the law state various kinds of termination (such as disciplinary action, end of probation period, etc.) that are not legally retrenchments. However, what is a retrenchment and what is not is a question that was left open by both the acts and the case laws until recently. In many cases, employees, irrespective of the nature of the contract, demanded that their dismissal from service was retrenchment under the length-of-service rule. Several court cases show that the Labor Courts are usually ready to grant such requests. In 2003, a Supreme Court judgment (*S.M. Nilajkar* v. *Telecom District Manager, Karnataka*) clarified that the natural coming-to-an-end of project-based, contractual employment was not retrenchment, provided the employee was pre-informed of the nature of the contract. In the meantime, the term 'retrenchment' had been broadened.

The Section 25 practically disallows retrenchments or lay-offs without compensation except when the owner dies. And a series of court cases made lay-offs and retrenchments with compensation on any ground impossible too. According to the IDA, lay-off is an inability of the firm to employ a worker on the muster, and retrenchment is termination of employment except on disciplinary ground. In one interpretation, the Section 25 makes it risky for the employer to promote anyone. In *Suraj Prakash Bhandari* v. *Union of India* (Supreme Court, 1986), an employee was promoted to a new position, and shortly thereafter retrenched on the ground that the new position was no longer needed. Section 25 also encouraged employees under a variety of fixed-term contracts, whether formal or informal, to claim the status of regular employees (entitled to retrenchment compensation), with a fair degree of success until recently. In two significant judgments (*Divisional Manager, Andhra Pradesh State Road Transport Corporation* v. P. *Lakshmoji Rao*, Supreme Court, 2004; and *Executive Engineer, Zilla Parishad Engineering Division* v. *Digambara Rao*, Supreme Court, 2004), the court ruled that serving one employer for 240 days continuously is not sufficient to claim the status of a regular employee.

The CLA has also seen a conflict between two tendencies in the sphere of case laws. On the one hand, the Act allows freedom to the employer denied him/her by the IDA. Some judges understood and respected that freedom. On the other hand, like in the case of 25-O, some judges saw this freedom as a failing and weakness of the Act, and judgments passed in that spirit led to a gradual crystallization of a job-security right within the Contract Labour Act. It is in this sphere that judicial rethinking has perhaps been the most striking. A series of cases in 2004 and 2005 reflected the interpretation that the fixed-term worker has no automatic right to demand regular employment on completion of 240 days of more or less continuous work. To demand a regular job, such a worker needs to make a case that the temporary status was a ploy to deprive him/her of a permanent status to which the person was in some sense entitled (for example, *Regional Manager, State Bank of India* v. *Raja Ram*, Supreme Court, 2005). An important judgment of 2004, delivered by the Bombay High Court observed that

> The other injurious effect of indiscriminate regularization has been that many of the agencies have stopped undertaking casual and temporary workers though they are urgent and essential for fear that those required to be continued for 240 or more days have to be absorbed. *Public interests are thus jeopardized.*
>
> (*Maharashtra Krishna Valley Development Corporation* v. *Tukaram Sahebrao Veer*, 2004)

The economic effects of selected key legislation

What was the effect of this complex and overly restrictive legislation on economic outcomes? Did the inefficiencies in enforcement and the *de facto* deregulation that took place reduce the impact of legislation? To answer this question requires performing statistical and econometric analysis to assess if and how legislation and, in particular, changes in legislation relates to variables such as output, employment creation, investment or workers' earnings.

While labor legislation is introduced with the objective of improving workers' welfare, there may be a number of adverse consequences on economic outcomes, and in turn, on workers' wellbeing, because it can generate: (i) price effects; (ii) hold-up effects; and/or (iii) rigidity effects. *Price effects* occur when legislation increases the cost of labor, thus reducing employers' incentives to hire workers. *Hold-up effects* occur when legislation makes it easier for one party to appropriate the return of the investment of the other party, thereby reducing the incentives of the latter to invest. This is the case, for instance, when legislation increases workers' ability to initiate and sustain industrial disputes, which may lead to lower returns on the investments of employers. Finally, *rigidity effects* occur when legislation makes the adjustment of labor (or other factors) more costly and difficult. Legislation that increases the price of labor or generates expropriation effects is expected to have a negative effect on the demand for labor. Instead, legislation that increases the cost of adjusting employment has ambiguous effects since it may cause a reduction of both job creation *and* job destruction (Bertola 1990).

Employers' opinions

Are employers constrained by labor legislation? An interesting source of cross-country information is provided by the Investment Climate Surveys (ICS). They collect firm level information on production, input use and the investment climate across a large number of countries.[7] Among other questions, ICS ask firms about how much labor-market regulations constitute an obstacle for their growth. Higher values of this answer imply higher obstacles for firms. The average of such responses by country yields a telling measure of differences in perceptions across countries (see Figure 11.7). According to this data, in India labor regulations are perceived to be a larger obstacle for firms' growth than in most other countries of the world.[8]

Moreover, larger firms tend to consider labor legislation as more of an obstacle than smaller firms (Figure 11.8). This is consistent with the fact that the most contentious labor law, chapter Vb of the Industrial Disputes Act, applies only to manufacturing firms that employ 100 or more regular employees. Interestingly, large firms consider labor legislation to be as constraining for their growth as electricity shortages, although not as constraining as taxes (rate and administration) or corruption.

The effects of dispute and retrenchment legislation

A number of studies have attempted to estimate the effects of job-security legislation, such as chapter Vb, on economic outcomes in India. In comparison, there is much less analytical work assessing the effects of the rest of laws contained in the IDA. Fallon and Lucas (1991) and (1993) studied the effects of the 1976 introduction of chapter Vb. They concluded that after the reform formal employment for a given level of output declined by 17.5 percent. In another study, Besley and Burgess (2004) found labor legislation to have important adverse effects on output and employment, particularly in the registered manufacturing sector. Hasan et al.(2003) examined whether differences in labor laws explain differences in the way labor markets adjusted to trade reforms. They found that states with more stringent labor legislation (measured as in Besley and Burgess 2004) had lower demand elasticities and these elasticities were less affected by trade reforms. Finally Lall and Mengistae (2005) examined the influence of labor-market legislation – as perceived by employers – on plant-productivity differences across Indian cities. They found that differences in legislation, jointly with differences in the severity of power shortages, explained a large share of the productivity differences between cities in India. Not all authors found results in the same direction. Dutta Roy (2004) examined the effects of a 1982 central amendment to the IDA, which extended the prohibition to retrench workers to firms that employ hundred or more workers and found evidence of substantial adjustment costs in employment but no evidence that such costs were driven or altered by the IDA legislative amendment.

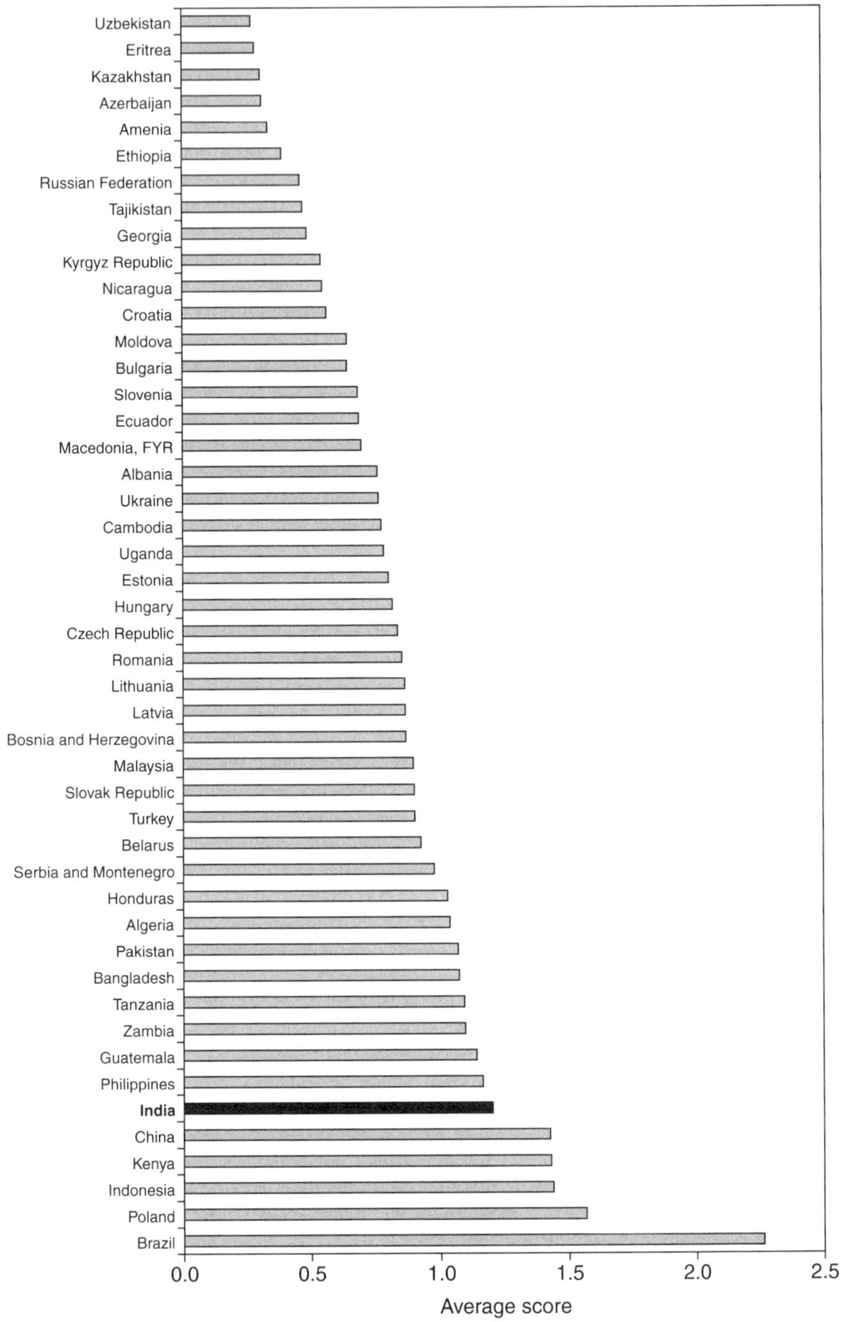

Figure 11.7 Average country perception on whether labor market regulations are an obstacle for growth (source: Investment Climate Surveys, the World Bank).

Notes
0 = No obstacle, 3 = Large obstacle.

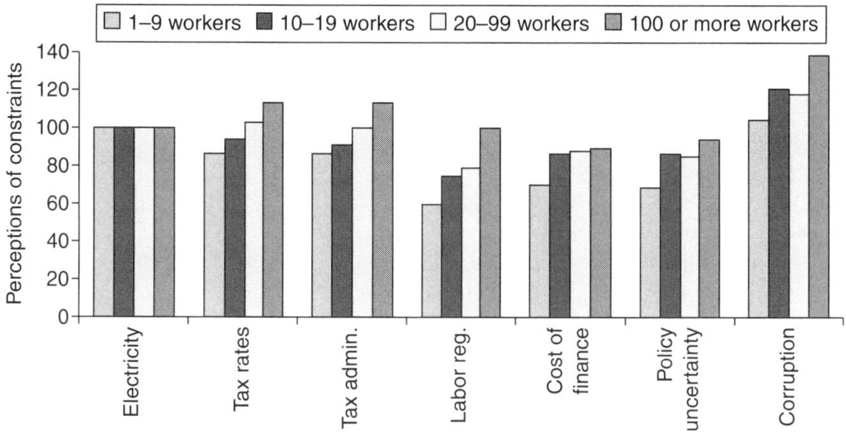

Figure 11.8 Ranking of perceptions of constraints (normalized to 100 for electricity) to firm growth of manufacturing firms, by firm size (source: Authors' computations from 2002 IIC-World Bank Investment Climate Survey data).

While the former results suggest that labor legislation can generate important adverse effects on economic outcomes, some of the former studies do not address important methodological issues. For example, while Fallon and Lucas find a decline in employment after the introduction of chapter Vb, this decline could be driven by factors contemporaneous to the introduction of the law, rather than by the law itself. Besley and Burgess control for this fact and still found an important effect of labor legislation, but since they use an aggregate measure of legislation, their results provide little evidence on whether all laws have similar effects, and if not, which labor laws are behind their identified adverse effects.

Using Annual Survey of Industries (ASI) data on manufacturing employment, output, investment, wages and number of factories by state and industry, Ahmad and Pagés (2006) estimate the effect of different laws on a number of economic variables distinguishing between job-security and dispute-related legislation. Within job security, they also distinguish between amendments to chapter Vb, and amendments in other laws that relate to the procedures for termination of the work relationship or the closure of firms. They also distinguish between labor reforms that involve amendments in the law (*de jure*) and de facto deregulation that occur, for example, by the increasing recourse of firms to contract labor.

Their methodology is based on constructing measures that track *de jure* and de facto labors reforms at the state level during the period 1959–1997. The construction of measures of *de jure* labor reforms follows Besley and Burgess (2004) procedure with some modifications. For the measure of job security, they construct a variable that takes a value of one when a state implements an amendment to the IDA that goes in the direction of increasing job security and –1 when labor reforms go in the opposite direction. Then they add up all these changes, so that in each period, the measure of labor legislation is the cumulative sum of all reforms to that given date. Higher positive values indicate that in a given state and year, job security is high because the reforms in the direction of increasing job security have not been outweighed by reforms in the opposite direction. An identical procedure is implemented for measuring reforms on laws that affect the resolution of industrial disputes.[9] During the period of study, some states implemented amendments to reduce the cost of labor disputes while other states passed amendments that made labor disputes more costly.[10] Instead, over time all amendments to lay-off, retrenchment and firm-closure laws were in the direction of making such actions more costly for the employer. De facto reforms are captured by the percentage of contract labor in each period and state, which as shown in Table 11.6, varies considerably across time and states. All these measures are then related to economic outcomes by estimating an econometric model that regresses economic outcomes on the labor-legislation measures, state and time dummies and controls at the state level.[11]

The results of this analysis strongly indicate that a state amendment that increases the cost of labor disputes or retrenchment above the cost stipulated by the Central Act results in declines in registered manufacturing employment and output in that state relative to the states that do not implement such changes. The main results are the following:

It is found that legislation both that (i) makes labor disputes costly and (ii) retrenchment costs high through the VB clause biases economic activity against registered manufacturing and in favor of sectors such as agriculture, construction or non-registered manufacturing, in which the IDA does not apply. Within manufacturing, legal amendments that slow down the resolution of industrial disputes or reduce firms' labor-adjustment possibilities lead to a reduction in registered manufacturing output of between 15 and 20 percent, and expand unregistered manufacturing output between 6 and 7 percent. The former underscores that while laws intended to increase job security, such as chapter Vb, draw most of the attention, dispute-related laws can also exert a large, if not larger, effect on economic outcomes. It is also estimated that both types of laws have important detrimental impact in manufacturing employment, for both total persons employed and also for production workers (Figure 11.9). It is estimated that India may have lost around 1,114,000 due to the introduction of chapter Vb, another 1,700,000 jobs due to the 1982 amendment of Chapter Vb, and 750,000 jobs due to different state amendments that made state acts more stringent than the central act.

In turn, results for capital indicate that much of the negative effects on employment and output are driven by a decline in investment rates and capital stocks, both in terms of capital per factory and capital per capita. Instead, and contrary to what is often predicted by economic theory, the capital–labor ratio within each firm declined. This again suggests that the reduction in investments and capital

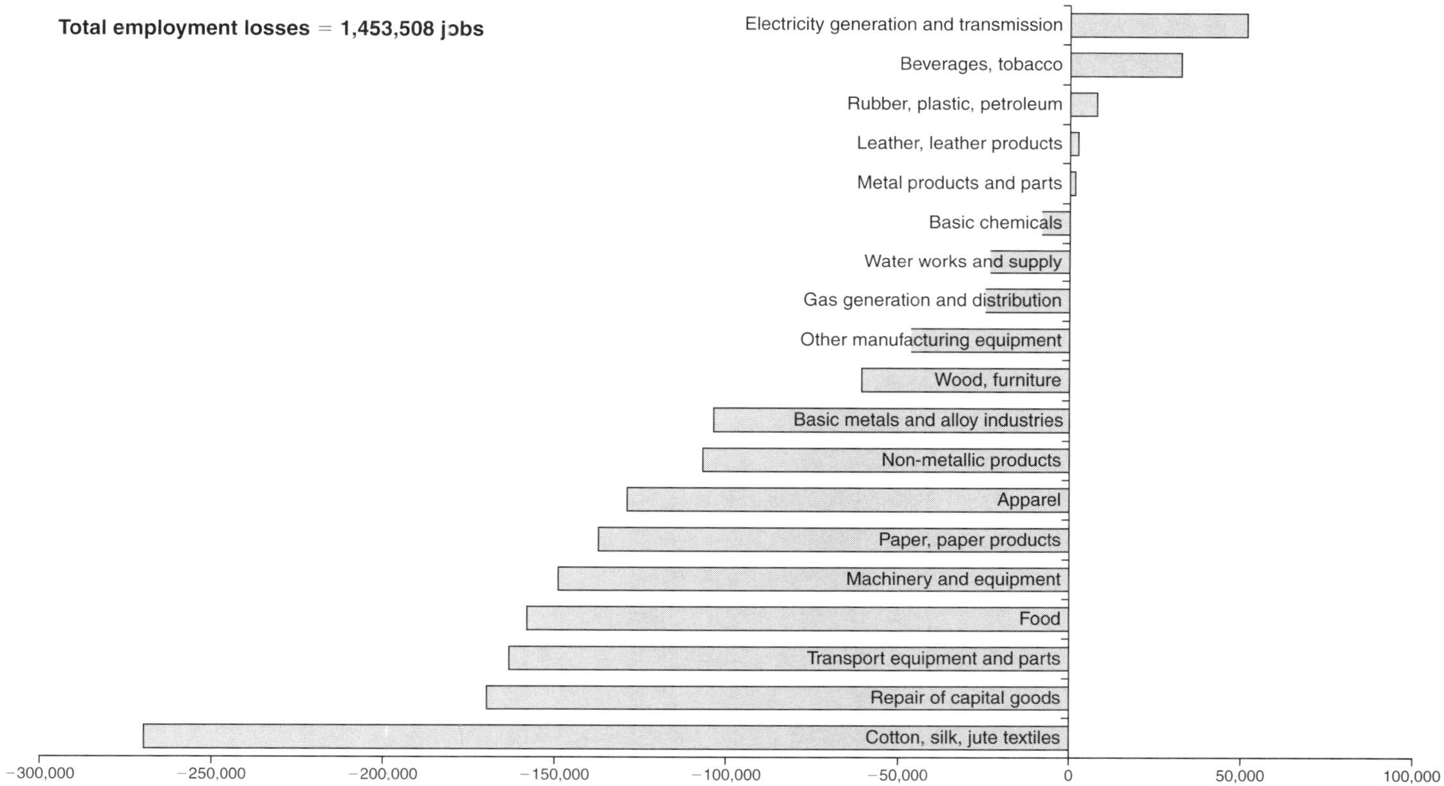

Figure 11.9 Measuring the cost of job security laws on employment by industries (Number of jobs lost due to state amendments in Job Security Legislation in IDA).

was driven by a fear that the returns of investments would be appropriation by part of labor and that this effect more than outweighed the price effect – which would go in the direction of substituting labor for capital. The effect on capital is much larger for laws that increase the cost of labor disputes (Figure 11.10).

In line with the results on capital, dispute-related regulations cost more jobs in capital-intensive industries (Figure 11.9), while retrenchment-related regulations have a higher job impact in labor-intensive industries. In addition, rather than a reduction in the number of jobs in existing plants, job losses are due to a decline in the number of factories. This suggests that labor laws are important in shaping incentives for new firms to enter the market. It also indicates that any positive gains in preserving jobs in existing factories were outweighed by the new factories that were not created.

Job-security regulations can lead to distributive conflicts. It is found that amendments that increase the cost of retrenchment have a positive effect on earnings per worker, although they do not have a positive effect on the total wage bill – that is the amount of resources that goes to workers – or the labor share – that is, the share of value added that goes to workers. This is because the increase in wages is offset by a decline in employment. This indicates that while some individual workers benefit by receiving higher earnings, others are worse off due to reduced access to manufacturing jobs.

Retrenchment-related regulations affect job losses in more states (Figure 11.10) than dispute-related regulations. This in part due to the fact that some states implemented laws reducing the cost of labor disputes, which resulted in employment gains – while no state implemented reductions in the cost retrenchment. West Bengal and Maharashtra pay, by far, the biggest costs in terms of jobs lost – accounting for more than half of gross job losses. States such as West

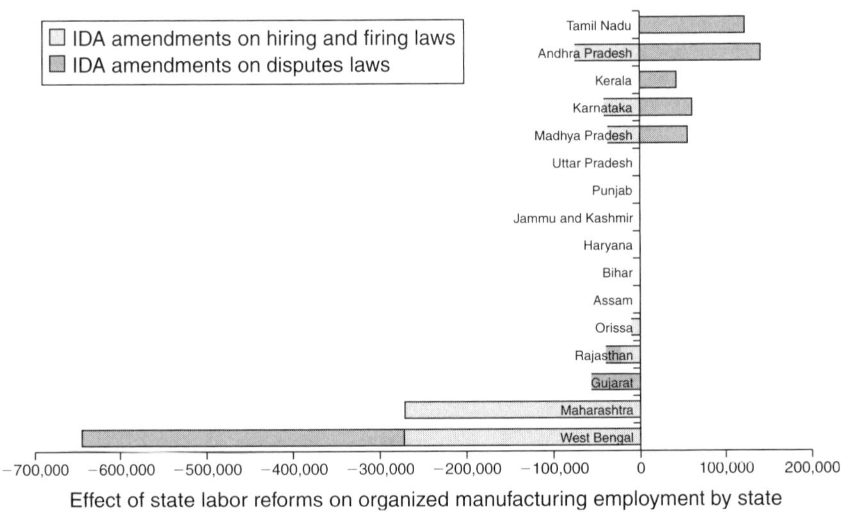

Figure 11.10 Measuring the costs of regulations on employment by states.

Bengal, Maharashtra, Gujarat and Rajasthan pay the costs in terms of thousands of factories that do not exist because of IDA regulations. This is because these states have more stringent labor regulations relative to the rest of states.

Finally, there is also some evidence that the use of contract labor across different states in the 1990s may have helped to reduce somewhat the costs of job-security regulations in terms of output but it has not done away with all the effects of regulations.

The adverse effects of labor laws in India do not circumscribe to the IDA. There are too many laws in place. A relatively large employer in western India would need to be knowledgeable about, on average, 28 acts. There are inevitably overlaps, and workers and employers have an incentive to seek protection not granted in one by recourse to another. The dynamics of legislation has been politically driven, with the result that a new demand for a specific law has usually been met by framing a new Act without changing the contents of the old one. Key concepts such as worker or factory have ambiguous meanings and are defined differently across Acts. For example, while the IDA excludes a number of undertakings including educational institutions from the concept of industry, the courts have held that skilled or unskilled workers in educational institution are employed by an industry, while teachers cannot be treated as workmen. As services are becoming increasingly important, it is unclear how the concepts of industry or workman are applied in the service sector.[12]

The former analysis is not to say that any labor regulations will have a negative effect on employment. But laws such as chapter Vb, which, as seen in the former section are more restrictive than anywhere else in the world, destroy, not protect, jobs. So it does the dispute-settlement mechanism. There has been a crowding out of the enterprise-level and local institutions by the state and the courts. It is not being suggested that firm-level institutions are necessarily more efficient than industry-level ones. However, the weakening of one of these levels limits the choice for both employers and workers, and, hence, potentially raises the costs of disputes. Sometimes legislation bears upon private contracts and squeeze private negotiations. Mechanisms at the firm level have often not been allowed to strengthen and grow; rather, these have been stifled. A third problem is that there is too much uncertainty regarding the interpretation of laws. For examples, in a 1970 case of a factory closure in Mumbai that progressed from the labor court to the Supreme Court, the legality of the closure was decided on the meaning of the word 'undertaking', and was decided in favor or the workers. In Premier Automobiles v. Engineering Mazdoor Sabha, 1971, the Bombay High Court ruled that the precise provisions of a contract depended on whether or not the matter under dispute (in this case 'ex-gratia payment') was *implied* by the parties when a contract was drawn.

The effect of minimum-wage laws

With individual states having as many as 40 or more minimum wages in place set by both central and state governments, minimum-wage regulations in India are as complex as other labor laws. Within the agricultural sector alone there are minimum wages for ploughing, weeding, sowing, transplanting harvesting, winnowing, threshing picking and herding. In the construction industry, stone breaking has eight minimum wages, set by the central government, differentiated by the thickness around an inch of the stone broken. There are also floor minimum wages set by the state governments for unskilled workers.

One result of this complexity is that minimum wages are not well enforced. A large share of workers, some 40 percent of agricultural workers and 21 percent of urban casual workers (top panel of Figure 11.11) get wages below the

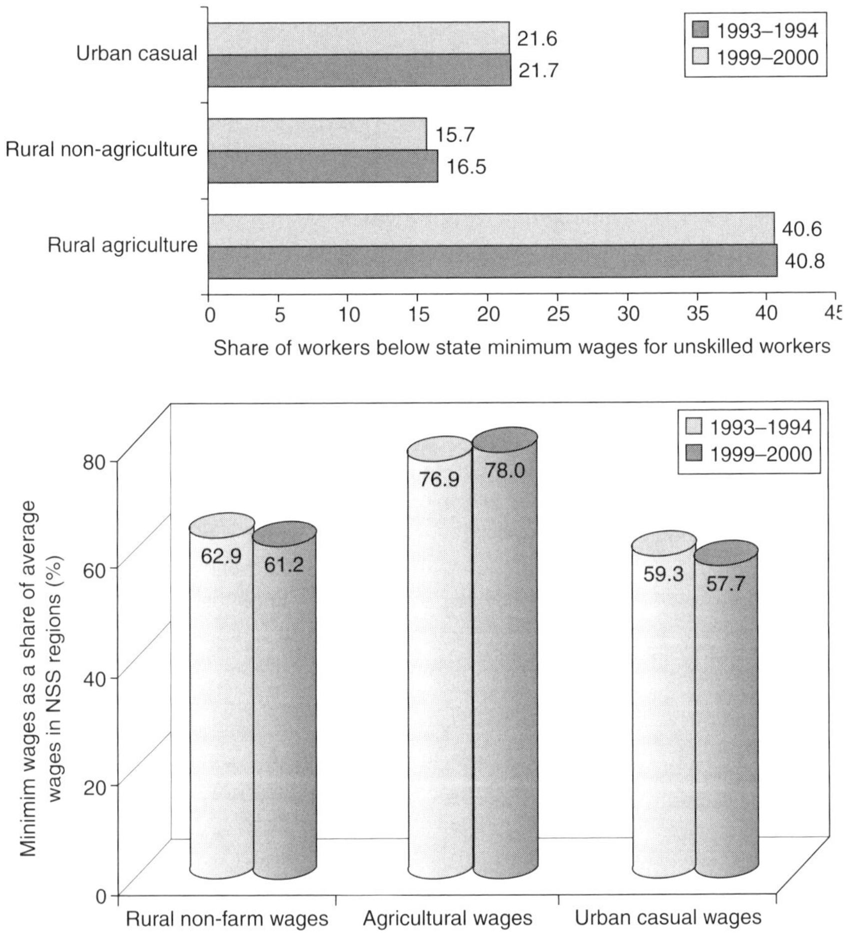

Figure 11.11 Minimum wages and employment (source: Wage data from NSS. Minimum wage data from Indiastat.com).

Notes
Top panel: Share of workers below state minimum wages for unskilled workers. Bottom panel: Minimum wages as a % of average wages in NSS regions.

lowest minimum wage (typically the one set for unskilled casual workers). Such figures, however, are likely to underestimate lack of compliance. Regarding the level, in most states, minimum wages are considerably below average wages for casual workers, both in agricultural activities and in urban jobs (bottom panel in Figure 11.11).

The data suggests a strong effect of minimum wages in supporting wages for unskilled casual workers in urban and rural areas. Such impact can be seen in the distribution of casual wages by states, presented in Figure 11.12, which show an important spike of rural and urban casual wages around the unskilled workers' minimum wage. The data also shows an important correlation between casual wages for agricultural and for urban workers and minimum wages across regions and over the periods in 1993–1994 and 1999–2000 (Figure 11.13). This is the case even after controlling for state fixed effects that can take into account other factors that determine the level of minimum wages.

Preliminary analysis suggests that minimum wages may be supporting the wages of less skilled workers without apparent costs on employment. A separate exercise indicate that unemployment (UPS) and underemployment rates (CDS) in the different states do not appear to be related to minimum wages even after we allow for fixed effects. A preliminary conclusion of this analysis is that minimum wages for unskilled workers could be welfare enhancing as they raise wages for unskilled poor workers without reducing employment or increasing unemployment significantly. Such a conclusion, however, is only tentative in that in need to be supported by further analysis. However, it points to an area of major policy importance that has been greatly under-researched as it can imply that a streamlined regime of minimum wages could be welfare enhancing for those in more need.

Conclusions and way forward

Markets need adequate institutional infrastructure to thrive.[13] This implies an appropriate set of regulations, effective law-enforcement institutions and a fair and efficient mechanism to settle disputes. In India, the labor-regulation debate is often portrayed as a choice between strict regulations and lawlessness. However, it should be more appropriately defined as a choice between keeping arcane regulations and institutions versus adopting a new market infrastructure that effectively advances the cause of workers. In this chapter, we have reviewed the system of regulations, law-enforcement and dispute resolution that supports Indian labor markets and found it to do very little to improve workers' welfare. By inhibiting job creation, capital accumulation and technology upgrades, this system deprives workers from employment opportunities while sustaining low productivity, low wages and poor work conditions. The complexity of the legal framework makes it impossible to enforce, which in turns leads to widespread corruption, a higher cost of doing business and no gains for workers. Labor disputes take forever to be resolved, creating inordinate amounts of uncertainty for all parties. This is not a status quo worth

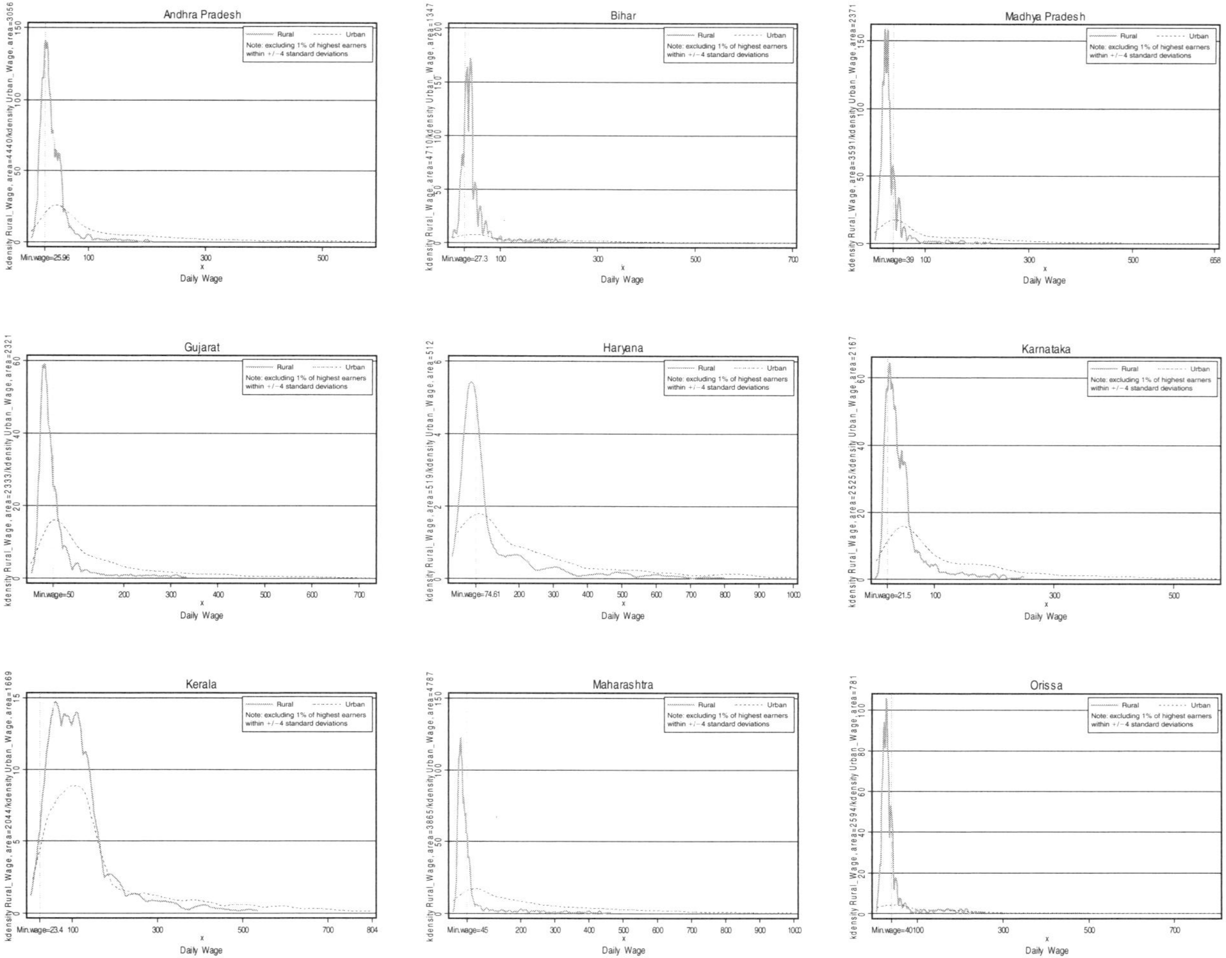
Andhra Pradesh
Bihar
Madhya Pradesh
Gujarat
Haryana
Karnataka
Kerala
Maharashtra
Orissa
Rural
Urban
Note: excluding 1% of highest earners within +/−4 standard deviations
Daily Wage
kdensity Rural_Wage, area=4440/kdensity Urban_Wage, area=3056
kdensity Rural_Wage, area=4710/kdensity Urban_Wage, area=1347
kdensity Rural_Wage, area=3591/kdensity Urban_Wage, area=2371
kdensity Rural_Wage, area=2333/kdensity Urban_Wage, area=2321
kdensity Rural_Wage, area=519/kdensity Urban_Wage, area=512
kdensity Rural_Wage, area=2525/kdensity Urban_Wage, area=2167
kdensity Rural_Wage, area=2044/kdensity Urban_Wage, area=1669
kdensity Rural_Wage, area=3865/kdensity Urban_Wage, area=4787
kdensity Rural_Wage, area=2594/kdensity Urban_Wage, area=781
Min.wage=25.96
Min.wage=27.3
Min.wage=39
Min.wage=50
Min.wage=74.61
Min.wage=21.5
Min.wage=23.4
Min.wage=45
Min.wage=40

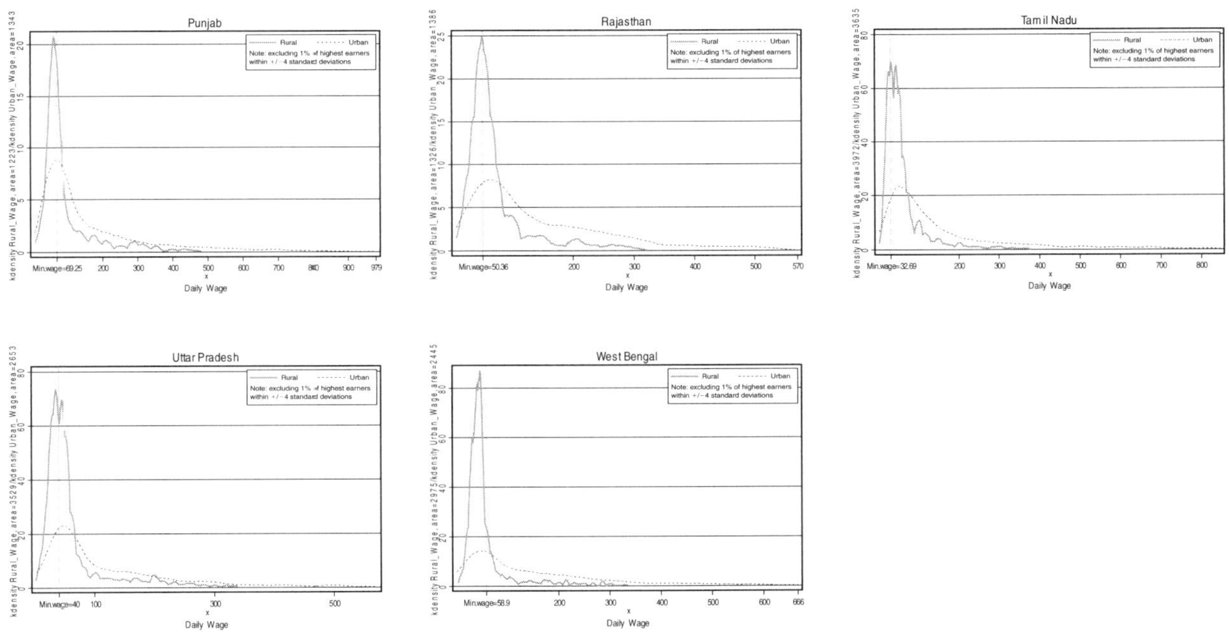

Figure 11.12 Clustering of urban and rural casual wages and minimum wages by state kernel distribution of urban and rural casual wages (source: Own estimates based on NSS and minimum wage data from Indiastat.com).

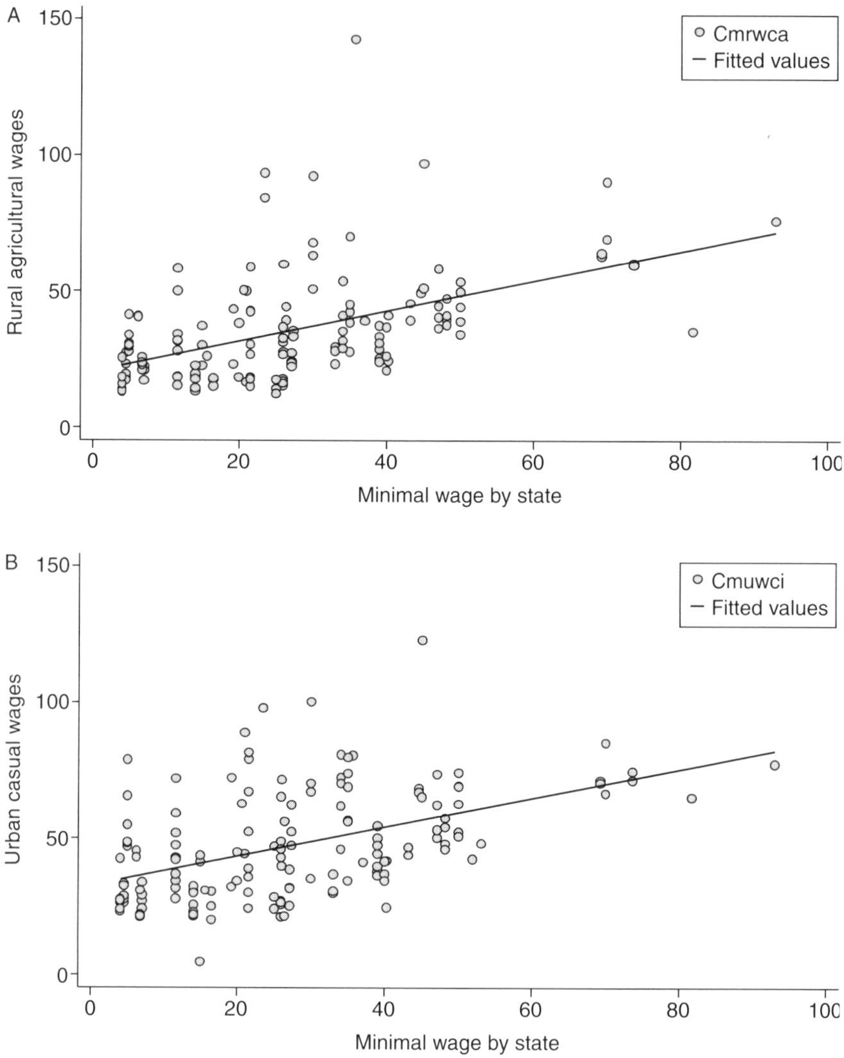

Figure 11.13 Rural and urban wages. (a) Rural agricultural wages and minimum wages regions in 50th and 55th rounds. (b) Urban casual wages and minimum wages by regions in 50th and 55th rounds (source: NSS and Ministry of Labor for minimum wages. Adjusted R squared for the two estimates at 0.85 and 0.75 respectively).

defending. To create a new institutional infrastructure that can truly advance the cause of workers and promote growth it is necessary to expand the reform debate beyond labor regulations to areas such as dispute resolution, adjudication, labor inspections and labor policy. Below, we describe what in our view would be some of the required transformations:

1 It is necessary to consolidate all Acts into a single law on labor relations dealing with the following aspects: (i) wages and conditions of work; (ii) social security; (iii) hiring and termination procedures; (iv) trade unions; (v) industrial disputes; (vi) health and safety provisions. In addition, key concepts such *workman* and *factory*, whose meaning and coverage is ambiguous and varies among Acts should be clarified and harmonized.

2 The resolution of industrial disputes should be rationalized in several ways. First, "*right disputes*" – that is those disputes that are based on a legal - right – and "*interest disputes*" – those which are not based on any existing rights – need to be distinguished. Only the first class of disputes should be a matter of adjudication. Disagreements belonging to the second class should be solved by means of collective bargaining, or if that fails, conciliation and arbitration mechanisms (Nath 2005). A corollary is that the machinery for conciliation should be strengthened, by giving conciliator officers powers currently awarded to the Board of Conciliator, making conciliation a compulsory step prior to adjudication, giving appropriate training and incentives to officers so they don't succumb to pressures from different groups (Hazra 2005), *addressing the shortage* of well-trained, high-caliber presiding officers in labor courts and tribunals (Hazra 2005), and *eliminating over-regulatory and impractical clauses and adopting procedures to expedite the resolution of disputes* (i.e., the possibility of adjournments and delays should be limited, the possibility that cases once rejected can be subsequently referred without new facts arising should be eliminated). Finally, the possibility of raising old disputes should be limited to one year (section 10 of the IDA) (Hazra 2005).

3 Regulation needs to evolve from protecting the job to protecting the worker. Change, transformation and upgradation are the engines of economic growth, and the legal framework requires to be sensitive to these needs. This in turn implies transforming current provisions aimed at ensuring job security into mechanisms that protect the incomes and welfare of those workers adversely affected by technological change or market fluctuations. More concretely such reforms would imply the following steps:

   a *Strengthening compensation for retrenchment and firm closure.* The current compensation contemplated in IDA is well below the standards of developing countries, and although in line with those prevalent in developed countries, workers in industrial countries have access to other forms of unemployment insurance. A compensation of one month per year of work, with an upper maximum of 8–11 months pay, would be in line with international standards.[14] However, it is necessary to trade off the insurance properties of such compensation with the possible disincentives for job creation. To minimize such disincentives, and quite importantly, to insure that workers receive the compensation in times of need, additional institutional mechanisms are required. One such mechanism is to mandate that firms regularly deposit a certain percentage of workers' wages in a financial institution account open for that purpose. Compensations to workers would then be paid out of the funds secured in the account or fund, which would prevent sick or closing firms from defaulting from their obligations. Building funds for a rainy day would allow increasing the very meager compensation that workers now received in case of closure to the same level that compensations awarded for retrenchment. To make these possible, firms who default from their contributions ought to be considered in serious breach of the law and penalized. A slightly different alternative, already in effect in some Latin American countries (Colombia, Peru, Ecuador and somewhat differently in Brazil), is to create individual accounts for each worker to which firms deposit a certain percentage of the worker's wage every month.[15] The funds in the account are the property of the worker and can be accessed in the event the worker is laid off, retrenched or quits the job. These funds then act as an unemployment insurance providing income support while the worker searches for another job.

b *Reduce incentives of parties to recur to adjudication.* Section 11-A of the IDA which gives discretion to labor courts and tribunals to reinstate the worker should be eliminated. Labor Courts should be endowed with the power to seek payments from firms to workers but not to direct reinstatement.

c *Eliminating section 25G which stabilizes procedure for retrenchment.* Section 25G establishes that when a worker is to be retrenched, the employer should start by the last person hired. In the current fast-changing environment, this section penalizes firms that seek to hire and maintain workers with the latest up-to-date skills, relative to firms that rely on experience. It does not do much for incentives as older, higher-experience workers have their posts secured even if they don't perform in their jobs.

d *Making job-search assistance and training available to workers affected by retrenchment.* The most successful income-support mechanism for a worker that loses his or her job is to find a similar or better job as fast as possible. Labor policy should assist workers to that end.

e *Eliminating the provisions related to seeking government permission for retrenchment and closure (Chapter Vb).* It has been proposed that chapter Vb be applicable only to industrial undertakings having 300 or more employees (report of second commission of Labor; Hazra 2005 among others). While such extension would reduce the adverse effects that this provision creates in the labor market, and make reform more acceptable to proponents of the status quo, it would still maintain strong disincentives for firms to grow above this size threshold. Yet, if firms are to seize the opportunities afforded by the global economy and take advantage of economies of scale, they will need to grow considerably in size. Inhibiting this process will cost India high paid jobs, since it is a well-established fact that wages increase with the size of a firm.[16] More generally, labor laws should avoid penalizing firms' growth.

4 Contract labor should not constitute a form of avoidance of labor laws. Contracting out work allows firms to concentrate in their core business and improve overall competitiveness. However, in very regulated labor markets, contract labor becomes a form of avoidance. Enacting comprehensive labor reforms is required to reduce the incentives to over-rely on this type of employment and improve the welfare of contract labor workers. As comprehensive reforms in the labor market take place, the use of contract labor becomes less distorted. Nonetheless, regulations on contract labor (and more generally on all those forms of work other than regular indefinite contracts) should strike a balance between the search for efficiency and the need to provide adequate protection to non-permanent workers. Labor laws should apply to the contractor in his/her relationship with the contract worker. Thus, for instance, in a reformed scenario along the lines proposed, contractors would have to make contributions to a Retrenchment Compensation Fund or to make regular contributions to workers' individual accounts. Such funds would be made available to the contract worker in the event the relationship between the contract labor worker and the contractor ends (see, however, that if a relationship between a principal employer and a contract worker ends but the contractor is prepared to place this worker in another firm at a similar wage then the end of the employment relationship between the contract worker and the principal employer would not be considered retrenchment)[17] It is also imperative to promote and facilitate training of contract workers.

5 Strengthen labor inspections and labor-law enforcement. Firms devote too much valuable time to deal with inspections, while inspectors enjoy inordinate powers to extract unofficial payments. Inspections should be targeted and publicly pre-announced. Firms to be inspected should be selected based on formal complaints raised by workers' representatives and for the group of firms where no complains are raised, inspections should be targeted based on which firms are more likely to evade the law. Inspectors should focus on technical assistance and not just sanctions, which in turn requires that inspectors be appropriately trained to be able to perform. On this issue, the ILO recommends not funding the inspectorate from revenue generated from fines, as it inhibits the educational/promotional role of the inspector. Some initiatives such as employer-generated implementation plans (EGIP) have produced good results in other countries. Employers can tailor an implementation plan and policies to suit their needs. They report to the inspectorate on progress against self-defined benchmarks in their annual plan for improving working conditions. Compliance is more likely since employers and often, as recommended, workers "own" the strategy. Other useful strategies are

providing special educational components and information provision to small and medium (SME) firms. Other important measures are to build a culture of compliance through mass-media campaigns and education in business schools and professionalize inspections providing adequate training and compensation.

12 Strengthening employment and social security for unorganized-sector workers in India

Philip O'Keefe and Robert Palacios[1]

Introduction

This chapter examines two approaches to promoting employment and social security for the labor force in India: (i) public works programs; and (ii) initiatives to provide social security for unorganized workers. A common objective of both types of interventions is consumption smoothing for unorganized-sector workers. While the modes of worker protection differ, the common theme is exploring the potential for public interventions to address market failures which may contribute directly and indirectly to poor welfare and labor-market outcomes in India.

The structure of the chapter is: the next section looks at public-works schemes in India. It first outlines the objectives of public works, before exploring spending trends and employment and other outcomes. A discussion of factors driving outcomes follows, before a review of the National Rural Employment Guarantee Act (NREG) and conclusions. The following section focuses on social security for unorganized workers. It first outlines international experience in expansion of social protection. A review of recent initiatives in India follows. This is followed by review of evidence on membership of intermediary organizations of unorganized workers. Conclusions and recommendations follow.

The motivation for this chapter includes the following:

- One of the factors driving chronic and transient poverty in India is uninsured risks faced by households. There is thus an equity rationale for understanding the role for public policy in helping households deal with risks and shocks related to unemployment, health and death, maternity and sickness, and unprotected old age.
- Uninsured risks and associated credit and insurance market failures may contribute to low productivity in the unorganized sector, particularly in agriculture. If this is so, there is a dynamic efficiency motive for understanding the role of policy in risk management.[2]
- GoI (Government of India) has placed an increased policy emphasis on both public works and social security for unorganized-sector workers in its CMP

(Common Minimum Program). This makes it important to understand what are the realistic expectations for public programs, in the light of experience in India and internationally.

- One objection to greater flexibility in labor regulations in India is the absence of a functional safety net. Understanding more about public interventions to provide social-security and employment support to workers may therefore be relevant to debates on labor regulation.

The objectives of the chapter are:

- To assess the role of both public-works and social-security initiatives in promoting consumption smoothing by unorganized-sector households in the face of predictable fluctuations in income-related to seasonal labor demand, and unpredictable fluctuations due to covariate and idiosyncratic shocks.
- To draw lessons for initiatives which may help in improving the impact of public interventions on the social risk-management strategies of unorganized-sector workers.

Public works schemes[3]

Objectives of public works

It is important to examine the objectives of public-works programs in order to assess workfare in India. They include:

- The transfer impact, i.e., direct transfer benefits to participating households. This impact is often equated with the employment impact, though the latter is properly considered as an intermediate activity.
- Impacts on overall wage levels, which may be felt by participating and non-participating households whose incomes are below the post-program area wage. The positive impact may be offset by negative impacts on labor demand from higher wages.
- Indirect impacts from the economic benefits of assets created under works schemes. These would typically be spread among a wider population than participants, so that the economic returns on assets to the poor will affect the distributional impact of workfare.
- The consumption smoothing or insurance function that schemes perform by acting as an effective wage floor. Whether or not households participate in the program, insurance benefits may promote less risk-averse behavior in production and portfolio choices.
- Skills development impacts for workfare participants, through work or training provided.[4]
- Impacts on gender and other socio-economic relations due to features such as equal pay for equal work, increased female labor-force participation, etc.

- Community-empowerment impacts which may arise through reliance on communities at different stages of sub-project planning and identification, beneficiary selection, works execution and monitoring.

Evolution of policy and expenditures on public works in India

Since the 1970s, public works have been an important component of the Indian safety net, with a succession of programs, both centrally sponsored and state-specific. This assessment focuses on the major central-works programs. While changes in programs have been frequent, much of the development has been rebranding rather than fundamental reform. The most significant policy shift in the 1990s has been the increased role for PRIs (Panchayat Raj Institutions). However, even this shift, which is clear in the guidelines of workfare programs (and very thorough in NREG) has been more mixed than policies might indicate. The more recent policy shift has been from scheme-based provision of works to a legislatively backed 100-day rural-employment guarantee under NREG.

Figure 12.1 shows spending for recent years on works schemes as a share of total central government expenditure and GDP, and in real terms. There was a clear fall in total spending as a share of GDP and government spending between 1995 and 2003–2004, to around a third of spending shares in the early 1990s. Spending in real terms tracked the decline in government spending share. While this trend has reversed in most recent years, spending shares remain below their high point. While the decline and recent reversal is the most notable feature, it is

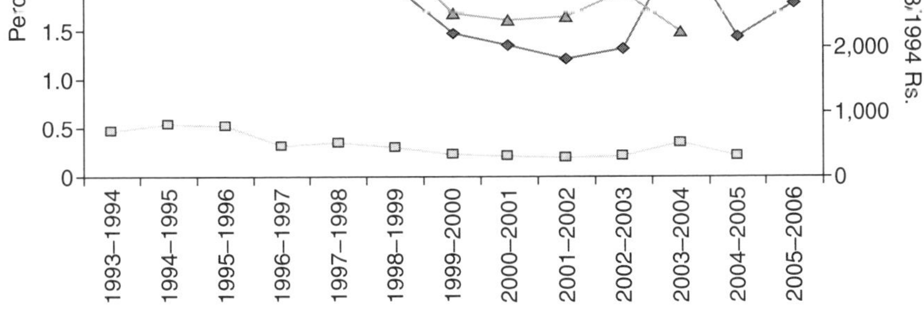

Figure 12.1 Spending on main public works programs, various indicators (sources: Rural Development Ministry to 2002/2003; MOF revised budget estimates for 2003–2005 and GoI total spending).

Note
Real 1993 Rs. adjusted by agricultural laborer consumer prince indices (CPI) (RBI series).

interesting to note the upticks in 1993–1994 and 2003–2004, i.e., years preceding national elections.[5]

Impacts of public-works schemes

What has been the performance of public-works programs with respect to their objectives? Unfortunately, both administrative and household data allow only partial answers. This is due to two reasons:

- Administrative data on employment generated are 'based only on arithmetic calculation' (CAG 1997), i.e., work days generated are calculated backwards from total spending on an assumed 60:40 split between wages and materials. Survey-based assessments throw doubt on these estimates.
- The NSS has to date asked households only about participation in public works of more than 60 days.[6] NSS coverage rates for public works can therefore be considered the lower bound.

Direct-employment effects

Figure 12.2 shows the administrative estimates of work days from the major works programs from 1993 to 2004, as well as aggregate rainfall data. As with spending share, employment-generation performance declined between the mid-1990s and early 2000s.

The level of public-works employment generated has been far lower than program objectives would suggest. Average annual employment per BPL household under SGRY in 2001–2004 came to only around 6.7 days, assuming that all workdays were for BPL.[7] The same work days spread across the agricultural workforce would mean around two days work per worker.[8] Such

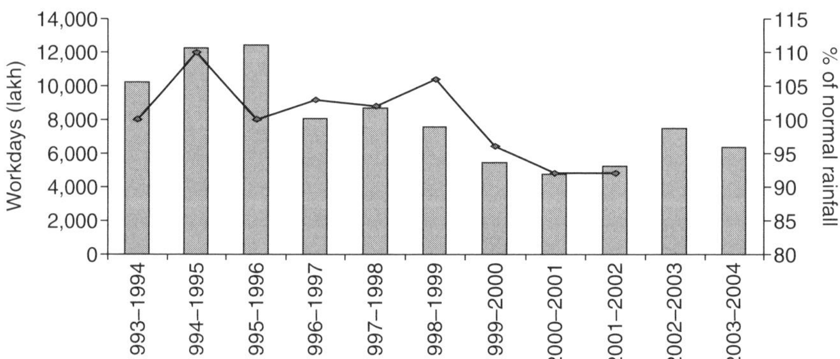

Figure 12.2 Work days of public employment and rainfall, various years (source: RD Ministry; Indiastat.com for rainfall data).

Note
Rainfall is measured by variation from annual mean rainfall.

employment-generation figures are lower than JRY and EAS, which had an average of 16 days employment per BPL household under JRY and 15 days per registered EAS worker in 1992–1999. The fall in employment seems broadly consistent with real spending since the mid-1990s.

Statewise employment-generation figures for SGRY suggest that the aggregate employment effect of workfare in all states is very low, with even outliers such as Assam and Orissa generating less than ten days work per agricultural worker, and none but Assam and Karnataka generating more than 15 days SGRY employment per BPL household.

At the household level, NSS allows for examination of works coverage. As noted, NSS is an imperfect source on the issue. Nevertheless, comparisons across states and time are possible, and include any public works undertaken. A few observations emerge:

- At the all-India level, the coverage rate is lower in each subsequent period, from 4.8 percent in 1987/1988, to 4.3 percent in 1993/2004 to 2.9 percent in 1999/2000. Given that works reliance is likely to vary by year depending on exogenous factors, not too much should be read in by way of a trend. This can be seen in state-specific coverage rates, which in a number of cases exhibit more pronounced inter-temporal variance, with a different pattern to the all-India.
- For 1987–1988, public works were able to respond well to a severe drought year. Drought data on a disaggregated basis needs to be explored to examine the responsiveness of works programs to more localized covariate shocks.
- Average coverage rates in the North-East have remained notably higher, reaching as high as 22 percent in Tripura and 30 percent in Arunachal Pradesh in some years.

Targeting of public works

Targeting of public works is more progressive than all other major anti-poverty programs with the relatively high coverage rate in the poorest quintile and among ST households.[9] Results from a 2004/2005 national survey for SGRY/FFW indicate progressive coverage across wealth groups, though low overall coverage even for the poorest. Nonetheless, the high relative coverage rates in the bottom quintile and among ST households places public works as the best program performer in distributional terms (see Table 12.1).

The positive targeting performance of public works from national data is supported by recent evidence from a three-state study in Orissa, Karnataka and MP in 2006. Particularly for the Food-for-Work program, coverage in the lowest quartile was relatively high (around 57 percent higher than the population average), while coverage among ST households was well above the population average, by almost 80 percent in the case of SGRY (Dev *et al.* 2001).

Table 12.1 Coverage of SGRY/FFW by wealth and social group, 2004/2005

	Beneficiary households	*% of all SGRY HHs from*	*Median daily wage rate*	*Benefit incidence (% benefit captured)*
Poorest	0.7	57.3	50	48.9
Q2	0.2	18.0	50	15.3
Q3	0.2	13.9	52	12.3
Q4	0.1	7.2	80	9.8
Richest	0.1	3.6	220	13.5
Brahmin	0.1	0.7	140	1.9
OBC	0.2	33.9	50	33.3
SC	0.3	23.6	50	23.1
ST	0.9	31.0	50	30.4
Other	0.1	10.9	52	11.1
All-India	0.3	100	50	100

Sources: NCAER HD survey 2004/05; Ajwad (2006) for estimates.

Note
Benefit incidence assumes equal number of work days.

Table 12.2 Average and marginal odds of participation in Indian workfare programs, 1993–1994

Quintile	*Average odds of participation in workfare (A)*	*Marginal odds of participation in workfare (M)*	*M/A*
1 (poorest)	1.23	1.16	94.2
2	1.13	0.93	82.3
3	1.04	0.80	76.9
4	0.86	0.92	107.0
5	0.83	0.55	66.3

Source: Lanjouw and Ravallion (1999).

The above analysis assesses targeting in terms of average incidence. This may be misleading where there are marginal adjustments in budgets. Analysis from 1993–1994 indicates that average benefit incidence underestimates the gains to poor households from increased spending on works (Lanjouw and Ravallion 1999). While the marginal odds of participation are lower for nearly all groups than averages, the relative reduction in odds is significantly less for the poor than for higher income quintiles (Table 12.2).

What has been driving employment outcomes in India's public works?

What are some of the explanations for such a wide gap between the employment commitments of public-works programs and outcomes? Several factors appear to be at work.

In employment terms, falling real spending since the mid-1990s has been reinforced by rising real wages on works in the 1990s (Table 12.3). Between 1993/1994 and 1999/2000, average annual growth in real earnings on works was 3.8 percent, which was higher than growth rates for casual rural laborers in and out of agriculture (Sundaram 2001). By the late 1990s, public-works wages were 21 percent (for men) and 38 percent (for women) higher than average wages in casual agricultural labor (Sundaram 2001b using NSS 1999–2000 data). While public-works schemes generally do not aim at paying less than minimum wages, around 75 percent of all work days on rural casual labor were below agricultural minimum wages, with the share above 90 percent in AP, Bihar and Orissa (Murgai and Ravallion 2005).

Although above-market wages should induce high demand for participation, budgetary resources are in practice constrained. Indian and international experience suggests that program wages above market rates result in rationing of employment on works (Ravallion *et al.* (1993); re Maharashtra EGS; and Subbarao 2003). It is interesting to compare information on wages in public works internationally, which shows mixed experience on the relationship. Generally, programs considered to be more successful (e.g., Trabajar; Korea; MEGS pre-1988) were more likely to have program wages below market wages. However, the position in India is subject to legal precedent that program wages below minimum wages are illegal (Papola 2005).

Public-works programs do not appear to have met the 60:40 labor to capital ratio, although the official method of calculating work days makes this hard to confirm. However, a survey-based EAS evaluation for 1993–1997 found that no category of works met the 60 percent wage component criterion, with the national average share of wages to total expenditure at 47.5 percent. Furthermore, only three of 14 major states (West Bengal, Orissa and Maharashtra) met the 60 percent wage target across activities. In contrast, several states had much lower wage shares, with Bihar at 27 percent, Haryana at 30 percent and Rajasthan at 33 percent (Program Evaluation Organization of Planning Commission 2002).

Another factor which may impact the labor intensity of public works is the extent of reliance on contractors. Though little evidence exists of contractors systematically using more labor-intensive methods, a GoI review of EAS indicates that even a 10–15 percent profit margin for contractors would reduce the labor budget per unit of spending.[10] Evidence in India on the extent of reliance on contractors in public works is mixed. A 2005 MRD evaluation of SGRY found use of contractors was substantially lower than previous evidence had indicated. At national level, contractors were reported to be involved in only 14 percent of assets, with significant state variations (e.g., Rajasthan, in only 2.4 percent of assets created, while Kerala reported for two-thirds of assets and Karnataka just over a third).

The findings should be viewed in light of other evidence, which seems difficult to reconcile. A 2005 study for RD [Rural Development] Department in Orissa found contractors in over 92 percent of SGRY assets (against a figure of

Table 12.3 Daily wages for various agricultural labor activities, 1993/1994 and 1999/2000

Work type	*Rural males (Rs/day)*			*Rural females (Rs/day)*		
	1993–1994	*1999–2000 (1993–1994 prices)*	*Annual rate of growth*	*1993–1994*	*1999–2000 (1993–1994 prices)*	*Annual rate of growth*
Public works	24.65	30.89	3.83%	18.52	24.87	5.04%
Casual agricultural labor	21.59	25.48	2.8%	15.12	17.99	2.94%
Casual non-agricultural labor	30.15	37.49	3.7%	17.46	23.49	5.07%
Casual labor all activities	23.18	28.65	3.59%	15.33	18.51	3.19%

Source: Sundaram (2001).

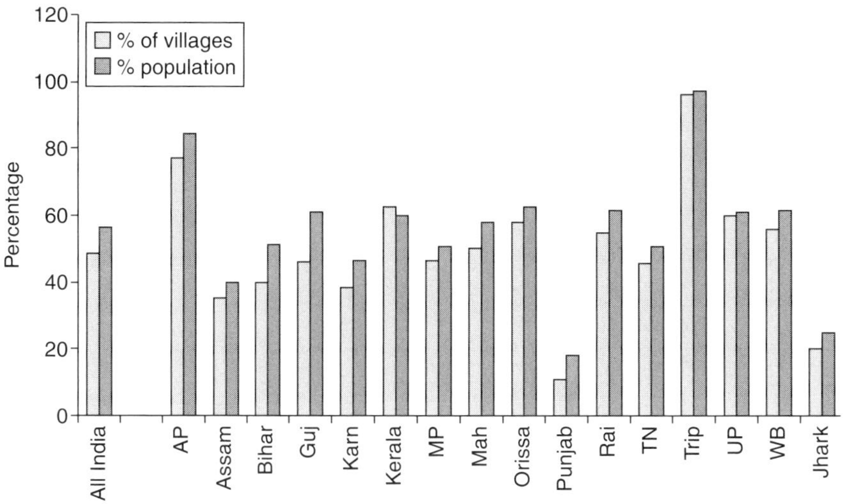

Figure 12.3 Share of villages and village population covered by public-employment programs in previous year, 2002 (source: NSS 58th round, 2001/2002. Bank staff estimates).

25 percent for Orissa in the national study).[11] A village study in AP of the state's food-for-work program in 2001–2002 found that all works were executed by contractors, and that, in the large majority of cases, sarpanches were the contractors.[12] Finally, a recent study of SGRY in Kerala, Karnataka, Rajasthan and West Bengal found regular use of contractors, despite the prohibition in guidelines (World Bank 2006).

Despite commitments to full rural coverage, the share of villages covered by works schemes has been far less than complete. Assessment of EAS for 1993–1997 found that only 53 percent of villages had any works, with some states much lower. More strikingly, the proportion of villages covered in all four years was only 5.4 percent.[13] Analysis from 2002 NSS village data confirms that partial spatial coverage has continued, with only 48.5 percent of villages (56.4 percent of population) reporting any public-employment program in the past year (Figure 12.3). Overall, there is substantial inter-state variation in coverage, with village (population) coverage as low as 20 (25) percent in Jharkhand and 11 (18) percent in Punjab. In addition, there is for all states (except Kerala) a higher likelihood of works having been available in the previous year in larger villages. At the all-India level, rural population coverage is around 16 percent higher than village coverage unweighted for population, with the large village effect particularly pronounced in states such as Bihar, Gujarat and Punjab.

Timing of public works has often not been well matched to seasonal employment needs, with difficulties in matching peak periods of public-works provision with periods of lowest market demand. This can be seen in Figure 12.4 for

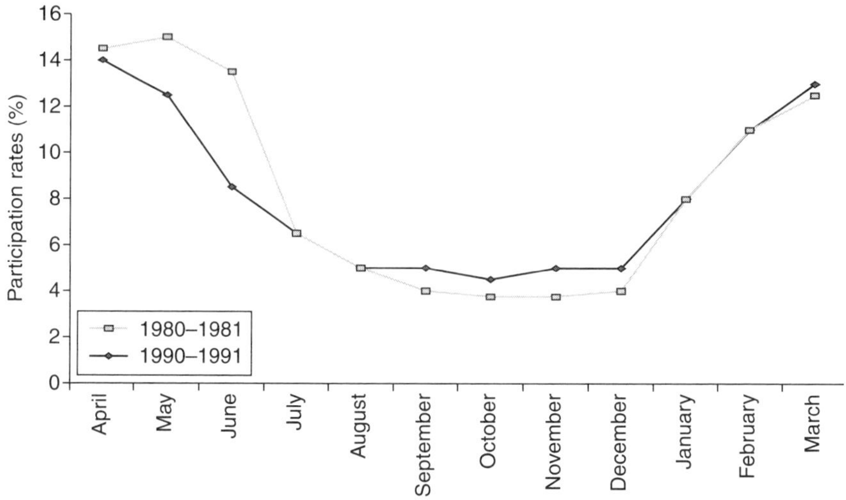

Figure 12.4 The seasonality of MEGS employment (source: Subbarao, 1993 and 1997).

Maharashtra, which shows public-works employment dropping sharply in the monsoon when market-based work is least available. Recent analysis of MEGS indicates that this pattern has continued.[14] It is consistent with findings in Rajasthan that works have typically been carried out during January–March, when opportunity costs of labor are high.[15] Part of the issue is that certain works cannot be executed during the lean season due to monsoon. This is reinforced by budgeting practices which concentrate disbursements for works in the final quarter of fiscal.

The persistence of implementation problems in public works has detracted from employment (and other) impacts. The problems are in general related to lack of accountability in workfare design, financing and management. Issues in GoI's assessments of public works and external assessments include (CAG 1997 and 2000; PEO 2000; Nayak *et al.* 2002; World Bank, forthcoming):

- Leakage and parking of funds. CAG reports point both to leakage of funds and parking of significant funds in deposit and other accounts. Parked funds show up in public accounts as executed but in fact remain undisbursed.
- Prioritization of works by line departments rather than PRIs.
- Lack of reliable records, in particular muster rolls. Survey evidence on the NFFW program from six states indicates that unavailable and fudged muster rolls continue to be a serious issue. At the same time, the study found that the practice had reduced sharply in Rajasthan in the face of better public information and community-level activism, suggesting that simple improvements in access to information can improve outcomes (Roy and Dreze, *The Hindu*, August 15, 2005).

- Lack of both strong administrative monitoring and evaluation and absence of "bottom up" monitoring through mechanisms such as social audits.

Other impacts from public-employment schemes

Measuring other impacts of public-employment schemes is more challenging. For several impacts, there are simply no data available. This includes impacts on overall wage levels, economic benefits of assets created, community empowerment and skill development impacts. On other indicators, research provides suggestions on the direction and scale of impacts, but is typically very much localized. The evidence on other impacts of works includes the following.

Female labor-force participation in SGRY appears to be lower than general rural female participation rates. Data from a 2005 evaluation of SGRY[16] show that the all-India share of SGRY female participants was only 12 percent, which is similar to CAG findings on JRY and EAS of only around 16 percent female beneficiaries (the target share was 30 percent). In states such as UP, Bihar and Punjab, females' participation in public works is very low, at less than 2 percent. Interestingly, the survey-based results above appear to diverge from administrative data for the same year, which report around 26 percent of person days generated for women.[17] The figures compare unfavorably with estimates of females by usual status in the rural workforce of around 35 percent in 2000.[18]

It is difficult to estimate the economic impact from assets in Indian works schemes. Given the importance of rates of return on assets in assessing program impact, this is unfortunate, though a common problem in workfare worldwide. Qualitative evidence available from GoI and other evaluations largely relates to quality of assets rather than rates of return.[19] A common criticism of public works is that they are 'washed away the next monsoon'. In light of this view, the findings of a beneficiary survey are intriguing.[20] Both at all-India level and in all states, beneficiaries finding the quality of works very good or good dominated. This needs to be interpreted with caution, both because of possibly low expectations of beneficiaries, and because the survey found that only 31 percent of respondents were aware of quality specifications for works. Evidence from EAS also indicates that public-works-assets maintenance is poor, so that even decent-quality assets may deteriorate quickly (CAG 2000). A challenge for the NREG will be developing cost-effective methods for estimating quality and rates of return on assets.

The insurance and associated productivity impacts of public works are also difficult to measure absent rigorous evaluations. However, what evidence there is for India suggests a positive insurance function of public works, with attendant impacts on production decisions. A study from the 1980s in Maharashtra found that income variability among landless agricultural households in villages where MEGS was available was half the level of villages where it was not (Walker *et al.* 1986). Farmer studies in Maharashtra also find greater adoption of higher risk/return agricultural practices (Devereux 2005), though how much this can be attributed to MEGS is unclear.

The national rural employment guarantee (NREG)

GoI has in recent years committed to major expansion in public works, initially with the National Food-for-Work program from 2004, and since 2006 through NREG. Overall, it is too early to make conclusions on the effects of NREG on parameters such as poverty, labor markets and the local economy. Nonetheless, relative to previous public-works schemes, there are a number of design features of NREG which are very sensible, and in many states there has been greater political and institutional commitment to trying to 'make the scheme work'. That said, the summary of initial implementation experience suggests that implementation is highly variable across (and even within) states, and that there remain major challenges in implementation.

Ex ante estimates of NREG impacts

Given the early stage of implementation, simulations of scheme impacts carried out prior to initiation remain worthy of consideration to look at the potential impacts of NREG. The main findings are the following (Murgai and Ravallion 2005).

ESTIMATED LABOR-SUPPLY EFFECTS

In terms of labor supply, an NREG wage rate close to Rs.60 at current prices[21] could induce a 5 percentage point increase in lean-season labor supply among casual rural workers. Interestingly, the incremental labor supply impact of a wage rate above Rs.60 is negligible for all groups. The overall wage elasticity of labor supply is estimated to be 0.17.

The estimated labor-supply impact can also be presented in terms of expected number of rural people presenting for work on a typical day in the lean season, and this can be broken down by gender. This is presented in Table 12.4, together

Table 12.4 Estimated labor-supply effects of lean season NREG

Expenditure quintile	*Pre-NREG lean-season employment rate*	*Casual labor supply at NREG wage rate (1999–2000 prices)*	
		Rs.50	*Rs.55*
Poorest 20%	34.5	41.7	41.8
Quintile 2	28.7	34.1	34.4
Quintile 3	24.5	29.3	29.4
Quintile 4	20.0	24.6	24.7
Richest 20%	12.2	15.6	15.7
Overall	23.8	28.9	29.0

Source: Murgai and Ravallion (2005).

Note
6/2005 equivalents of Rs.50 and 55 at 1999–2000 wages = Rs.63 and 69, using CPIAL index, adjusting base by 13 percent to allow for differences in NSS casual male agricultural wages and AWI series.

Table 12.5 Estimated labor supply by gender and as share of total casual labor, and fiscal costs

Wage rate (1999/2000 prices	*Estimated number of EGS applicants on typical day*			*As % of total casual labor*	*Estimated fiscal cost (% GDP)*
	Males	*Females*	*Total*		
Rs.45	24.4	14.0	38.4	35.7	1.5
Rs.50	25.0	14.0	39.0	36.2	1.7
Rs.55	25.3	14.0	39.3	36.6	1.9

Source: Murgai and Ravallion.

Notes
6/2005 equivalents of Rs.45, 50 and 55 1999/2000 wage rates = Rs.57, 63, and 69.

with estimated fiscal costs at three wage rates. Some interesting observations emerge:

- If the estimated supply response is realized, it would imply a total annual provision of work days of around 3.9 billion once NREG is rolled out nationwide. This compares to an annual average in 1999–2004 of closer to 600 million days annually on workfare programs – a more than six times expansion once NREG reaches scale. Such expansion would not happen immediately, due to initial implementation in backward districts, and other factors. NREG thus implies huge additional demands on public-works delivery systems in India.
- Fiscal costs are potentially substantial for a nationally implemented scheme. The wage rates for NREG suggest fiscal costs of a nationwide program of around 1.7–1.9 percent of GDP. The costs estimates are gross, and there would be netting out of SGRY and NFFWP spending (which nationally ran to around 0.2 percent of GDP in 2004–2005).
- The benefits of inducing higher female labor supply are fully realized at a wage rate lower than state minimum agricultural wages. Nonetheless, in absolute terms, more men than women would be expected to take up NREG lean-season employment (though predicted female share is higher than under SGRY) – see Table 12.5.

Poverty and distributional impacts of NREG

The estimated lean-season poverty-reduction impacts of NREG are significant, and the distribution of gains progressive. At a wage equivalent to Rs.63 in 2006 prices, lean-season rural poverty could be reduced from 37 percent pre-NREG to 23 per cent or from 34 percent to 30 percent on an annualized basis. The distribution of gains would also be progressive, with around 54 percent of gainers in the bottom two expenditure quintiles, and less than 10 percent in the top quintile.

More notably, direct income gains from NREG would be around 51 percent of pre-NREG lean season income for the bottom expenditure quintile (Murgai and Ravallion 2005).

How has NREG done so far in practice?

This section presents administrative data on performance, before a summary of several studies on initial implementation experience with NREG. Looking at administrative data for the end of 2006 (as given in the organization's website), a few points are worth noting:

- NREG generated significant demand from rural households in its first nine months of implementation, with 33.7 million rural households issued with a job card, or approaching one quarter of all rural households. Even the lower figure of 13.7 million households being provided employment approaches 10 percent of rural households. This is a major achievement in program coverage relative to prior public-works schemes.
- There is a wide gap between those registered with NREG job cards and those actually demanding work, with the latter around 42 percent of the former. At the same time, the gap between those demanding and provided work is negligible. This points to two features of demand manifestation. The first is that households may register with no current intent to undertake public works, exercising an implicit insurance function of the program. The second – and more worrying – is the process through which work is "demanded" under NREG. While the scheme is framed as on-demand, in practice worksites have to be opened in a locality before people are likely to come forward for work. This in turn requires a quorum of people expressing a demand for work. This 'chicken and egg' issue suggests the importance of the supply side even in such a demand-driven program.
- Program outcomes have been quite variable across states. Coverage of NREG registration is high in absolute terms largely where one would expect based on district concentration across states, though AP, MP and West Bengal stand out on the upside, and North-Eastern states as laggards. Greater variability can be seen on the supply of actual employment to those registered, which may reflect both demand - and supply-side effects. Of particular note is Rajasthan, with easily the highest employment ratio of major NREG states, reflecting a massive public awareness effort on the part of CBOs.
- Administrative data also indicate impressive inclusion of ST (scheduled Tribe) households, and of women relative to previous public-works schemes. Nationally, ST households account for around 39 percent of work-days generated in 2006 (and as high as two-thirds in Rajasthan), a share that far outstrips their general population share. In addition, the share of women in total work days generated in 2006 was around 38.5 percent, and as high as two-thirds in Rajasthan. This is a major improvement in female participation relative to SGRY.

Beyond the administrative data, survey results from initial NREG implementation experience in a number of states provide useful insights, and identify several key challenges in ensuring program effectiveness. The studies were carried out in the first six months of implementation, so should be seen as identifying very initial performance.

In the states surveyed, the composition of households who had received job-card work under NREG indicates that the program has managed to sustain good penetration among ST households that is seen in previous schemes. The coverage rate among ST households is high in absolute and relative terms (though not in Bihar, where ST are a much smaller share of the population). Overall, it is too early to comment reliably on the targeting outcomes of NREG, but the results are promising.

Apart from the above, the surveys identify several implementation challenges that are consistent with anecdotal reports from other NREG districts. They include:

- Program wage rates. There has been tension between the program commitment to payment of agricultural minimum wages and the reliance on piece rates for wage payment. This has resulted in most states in actual wage payments which fall short of official minimum agricultural wages (Table 12.6). This is due to rural schedules of rates for work which assume a level of capital intensity not appropriate to a labor-intensive scheme such as NREG. A number of states – e.g., Gujarat, AP, and Rajasthan – are addressing this issue through general revisions of rural schedules of rates or setting of NREG-specific rates (based on new time and motion studies), including in AP a specific time and motion study for disabled workers.
- Role of communities in selection of works. In principle, gram sabhas have a key role to play in identification of works under NREG. As of mid-2006, such consultation was happening rarely in MP, Chhattisgarh and Jharkhand, and in AP the GP role was being undertaken by the Village Organization which operates a CDD initiative (CBGA 2006). In Bihar, most GP-level

Table 12.6 NREG wages received and agricultural MW by state, 2006

State	*Wage received*	*Official minimum wage*	*Actual as % of official*
Chhattisgarh	15.5	58.8	26.4
Jharkhand	17.5	73.0	24.0
AP	44.5	88.0	50.6
Bihar	60.7	68.0	89.3
MP	18.0	61.4	29.3
Gujarat	49.2	60.0	82.0

Sources: CBGA (Chattisgarh, MP, AP and Jharkhand); IHD (Bihar); CDA (Gujarat), all 2006.

Notes

State averages are unweighted district averages.

sub-projects were selected by the mukhiya without gram sabha consultation, and in Gujarat, households reported a gram sabha input to works identification in only about a third of cases.

- The generally low capacity of PRIs to carry out a range of NREG functions expected of them is a difficult challenge. Apart from works selection, GPs are expected to mobilize field assistants and beneficiaries, keep asset, beneficiary and financial records, and play an important role in social audits.
- There is no evidence of any state having paid an unemployment allowance (UA) in cases where work has not been provided within the specified period. This is important for two reasons. The first is that the 'guarantee' of the Act is ineffective unless UA is paid in a timely manner. The second is that states – which have to finance UA from their own budgets – will have stronger incentives to improve implementation if UA is implemented.

Conclusions and recommendations on public works

Many of the appropriate reforms of public-works policy are reflected in NREG, which represents the most serious effort to date to address the institutional and implementation problems encountered in works schemes. Nonetheless, areas that warrant particular attention as the program matures include:

- Continue and deepen awareness raising efforts on NREG entitlements, in close collaboration with civil society. Initial results indicate that basic awareness is still lacking in several states, and even in well-performing states that knowledge of specific entitlements can be improved.
- Complete time and motion studies in major NREG states to assess the appropriateness of piece-rate-payment schedules. The experiences of AP, Gujarat and others are useful.
- Explore options for a wider range of authorized work activities which may be done under NREG, in particular for those not capable of hard manual labor. The NREG Act allows for this, but the option of expanding categories of works has yet to be exercised. As experience grows, this would be worth looking at from several perspectives. The first is whether 'softer' work options – e.g., provision of community services for vulnerable populations – could be introduced which have high positive externalities. The second is looking at the needs of sub-groups of job-card holders for whom special efforts may be needed to provide appropriate work, e.g. disabled people.
- Deepen the direct involvement of communities in identification of works undertaken under NREG. While it is understandable that the initial implementation would rely on shelves of works already identified, it will be important to ensure that the role of gram sabhas anticipated under the Act is made a reality, and that groups such as SHG and CBOs (Community-based organizations) are mobilized to have their priorities reflected through the gram sabha process.

- Assess the ways in which demand for work is manifesting itself, and the constraints – formal and informal – on matching that with supply of work-sites and employment opportunities. This is probably the most difficult area of NREG to operationalize effectively, and goes to the heart of what a demand-driven approach means in practice. This will involve a principled but practical look at such questions as the minimum number of workers required at a worksite, how the bureaucratic demands of authorizing work-site opening can be matched to demand, etc.
- Make states and communities aware of the unemployment allowance provision in the Act. This is essential if the guarantee function is to be credible.
- Continue to develop the capacity-building function allowed for under NREG. Under the Act, a portion of funds are available for capacity building of PRIs and others involved in NREG implementation. To date, this is still to be developed, but will be a critical element of program success.
- Get 'baselines' in place for impact assessment. Unfortunately, there is no solid pre-program baseline on NREG. However, efforts are being made to provide for credible impact evaluations of poverty, labor-market and other outcomes.
- Operationalize the central and state NREG councils to oversee implementation, and use them to promote exchange of good practice between states.

An additional issue for consideration is whether any element of direct human-capital formation can be factored into NREG as it matures. Presently there is no provision under NREG for skill formation among workers. This could be considered, along the lines of the South African public-works scheme. While such an approach obviously requires a supply side – probably on a contracted basis – which can provide useful training, it seems an interesting option to consider.

A final issue is that public works for the poor remain restricted to rural areas. An issue for the consideration of policymakers is whether an expanded self-targeted public-works program could be designed for implementation among the urban poor. Such programs exist in the works schemes of a number of developing countries. While a small scheme (SJSRY) exists, its impacts to date appear negligible and funding remains marginal (World Bank forthcoming).

Social insurance for the unorganized sector

As in many developing countries, unorganized-sector workers in India face an array of uninsured risks, making them highly vulnerable to both idiosyncratic and covariate shocks. While family, *jati* and other informal support networks play an important role in smoothing consumption in the face of shocks, the risk-sharing function they perform is far from perfect (and more effective for idiosyncratic than covariate shocks, and for small as opposed to catastrophic shocks).[22] Recent work also demonstrates a link between reliance on *jati* (caste) networks of mutual informal insurance and low rates of occupational and geographical mobility found in rural India, with migration and marriage outside the *jati* triggering loss of access to finance in the face of shocks (Munsi and Rosenzweig 2005). Credit- and insurance-market failures may thus be limiting the ability of rural workers to seek more productive employment opportunities.

Survey evidence confirms the impact of uninsured shocks on household welfare. This is particularly the case for health shocks, and for the poor.[23] For example, at least 24 percent of Indians who are hospitalized fall into poverty as a result (Peters *et al.* 2002). There are also concerns that credit-market failures drive coping mechanisms which may turn transient into long-term and even inter-generational poverty, e.g. withdrawal of children from school, debt-bondage, etc. Such effects have been analyzed for countries such as Indonesia, which stress that the benefits of social insurance in poor countries may come less from the direct contribution to consumption smoothing than the reduction of coping strategies to smooth consumption (Chetty and Looney 2005).

International context

Despite efforts, many developing countries have failed to extend insurance coverage to the majority of workers typically found in the unorganized sector. At the same time, international evidence since the nineteenth century indicates that social security spending tends to increase sharply with rising income levels,

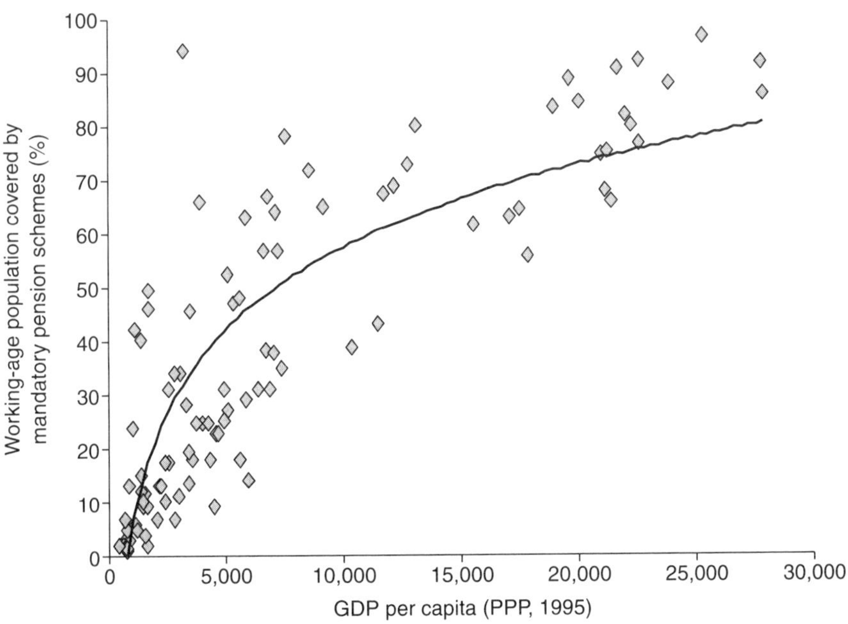

Figure 12.5 Social insurance and assistance spending shares by region, and pension coverage by GDP (sources: WDR (2006)).

or at least to increase sharply once a threshold level of GDP is attained (Lindert 2004). Important facts on this transition include:

- As countries become richer, the share of social protection spending in GDP and total public spending tends to increase (Palacios and Paralles 2002; Lindert 2004).
- Within social protection spending, social insurance typically accounts for an increasingly higher share of GDP as countries become richer, while the share of social assistance stabilizes at 2–3 percent of GDP (a level India already approaches). The transition also involves an increased role for cash-based interventions relative to food-based.
- Voluntary social-insurance systems have not resulted in major coverage expansion, indicating that more formalized labor markets – where mandated participation can better be enforced – are closely associated with higher coverage rates. The association between GDP per capita and mandatory pension coverage is shown in Figure 12.5.[24] Experience with health-insurance expansion in East Asia conforms to this pattern, with universal coverage being achieved at income levels between US$5,000 and $10,000 and where formal-sector employment dominates.[25]

Current status of unorganized-sector social security in India[26]

Given the high rate of informality in Indian labor markets and level of income, coverage of social insurance is predictably low and concentrated heavily in the organized sector. Figure 12.6 provides coverage estimates of different social insurance types for 2004/2005 across the distribution, showing not only the failure of formal health and pension insurance systems to expand coverage, but also the growing penetration of life insurance driven by the commercial-insurance sector.

Recent approaches to social insurance (SI) for the unorganized sector

In the face of very low SI coverage of unorganized-sector workers, the public (central and state), non-government and private sectors are all involved in efforts to expand coverage. Various approaches are being tried with differing degrees of success, in terms of reaching scale, achieving financial viability, and providing financial protection to households. Each approach has advantages and drawbacks, some inherent (e.g. viability in the face of covariate or catastrophic idiosyncratic shocks for community-based initiatives), and others a product of specific design and implementation features. The main initiatives described are:

- Welfare and provident funds for unorganized-sector workers at central and state levels, which include both occupation-specific and generalized unorganized sector funds.

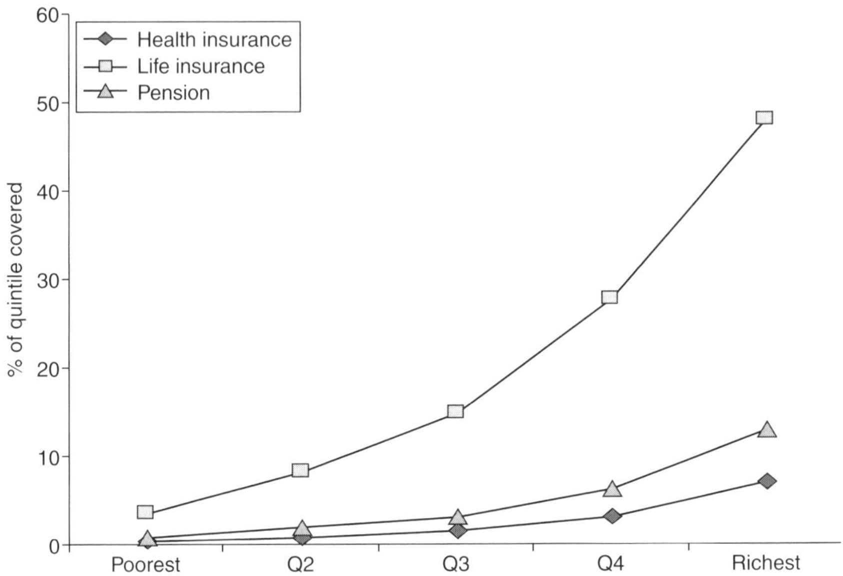

Figure 12.6 Coverage rates of health, life and pension insurance by quintile, 2004/2005 (source: World Bank (forthcoming)).

- GoI national schemes for unorganized-sector workers outside the welfare-fund model.
- NGO and community-based initiatives, which range from coverage of specific SI types (usually health) to more bundled social-insurance packages.

Welfare and provident funds

Welfare funds (ILO 2004) have traditionally been occupation-specific schemes providing a range of benefits for members. The earliest fund dates to 1946, though they have proliferated since the late 1970s. It is difficult to obtain a comprehensive picture of funds due to their decentralized nature, both geographically and occupationally. Despite the lack of comprehensive coverage, patterns emerge in terms of key features and challenges of welfare funds.

Most attention in discussion of welfare funds has been paid to the Keralan funds, of which there were more than 20 by 2000. (Dev 2000; Kannan 2002), and central government funds, of which there are five with central financing and another with a central act but to be implemented and financed at state level.[27] However, in terms of total coverage, funds in other states – initially in southern and western states, but spreading in recent years to the north and east – have accounted for an increasing share of participating workers since the 1990s.

The financing of welfare funds follows two basic models: (i) cess-financing, which is used for all the central government funds, and may be a cess-proper or excise duty; and (ii) contributory financing, which is either tripartite between government, employers and workers, or from employer and employee only.[28] In cases where government contributes to the second category of funds, the dominant method is direct contribution. Management of the funds is either tripartite or government only (in roughly equal proportion for documented funds). A few things are apparent from looking at contribution rates and benefits of funds:

- Contribution rates exhibit dramatic variations across funds, from very low amounts (e.g. AP and Karnataka Labor Welfare Funds), through more significant absolute amounts (e.g. Kerala Cashew Workers), to quite substantial shares of worker compensation more akin to formal sector contribution rates (e.g. Maharashtra Mathadi Boards). More detailed analysis is needed of the correlation between contribution rates and benefits offered. However, initial examination suggests no systematic relationship.
- It appears that no financial/actuarial analysis has preceded the setting of contribution rates and packages of entitlements. This is likely to show up more starkly as the membership of funds ages. The long-term finances of the Beedi Workers' Fund demonstrate the impacts of membership ageing, with expenditures in most of the 1980s well below income, but moving into significant deficits after 1992 (Rajan 2001).

Although welfare funds tend to be characterized primarily as instruments of social insurance, the picture with respect to benefits and services offered is more complex. Education is the most commonly provided entitlement across funds, followed by medical cover and then pensions. The benefits provided spread beyond typical social insurance, raising concerns about the ability to provide financial protection in the face of shocks. For the pensions portion of schemes, the large majority are defined benefit programs, typically with benefits expressed in nominal rupees and hence subject to deterioration in real value.

There is also major heterogeneity in the generosity of entitlements provided by different funds. Given this, establishing typical expenditure patterns is not straightforward, as detailed spending information is available only for a limited number of funds. For the central funds, the available data suggest the following (Rajan 2001):

- Health overwhelmingly dominates spending for all central funds except Mica, where education is significant. This has been the case since at least the early 1990s also.[29]
- Administrative costs are extremely high in the smaller funds. This poor performance is remarkable given that financing is cess or excise based, and should not demand the intensity of administration of funds based on contributions.
- None of the central funds provide for old age, disability, sickness or life insurance. The exception is the Building and Construction Workers' Fund, which is delegated to states. Below gives a recent example of a state-level initiative to promote old-age pensions: a defined contribution provident fund for unorganized-sector workers in West Bengal.

Since 2001, West Bengal has operated a Provident Fund for workers in the unorganized sector, not including agricultural workers. In 2006, enrolment was around 700,000. Membership is open to wage and self-employed workers in designated industries/activities (which are expanding over time) whose family income is no more than Rs.3,500 per month (though the means test appears to be rather informal). The key feature of the Fund is that it is a defined contribution scheme. Members contribute Rs. 20 per month, with a matching contribution from the state government. Interest accrues on the account at a rate designated by government (the EPFO [Employee Provident Fund Organization] rate to date). Accrued principal and interest is paid to the worker at age 55 or at death or when there is no account activity for six months.

Rapid expansion has been driven by a highly decentralized distribution network and governance structure, with support from trade unions and political parties in mobilizing awareness and interest. Collection agents are typically public workers who are incentivized by a one rupee payment for each enrollee. The state government covers the administration costs of the Fund. While the West Bengal experience has great promise, particularly given its DC basis, it remains to be seen whether the promotion and distribution success achieved is replicable in states with less stable political institutions (LO 2004).

Welfare funds have potential as vehicles for expanding social insurance to some segments of the unorganized sector, i.e. those amenable to a cess and/or with strong presence of intermediary organizations which can share the transaction costs of wide membership/low contribution schemes. They provide interesting parallels to occupational social-insurance schemes in OECD countries at earlier stages of development. Despite their potential, however, the evidence suggests that they face a number of design and implementation challenges which may constrain their ability to provide adequate and sustainable financial protection for members, including:

- The small and occupationally concentrated risk pools of a number of funds risk driving high administrative costs and weak capacity to absorb significant covariate shocks. These challenges can be surmounted through group insurance with commercial insurers, but it remains unclear to what extent this has been exploited.
- The scope of benefits in many funds is likely to contribute to inadequate financial protection for any specific type of benefit. This in turn risks benefits becoming supplements to smaller and/or more predictable expenditures rather than being focused on larger shocks.
- For the insurance-like benefits in welfare-fund-benefit packages, there appears to be no actuarial basis for contribution determination. In light of this, the extent to which the schemes can be considered insurance rather than partial pre-payment schemes is an issue.
- There appears to be no example of a rigorous impact study of welfare-scheme participation.

Other government initiatives on social security for the unorganized sector

The government has in recent years increased efforts to expand social security to unorganized-sector workers through non-welfare fund mechanisms (Planning Commission 2002). This section provides a brief review of initiatives in recent years.[30] By way of context, it is important to note a couple of points on the insurance industry in India. First, public and private insurance companies have obligations under the IRDA (Insurance Regulatory and Development Authority) for a minimal level of both social and rural coverage (Breman and Ahuja 2005). Second, to date life and non-life insurance provision remains separated.

In 2004, GoI introduced a social-insurance scheme for unorganized-sector workers (excluding agriculture), piloted in 50 districts nationwide and targeting around 2.5 million workers.[31] The scheme was managed by EPFO in collaboration with ESIS for health services. It was voluntary and contributory for those with monthly incomes under Rs.6,500 and provided for old-age, medical and accident insurance. GoI contributed around Rs.250 annually per worker. Premia for workers were Rs.50 per month for workers to 35 years and Rs.100 above that. Employers were meant to contribute Rs.100 monthly. Workers covered the employer contribution themselves in addition to their basic contribution when no employer is identified. The scheme appears to have had negligible penetration, with an estimated enrollment in mid-2005 of less than 10,000 and the scheme is now dormant.

Another major initiative was the Universal Health Insurance Scheme (UHIS), launched in 2003 (Ahuja and Narang 2005). This is a voluntary contributory scheme for BPL households, covering medical costs of hospitalization, loss of income during short-term-illness and death. There is a contribution subsidy from GoI ranging from Rs.200–400, with net contribution from the worker ranging from Rs.165 to Rs.300, depending on household size. In parallel, a scheme for unorganized non-BPL households was introduced. Outcomes on UHIS appear also to have been limited in the initial phases, with only around 400,000 households covered in the first year of operation (less than 5 percent of them BPL) and a further 31,000 households up to January 2005.

Another important scheme targeted to the unorganized sector is offered by the government-owned Life Insurance Corporation (LIC) called the Janashree Bima Yojana (JBY) scheme. It covers 44 occupational groups, chosen to target those living near the poverty line. The scheme pays Rs.20,000 for natural death, 50,000 for accidental death or permanent disability and 25,000 for partial permanent disability. There is also a scholarship of Rs.300 per quarter per child paid to workers who send their children (up to two) to grades 9–12 for a maximum of four years. The package is financed by a premium of 200 rupees collected through 'nodal' agencies, i.e., groups that must include at least 25 workers. A number of groups, ranging from SHGs to small occupational groups, have signed up as 'nodal agencies', reflecting a growing tendency to rely on the partner–agent model.

As in West Bengal, there is a matching premium payment, in this case subsidized by the central government. Financing comes from a social-security fund at LIC that was set up in 1989 and has received two grants from the central government. In 2005, there were approximately 3.5 million lives covered. There was a massive expansion of the program in mid-2006 when the state government of Rajasthan purchased the policy on behalf of workers in all 2.2 million Below Poverty Line (BPL) households.

JBY is undoubtedly the single largest insurance scheme for the informal sector in India. The design of the scheme is interesting from a policy perspective in several ways. First, it is an attempt incrementally to increase coverage, in this case on the basis of occupations or groups considered to have lower incomes, but with a capacity to contribute. Second, there is a transparent subsidy intended to incentivize voluntary take up. On the other hand, the target group-size – 25 – seems small, and financing of the subsidy over the long run does not seem to have been considered carefully. Moreover, the government subsidy has only been available to one (state-owned) provider and there is no record keeping mechanism to allow the government to monitor whether its money is reaching the intended target.

The above schemes are by no means a comprehensive picture of central and state government initiatives to expand social insurance. However, even the selective presentation suggests a few preliminary conclusions:

- The rollover of insurance schemes at central level has been frequent. When trust in the notion of insurance may be low and information dissemination is weak, such policy uncertainty is problematic. The frequent introduction of schemes appears to be driven more by political imperatives than a strategic approach to expansion.
- While the need is high, taking on health insurance confronts the most challenging area of social insurance first, where moral hazard risks and administrative demands are high.
- Most central schemes have to date failed to address the fundamental issue of high transactions costs and the need for decentralized distribution networks.
- As with welfare funds, it is not apparent that the contributions for various schemes are based on an informed assessment of claims information from existing insurance products.

NGO and community-based social-insurance initiatives for the unorganized sector

Estimates on the scale of social-insurance provision by NGOs and other community-based actors (e.g. microfinance institutions, health facilities) vary from around three to around five million (Breman and Ahuja 2005). Given the very low coverage rates achieved by government initiatives, community-based micro-insurance (CBMI) initiatives assume significance as a potential channel for expansion of social security. At the same time, the experience to date is mixed, with questions on the capacity to go to scale, given the reliance on subsidies from founding institutions and donors. In addition, CBMI to date have focused primarily on health insurance, and not yet addressed other types of insurance, particularly old age. Finally, there are legal issues with respect to CBMI, as the IRDA Act does not provide for such schemes as part of the broader insurance market (Devadasan *et al.* 2004). There are a few basic models of community-based social insurance:[32]

- The insurer–agent model, where the NGO/MFI or other founder acts as intermediary between members and the insurer, in India typically one of the public insurance companies (though SEWA has also involved a private commercial insurer). This model has been relied on by large organizations such as SEWA and Buldhana, and smaller ones such as Navsarjan in Gujarat and BAIF in Maharashtra (Acharya and Ranson 2005).
- The founding organization acts as the direct insurer, but is not the provider of the insured services. This applies both to some NGO schemes (Yeshasvini in Karnataka; Dhan in TN) and occupationally based programs (e.g., Tribhuvandas Foundation).[33]
- The founding organization is the direct insurer and the main provider of the insured services. Examples include ACCORD in TN, Kasturba Hospital scheme in Maharashtra; Students' Health Home in West Bengal.

The different approaches exhibit both common features and differences. They include:

- In terms of types of risks covered, the primary focus has been health insurance. Some schemes cover associated costs such as loss of income, and life and accident insurance.[34] However, old-age insurance is not a CBMI product.
- Nearly all CBMI work on voluntary participation. This approach is consistent with the experience from Asia on coverage of health-insurance schemes for the informal sector (Bernett *et al.* 1998).
- In terms of financing, all CBMI schemes require a contribution. However, there is a range in the level of contribution required and the extent to which it is subsidized. In the best cases, contributions cover the bulk of medical claims and administration is covered by donor support (e.g., SEWA Vimo). At the other end of the spectrum, contributions are covered for many of the members from the NGO/funder's own resources. An additional innovation in some schemes is provision for deposit of a lump sum by the participant, from which interest generated covers the annual premium.
- Although community/NGO involvement controls administrative costs, most schemes rely on an external subsidy. The subsidy may come from Government, the NGO or donors, cooperatives or other sources. This is very typical of rural health-insurance initiatives in developing countries, virtually none of which cover services from contributions only (O'Keefe 2003).

- The experience on whether benefits are provided on reimbursement or up-front deduction/exemption is mixed. The majority of schemes are based on reimbursement, but those that both insure and provide services are cashless, as is the Yeshasvini scheme in Karnataka, which uses a third-party administrator. Experience internationally suggests that reimbursement-based schemes dominate in community health insurance (Bennett *et al.* 1998).
- While most of the schemes are relatively small, the largest have achieved significant membership (e.g., Yeshasvini had around two million farmers registered in 2004–2005, having started in 2003; the West Bengal Students' Health Home, which covers around 1.6 million students).
- Many of the schemes are relatively new and yet to be evaluated, both in terms of short-term impacts and with respect to financial trajectory.

Of the prevailing models, the insurer–agent approach appears to have the most potential for broadening coverage of social insurance. It appears to combine the benefits of large-scale pooling of risks (both within the membership group when group insurance is purchased, and beyond through the risk pool of the end-insurer), and the cost-reducing benefits of an intermediary organization close to the client. At the same time, the Yeshasvini experience cautions against being very prescriptive on a preferred model.

A further important recent development is the 'micro-pension' product of the Unit Trust of India (UTI). The first client in this partner–agent arrangement was SEWA. In 2006, around 30,000 women joined their DC pension scheme where contributions of around 200 rupees per month are invested in a balanced fund invested in bonds and equities. Individuals must maintain a savings account with SEWA Bank. The SEWA experience may not be easy to replicate on a large scale, however. First, preliminary analysis shows that administrative costs are still relatively high given the flows involved. Second, the arrangement relies on one provider, UTI, which is the only asset manager licensed to offer this kind of product. Nevertheless, the scheme was recently taken up by a dairy cooperative in Bihar and other groups of unorganized sector workers are considering it.[35]

Looking ahead: new GoI initiatives on unorganized-sector social security

The GoI in its Common Minimum Program has committed itself to expansion of social security. To this end, the National Commission for Enterprises in the Unorganized Sector (NCEUS) produced a report in 2006 on behalf of MoLE, which recommended the introduction of a national social-insurance scheme offering old-age pensions, health insurance and maternity benefits, as well as life and disability insurance.

The NCEUS proposal is ambitious in that it seeks to offer insurance for several major risks to 300 million informal sector workers in a span of five years. The ultimate objective of universal coverage is shared by many developing-country governments as well as donors. However, such an expansion of coverage through voluntary participation is unprecedented in terms of international and Indian experience. The administrative and recordkeeping challenges alone suggest that the proposed time frame is not feasible (O'Keefe and Palacios 2006).

In addition to the scope of the proposal, elements of the design require closer consideration. In the area of old-age pensions, for example, the proposal would pay an indexed monthly pension of Rs.200 to all individuals aged 65 and over that were BPL card holders. Conceptually, the idea of providing a transfer to those that cannot afford to participate in a contributory scheme is sensible and many countries have chosen to implement this type of program.[36]

On the positive side, for the first time, there is an effort to grapple with the issue of high transactions costs in unorganized-sector social security, through allowing a role for intermediary organizations such as NGO/MFIs, PRIs, unions and worker associations between the state/insurer and workers in raising awareness of the scheme, identifying and registering workers, collecting contributions and payment of benefits. The scheme recognizes the need for a significant contribution subsidy to incentivize participation.

Building on the NCEUS report, the GOI is currently considering various options both in terms of program design as well as sequencing. In some areas, there appears to be growing consensus. For example, there appears to be support for scaling up the NOAPS social-pension program so that it would reach a larger proportion of the elderly in India. There is also an emerging vision that involves combining government subsidies with provision by non-governmental entities on a competitive basis, perhaps through the partner–agent model. For example, MoLE is studying programs like the JBY scheme for life insurance.

Membership of potential intermediary organizations

One of the key facilitating preconditions for participation in contributory social-insurance schemes is membership of some organization which could play an intermediary role between workers and the ultimate insurer. As a result, membership in potential intermediary organizations is of interest in assessing the institutional scope for SI expansion.[37] Figure 12.7 presents survey-based findings on membership at the all-India level. Group membership remains low, and distributional analysis confirms that coverage is concentrated in the upper end of the distribution for all but SHGs.

Most states also have very low membership of organizations, though with standouts. The most significant is Kerala, with high union and coop/SHG membership rates, and higher welfare fund membership. AP also stands out for the high share of workers in SHGs. There are also a number of states with higher than average membership rates of specific types of organization,

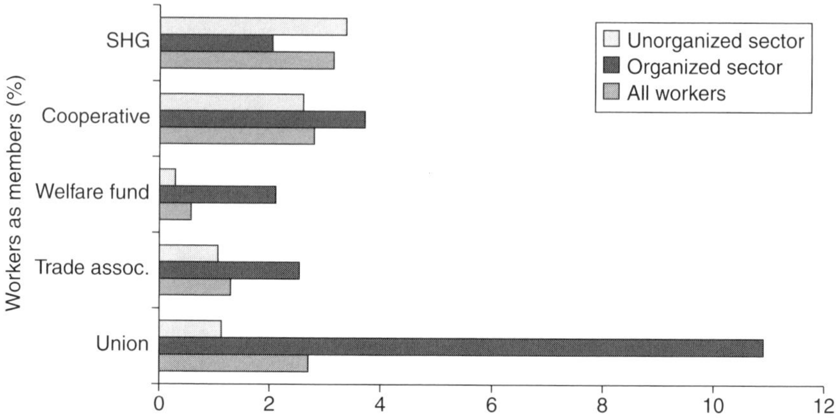

Figure 12.7 Membership rates in organizations, all workers and by organized/unorganized, 2004 (source: ADB/MOF survey, 2004. Author estimates).

including West Bengal for unions/associations, and Orissa and Chattisgarh on coops/SHGs.

Conclusions and recommendations

While the market failures that suggest a role for public intervention in social insurance for unorganized-sector workers are clear, it is not axiomatic that 'more is better'. Badly designed schemes can have negative impacts for the poor (Gertler 1998). A common problem is health-service-cost escalation if moral-hazard problems among users and providers are not controlled. The losses from moral hazard are higher where the price elasticity of demand for services is significant, which international evidence suggests is the case in developing countries.[38]

With respect to types of social insurance, there is a tension between household needs, and operational feasibility of rapid expansion coverage for different types of insurance. The profile of household shocks reveals a high demand for income smoothing due to health shocks. However, due to supply-side constraints, moral hazard and adverse selection, as well as the complexities of administering health insurance, this type of scheme is the most difficult to implement. In India, experience with the Universal Health Insurance Scheme illustrates these difficulties. In comparison, life insurance and defined contribution pensions are easier (and with life insurance, cheaper) to design and implement. The contingencies involved, age and death, are easier to monitor and less subject to moral hazard and adverse selection. Unlike health care, the benefits are simple and standardized cash payments. Disability insurance lies somewhere in between, given the need to verify the condition and potential for moral hazard. GoI has implicitly recognized the relative difficulties in its

2007/2008 budget, which seeks expansion of social security starting with life and permanent disability insurance for rural landless workers under the proposed Aam Admi Bima Yogana (though the scheme does not unfortunately have a clear strategy on aggregation of workers through groups to control transactions costs and raise awareness).

In addition, large-scale coverage expansion will require government subsidies to address the question of affordability, and oversight to mitigate fraud and/or mismanagement. However, this does not necessarily suggest a 'top-down' approach whereby new layers of bureaucracy are created to implement schemes. On the other hand, given likely economies of scale, the need for portability of benefits and the exigencies of supervision, the government's role may include creating robust and harmonized record-keeping and payments/collection infrastructure.

The second dimension of sequencing to be considered relates to the target-covered population. In this regard, it is necessary to recognize that some individuals are past the point where insurance or savings instruments are useful. For households with disabled, elderly, widows and already suffering from catastrophic health shocks or disease, the appropriate intervention is to alleviate poverty through direct transfers and other types of assistance. This distinction between those too poor to contribute and others is less obvious in the case of certain approaches to health insurance.

For most households with unorganized-sector workers, insurance is possible, at least with a degree of subsidy. However, voluntary schemes that require individuals to make contributions or pay premia in order to be eligible for coverage may not be easily expanded to the lowest income workers unless they are heavily subsidized. At the same time, experience of NGO and other schemes in India and internationally suggests that some small contribution even for the poorest is an important tool in improving the accountability of schemes to their beneficiaries.

The main alternative to direct public provision and administration is to use existing non-governmental entities and restrict the role of government to: (i) providing targeted subsidies; and (ii) regulating these entities and setting basic standards. This model already exists in India in several forms. In addition, many CBMI schemes could be incorporated under an umbrella program that provided matching contributions or premia but set standards in terms of minimum-benefit targets, eligibility conditions, investment policy and record-keeping, among others.

This coordinated partner–agent approach has recently become more attractive due to financial-sector reforms that have resulted in dynamic asset-management and insurance sectors as well as supervisory agencies that are becoming more experienced. There are several potential advantages to this approach. First, by harnessing existing groups including SHGs, cooperatives and MFIs, transaction costs could be kept low, especially where individual recordkeeping is already taking place. A second advantage would be the promotion of competition on the basis of cost and quality of services. Third, many unorganized-sector workers have no experience with formal financial-sector institutions so that groups can serve as an effective intermediary.

For health, pension, life and disability insurance, a viable plan to extend coverage based on unorganized-sector workers paying premiums or making contribution would need to meet the following criteria:

- long-term financial sustainability;
- transparent costing based on actuarial principles;
- reasonable incentives to encourage widespread take up on a voluntary basis;
- ability to cope with irregular income streams;
- harmonization, in terms of incentives and portability, with formal-sector programs;
- low transaction costs;
- accurate and timely record-keeping;
- effective risk pooling (in the case of insurance);
- effective asset management (in the case of long-term savings/pensions);
- accessibility on a national scale.

Perhaps the greatest challenge for any approach will be that of tracking participants and the financial flows associated with each of them. While universal national registration in India in the near future appears unlikely, alternative solutions could be explored in the meantime. Computerized record management makes any program more transparent and flexible. Programs with systematic personalized record-keeping provide much greater capacity for adding new benefits and improving existing schemes. The access gap can further be reduced by means of various technological innovations.

Cash-collection and disbursement systems in the unorganized sector pose serious challenges. Conventional financial intermediaries are often ill prepared to deal with mass transactions of very small amounts in remote, disbursed and poorly educated communities. Penetration of commercial banks in the rural areas in India remains low. While India's extensive postal system operates in almost every corner of the country, the adequacy of its accounting mechanisms and capacity to assume new tasks remains to be evaluated. Both in India and abroad, a number of interesting and relevant innovations provide lessons for adapting to the needs of both public and private sector in extending the coverage of financial services.

Conclusion

This chapter has reviewed evidence on two tools for promoting consumption smoothing among unorganized-sector households in India. While public works and social security for unorganized workers have considerable potential, this has yet to be realized for the large majority. Moving from the big picture of policy initiatives to the 'nuts and bolts' will remain the biggest challenge in realizing this potential and the benefits it may hold for the poor. At the same time, even well-designed and executed programs will remain only some tools in a much wider array of policy initiatives needed to improve the lot of unorganized-sector workers.

Appendix 1

Major central rural-employment programs

- *Jawahar Rozgar Yogana* (JRY – from 1989–1999), a CSS targeted to BPL households in rural areas, with preferences for SC/ST and women, and 80:20 financing split between centre and states. The wage/material ratio was 60:40, and DRDA/ZP the main implementing agencies through line departments and GPs.
- *Employment Assurance Scheme* (EAS – from 1993–2001), a CSS initially focused on 261 districts, and gradually extended to nationwide rural coverage by 1997. EAS committed to 100 days of lean-season employment for up to two adults per rural family, and was also financed on an 80:20 central and state split. As with JRY, the wage/material ratio was 60:40 and DRDA/ZP the main implementing agencies through line departments and GP.
- In 1999, JRY was restructured into the *Jawahar Gram Samidhi Yogana* (JGSY), with the main difference being that creation of demand-driven community infrastructure moved from being a secondary objective to the primary objective, with rural-employment generation conversely becoming the secondary objective.
- From 2001, the EAS and JGSY were merged into *Sampoorna Grameen Rozgar Yogana* (SGRY), which had a target of 100 days employment (per rural household). Financing is split 75:25 between the centre and the states, and PRIs have in principle been given an increased implementation role.
- In late 2004, the *National Food for Work Program* (NFFWP) was introduced in 150 backward districts, with a massive increase in funding to Rs.5,400 crore in the 2005–2006 budget.
- The *National Rural Employment Guarantee Act* (NREG) was passed in August 2005 and implemented from 2006. It initially covers 200 backward districts, with commitment to national rural coverage within five years. This is the first legislated national rural-employment program, and commits to 100 days guaranteed employment per rural household annually. The funding split is 90:10 between centre and states, and PRIs are considered the primary implementing agencies.

Appendix 2

Abbreviations used in this chapter

BAIF	Bharatiya Agro Industries Foundation
CBMI	Community-based Micro-insurance
CBO	Community based Organization
CMD	Centre for Management Development
EPFO	Employee Provident Fund Organization
ESIS	Employee Social Insurance Scheme
GoI	Government of India
GP	Gram Panchayat
IRDA	Insurance Regulatory and Development Authority
MFI	Microfinance Institution
MoLE	Ministry of Labor and Employment
NCEUS	National Commission in Enterprises in the Unorganized Sector
OBC	Other Backward Castes
RD	Rural Development
SEWA	Self-Employed Women's Association
ST	Scheduled Tribe
SC	Scheduled Caste
SI	Social Insurance
SHG	Self-Help Group
UHIS	Universal Health Insurance Scheme

Part V

Epilogue and conclusions

13 Epilogue

The analysis presented in much of the book made use of the detailed unit-level data available from the 'thick' rounds of the NSS. The last of these quinquennial rounds which were available to us was for the year 1999–2000 (the 55th round). Thus we were unable to cover the current trends in the early years of the century. Another 'thick' round of the Survey was completed by the NSS for 2005–2006 (the 61st round). At the time of completing this manuscript (April 2007) the unit-level data sets from this survey are available only in part. But the NSS has released two reports on the some basic tables both for the Employment and Unemployment (EUS) part and the Consumer Expenditure (CES) part of its survey. In what follow we have made use of these published reports to discern some of the trends emerging in the most recent years and see how they fit into the picture emerging from our detailed work for the period ending 1999–2000.

Trends in employment and earnings

India's growth rate accelerated towards the end of the period between the 55th and the 61st rounds. While the *average* growth rate over the decade 1992–1993 to 2002–2003 was 5.9 per cent, it touched 8.5 per cent in 2003–2004 and 7.5 in 2004–2005 (World Bank 2006, Table 1.2, p. 14). As in the late nineties the service sector continued to lead the growth process. Also the lagging growth in the agricultural sector persisted. If anything the growth in the agricultural sector decelerated from 3.2 percent in the period 1980–1992, to 2.4 per cent in 1992/1993 to 2002/2003 and even lower in the last few years. However, industry recovered somewhat from the slump of the second half of the 1990s. Manufacturing grew at the rate in excess of 6 percent per annum. But the basic structural problems of manufacturing, identified in the book continued to be significant, posing serious problems for sustained growth. These include the persistence of 'dualism' and employment stagnation in the formal (organized) sub-sector.

Recovery of participation rates

The new evidence suggests a major development on the labor-market front between the 55th and the 61st rounds. This is the recovery of participation rates which affect the trends in employment. The slow-down in employment growth in the 1990s discussed in Part I of the book was traced to: (i) a withdrawal of labor of principal status in the young-age groups because of expanded schooling; but (ii) more importantly to the withdrawal of female labor of subsidiary status, particularly in the rural labor market. A good deal of attention was paid to the possible reasons for this withdrawal (Chapter 4). While no definitive conclusion could be reached, there was a strong suggestion that this decline in PRs was due to a shift in demand conditions in the agricultural economy. The 1980s had seen an upsurge in the demand for labor due to the second phase of the green revolution spreading to the eastern states. Prime-age females were pulled into the labor market due to a sudden upsurge of labor. With the passing of this wave of technological change the labor market adjusted to a more stable pattern: the subsidiary workers who met the upsurge in labor demand seem to have been substituted by more permanent labor arrangements, such that while there was a pronounced fall in PRs of subsidiary females, the principal status females increased their participation to some extent.

What caused the recovery in participation in the latest period between the 'thick' rounds? An overview of the changes in broad categories of labor is presented in Figure 13.1. A perusal of the bar chart and the figures attached to it suggest that, while all four groups of labor distinguished increased their participation, the bigger

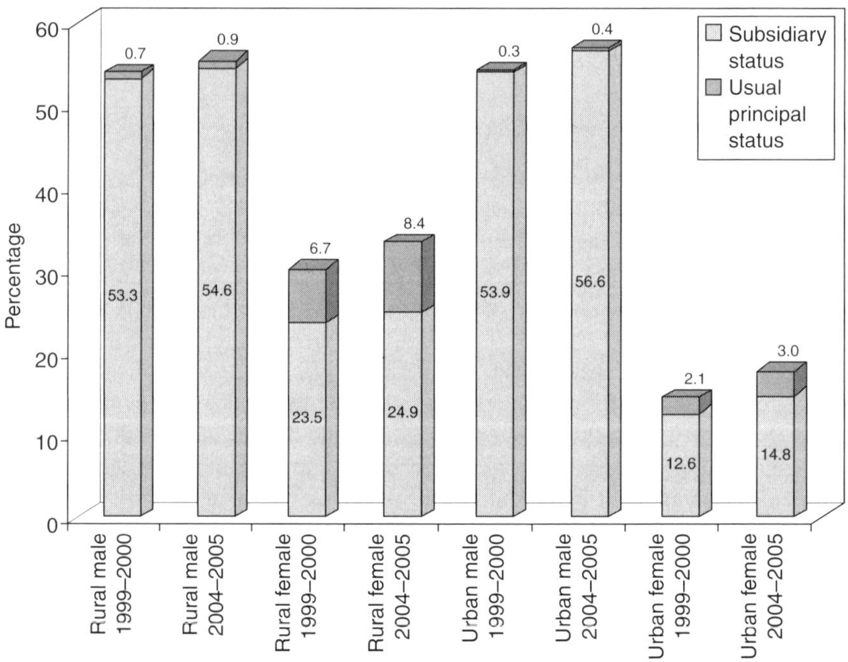

Figure 13.1 Labor-force participation rates, 1999–2000 and 2004–2005 (source: NSS Report number 515, 2007).

contribution has been made by females – and more so in the rural areas. The increase in female participation has been both in the principal and subsidiary categories. Subsidiary females played a bigger role in the *increment* to the participation rate in the rural sector but in the urban areas it is the female principal workers who are more important in the change. Subsidiary females are, however, a substantial part of the change in the urban areas as well. The following graphs depict the age profiles of participation rates of females of subsidiary status for all three of the last quinquennial rounds of the NSS.

We see that there is an interesting difference between the changes in the profiles in the rural and the urban areas. In the rural sector the increase in the subsidiary participation in the 61st round is concentrated in the prime-age group, and the recovery brings the profile up but not as far as the level of the 50th round (1993–1994). Figure 13.2 depicts it. In the urban areas by contrast the increase in participation is stronger among female subsidiaries of the younger age groups, and in fact their PRs in the 61st round exceed what had been achieved in 1993–1994 (Figure 13.3). Generally, the age-profile of female participants of subsidiary status has shifted to the left in the 61st round. It suggests that in the urban sector young females are tending to enter the job market more strongly than in the earlier rounds.

It is not possible with the summary data available so far to examine the proximate causes of the change described above. It is doubtful if the shift in the demand for labor in agriculture, which apparently explained a significant part of the decline in female participation in the 1990s, could be the cause of the recent recovery. As we have already pointed out the agricultural sector has continued to suffer from stagnation and slow growth. Is it possible that the strong growth in

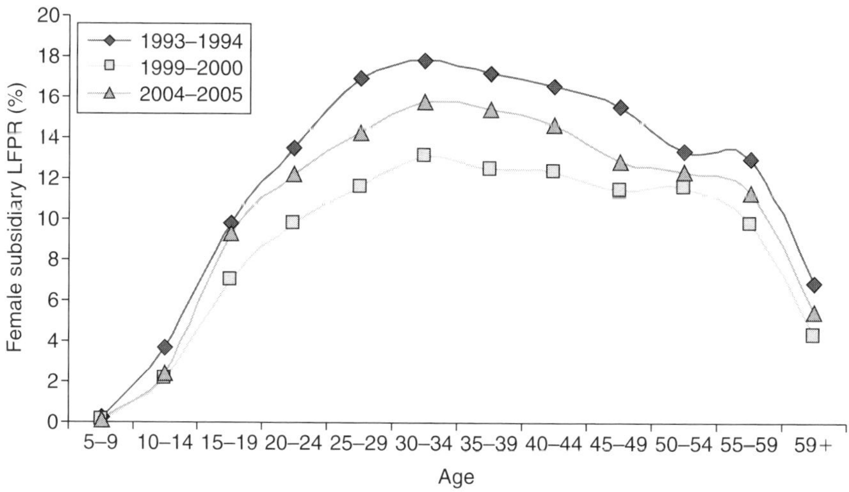

Figure 13.2 Female subsidiary labor-force participation rate (in %) across age groups, rural areas (source: Same as Figure 13.1).

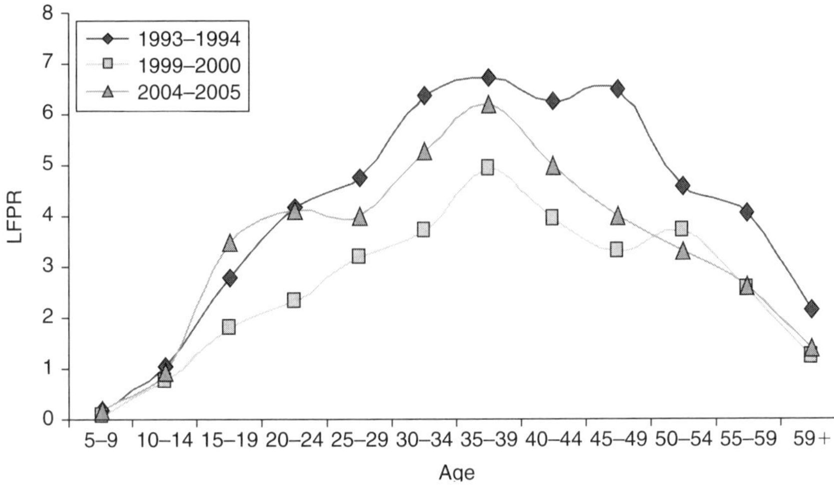

Figure 13.3 Female subsidiary labor force participation rate (in %) across age groups, urban areas (source: Same as Figure 13.1).

the non-agricultural, and particularly the service sector, which has propelled the demand for female labor inducing an increase in PRs? The fact that females of principal status and of the younger age groups are important in the increase in participation in the urban economy might give some strength to this hypothesis, since non-agriculture is of much greater importance as a source of job growth in the latter.

The change in participation rates is of course not the same as the change in employment rates. The gap between the two is accounted for by any change in unemployment rates. Here the evidence as far as males are concerned is that there has been little change in unemployment rates in the UPS count but that the unemployment rate in the CDS count has increased only in the rural sector. Much the more important change has been in the female labor market. The rates for females have gone up significantly. This is true of both the rural and urban sectors, and also for the longer-term unemployed (as measured by the UPS count) and the shorter-term ones (the CDS count). The figures are given in the Table 13.1.

It seems very likely that the increase in female PRs and the increase in unemployment rates are parts of the same phenomenon. As women job seekers enter the labor market their job search pushes up the unemployment rate. The increase in the unemployment rate is, however, less than the increase in participation rate.

As discussed at length in Chapter 3, this development might be due to supply- or demand-side changes, or to both. The problem now, however, is to explain the change in the direction opposite to what was discussed in the chapter. The movement in participation is in the upward direction – which might be caused by the supply curve shifting *downwards*, or the demand curve shifting

Table 13.1 Unemployment rates (per 1,000) for three rounds (UPS)

	Rural		*Urban*	
	Males	*Females*	*Males*	*Females*
Usual status				
1993–1994 (50th)	20	13	58	83
1999–2000 (55th)	21	15	48	71
2005–2006 (61st)	21	31	44	91
Current daily status				
1993–1994	56	56	67	104
1999–2000	72	70	73	94
2005–2006	80	86	75	116

Source: NSS Report Number 515, 2007.

Table 13.2 Absolute change in the share of the self-employed among principal-status workers

Year	*Rural*			*Urban*		
	Male	*Female*	*Total*	*Male*	*Female*	*Total*
1983–1993	–2.8	–2.8	–2.7	0.9	–0.1	0.7
1993–1999	–2.3	–1.3	–2.0	0.1	1.2	0.3
1999–2004	3.2	6.4	4.1	3.4	2.0	3.1

Source: NSS Report Number 515, 2007.

upwards, or to both. No conclusion on this issue is possible without detailed work with unit-level data. We will now discuss the changes in employment structure, wage rates and household welfare levels to come up with some plausible hypotheses for future research.

While the period of the 1980s and the 1990s had seen an increase of the share of casual workers – more so in the rural areas – the latest period saw a decline in this share in both sectors, and both for males and females (Table 13.4). In fact, the decline in the share of casuals in female employment has been going on in the urban sector for a long time, and gathered momentum in the latest period. What is a new development is the decline of the casual share among rural females and among males in both sectors. What type of employment did increase to compensate for the decline in the casual share? Females in the urban labor market increased the share of regular wage workers – reinforcing again the trend which had already been under way since the 1980s (Table 13.3). All other groups – males in both rural and urban areas, and females in rural areas – increased their share in self-employment (Table 13.2).

While the movement from casual to regular workers among the body of female urban job seekers signifies an improvement of labor-market conditions, the same cannot be said unambiguously about the increase in the share of self-employment

Table 13.3 Absolute change in the share of the regular workers among principal-status workers

Year	*Rural*			*Urban*		
	Male	*Female*	*Total*	*Male*	*Female*	*Total*
1983–1993	–1.9	–0.3	–1.3	–1.8	3.7	–0.8
1993–1999	0.3	0.5	0.3	–0.8	3.0	–0.1
1999–2004	0.1	0.9	0.3	–1.1	3.7	–0.3

Source: NSS Report Number 515, 2007.

Table 13.4 Absolute change in the share of the casual workers among principal-status workers

Year	*Rural*			*Urban*		
	Male	*Female*	*Total*	*Male*	*Female*	*Total*
1983–1993	4.7	3.1	4.0	0.9	–3.6	0.1
1993–1999	2.0	0.8	1.7	0.7	–4.2	–0.2
1999–2004	–3.3	–7.2	–4.4	–2.3	–5.7	–2.8

Source: NSS Report Number 515, 2007.

without further information of incomes earned (Table 13.2). It might represent the growth of a dynamic informal sector, or alternatively could signify accumulation of job seekers at the low end of the earnings spectrum.

Changes in the structure of employment by industry

It was seen in earlier chapters that in Indian economic development the tertiary sector had led the way in absorbing labor which had been increasingly diverted from the agricultural sector. Further, even the limited amount of labor finding employment in the secondary sector was mostly absorbed in its informal sub-sector. What is the evidence in the recent period while the post-reform changes had some time to take root? The relevant data are presented in Table 13.5. It is seen that the increase in employment share in the secondary sector in the recent period has been higher than in the tertiary. However, the secondary sector in the table includes construction – and this sub-sector accounted for fully half of the incremental share of employment. Further, the dominance of the informal sector in the growth of manufacturing employment has persisted.

Table 13.6 gives the figures given by the DGE&T (Labor Bureau) for the latest years available. They show an absolute decline in employment in the formal sector as a whole – even taking the private sector on its own. The percentage decline in manufacturing – including the private part of it – is much higher, two-and-half times as much.

Table 13.5 Distribution of employment by broad sectors

Principal status workers		
Sector	*55th*	*61st*
Primary	59.2	54.8
Secondary	16.1	18.8
Tertiary	24.7	26.4
All workers		
Primary	60.9	57.0
Secondary	15.7	18.2
Tertiary	23.5	24.8

Source: NSS Report Number 515, 2007.

Educational upgrading: the role of college graduates

We would expect significant upgrading over time of the labor force in terms of formal education. This is indeed what we see in Table 13.7. But a striking feature of the table is that the expansion is relatively more pronounced for college graduates. There is indeed a curious dent in the middle level of education. There is a decline in the share of workers with middle to higher secondary education in most of the groups distinguished in the table. Even the rural females, the sole group to register an increase in its share in the recent period, did so only to a minuscule percentage. By contrast the increase in the share of workers who are college graduates is large and impressive – particularly for urban females. This is an important development in the labor market, and obviously related to the strong growth of skilled tertiary-sector jobs, particularly in the urban economy (and more for females).

Wage trends

Consistent with the above developments in job trends – and the shifts in the demand for labor – we find that the wage structure in the recent period has tilted in favor of the relatively well educated. Their higher returns to education – which has already been noticed in the 1993–1999 period (see Chapter 3 above in particular), would of course affect the *regular* wage workers, who also show diversity in educational attainment. The data presented in Table 13.8 bear this out. It suggests an increase in wage inequality in the recent period, reinforcing the trend in the previous period analyzed in Chapter 3.

A rather striking and perhaps disturbing result in the table is the decline overall of real wages. The more educated groups have indeed had a positive trend but it is quite low. The growth rate of mean earnings for the illiterate and those with less than middle level education has been substantially negative. This trend in mean earnings does not necessarily imply that there has been absolute

Table 13.6 Employment in organized sectors, 1999–2003 (in hundred thousand)

Industry groups	*Public*		*Private*		*Total*		*Growth of employment (in %)*		
Year	*1999*	*2003*	*1999*	*2003*	*1999*	*2003*	*Public*	*Private*	*Total*
Agriculture	5.15	5.06	8.71	8.95	13.86	14.01	–0.44	0.68	0.27
Mining and quarrying	9.26	8.47	0.87	0.66	10.13	9.13	–2.20	–6.67	–2.56
Manufacturing	15.69	12.6	51.78	47.44	67.47	60.04	–5.34	–2.16	–2.87
Electricity, gas and water supply	9.62	9.13	0.41	0.5	10.03	9.63	–1.30	5.09	–1.01
Construction	11.07	9.48	0.71	0.44	11.78	9.92	–3.80	–11.27	–4.21
Trade	1.63	1.82	3.23	3.6	4.86	5.42	2.79	2.75	2.76
Transport, storage and communication	30.84	29.39	0.69	0.79	31.53	30.18	–1.20	3.44	–1.09
Finance, insurance and real estate	12.95	13.77	3.58	4.26	16.53	18.03	1.55	4.44	2.20
Community, social and personal services	97.94	96.09	17	17.56	114.94	113.65	–0.48	0.81	–0.28
Total	194.15	185.8	86.98	84.21	281.13	270.01	–1.09	–0.81	–1.00

Sources: DGE&T, Labor Bureau, Ministry of Labor, Government of India.

Table 13.7 Absolute change in employment share in UPS workers (15+) across education categories

Educational level	*Rural male*		*Rural female*		*Urban male*		*Urban female*	
	50th to 55th	*55th to 61st*	*50th to 55th*	*55th to 61st*	*50th to 55th*	*55th to 61st*	*50th to 55th*	*55th to 61st*
Not literate	–4.4	–5.8	–4.4	–7.6	–2.3	–3.1	–4.8	–6.0
Literate and up to primary	–2.0	2.2	1.3	3.0	–4.0	0.9	–1.4	2.7
Middle	2.7	1.9	2.0	2.3	1.5	0.6	2.0	1.2
Secondary	2.0	–0.2	0.8	0.9	1.6	–2.0	0.9	–1.8
Higher secondary	1.0	0.3	0.1	0.6	0.7	–0.2	0.7	–0.9
Graduate and above	0.7	1.6	0.2	0.8	2.5	3.8	2.6	4.8

Source: NSS Report Number 515, 2007.

Table 13.8 Levels and growth of average daily earnings of regular workers (15–59) across education level (at constant 1999–2000 prices)

Education Level	*Rural*		*Urban*		*Growth rates*	
	55th	*61st*	*55th*	*61st*	*Rural*	*Urban*
Not literate	62.4	54.5	75.3	63.7	–2.7	–3.3
Literate and up to middle	99.6	82.3	101.0	86.6	–3.7	–3.0
Secondary and higher secondary	145.3	145.1	165.2	165.6	0.0	0.1
Graduate and above	212.7	228.5	272.4	277.8	1.4	0.4
All	125.3	120.8	165.1	159.5	–0.7	–0.7

Source: NSS Report Number 515, 2007.

decline in all wage groups. We do not have the distribution of wages within each educational category. The decline in mean earnings would be consistent with a shift in the distribution to the lower end – as with the development of a bi-modal structure with relatively more jobs being created at the low and the upper end of the distribution. Further examination of these possibilities must await the availability of unit-level data which will enable us to study the shapes of the wage distribution within skill or education groups.

Table 13.9 presents the data on trends for casual wage earners. The rate of growth although positive only in the rural areas, shows a marked deceleration relative to the previous period and indeed relative to the 1980s as well (see Chapter 3).

Interpreting the wage–employment trends

The clear evidence about the deceleration of the wage rate at the same time when participation and employment rate increased is a puzzle which needs

Table 13.9 Average wage earnings per day received by casual workers (15–59) at 2004–2005 prices

Category	*55th round*	*61st round*	*Growth rate*
Rural male	52.5	55.0	0.96
Rural female	34.7	34.9	0.16
Rural person	47.2	48.9	0.72
Urban male	76.8	75.1	–0.46
Urban female	46.4	43.9	–1.13
Urban person	70.4	68.7	–0.51

Source: NSS Report Number 515, 2007.

careful analysis. It contrasts dramatically with the experience of the previous period between the 50th and the 55th rounds, when decline in employment rates was associated with a higher rate of wage growth. At first sight both these phenomenon might suggest significant shifts in the supply curve of labor. The observed trends are consistent with a shift upwards of the supply curve in the 1993–1999 period followed by a reverse movement of the function upwards in the 1999–2004 period. Quite apart from the fact that these opposite movements of the supply curve need explanation, two points need to be emphasized which need to form part of any composite hypothesis:

1 The cyclical behavior of the demand for labor. Evidence has been produced in Chapter 3 that the 1993–1999 period saw a contraction in the demand for labor, particularly in the rural sector. It followed the passing of the second wave of the green revolution in agriculture, particularly in the rice-growing states, and was also accompanied by a shift to the use of labor of principal rather than subsidiary status. We have now seen in this Epilogue that there is strong suggestion in the data that the latest period between 1999/2000 and 2004/2005 has witnessed another upsurge in the demand for labor – this time most likely caused by the growth of the non-farm sector both in the rural and urban labor markets. There has also been a significant change in the composition of labor demand – with a marked shift to regular and more educated labor, and away from market for casual labor.
2 It is difficult to distinguish the movements along a fixed supply curve of labor and a movement of the supply curve itself when demand is fluctuating so much in a cyclical pattern. This is because labor is offered in the market – particularly by female workers who have alternative use of their time within the household – not only by changes in the wage rate (movements along the supply curve) but also by changing *expectations* about employment in the labor market (movements of the supply function itself). Demand and supply curves are interrelated. It is possible that stronger expectations about the labor market might cause rightward shift in the supply curve of labor which might compensate partly for the upward pressure on wage rates.

3 The last point is related to the wider issue of the response of labor supply to *the period of time* over which wage earnings are being considered. An important statistical issue needs to be stressed in this connection. The daily-wage rate in casual labor market reported by the NSS (and used in this work) is really the derived daily earnings calculated by dividing the total labor earnings over a longer period of time (a week), and hence depends on the number of person-days of employment obtained during the week. Thus the data might show higher growth rate of weekly earnings than that of daily earnings (or what has been called the wage rate in some parts of the discussion). The supply function of labor might be related to earnings over a longer period if time (week, month or season) than the average day.

The upshot of this discussion is that the rate of growth of earning per week or season might show a different trend than that of average daily earnings, and indeed might have been higher in the recent 1999–2004 period. This should be reflected in higher incomes over the month for agricultural laborers. The NSS does not collect data on income. But the trends might be reflected in the data on expenditure per household collected by the NSS. Since agricultural laborers are at the bottom of the income ladder and suffer disproportionately from the incidence of poverty, a relevant variable to examine is the trends in poverty as calculated from the NSS data from the Consumer Expenditure Survey (CES). This is the topic to which we now turn.

Trends in household expenditure, poverty and inequality

The summary report of the NSS, giving selected tables from the Household Expenditure Survey, has given a rough idea of changes in household welfare (mean expenditure per capita) for different parts of the distribution.

Table 13.10 reveals that for the five-year period between the 55th and the 61st rounds there has been an increase in MPCE for all percentile groups, but that the increase is equalizing in the rural sector, but non-equalizing in the urban. In the rural areas the percentage increase is highest in the poorest slab, and declines gradually from 13 to 14 percent increase in the '5 percent or less' group to 6 percent or less in the 80–90 and the 90–95 groups (although the highest slab shows an increase of more than 10 percent). By contrast in the urban areas the percentage increase in MPCE is low in the bottom slab. In fact it is only 2–3 percent for the poorest group (based on column 7 of the table) for the lowest *five* groups rising to 7–9 percentage for the 80–90 and 90–95 slabs.

The overall impression from these figures and graphs is that the trend observed in the 1990s between the 50th and the 55th rounds is continuing steadily, with a decline in low incomes and the incidence of poverty, but an increase in inequality in the urban areas.

Mahendra Dev and Ravi (2007) in fact have used the 61st round to calculate poverty ratios over the two periods, using the official poverty line and

Table 13.10 Comparison of APCE between 55th and 61st rounds

Percentile group of population	*APCE at constant (1993–4) prices*				*% change between 55th and 61st*	
	Rural		*Urban*			
	55th	*61st*	*55th*	*61st*	*Rural*	*Urban*
0–5%	121	137	159	164	13.2	3.1
5%–10%	153	169	203	210	10.5	3.4
10%–20%	176	193	242	248	9.7	2.5
20%–30%	203	220	288	294	8.4	2.1
30%–40%	228	245	334	342	7.5	2.4
40%–50%	252	271	385	396	7.5	2.9
50%–60%	281	299	447	461	6.4	3.1
60%–70%	313	333	523	545	6.4	4.2
70%–80%	358	380	628	657	6.1	4.6
80%–90%	433	455	800	854	5.1	6.8
90%–95%	537	569	1052	1144	6.0	8.7
95%–100%	849	938	1912	1985	10.5	3.8
All	307	331	532	555	7.8	4.3

Source: NSS Report number 508, 2007.

Table 13.11 Percentage of poor in rural and urban areas (survey of mixed-reference period)

	Poverty ratios			*Changes in poverty (% points per annum)*		*Changes in poverty (per annum changes as % of base year)*	
	1993–1994	*1999–2000*	*2004–2005*	*1993–2000*	*1999–2005*	*1993–2000*	*1999–2005*
Rural	31.6	27.5	21.9	–0.7	–1.1	–2.2	–4.1
Urban	28.5	24.3	20.7	–0.7	–0.7	–2.5	–3.0
Total	30.8	26.6	21.5	–0.7	–1.0	–2.2	–3.8

Source: Mahendra Dev (2007), Table 5.

mixed-reference periods (Table 13.11).[1] The data bears out the surmise mentioned at the end of the last section. There has indeed been a reduction in poverty ratios, and it is seen that at least one estimate from the new data suggest that there has been *an increase* in the rate of poverty reduction in the latest period in both sectors, but more so in the rural areas.

The results given above are based on the consumer expenditures based on the 'mixed-reference period', There is, however, thc presumption that for an assessment of trends over longer periods of time, there is some case for ignoring the change in the reference period introduced for the first time in the 55th round. Sticking to the original NSS practice of the 30-day reference period it is possible

Table 13.12 Percentage of poor in rural and urban areas (survey of 30-day reference period)

	Poverty ratios			*Changes in poverty (% points per annum)*		*Changes in poverty (per annum changes as % of base year)*	
	1983	*1993–1994*	*2004–2005*	*1983–1994*	*1993–2005*	*1993–1994*	*1999–2005*
Rural	45.7	37.3	29.2	–0.8	–0.7	–1.8	–2.0
Urban	42.3	32.6	26.0	–0.9	–0.6	–2.2	–1.8
Total	44.9	36.0	28.3	–0.9	–0.7	–1.9	–1.9

Source: Mahendra Dev (2007), Table 1.

to compare the trends over two decades – the first over the period 1983 and 1993 (between the 43rd and the 50th rounds) and the second between 1993 and 2004 (the 50th and the 61st rounds). Along with many other authors Mahendra Dev considers the first period to be the 'pre-reform' one, and the second the 'post-reform' years. Although based on simple applications of the official poverty lines and on data published by the NSS rather than the original analysis of unit-level data the differences in the trends between the two decades is intriguing. Mahenrda Dev's figures are reproduced in Table 13.12.

The difference between the rural and the urban sectors is confirmed in this table. The reduction in the rate of poverty decline (normalized by base-year values) increased marginally in the rural sector in the post-reform decade, but it was distinctly reduced in the urban. Consistent with results obtained in the book, the increase in inequality was much more pronounced in the urban sector in the post-reform decade (ibid., table 3, p. 510).

Further confirmation of this and other suggestions emerging from the summary tables must await detailed analysis of the unit-level data from the 61st round of the NSS.

14 Conclusions

The book is concerned with the impact of growth on poverty reduction and inequality. The experience of India in the post-reform years of 1993–2000 – in the period covered by the 50th and the 55th rounds of the NSS – has been examined in detail against the backgrounds of trends in earlier periods. As in studies in other countries and periods, growth is the key factor in poverty reduction. The growth rate of mean household income (or expenditure) – which is the more proximate factor in poverty reduction – can be expected to be less than growth rate in GDP in periods of expansion since savings and investment typically increases in such periods. The other factor is the trend in inequality. An increase in inequality not only slows down the growth of income of the poorer groups, but it might have an adverse impact on growth itself. Quite apart from increasing social tensions, a growth pattern that exacerbates inter-regional, inter-sectoral as well as intra-regional inequality create bottlenecks which put a drag on sustainable growth.

The post-liberalization period in the nineties saw a continuation of the trend in poverty reduction – at about the same rate as the previous six-year period. It was accompanied by an increase in inequality, particularly in the urban sector. The evidence for the rising inequality came both from the data on household expenditure per capita (household welfare level) as well as those on wage earnings. This scenario is no different from that of China (although the magnitudes are much larger in China), and perhaps several other newly developing countries of Asia, though it differs markedly from the 'East Asia model' of growth with equity.

The increased inequality in the urban sector has exacerbated rural–urban dualism, which was already a feature of Indian development, in spite of the marked tilt of urban growth towards smaller towns. The share of the urban sector in poverty reduction, however, has gone up, not because of increased rural-to-urban shift of labor, but because of the higher rate of growth in this sector. An interesting difference was found between states which had a greater FDI inflow and the others – in spite of the generally low level of FDI in India compared with China, for example. FDI seems to have had two opposite effects on poverty reduction: it enhanced the process through higher growth, but seemed to have less of a 'trickle-down effect' as its impact was felt disproportionately on metro towns, Thus some states with higher than average FDI inflow appears in the list of high poverty decline states like Karanataka and Tamil Nadu, but others like Andhra Pradesh and Madhya Pradesh are not.

The higher return to education – particularly in college education – is a major cause of the rising urban inequality, but other features of the evolution of the employment structure are also of importance. Particularly significant is the extreme dualism in the manufacturing sector – with the striking phenomenon of the 'missing middle' which has been highlighted in this study as a distinguishing feature of Indian industrialization.

It is only to be expected that a big country like India has vast regional differences. Although the degree of inter-regional inequality is not as great as in China the evidence suggest a certain inertia and persistence of spatial differences. Labor-market outcomes are widely different – in terms of earnings levels, employment rates and female participation – across the major states and regions of India. The econometric exercise presented in Chapter 5 has a strong message that state-level GDP and economic growth has significant impact on employment rates, particularly of females. While higher incomes might lead to some withdrawal of females from labor-market activity, regions that can provide greater economic opportunities have significantly higher participation rates.

In Chapter 6 a novel attempt has been to demarcate India into seven 'broad regions' based on agro-ecological differences – an attempt which goes beyond the political demarcation of 'states' to more meaningful regions distinguished by factors which have a persistent effect on land productivity in particular. Our analysis of the components of the difference in mean consumption per household across regions, and in the trends over time, do bring out the quantitative importance of inter-regional differences in land productivity. It was seen that the low-poverty region of the North-West (region 1) was in fact losing in advantage over the other regions in terms of the growth of land productivity in the period 1983–1993, but that this equalizing trend has been reversed in the post-reform years of 1993–1999. Over the entire 1983–1999 period the maintenance of the leading role of region 1 in poverty reduction has not been entirely due to differential growth in land productivity (relative to the offsetting trend in land–man ratio). The growth of off-farm employment, both in the rural and the urban areas of this region, has contributed at least half of the differential growth in rural income (household expenditure) relative to regions 2 and 3. While the process of cumulative growth, in which agricultural growth seems to stimulate non-farm growth, is the dominant scenario in much of North India, somewhat different outcomes are observed in the South. The rural non-farm and urban sectors played a larger role in determining the level of rural incomes in the Southern regions in the 55th round. These sectors grew at a relatively high rate over our period not because of, but to compensate for, the low growth of land productivity.

Part III of the book turns to an examination of the issues in the major industrial sectors of the economy. Agricultural productivity, as we have just mentioned, holds the key to growth of incomes. The reform process has not gone very far in the agricultural sector, and it is a matter of concern that agricultural growth actually slowed down in the post-reform years. Major breakthroughs in this sector, like the green revolution of the sixties and the seventies, are not yet in the horizon. While accelerating growth in agriculture remains a key concern of policy, it would be wrong to assume that such growth would increase the gainful absorption of labor in agriculture. The evidence analyzed in Chapter 7 suggests that employment elasticity is higher in regions of *low* agricultural productivity, implying that the greater degree of labor absorption is really due to agriculture serving as the sponge for labor with no viable alternative. The role of high agricultural growth is to stimulate off-farm employment – both in the rural and the urban sectors – through the process of cumulative development. Our econometric work in this chapter confirms that this relationship of complementarily between agricultural productivity and off-farm employment (and incomes) for All-India, although, as we have mentioned, some land-poor regions in the South have succeeded in developing off-farm employment as an *alternative* to agriculture. One other important result from the chapter on agriculture is worth re-emphasizing. There is some disturbing evidence supporting the widespread concern that the post-reform years has seen a deterioration in the conditions of smaller and landless farmers relative to larger farmers. The warnings about 'distress inducing growth' given in the literature with respect to some cash crop oriented districts in Andhra Pradesh do seem to have some validity at the all-India level.

Employment growth outside agriculture in the Indian economy has been led in recent decades not by manufacturing but by the tertiary sector. This is a pattern historically observed in today's developed countries at a much later stage of their development. On the other hand, the relatively larger role of the tertiary sector in labor absorption in the nineties have been observed, not only in the more developed countries of Asia like Korea and Taiwan, but also in Thailand, Indonesia, Malaysia and the Philippines. But the other developing Asian counties, with the possible exception of the Philippines, have not shown the dominance of the tertiary sector in the absorption of labor in non-agriculture that India does. The pertinent question from the employment angle is to ask: is labor being pushed or pulled into the tertiary sector? Our detailed exploration of this issue in Chapter 9 shows that the marginal absorption of labor in the tertiary sector has been taking place at the two ends of the earnings spectrum – the first and the last quintiles.

Comparing, however, mean income per worker in the major sectors for a number of Asian countries we find that India is an outlier in terms of a higher productivity of the tertiary sector relative to the industrial. Furthermore the productive differential in favor of the tertiary sector in India seems to have increased between 1960 and 2002, while it has fallen in all the other comparator countries. It shows that service-sector growth in India has been productivity led and not employment led contradicting views of some economists that employment grew in services because this sector has been a repository of low income labor "pushed out" of agriculture. The heart of the employment problem in India would thus seem to be not an excess absorption of labor in the tertiary sector, but the low productivity of the manufacturing sector, and its persistence over time. It is this low performance of manufacturing which has prevented it from being the dynamic sector – playing a central role in productivity growth as well as the reallocation of labor as in other countries in the history of successful economic development. It has been argued that this disappointing role of the manufacturing sector can be traced, at least to a significant part, to the persistence of dualism in the sector. It is this which perpetuates the tremendous difference in relative labor productivity between the small and large size groups. The very low level of labor productivity in the manufacturing sector can be traced to this dualism.

Chapter 8 analyzed the various factors explaining the low employment elasticity in the high-productivity formal sector of manufacturing. Thus, in spite of a healthy growth of output in this sector, employment growth has been very low. Much of the labor in Indian manufacturing has been absorbed in the informal and the small-scale part of the modern manufacturing sector – the so-called DME sector employing between five and ten workers. It was shown in Chapter 10 that, quite apart from the informal sector, the distribution of employment in formal manufacturing is bi-polar with strong modes at the 6–9 and 500+ size groups, and a marked "missing middle". It was also seen that this is very much a peculiar phenomenon of Indian manufacturing development – and not seen in other comparator countries in Asia. The relatively low productivity of the Indian manufacturing sector – even if we look specifically at the formal part of it – and its lack of dynamism can be traced in a significant way to this problem. Historically this problem arose partly from past policies, particularly the way the policy of reservation for the small scale was handled, and the bias in education policies towards the development of tertiary education at the cost of more general development at the lower end of skills. The problem of the missing middle, however, continues even after reforms have mitigated the more adverse effects of these policies. Apart from the persistence of labor and capital market segmentation, trade and infrastructure links which have supported the older system are slow to change.

A relevant set of considerations on this point is the complexity and rigidity of labor legislation protecting workers in large factories. The low employment elasticity of the large-scale manufacturing sector (the so-called ASI sector), analyzed in detail in Chapter 8 demonstrates the prevalence of an effective tax on increasing the number of workers employed per unit of output. Chapter 11 examined the issue of labor legislation. While it is sometimes argued that this set of legislation cannot be that important for it affects only a small portion of India's total labor force, the pertinent point to emphasize is that it is a serious impediment to the entry of new workers into the protected sector, and ultimately is detrimental to the process of raising income levels of workers outside the protected sector. It is, however, recognized that reforms of labor laws in the formal sector is not likely to be acceptable politically unless more attention is paid to labor institutions that might affect the conditions of workers in India's vast informal sector. Recent initiatives on this point, which are very much in the forefront of public discussion in the country, are critically reviewed in the last chapter of the book.

Notes

1 Introduction: an overview of globalization, reforms and macro-economic developments in India

1 There is a large literature on this subject. Here it is sufficient to note that, while institutional factors might exacerbate the wage differential between the formal and the informal sectors, the original cause of the emergence and persistence of the differential are likely to be economic (see Mazumdar 1989).

2 Poverty, growth and inequality in the pre- and post-reform periods and the patterns of urbanization in India: an analysis for all-India and the major states

1 We are thankful to Niranjan Sarangi for decomposition exercises done from NSS Unit Level Data.

2 The quinquennial rounds are known as thick surveys constituting hundreds of thousands of households that allows analysis to be taken down to major state level as well.

3 We adopted the procedure followed by Sundaram and Tendulkar (2003a). We could reproduce the APCE figures by fractile group for URP for both rural and urban areas as presented in their revised calculations (Sundarm and Tendulkar 2003a). The changes in APCE by fractile group due to changes in the reporting period of five items from 30-day to 365-day (MRP) differs marginally. The details of the difference are given in Appendix 2. In this appendix we also discuss briefly the revised estimates of head count ratio (HCR) as obtained by Sen and Himanshu (2004).

4 This point was made by Professor Angus Deaton in correspondence with us.

5 Unlike the official price index, the Tornqvist price index is calculated using the information from the consumer expenditure surveys itself, and, hence, it allows for substitution behaviour as households adapt to relative price changes over time. It is also considered superior to Laspeyre's or Paasche's index as it satisfies both time-reversal and factor-reversal tests. These indexes, however, differ from official indexes in a number of ways. In particular, they rise somewhat more slowly over time than do the official price indexes, especially in the rural sector. This implies that poverty estimates will remain below that of the official estimates in subsequent periods.

6 Equation (Figure 2.5): $y = 2.72 + 0.21^{***} x$; $R^2 = 0.386$; Equation (Figure 2.6): $y = 3.41 + 0.06 x$, $R^2 = 0.015$.
(2.97)
(0.47)

Equation (Figure 2.7): $y = 3.57 + 0.37^{***} x$; $R^2 = 0.859$; Equation (Figure 2.8): $y = 0.22 + 0.29^{**} x$, $R^2 = 0.253$.
(9.26)
(2.17)

Figures in parentheses () are t-values and *** and ** denote significance at 1 and 5 per cent levels respectively.

7 Datt and Ravallion (1992) had criticized an earlier formulation by Kakwani and Subbarao (1990) in which the change in poverty was decomposed into the growth and inequality components by taking the former as resulting from a change in mean income between the two years of comparison. The difference between this and the actual change in poverty was assumed to be that due to change in inequality. This procedure is equivalent to assuming that the Lorenz curve of the initial period is constant in calculating the growth component. Datt and Ravallion correctly point out that in this formulation the decomposition is not an exact one, but contains a residual term – which has been arbitrarily allocated to the redistribution component. It is shown that the residual vanishes if the Lorenz curve remains unchanged.

3 Trends in employment and earnings 1983–2000

1 In some official statements (e.g., the *Economic Survey 2004*) employment is calculated on the basis of numbers estimated by the NSS on the basis of 'current daily status' (CDS). This gives a much sharper decline in the growth rate of employment. But this procedure is inappropriate because the CDS measures *person-days* not persons (see the Appendix 1 to this chapter).

2 Gordon and Gupta (2003) also reached similar conclusions. They found that compared to the general trend in developing countries, India's service sector absorbed far less labor (relative to other similarly placed countries in Asia). In terms of services' share in GDP, India moved slightly above the general trend during the nineties. This was accompanied by a fall in the share of services in gross capital formation (Chandrasekhar and Ghosh 1999). Labor productivity increase without any increase in capital intensity in services might have occurred because of a faster rise in sub-sectors that depend on skilled labor (Gordon and Gupta 2003). Hansda (2001) found (from input–output tables) that the proportion of intermediate use of services output to be declining slightly between 1978–1979 and 1993–1994. There also exists a widespread view (Virmani 2002) that the increase in the salaries of public administration and defense contributed substantially in increasing contribution of services in GDP in India. In other words, it is largely spurious. But this interpretation has been challenged by Nagaraj (1999, 2000). He did not find that these components made any positive contribution to the acceleration in service-sector growth during the nineties.

4 Accounting for the decline in labor supply in the nineties

1 The age-specific LFPR are explained in detail in Appendix 2.

2 In West Bengal, there is clear evidence of increased absorption of labor in the 1980s as evident from workforce data of both NSS and Census. NSS also reports substantial contraction of employment in agriculture in the 1990s in this state. For Madhya Pradesh, under oilseed development program in the 1980s, there was huge expansion of oilseed cultivation. In the 1990s it faltered and downturn in oilseed was further compounded by allowance of import of cheap palm oil.

3 There might be an 'endogeneity problem' in this analysis in that a fall in PR itself reduces the household welfare level as measured. In this case, in the classification by household expenditure levels for the 55th round, there would be relatively more households in the lower welfare groups with less participation of females. But in this case we would expect to see a relative increase in the higher welfare groups for the participant households – not a fall as we in fact find.

5 Some implications of regional differences in labor-market outcomes in India

1 Ahmad Ahasan and Carmen Pages are staff members of the World Bank and the Inter-American Development Bank respectively, both working at their headquarters

in Washington DC. The findings, interpretations and conclusions of this chapter are those of the authors and should not be attributed to the World Bank, its Executive Directors, or the countries they represent. All errors are ours. The authors thank Sergiy Biletsky, Zhaoyang Hou and Mikhail B. Oslmolovski for excellent research assistance and the World Bank's Human Development team for providing the NSS region map coordinates, and members of the India Labor and Employment study team for their valuable comments in discussions held in September 2005.

2 The latest thick round data is from the 2004–2005 survey.

3 Employment rates are defined as the share of workers (i.e. with status codes of 11 to 51 in Question 3, Block 5.1 in Schedule 10 questionnaire of the NSS) in the age group of 15 to 59. Participation rates are defined as the share of worker and population looking for jobs (i.e. with status codes from 11 to 81) in the 15 to 59 age cohort. Finally, unemployment rates are defined as the ratio of those unemployed but searching for jobs (Code 81) as a proportion of the population participating in the labor market, i.e. those working and unemployed but searching for jobs.

4 As the fourth section explains, most of these estimates have taken into account endogeneity of labor-market outcomes, wages, earnings and GSDP.

5 For instance, Duryea, Edwards and Ureta (2004) find that increases in education explain 30 percent of the increase in female participation rates in Latin America.

6 U.S. Bureau of the Census, Geographic Mobility: March 2000 to March 2001

7 Mohan and Dasgupta (2004).

8 It is true though that part of the answer may lie in the lack of updating of rural areas due to which many actually urban areas may be classified as a rural area – such as environs of Delhi. Thus higher "rural" wages may be partly reflecting this misclassification and the migration may be being under-reported. Still, it would be hard to ascribe all the changes to this fact.

9 We account for differences between urban and rural areas by including an urban dummy. In addition, we account for the fact that output only varies at the state and not at the regional level by computing robust standard errors clustered at the state level.

10 We estimate specifications of the following kind:

$$E_{ijt} = \tau_t + \beta Y_{jt} + \delta w_{ijt} + \gamma X_{ijt} + \varepsilon_{ijt} \tag{1}$$

Where E_{ijt} denotes log of employment in state i, region j, round t, Y_{jt} is log of state GDP, w_{ijt} denotes log of wages and X_{ijt} is a vector of additional controls. We also control for aggregate, round effects by means of time (round) dummies, denoted as τ_t.

11 As in the first differences estimates, we account for the fact that GDSP only varies at the state level by computing robust standard errors clustered at the state level. We also account for a likely endogeneity of GSDP and wages by instrumenting wages and GSDP with the following set of variables: share of industry in the state economy, log of state credit to industry per capita, log of state credit to agriculture per capita, log of power (measured as percentage of villages that are electrified) and log of km of roads per 100 square km per state. These variables capture differences in state development and output that are uncorrelated with contemporaneous labor supply.

12 We estimate specifications parallel to specification (1) but substituting employment at the regional level by average regional weekly earnings. As usual, we compute robust standard errors clustered at the state level to account for the lack of within state variation of GSDP.

13 The difference between the predicted increase and the actual decline indicate that a part of the participation decline is not accounted for by substitution effects and that other causes, beyond lack of opportunities or increased husband incomes, are behind the participation decline. Understanding which additional factors are behind should be an important priority for future research.

6 Trends in the regional disparities in poverty incidence: an analysis based on NSS regions

1 For 1972–1973, Jain and Tendulkar have obtained the poverty line a) by using a poverty line of Rs.15 per capital per month at 1960–1961 prices and b) by converting this poverty line at 1972–1973 prices by using the consumer price index for the agricultural laborers (CPIAL). For 1999–2000 we have used poverty line as obtained by Deaton (2002). He has taken poverty line of each state separately obtained from 'expert group on poverty line' by planning commission for the year 1987–1988. He updated it to the current (1999–2000) year from the higher prices that rural consumers pay in 1999–2000 for various items (obtained from unit level data) compared with 1987–1988.

2 For the triennium ending 1982 and 1992 value of output and net sown area figures at district level (1961 classification) was obtained from Bhalla and Singh, 2001. From district level we aggregated to NSS region level and further to broad-region level. For the late nineties we managed to get district-level crop-wise season-wise data for two years 1997–1998 and 1998–1999 from Govt. of India, Ministry of Agriculture, District-wise Area and Production of Crops in India, 2001. These production data of different crops were converted to value by using crop wise price data (for the year 1993–1994) used by Bhalla and Singh (2001) to maintain comparability. These were aggregated to all crop NSS region level and further to broad region level. For two crops, rubber and coffee, we collected value of output and net-sown area from the Rubber Board of India and Coffee Board of India. For net-sown area we collected data from several issues of IFFCO, Agricultural and Fertilizer Statistics. The two years data were aggregated to get data for 1997–1999.

7 Agricultural productivity, off-farm employment and rural poverty: the problem of labor absorption in agriculture

1 The non-specified activities could be irrigation, spraying of fertilizer and pesticides, post harvesting operations, etc.

2 First we distinguished rural households dependent on agriculture in two categories cultivators and agricultural-labor households, on the basis of main source of earnings – labor income and self-employment in agriculture. Households whose main income comes from self-employment in agriculture (i.e. cultivators) are further divided on the basis of operational landholding size. These are divided into marginal (0–1 hectare), small (1–2 hectare), medium (2–4 hectares) and large (more that four hectares). Vakulbrahmanam's (2005) land classification is based on landownership whereas our land classification is based on operational landholding.

8 Employment elasticity in organized manufacturing in India

1 See, e.g., Eichner (1973). The author notes the affinity of the theoretical tradition to the empirical literature which has found from surveys of business-pricing decisions that firms set prices on the basis of the 'cost plus' concept. The 'plus' margin is in its turn set by the necessity to generate the profit share which finances the investment ratio. The affinity of these ideas to the Kalecki models of the firm has been stressed by Asimakopoulos (1971) among others.

2 See Mazumdar (2003b) for a more extended discussion of the labor-market theories relevant to this set of decisions.

3 We are grateful to Ahmad Ahsan of the World Bank for providing the ideas and calculations for this sub-section.

4 The data period of this section ends at 1994–1995.

5 Our data period for this section ends at 1994–1995.

9 Dualism in Indian manufacturing: causes and consequences

1 The term "directory" and "non-directory" establishments presumably refer to the 'supposed' registration practice of the government that never materialized.
2 Data on average earnings for the two countries can be found in the same national sources as are cited for Table 9.1.
3 It is apparent that the reason why the difference in value added per worker between the largest and the smallest size groups in Taiwan is larger than that in wages per worker is because Taiwan has a fair presence of large conglomerates, with a large share of capital, along with the small- and medium-scale firms. Such conglomerates play a smaller role in Hong Kong's manufacturing economy.
4 It should be emphasized once again that the sets of data considered here exclude the very large household and other parts of the informal sector in establishments employing less than five workers.
5 But under WTO agreement India was under obligation to remove quantitative restriction by 1 April, 2001. So by 2001–2002, all remaining 799 items reserved in the SSI list has been put under OGL. However, through a series of de-reservation over the years, the number of reserved items in small scale has been pruned to 239.
6 For more detailed examination of the origins and consequences of the Indian industrial policy affecting the small-scale sector see Mazumdar (1991) and Little et al. (1987)
7

> For a poor country spent and still spends much more on tertiary education. In 2000 India spent 86 percent of per capita GDP per student on tertiary education, and only 14 percent on primary education. The corresponding percentages for China were 10.7 and 12.1 respectively. The Indian level of expenditure on tertiary education was even higher than Korea or Indonesia.
>
> (IMF, WP 06/22 2006, pp. 6–7)

8 The contents and impact of this set of policies have been discussed in detail in Little et al. (1987). See also Mazumdar 2003b.

10 Growth of employment and earnings in the tertiary sector

1 The APCE (Average Per Capita Consumption Expenditure) that we have used for the 55th round comes from employment schedule. It is an abridged questionnaire compared to the consumption-expenditure schedule. Consequently APCE in abridged employment schedule is underestimated. When APCE of both these questionnaires was compared across percentile APCE distribution, APCE from employment schedule was uniformly lower by 9–11 percentages compared to consumption-expenditure schedule. The distribution of APCE in both these series would be similar.

11 Legislation, enforcement and adjudication in Indian labor markets: origins, consequences and the way forward

1 Ahmad Ahasan and Carmen Pages are staff members of the World Bank and the Inter-American Development Bank respectively, both working at their headquarters in Washington, DC. Tirthankar Roy is a Professor at the Gohkale School of Economics in Poona. The views expressed in this chapter are the personal views of the authors, and in no way represent the position of their respective organizations.

The authors would like to thank Gautam Mehta for valuable research assistance, Farah Zahir for her indispensable help in gathering the data used in this study, and K.V. Ramaswamy for very helpful discussions. The authors also thank the Labor Bureau and the Central Statistical Organization for kindly sharing their data.

2 There was a surge in the share of factories inspected in the year 2001. Given the existent data is impossible to determine whether this is a short-term reversion or a more permanent effect.
3 If a firm did not report a change in behavior, the reduction in the number of visits is zero. To compute the adjusted number of inspections the reported number of inspections is divided by (1 percent reduction in visit due to unofficial payments/100).
4 Notice, however, that a positive relation between the number of inspections and the perceived stringency of labor laws is not sufficient to conclude that inspections increase compliance. This is because inspections could concentrate in firms for which the law is more binding.
5 Conversations with Labour Commissioners in a number of states suggest that the grip of Chapter Vb is still very high. In the year 2004 there were six applications for permission to retrench in Karnataka, out of which only one was granted. In Tamil Nadu, there were three. One was granted, one was denied and the other one was still pending. In West Bengal, only one case was granted out of 20 applications.
6 Systematic data on the use of contract labor is only available from the Annual Survey of Industries (ASI) which only covers the manufacturing sector.
7 At the time of this study, the Investment Climate Survey data (ICS) provided firm level information for 25,582 firms from 55 emerging countries, but data for additional countries are periodically added to the data set. Surveys are administered in each country to a sample of firms stratified by size, sector and location, following a common framework. The surveys contain a number of questions regarding firms' characteristics, outcomes and perceptions about the business environment. The sample size for each country ranges from less than 100 establishments, for countries with a small private sector like Bhutan and Eritrea, to more than 1,500 for China, India, and Brazil. Information on ICS data can be obtained at http://rru.worldbank.org/external/cicic/portal.htm.
8 Firms' perceptions about labor-market legislation may be colored by the overall degree of optimism or pessimism about the economic outlook in each country. However, accounting for this factor by measuring each employer's response in relation to her average response to all other obstacles does not change the results. India still remains among the countries in which labor legislation is perceived to be more binding.
9 See Ahsan and Pagés (2006) for further details.
10 For example, in 1988, Tamil Nadu introduced an amendment increasing the power of conciliation officers in terms of enforcing attendance, compelling the production of documents and issuing commissions for the examination of witnesses. Other examples of laws that reduce the cost of disputes are (i) eliminating the need for the parties to refer labor disputes to the government prior to referring them to a Tribunal. or (ii) granting the government the power to transfer any industrial dispute pending before a tribunal to any other tribunal constituted by the state government for adjudication.
11 They relate labor regulations to economic outcomes, by estimating the following specification:

$$Y_{it} = \tau_i + \tau_t + \beta X_{it} + \phi_a L_{it-1} + \varepsilon_{it} \quad (1)$$

where Y_{it} is an economic outcome such as manufacturing output, employment or wages in state i in period t, X_{it} is a vector of state controls, and τ_i and τ_t denote a state and time dummy, respectively. L_{it-1} is a vector of legislation measures, which refer to the accumulated sum of amendments in a given type of laws over time in a state up to period t. In some specifications, outcome variables vary at the industry–state level. They lag regulatory variables one period to account for the average lag between enactment and implementation of the law and to reduce the possible endogeneity of labor laws.
12 For instance, there is a large degree of uncertainty and ambiguity regarding whether business processing operations, calling centers or software companies are included in the definition of industry.

13 The term market infrastructure is adopted from Rajan and Zingales (2003).
14 It should be noted that a level of compensation of 45–60 days of compensation per year of service in case of a restructuring sick industries or profit-making companies, respectively, are above the norm in both developing and developed countries.
15 For more information on the operation of these schemes see Heckman and Pagés (2004), IADB (2004), Kugler (2004, 2005), Saavedra and Torero (2004) and Paes de Barros and Corseuil (2004).
16 See for example Brown and Medoff (1989).
17 An example is useful to clarify this issue. Assume a certain firm hires a contractor to run a cafeteria. Workers employed in the cafeteria are the employees of the contracted firm, which would then be responsible for abiding by all labor regulations with its employees. Nonetheless, the contracting firm could have a subsidiary responsibility if it hires a contractor that is not abiding by the law.

12 Strengthening employment and social security for unorganized-sector workers in India

1 Philip O'Keefe and Robert Palacios are currently working at World Bank office in New Delhi. The views expressed in this chapter are the personal views of the authors, and in no way represent the position of their respective organizations.

We are grateful to Ihsan Ajwad, Corinne Siaens and Sangeeta Goyal for analysis of NCAER, NSS and ADB/MOF data respectively, and to Rinku Murgai and Martin Ravallion for discussions of their work on NREG. Thanks also to Dipak Mazumdar for comments on an earlier version.

2 WDR 2006; Munshi and Rosenzweig (2005) for empirical evidence of credit and insurance-market failures driving limited mobility in rural areas in India.
3 For summaries of international experience, see Ravallion (1991); Devereux (2002); Subbarao (2003).
4 South Africa's Special Public Works Programme (SPWP) provides a good example of the latter, with participants required to undertake two days training for every 22 days worked, and 2 percent of each sub-project budget allocated to worker training (Devereux and Solomon 2005).
5 This did not happen in the lead-up to the 1999 national election, though spending may have been unusually constrained in the aftermath of the 5th Pay Commission.
6 This is to change in the 62nd round, which has revised questions on participation in works.
7 Based on estimates of around 65 million BPL households in 2000 (Indiastat.com).
8 Based on a usual status (PS+SS), workforce of just over 300 million. Sundaram, 2001.
9 This is consistent with international evidence of targeting of public works. For example, in Argentina's Trabajar program, 80 percent of beneficiaries were from the poorest quintile, while in Chile the share was close to 100 percent. In Bangladesh, around 70 percent of beneficiaries of the Food-for-Work Program were in the lowest income bracket, while in Indonesia, the post-crisis public works program was more likely to reach household who had suffered large shocks (Subbarao 2003).
10 CAG 1997. The CAG report on EAS from 2000 estimated that 10.9 million workdays were lost due to contractor margins, assuming a 10 percent margin.
11 AFC SGRY program assessment for Orissa, 2005.
12 Deshingkar and Johnson (2003). The statewide figure for AP for 2002–2003 in the MRD evaluation was 25.3 percent of works with contractor involvement.
13 In the last year of the period, the village coverage rate for EAS was 32 percent.
14 Acharya (2005) for seasonal MEGS employment data up to 2002–2003.
15 IDS for Planning Commission (2002) which found 80 percent of works occurring in this period.
16 CMD evaluation of SGRY on behalf of MRD, 2005.

17 The two shares are not necessarily inconsistent, but one would need to assume that female participants worked more than twice as many days.
18 General rate based on Sundaram revised estimates from 2001. Swamy (2003) on gender and workfare schemes internationally.
19 CMD study for MRD on SGRY (2005); PEO EAS evaluation (2000); and for Rajasthan an IDS evaluation of employment programs (2002).
20 CMD for MRD 2005.
21 This is a rate of Rs.50 in 1999–2000 prices, scaled up for subsequent movements in the CPI for agricultural and rural laborers (RBI series).
22 Townsend (1994); Munshi and Rosenzweig (2005); Ravallion and Chauduri (1997). Gertler and Gruber (1997) re Indonesia.
23 Peters *et al.* (2002); Dev *et al.* (2001); World Bank, op. cit.; and Duflo (2005).
24 Though note the collinearity between society ageing and country income levels.
25 Gertler (2001) re Korea, Taiwan, Singapore and Japan. O'Keefe and Palacios (2006).
26 Dev *et al.* (2001); Jhabvala and Subrahmanya (2000) and World Bank, op. cit. This section focuses on contributory schemes. Dev *et al.* demonstrate the value of a wide-ranging consideration of social security.
27 The central funds are: Mica Mines Welfare Fund (1946); Limestone and Dolomite Mines Labor Welfare Fund (1972); Beedi Workers' Welfare Fund (1976); Iron Ore, Manganese Ore and Chrome Ore Labor Welfare Fund (1978); Cine Workers' Welfare Fund (1981); Building and Other Construction Workers' Welfare Fund (1996). ILO, op. cit., and Rajan (2001).
28 Among funds based on contributions, 12 had tripartite financing, ten were funded from employer and worker contributions, and two from employer contributions only. See ILO (2004).
29 In contrast, for the Karnataka and AP Labor Welfare Funds, education has been the dominant expenditure – in Karnataka, accounting for around 98 percent of non-administration spending in 1997–2000, and in AP for 74 percent in 1998–2001. Rajan 2001.
30 In addition to central initiatives, many states and specific national ministries have schemes of social insurance. They are not addressed here.
31 Berman and Ahuja 2005; Gupta and Trivedi (2005).
32 Devadasan *et al.* 2004, gives a typology; Ahuja and Narang (2005).
33 Kuruvilla *et al.* (2005) re Yeshasvini, and ILO (2005).
34 There are also revolving funds, often for drug costs, but these are not covered here.
35 Another limitation is the regulatory obstacles for deposit taking. SEWA did not face this problem because it is also licensed as a banking institution.
36 For a review of international experience with social pensions, Palacios and Sluchynsky (2006).
37 Other factors such as savings capacity, risk preferences, and other demands on disposable income are also crucial (Palacios and Goyal forthcoming).
38 Gertler and Hammer (1997), which finds price elasticities of demand for health services in developing countries of –0.5 to –1.0, again an average of around –0.2 from developed countries.

13 Epilogue

1 The published report for the 61st round does not give expenditure distribution for the MRP at the state level. Therefore the authors

> estimated the MRP poverty ratios using the Lorenz curve method based on URP distribution of persons and MRP per capita expenditures. This assumes that MRP expenditure levels are monotonic with URP levels for all observations. Since this is unlikely to hold strictly, it may marginally affect the poverty estimates.
>
> (Ibid., p. 509)

References

Abe, Makoto and Momoko Kawakami (1997) 'A distributive comparison of enterprise size in Korea and Taiwan', *Developing Economies*, 35 (4): 382–400.

Acemoglu, D. (2002) 'Technical change, inequality and the labor market', *Journal of Economic Literature*, XL (1): 7–72.

Acharya, A and Ranson, K. (2005) 'Health care financing for the poor: Community-based health insurance schemes in Gujarat', *Economic and Political Weekly*, 40 (38): 4141–4150.

Acharya, S. 'Employment guarantee in rural India: Issues in productivity and quality of assets created', Round Table on NREGP in India, August 30–31, 2005, New Delhi, ILO.

Ahsan, A. and Pages, C. (2005) 'Helping or hurting workers?: Assessing the effects of de jure and de facto labor regulation in India', paper presented in the conference on Labor and Employment Issues in India, 27–29 July, Institute for Human Development, Delhi, 2006.

Ahluwalia, M. (2002) 'Economic reforms in India since 1991: Has graduation worked?', *Journal of Economic Perspectives*, 16 (3): 67–88.

Ahuja, Rajeev. and Narang, Alka (2005) 'Emerging trends in health insurance for low-income groups', *Economic and Political Weekly*, 17–23 September, 40 (37): 4151–4159.

Anant, T.C.A., Sundaram, K. and Tendulkar, S.D. (1999), 'Employment and labor in south Asia', processed, ILO, Geneva.

Asimakopoulos, M. (1971) 'The determinants of investment in Keynes's model', *Canadian Journal of Economics*, 4 (3): 382–388.

Bamoul, W.J. (1967) 'Macroeconomics of unbalanced growth: the anatomy of urban crisis', *American Economic review*, Vol. 57.

Beng, Chew Soon (1988) *Small Firms in Singapore*, Singapore: Oxford.

Bennett, S, A. Creese and Monasch, R. (1998) 'Health insurance schemes for people outside formal sector employment', *ARA Paper No. 16*, World Health Organization.

Berman, P. and Ahuja, R. (2005) 'Exploring the feasibility of financing private voluntary health insurance in India', mimeo, World Bank, New Delhi.

Berry, Albert and Mazumdar, Dipak (1991) 'Small-scale industry in the Asian-Pacific region', *Asian Pacific Economic Literature*, 5 (2): 35–67.

Berry, Albert (2006) 'India's complicated acceleration', processed, Munk Center for International Studies, University of Toronto.

Bertola, G. (1990) 'Job security, employment and wages', *European Economic Review*, June, 34 (4): 851–879.

Besley, T. and Burgess, R. (2004) 'Can labor regulation hinder economic performance? Evidence from India', *Quarterly Journal of Economics*, February, 119: 91–134.

Besley, T., Burgess, Robin and Esteve-Bolart, Berta (2004) 'Operationalizing pro-poor growth: India case-study', processed, Department of Economics, London School of Economics

Bhall, G.S. and Singh, Gurmail (2001) *Indian Agriculture: Four Decades of Development*, New Delhi: Sage Publications.

Bhalla, Sheila (2005) 'India's rural economy: issues and evidence', *IHD Working Paper no. 25*, New Delhi.

Bhalotra, Sonia R. (1998) 'The puzzle of jobless growth in Indian manufacturing', *Oxford Bulletin of Economics and Statistics*, 60 (1): 5–32.

Bhattacharya, B.B. and Sakthivel S. (2004) 'Economic reforms and jobless growth in India', *Working Paper Series no. E/245/2004*, Institute of Economic Growth, Delhi.

Brown C. H. and Medoff, J. (1989) 'The employer-size wage effect', *Journal of Political Economy*, 97 (5): 1027–1059.

Chadha, G.K. and Sahu. P.P. (2002) 'Setback in rural employment: Issues for further scrutiny', *Economic and Political Weekly*, 37 (2): 1998–2026.

Chandrasekhar, C.P. and Ghosh, J. (1999) 'Services sector growth: What does it mean?', *Hindu Businessline*, 16 November.

Centre for Management Development, (2005) *Concurrent Evaluation of SGRY*, on behalf of Ministry of Rural Development, Government of India.

Chetty, R. and Looney, A. (2005) 'Consumption smoothing and the welfare consequences of social insurance in developing countries', *NBER Working Paper No. 11709*, Cambridge, Massachusetts.

Comptroller and Auditor General of India (1997) *Performance Audit Report of Jawahar Rozgar Yogana*, New Delhi.

Comptroller and Auditor General of India (2000) *Performance Audit Report of Employment Assurance Scheme*, New Delhi.

Confederation of Indian Industry (CII) (2003) 'Industrial policies of northern region states: A comparative study', October.

Dahlman, C. and Utz, A. (2005) *India and the Knowledge Economy: Leveraging Strengths and Opportunities*, WBI Development Studies, Washington, DC: World Bank.

Datt, G. and Ravallion, M. (1992) 'Growth and redistribution: components of changes in poverty measures – a decomposition with applications to Brazil and India in the 1980s', *Journal of Development Economics*, 39: 275–295.

Datt, G. and Ravallion, M. (2002) '*Is India's Economic Growth Leaving the Poor Behind*?', mimeo, Washington DC: World Bank.

Deaton, A. (2003), 'Prices and poverty, 1987–2000', *Economic and Political Weekly*, 25 January, 38: 362–368.

Deaton, A. and Dreze, J. (2002) 'Poverty and inequality in India – a re-examination', *Economic and Political Weekly*, 7 September, 37: 3729–3746.

Debroy, B (2005) 'Issues in labor law reform' in B. Debroy (ed.) *Reforming the Labor*, New Delhi: Academic Foundation.

Deshingkar, P. and Johnson, C. (2003) 'State transfers to the poor and back: The case of FFW program in Andhra Pradesh', ODI Working Paper No. 222.

Dev, M. (2000) 'Kerala's Development Experience: Economic Growth and Human Development', *WP series No. 39, Centre for Economic and Social Studies*, Hyderabad.

Dev, M., Antony, P., Gayathri, V. and Mamgain, R.P. (eds) (2001) *Social and Economic Security in India*, New Delhi: Institute for Human Development.

Dev, S. Mahendra (2002) 'Pro-poor growth in India's employment challenge: what do we know about the employment effects of growth 1980–2000?', *Centre for Economic and Social Studies Working Paper no. 161*, Hyderabad, India.

Dev, Mahendra S. and Ravi, C. (2007) 'Poverty and inequality: All-India and states, 1983–2005', *Economic and Political Weekly*, 10 February, 42: 509–521.

Devadasan. N., Ranson, K., Van Damme, W. and Criel, B. (2004) 'Community health insurance in India: An overview', *Economic and Political Weekly*, 39: 3179–3183.

Devereux, S. and Solomon, C. 'Employment Creation Programs: The international experience', Round Table on NREGP in India, August 30–31, 2005, New Delhi, ILO.

Dollar, David, Iarossi, Giuseppe and Mengistae, Taye (2001) 'Investment climate and economic performance: some firm level evidence from India?', mimeo, World Bank.

Duryea, S., Cox-Edwards A. and Ureta, M. (2004) 'Women in the Latin American labor market: The remarkable 90s', in C. Piras (ed.) *Women at Work*, Washington, DC: Inter-American development Bank.

Duflo, A. (2005) 'Health shocks and economic vulnerability in rural Rajasthan', mimeo, Harvard University.

Dutta Roy, Sudipta (2004) 'Employment dynamics in Indian industry: adjustment lags and the impact of job security regulations', *Journal of Development Economics*, 73 (1): 233–256.

Eichner, Alfred S. (1973) 'A theory of the determination of the mark-up' *Economic Journal*, 83 (332): 1184–1200.

Fallon, P. and Lucas, R. (1991) 'The impact of changes in Job security regulations in India and Zimbabwe', *The World Bank Economic Review*, 5: 395–413.

Fallon, P. and Lucas, R.E.B. (1993) 'Job security regulations and the dynamic demand of industrial labor in India and Zimbabwe', *Journal of Development Economics*, 40: 241–275.

Feenstra, R. and Gordon, H. (1999) 'The impact of outsourcing and high-technology capital on wages: estimates for the United States, 1979–1990', *Quarterly Journal of Economics*, 114 (3): 907–940.

Fields, G. and Yoo, G. (2000) 'Falling labor income inequality in Korea's economic growth: patterns and underlying causes', *Review of Income and Wealth*, 46 (2): 139–159.

Fong, Chan Onn (1990) 'Small and medium enterprises in Malaysia: Economic efficiency and entrepreneurship', *Developing Economies*, 28 (2): 152–179.

Foster, D. Andrew and Rosenzweig, Mark P. (2004) 'Agricultural productivity growth, rural economic diversity and economic reforms: India 1970–2000', *Economic Development and Cultural Change*, 52 (3): 509–542.

Fuchs, V.R. (1968) *The Service Economy*, New York: National Bureau of Economic Research (NBER).

Gertler. P. (1998) 'On the road to social health insurance: The Asian experience', *World Development*, 26: 717–732.

Gertler, P. and Gruber, J. (1997) 'Insuring consumption against illness', *NBER Working Paper No. 6035*.

Gertler, P. and Hammer, J. (1997) 'Strategies for pricing publicly provided health services', World Bank Policy Research Working Paper No. 1762, World Bank.

Ghose, Ajit K. (1994) 'Employment in organized manufacturing in India', *Indian Journal of Labor Economics*, April–June, 37 (2): 141–162.

Ghose, Ajit K. (2003) *Jobs and Income in a Globalizing World*, Geneva: ILO.

Gordon, J. and Gupta, P. 'Understanding India's Services Revolution', paper prepared for the IMF–NCAER Conference 'A tale of two giants: India's and China's experience with reform', New Delhi, 14–16 November 2003.

Gottschalk, P. and Smeeding, T.M. (1997) 'Cross-national comparisons of earnings and income inequality', *Journal of Economic Literature*, 35: 633–687.

Government of India (2001) 'Report of the task force on employment opportunities' (Ahluwalia Committee), reprinted in *Planning Commission Reports on Labor and Employment* (2002), New Delhi: Academic Foundation.

Government of India (2002) 'Report of the special group on targeting ten million employment opportunities per year over the Tenth plan period', in *Planning Commission Reports on Labor and Employment*, New Delhi: Academic Foundation.

Government of India (2003) 'Statistical abstract – India 2002', *Central Statistical Organisation* (CSO), New Delhi: Controller of Publications.

Government of India (2006) *Economic Survey 2005–06*, Delhi: Ministry of Finance.

Gulati A. and Narayanan, S. (2002) 'Demystifying fertilizer and power subsidies in India' in R.P. Kapila and U. Kapila (eds) *Indian Agriculture in the Changing Environment*, Volumes 1 and 2, New Delhi: Academic Foundation.

Gupta, Indrani and Trivedi, Mayur (2005) 'Social health insurance redefined: Health for all through coverage for all', *Economic and Political Weekly*, September 17–23, 40 (38): 4132–4140.

Hansda, S.K. (2001) 'Sustainability of services-led growth: an input–output exploration of the Indian economy', *RBI Occasional Papers*, 22 (1–3).

Hanumantha Rao, C.H. (2004) Preface to 'state of Indian farmers – a millennium study', Ministry of Agriculture, Government of India, New Delhi: Academic Foundation.

Hasan, R, Mitra, D. and Ramaswamy, K.V. (2003) 'Trade reforms, labor regulations and labor–demand elasticities: empirical evidence from India', *NBER Working Paper 9879*, Cambridge MA.

Hazra A. (2005) 'Labor Laws and Industrial Relations', in B. Debroy (ed.) *Reforming the Labor*, New Delhi: Academic Foundation.

Heckman, James and Pagés, Carmen (2004) 'Introduction to law and employment: lessons from Latin America and the Caribbean', in J. Heckman and C. Pagés (eds) *Law and Employment: Lessons from Latin America and the Caribbean*, Chicago: National Bureau of Economic Research, University of Chicago Press.

Hill, Hal (1983) 'Choice of Techniques in the Indonesian Weaving Industry', *Economic Development and Cultural Change*, 31 (2): 337–353.

Indian Law Institute, *Annual Survey of Indian Law*, various years.

Institute of Development Studies (2002) *Evaluation for the Planning Commission of Employment Programs in Rajasthan*, Jaipur.

International Labor Organization (2004) *Welfare Funds in India*, New Delhi: ILO.

International Labor Organization (2005) *Case Study of Yeshashvini Health Insurance Scheme*, New Delhi: ILO.

International Monetary Fund (IMF) (2006) 'India's pattern of development: what happened, what follows', *IMF Working Paper* 06/22, Washington, DC.

Ishikawa, Shigeru (1967), *Economic Development in Asian Perspective*, Tokyo: Kinokumiya Bookstore.

Ishikawa, Shigeru (1978) *Labor Absorption in Asian Agriculture*, Bangkok: International Labor Organization.

Jain, L.R., Sundaram, K. and Tendulkar, S.D. (1988) 'Dimension of rural poverty – an inter-regional profile', *Economic and Political Weekly*, Special No.: 2395:2408.

Jhabvala, R. and Subrahmanya, R.K.A. (eds) (2000) *The Unorganized Sector: Work Security and Social Protection*, New Delhi: Sage.

Joshi, V. and Little, I.M.D. (2000) *India's Economic Reforms*, New Delhi: Oxford University.

Kakwani, N. and Subbarao, K. (1990) 'Rural poverty and its alleviation in India', *Economic and Political Weekly*, 25: A2–A16.

Kakwani, N. and Pernia, E.M. (2000) *Pro-poor Growth and Income Inequality*, October, Bangkok: Asian Development Bank.

Kalecki, M. (1938) 'The determinants of distribution of the national income', *Econometrica*, 6 (2): 97–112.

Kalecki, M. (1941) 'A theory of the long-run distribution of the product of industry', *Oxford Economic Papers (Old Series)*, 5: 31–41.

Kalecki, M. (1954) *Theory of Economic Dynamics*, London: Allen and Unwin.

Kalecki, M. (1971) *Selected Essays on Dynamics of the Capitalist Economy: 1933–1970*, London: Cambridge University Press.

Kaneda, Hiromitsu (1980) 'Development of small and medium enterprises and policy responses', *Studies in Employment and Rural Development no. 32*. Washington, DC: World Bank Economics Department.

Kannan, K.P. (2002) 'The welfare fund model of social security for informal sector workers: The Kerala experience', *Indian Journal of Labor Economics*, 45 (2): 243–272.

Kapila, R.P. and Kapila, U. (eds) (2002) *Indian Agriculture in the Changing Environment*, Volumes 1 and 2, New Delhi: Academic Foundation.

Kijima, Yoko and Lanjouw, Peter (2004) 'Agricultural wages, non-farm employment and poverty in rural India', presented in international seminar on Wages and Income organized by IGIDR and IHD, Mumbai.

Koshiro, Kazutoshi (1990) in Chapter 5 (Chapter on Japan) of W. Sengenburger, G. Lovemen and M.J. Piore (eds) *The Re-Emergence of Small Enterprises: Industrial Restructuring in Industrialized Countries*, Geneva: International Institute of Labor Studies (ILO).

Kugler, A. (2004) 'The effect of job security regulations on labor market flexibility: evidence from the Colombian labor market reform' in J. Heckman and C. Pagés (eds) *Law and Employment: Lessons from Latin America and the Caribbean*, Chicago: National Bureau of Economic Research, University of Chicago Press.

Kugler, A. (2005) 'Wage shifting effects of severance payments accounts in Colombia', *Journal of Public Economics*, 89: 487–500.

Kuruvilla, S., Liu, M. and Jacob, P. (2005), 'The Yeshaswini health insurance scheme for rural farmers and peasants: Towards health care for all?', mimeo, School of Industrial Relation Cornell University.

Lall, S. and Mengistae, T. (2005) 'The impact of business environment and economic geography on plant level productivity: an analysis of Indian industry', *World Bank Working Paper WPS 3664*, Washington, DC.

Lanjouw, P. and Ravallion, M. (1999) 'Benefit incidence, public spending reforms, and the timing of program capture', *World Bank Economic Review*. 13 (2): 257–274.

Lindert. P. (2004) *Growing Public: Social Spending and Economic Growth since the Eighteenth Century*, Cambridge: Cambridge University Press.

Little, I., Mazumdar, D. and Page, J. (1987) *Small Manufacturing Enterprises*, New York: Oxford.

Mahotra, O.P. (2001) 'Arbitration of labor disputes', in Z.M.S. Siddiqui and M.A. Wani (eds) *Labor Adjudication in India*, Delhi: Indian Law Institute.

Mazumdar, Dipak (1989) 'Micro-economic issues of labor markets in developing countries' *Seminar Paper no. 40, Economic Development Institute*, Washington, DC: World Bank.

Mazumdar, Dipak (1991) 'Import-substituting industrialization and protection of the small-scale', *World Development*, 19 (9): 1197–1213.

Mazumdar, Dipak (1997) 'Structure, growth and productivity of the small-scale manufacturing sector in India: An overview', processed, National Council of Applied Economic Research (NCAER), New Delhi.

Mazumdar, Dipak (2001)'Small–medium enterprise development in equitable growth and poverty alleviation', paper presented in Program for Asia Pacific Forum on Poverty 5–9 February, Asian Development Bank, Manila.

Mazumdar, Dipak (2003a) 'Trends in employment and the employment elasticity in manufacturing, 1971–92: An international comparison', *Cambridge Journal of Economics*, 27 (4): 563–582.

Mazumdar, Dipak (2003b) 'Small and medium enterprise development in equitable growth and poverty alleviation', in Christopher M. Edmonds (ed.) *Reducing Poverty in Asia; Emerging Issues in Growth, Targeting and Measurement*, Cheltenham, UK: Asian Development Bank.

Mazumdar, Dipak 'Trends and employment and earnings in the formal sector of India', background paper in *India's Employment Challenge: Creating Jobs, Helping Workers*, Draft World Bank Report, 2005.

Mazumdar, D. and Basu, P. (1997) 'Macroeconomic policies, growth and employment: the east and south-east Asian experience' in Khan and Muqtada (eds) *Employment Expansion and Macroeconomic Stability under Increasing Globalization*, London: Macmillan.

Mazumdar, Dipak and Sarkar, Sandip (2004) 'Measurement and determinants of poverty in pre and post reform period in India: An analysis for India and major states', *IHD Working Paper Series No. 22*, New Delhi.

Mazumdar, D. and Son, H.H. (2002) 'Vulnerable groups and the labor market in Thailand – impact of the Asian financial crisis in the light of Thailand's growth process', mimeo, September, University of Toronto.

Mohan, R. and Dasgupta, S. (2005) '21st Century: Asia becomes urban', *Economic and Political Weekly*, 15 January, 40 (3): 213–223.

Morawetz, D. (1974) 'Employment implications of industrialization in developing countries', *Economic Journal*, 84 (335): 491–542.

Mukhopadhyay, S.K. (2005) 'Conciliation – main obstacles and strategies for overcoming them', Awards Digest, *Journal of Labor Legislation*, 31: 5–6.

Munshi, K. and Rosenzweig, M. (2005) 'Why is mobility in India so low? Social insurance, inequality and growth', *BREAD Working Paper No. 97.*

Murgai, R., and Ravallion, M. (2005) 'Is a guaranteed living wage a good anti-poverty policy', *World Bank Policy Research Working Paper No. 3640.*

Nagaraj, R. (1990) 'Growth rate of India's GDP, 1950–51 to 1987–88: examination of alternative hypotheses', *Economic and Political Weekly*, 30 June, 25: 1396–1403.

Nagaraj, R. (1994) 'Employment and wages in manufacturing industries: trends, hypotheses and evidence', *Economic and Political Weekly*, 22 January, 29 (4): 177–186.

Nagaraj, R. (2000) 'Indian Economy since 1980: virtuous growth or polarization?', *Economic and Political Weekly*, 5 August, 35: 2831–2838.

Nayak, R., Saxena, N.C. and Farrington, J. (2002) 'Reaching the poor: The influence of policy and administrative processes on the implementation of government poverty schemes in India', *ODI Working Paper 172.*

Nath, S. (2005) 'Labor policy and economic reforms in India', in B. Debroy (ed.) *Reforming the Labor*, New Delhi: Academic Foundation.

Nayar B. R. (2006a) *Globalization and Nationalism: The Changing Balance in India's Economic Policy, 1950–2000*, New Delhi: Sage.

Nayar, B. R. (2006b) 'India's globalization: evaluating the economic consequences', *Policy Studies 22*, Washington, DC: East-West Centre.

O'Keefe, P. (2003) 'Rural health finance: Issues and experience with particular reference to Asia', mimeo, Institute for International Health, University of Sydney.

O'Keefe, P. and Palacios, R. (2006) 'Evaluating the NCEUS social security proposals in light of international experience', *Economic and Political Weekly*, August 12, 41: 3483–3487.

Paes de Barros, R. and Corseuil, C.H. (2004) 'The impact of regulations on Brazilian labor market performance', in J. Heckman and C. Pagés (eds) *Law and Employment: Lessons from Latin America and the Caribbean*, Chicago: National Bureau of Economic Research University of Chicago Press.

Palacios, R. and Goyal, S. (2006) 'Extending social protection to the unorganized sector: The challenges for India', mimeo, World Bank, New Delhi.

Palacios, R. and Sluchynsky, O. (2006) 'Social pensions part 1: Their role in the overall pension system', *World Bank Social Protection Discussion paper No. 601.*

Palmer-Jones, Richard and Sen, Kunal (2003) 'What has luck got to do with it? A regional analysis of poverty and agricultural growth in rural India', *Journal of Development Studies*, 40 (1): 1–31.

Papola, T.S. (1992) 'Labor institutions and economic development: the case of Indian industrialization', in T.S. Papola, and G. Rodgers (eds) *Labor Institutions and Economic Development in India*, IILS Research Series no. 97, Geneva: ILO.

Papola, T.S. 'Emerging structure of Indian economy – implications of growing inter-sectoral imbalances', presidential address of 88th annual conference of Indian Economic Association, 27–29 December, 2005, Vishakhapatanam.

Papola, T.S. (2005), 'A universal program is feasible', *Economic and Political Weekly*, 12–18 February, 40 (7): 594–598.

Program Evaluation Organization of Planning Commission (PEOPC) (2002) *Study on Employment Assurance Scheme*, New Delhi.

Peters, D.H., Yazbeck, A.S., Sharma, R., Ramana, G.N.V., Pritchett, L. and Wagstaff, A. (2002) 'Better health systems for India's poor: Findings, analysis, and options', mimeo, World Bank.

Rao, K.S.C. and Murthy, M.N. 'Locational aspects of FDI in the post-liberalization period: some tentative observations', paper presented at the workshop on Urban Agenda for the New Millennium, Centre for Environmental Planning & Technology, Ahmedabad, 23–24 July 1999.

Rajan, S.I. (2001) 'Social Assistance for Poor Elderly: How Effective?', *Economic and Political Weekly*, 24 February, 33 (8): 613–617.

Rajan, R. and Zingales, L. (2003) *Saving Capitalism from the Capitalists*, Princeton: Princeton University Press.

Rajeev, M. and RoyChowdhuri, S. (2005) 'Contractual employment in selected manufacturing enterprises in Karnataka', Project no. SRTT/4, Institute for Social and Economic Change, Bangalore.

Ramaswamy, K.V. 'Employment in Indian manufacturing and new services: impact pf trade and outsourcing', paper presented in the conference on Labor and Employment Issues in India, 27–29 July, Institute for Human Development, Delhi, 2006.

Rastogi, Avih (2002) 'Inspector Raj for garment export businesses, Center for Civil Society, Delhi.

Ravallion, M. (1991) 'Reaching the Rural Poor through Public Employment: Arguments, Evidence and Lessons from South Asia', *World Bank Research Observer*, 6 (2): 153–175.

Ravallion, M. and Datt, G. (1995) 'Is targeting through a workfare requirement efficient? some evidence for rural India', in D. Van de Walle and K. Nead (eds) *Public Spending and the Poor: Theory and Evidence*, World Bank.

Ravallion, M. and Datt, G. (2002) 'Why has economic growth been more pro-poor in some states in India than others', *Journal of Development Economics*, 68: 381–400.

Ravallion, M., Datt, G. and Chauduri, S. (1993) 'Does Maharashtra's 'employment guarantee scheme guarantee employment?', *Economic Development and Cultural Change*, 41: 251–76.

Rodrik, Dani and Subramanian, Arvind (2004) 'From Hindu growth to productivity surge: the mystery of Indian growth transition', processed, Cambridge, MA and Washington, DC.

Roy, Tirthankar (2002) 'Social Costs of Reforms: A study of job loss with special reference to declining industries in 1990–98', chapter in Uchikawa (ed.) *Economic Reforms and Industrial Structure in India*, New Delhi: Manohar Publishers.

Rustagi, Preet (2005) 'Understanding Gender Inequalities in Wages and Incomes in India', *Indian Journal of Labor Economics*, 48 (2): 319–324.

Saavedra, J. and Torero, M. (2004) 'Labor market reforms and their impact over formal labor demand and job market turnover: The case of Peru', in J. Heckman and C. Pagés (eds) *Law and Employment: Lessons from Latin America and the Caribbean*, Chicago: National Bureau of Economic Research, University of Chicago Press.

Sachs, Jeffrey D., Bajpai, Nirupam and Ramiah, Ananthi (2002) 'Understanding Regional Economic Growth in India', *CID Working Paper No. 88*, Harvard University.

Saha, B. (2005) 'Labor regulation in India and China', processed, Ministry of Finance, Government of India, New Delhi.

Sarkar, Sandip (2006), 'Trends and Patterns of Labor Supply and Unemployment in India', processed, ILO, Delhi.

Sarkar, Sandip and Mehta, Balwant Singh (2006) 'Employment profile of ICT Sector', paper presented in seminar on Knowledge based Industries, Employment and Global Competitiveness, 6–7 October, Forum for Global Knowledge Sharing.

Sen, A. and Himanshu (2004) 'Poverty and inequality in India – getting closer to the truth', mimeo, Jawaharlal Nehru University.

Silberston, Aubrey (1970) 'Surveys of Applied Economics: Price Behavior of Firms', *Economic Journal*, 83 (332): 511–582.

Srinivasan, T.N. 'Employment and unemployment since the early seventies', in S. Mahendra Dev (ed.). Forthcoming, *India Development Report*, New Delhi: Academic foundation.

Subbarao, K. (2003) 'Systemic Shocks and Social Protection: The Role of Public Works Programs', *Social Protection Discussion Paper Series no. 302*, World Bank.

Sundaram, K. (2001) 'Employment and poverty in 1990s: Further results from NSS 55th Round Employment–Unemployment Survey 1999–2000', *Economic and Political Weekly*, 11–17 August, 36 (32): 3039–3051.

Sundaram, K. and Tendulkar, S.D. (2000) 'Poverty in India: an assessment and analysis', draft report for the Asian Development Bank, mimeo, Delhi School of Economics, Delhi.

Sundaram, K. and Tendulkar, S.D. (2003) 'Compatibility problems in NSS data', *Economic and Political Weekly*, 25 January, 38: 327–337.

Sundaram, K. and Tendulkar, S.D. (2003a) 'Poverty in India in the 1990s – revised results for All-India and 15 major states for 1993–94', *Economic and Political Weekly*, 15 November, 40: 4865–4872.

Sundaram, K. and Tendulkar, Suresh D. (2004) 'Poor in the Indian labor force: scenario in the 1990s', *Economic and Political Weekly*, 27 November, 39 (48): 5125–5132.

Sundaram, K. and Tendulkar, Suresh D. (2006) 'Trends in labor and employment in India, 1983–2003: some fresh results?', paper presented in the conference on Labor and Employment Issues in India, 27–29 July, Institute for Human Development, Delhi; *India's Employment Challenge: Creating Jobs, Helping Workers*, Draft World Bank Report, 2005a.

Sundaram, K. and Tendulkar, Suresh D. (2006) 'Changing structure of Indian workforce, quality of employment and real earnings?', paper presented in the conference on Labor and Employment Issues in India, 27–29 July, Institute for Human Development, Delhi; *India's Employment Challenge: Creating Jobs, Helping Workers*, Draft World Bank Report, 2005b.

Swamy, G. (2003) 'Gender dimensions of public employment schemes', processed, World Bank.

Tendulkar, S.D. (2003) 'Organized labor market in India: pre and post-reform', paper presented at Conference on Anti-Poverty and Social Policy in India.

Timmer, C. Peter (2005) 'Agriculture and pro-poor growth: An Asian perspective', *Working Paper 63*, Center for Global Development, Washington, DC.

Townsend, R. (1994) 'Risk and Insurance in Village India', *Econometrica*, 62 (3): 539–591.

Uchikawa, Shuji (2001) 'Investment boom and underutilization of capacity in the 1990s', *Economic and Political Weekly*, August 25, 36: 3247–3254.

Uchikawa, Shuji (ed.) (2002) *Economic Reforms and Industrial Structure in India*, New Delhi: Manohar Publishers.

Uchikawa, Shuji (ed.) (2003) *Labor Market and Institutions in India: 1990s and Beyond*, Tokyo: Institute of Developing Economies.

Unni, Jeemol (2006) 'Employment trends and earnings in the informal sector', paper presented in the conference on Labor and Employment Issues in India, 27–29 July, Institute for Human Development, Delhi.

Vaidyanathan, A. (2001) 'Employment in India 1977–78 to 1999–00: characteristics and trends', *Journal of Indian School of Political Economy*, 13 (2): 217–254.

Vakulbrahmanam, Vamsi (2005) 'Growth and distress in a South Indian peasant economy during in the era of economic liberalization', *Journal of Development Studies*, August 41 (6): 971–997.

Vasudeva-Dutta, P. (2005). 'Accounting for wage inequality in India', *PRUS Working Paper No. 29*, Department of Economics, University of Sussex.

Virmani, Arvind (2002), 'India's economic growth: from socialist rate of growth to Bharatiya rate of growth', *ICRIER Working Paper no. 122*, New Delhi.

Walker, T.S., Singh, R.P. and Asokan, M. (1986) 'Risk benefits, crop insurance and dry land agriculture', *Economic and Political Weekly*.

Wood, A. (1994) *North–South Trade, Employment and Inequality: Changing Fortunes in a Skill-Driven World*, Oxford: Clarendon Press.

Wood, A. (1997) 'Openness and wage inequality in developing countries: the Latin American challenge to East Asian conventional wisdom', *World Bank Economic Review*, 11 (1): 33–57.

World Bank (1989) *India: Poverty, Employment and Social Services: A World Bank Country Study*, Washington, DC: World Bank.

World Bank (1996) 'Thailand: Growth, poverty and income distribution', World Bank Report No. 15689-TH.

World Bank (2003) 'India: Sustaining Reforms, Reducing Poverty', *Development Policy Review*, 14 July, Washington, DC.

World Bank (2005) *India: Re-energizing the Agricultural Sector to Sustain Growth and Reduce Poverty*, Agricultural and Rural Development Unit, South Asia Region, New Delhi: Oxford University Press.

World Bank (2006) *Development Policy Review, India: Inclusive Growth & Service Delivery: Building on India's Success*, New Delhi: Macmillan India Ltd.

World Bank (2006) World Development Report 2006: Equity and Development, Washington, DC.

Index